The Original Lists

OF

PERSONS OF QUALITY;

EMIGRANTS; RELIGIOUS EXILES; POLITICAL REBELS;
SERVING MEN SOLD FOR A TERM OF YEARS; APPRENTICES;
CHILDREN STOLEN; MAIDENS PRESSED; AND OTHERS
WHO WENT FROM GREAT BRITAIN TO THE
AMERICAN PLANTATIONS

1600-1700.

WITH THEIR AGES, THE
LOCALITIES WHERE THEY FORMERLY LIVED IN THE MOTHER COUNTRY,
THE NAMES OF THE SHIPS IN WHICH THEY EMBARKED,
AND OTHER INTERESTING PARTICULARS.

*FROM MSS. PRESERVED IN THE STATE PAPER DEPARTMENT OF HER
MAJESTY'S PUBLIC RECORD OFFICE, ENGLAND.*

EDITED BY

JOHN CAMDEN HOTTEN.

Southern Historical Press, Inc.
Greenville, South Carolina

This volume was reproduced from
a personal copy located in the
Publisher's private Library

Please direct all correspondence and orders to:

www.southernhistoricalpress.com
or
**SOUTHERN HISTORICAL PRESS, Inc.
PO Box 1267
375 West Broad Street
Greenville, SC   29601
southernhistoricalpress@gmail.com**

Originally published: London, England 1874
ISBN #0-89308-178-7
All rights Reserved.
Printed in the United States of America

To the Members of the

GENEALOGICAL AND HISTORICAL SOCIETIES

OF THE

UNITED STATES OF AMERICA,

THIS COLLECTION OF THE NAMES OF THE EMIGRANT
ANCESTORS OF MANY THOUSANDS OF AMERICAN FAMILIES,

IS RESPECTFULLY DEDICATED

BY THE EDITOR,

JOHN CAMDEN HOTTEN.

CONTENTS.

INTRODUCTION.

ITTLE could even the most sanguine of the early emigrants to America have contemplated the subsequent effect which their action would work upon the world's history. Some of them, it is true, were men of position at home, with wealth and all its concomitant advantages at their disposal, but by far the greater number was composed of comparatively obscure men—men of little means, but possessed of hearts and consciences of too honest a nature to permit them quietly to submit to the intolerance which was forced upon them at home. But those whose names are recorded in the following pages, with many others of whom no such minute particulars have come down to us, were the seed-grains from which the mighty Republic has sprung—the rapid growth of which has no parallel in the world's history. Colonization was but imperfectly developed in those early days, and many attempted settlements proved abortive; but the first settlers in Virginia, and subsequently those in New England, carried with them the elements of success, resulting in permanent establishments.

Of the history of the Colonies, and the eventual establishment of Independence, I have nothing to say. My object is simply and briefly to point out some of the causes which contributed to the early emigration of English families to America; and then to estimate the practical value of the contents of the present volume as a means of assistance in making genealogical researches in the mother country.

One of the earliest acts of Charles the First,—an act which raised a storm of indignation throughout the country,—was the imposition of a forced loan without the grant of Parliament. The manner in which this unconstitutional measure was treated by those called upon to contribute towards the assessment, is well illustrated by the events which took place in Lincolnshire; and a relation of the part taken by the leading men of that locality, some of whom were related to, or intimately associated with, the principal agents in the subsequent emigration to Massachusetts, under JOHN WINTHROP, in 1630, will be of some interest to the descendants of the New England emigrants.

One of the richest men in the county of Lincoln, who strenuously opposed the forced loan, was ISAAC JOHNSON, who, as is well known, married the Lady ARABELLA FYNES, sister to THEOPHILUS, Earl of LINCOLN, who himself married a sister of the Lord SAY and SELE. These two noblemen took a very active part in denouncing the loan as dangerous and unconstitutional. Lord SAY and SELE, who, during the civil war, some years later, commanded a Parliamentarian regiment, openly asserted that he would rather lose half his estate than risk the impoverishment of his posterity by the establishment of so dangerous a precedent as a loan without the sanction of Parliament. But Lord LINCOLN'S opposition to the loan was more immediately productive of dissatisfaction. As soon as it was proposed he took upon himself to have an Abridgment of the Statutes prepared for distribution; and it is not unlikely that in the compilation of this document he was aided by his former steward, THOMAS DUDLEY, who subsequently went over to New England, and became Governor of Massachusetts. DUDLEY had received a legal education, under his relative, Sir AUGUSTINE NICHOL, one of the Justices of the Common Pleas, and was therefore peculiarly fitted for the work. The immediate result of this act on the part of Lord LINCOLN, was to bring down upon himself and his servants the resentment of the King and his party, and the Abridgment was rigorously suppressed. Not only was his lordship proceeded against in the Star Chamber, but more completely to crush out the attempts made to incense the people, a proclamation was issued for the apprehension of JOHN HOLLAND, Steward to the Earl, and ROBERT BLOW, the Clerk of his kitchen; and further, a Groom in the household of his lordship was condemned in the Star

Chamber to pay a fine of £3000 for his share in distributing the obnoxious work. The Earl was soon after committed a close prisoner to the Tower, where he remained in custody for some years. I have not found any evidence of what was the result of the attempts made to apprehend HOLLAND and BLOW, but there are reasons for supposing that both escaped detection. A ROBERT BLOW, in all probability the same person, was subsequently an ensign in the regiment of Lord SAY and SELE, the nobleman before mentioned. The only trace of HOLLAND we have met with brings out some information respecting the residence, at Boston, of THOMAS DUDLEY, and the estimated value of his yearly income.

Letter from Sir EDWARD HERON, addressed to Sir HUMPHREY MAY, Chancellor of the Duchy of Lancaster :—

"Cressye, 28 July, 1627.

"RIGHT HONORABLE,

"I had rather offende in too much officiousnes, then negligence, especially to the king's ma^tie. I have hearde that Mr. HOLLANDE who attended the earle of Lincolne, hath been in quest by the state ; yf it be soe, I doe heare for certeine, that he was seene dyvers tymes, about a month or six weekes past vpon the terras-walkes at Sempringham ; but since that tyme it is privatly whispered that he is now removed to the house of one Mr. THOMAS DUDLYE, in Boston, whoe did allsoe of late tymes wayte vpon the sayde earle ; and it is very p'bable, because Mr. HOLLANDS wyfe is observed to make often viages frome Sempringham vnto Boston, and there to abide sometyme 2 or 3 dayes, sometyme a weeke together. *   *   *   "EDWARD HERON.

"Yet maye you please further to vnderstande, that this Mr. DUDLYE beynge reported to have 300li p. an., some saye 400li, refused vpon our earnest request to beare 30s. towards the loane with a neyghbourgh that was deeply charged as we have informed in our certificatts vnto the lords of the councell, whereof I beseech your honor to direct the delyverye.

"Since the writinge hereof, I vnderstande that one ADDAM RESTON' brother in law vnto the s^d Mr. HOLLANDE, came ridinge through our streete on fridaye in the nyght, the 20th of this month, with a gentlewoman behinde him, supposed to be the wyfe of Mr. HOLLANDE goeynge towards Boston; and an other gent, seeminge vnwillinge to be knowne.

"You maye allsoe please to take into your consideration that one BENIAMINE DICKOSON of Boston adviseth, that the toune of Boston is able and ought to contribute to the charge and expence of theyre late mayor & EDW. TILLSON, or anye else, that suffer trouble in cause of the loane; and to helpe towards theyre losses. p JOHAN HOBSON, Collector.

"The same DYKCONSON was 3li lands, yet sett vnto 1li by the lords at Lincoln."*

A long list of Lincolnshire men who refused to contribute to the loan, has been preserved. Ten of the principal of them were immediately committed to prison :—Sir JOHN WRAY, Sir THOMAS GRANTHAM, and Sir EDWARD ASCOUGH, to the Gate House; Sir WILLIAM ARMYN, Sir THOMAS DARNELL, WILLIAM ANDERSON, Esq., the Mayor of Boston, and Alderman (EDWARD) TILSON of that town, to the Fleet; and WILLIAM TAROLD (THOROLD), Esq., and —. HORWOOD, Esq., to the Marshalsea. The Boston men who refused to lend, or to enter into bond for their appearance before his Majesty's Privy Council, beside the Mayor, and Alderman TILSON, were ATTERTON HOWGHE (ATHERTON HOUGH), EDMOND JACKSON, BENJAMIN DICONSON, THOMAS LEVERETT, THOMAS LOWE, THOMAS TOOLY, JOHN COPPYN, WILLIAM COTTINGTON (CODDINGTON), WILLIAM CONDY, and RICHARD WESTLAND. Of these, LEVERETT, CODDINGTON, and HOUGH subsequently went out to New England, and there attained positions of eminence. The London prisons were soon filled with the more important of the objectors, from various parts of the country, but chiefly from the city of London, Lincolnshire, Northamptonshire, Essex, and Gloucestershire. The

---

* State Papers, Chas. I., Domestic Series, Vol. 72, No. 36, Record Office.

gaols being filled to repletion, and moreover the expense of maintaining
the prisoners proving a heavy charge upon the State—already impove-
rished—the great majority were liberated from confinement, but were not
allowed, however, to return to their own homes for fear of their stirring
up fresh disaffection among their neighbours. Thus a delinquent belonging to Essex would be sent, perhaps, to Wiltshire, or Yorkshire, and
under pain of severe punishment, forbidden to leave the town in which
he was located, where, by-the-way, under the semblance of being a free
man, he was compelled to earn, or at least procure, his own living.

This was a very ill-advised proceeding on the part of the Government, for each man thus removed to a distant town soon formed a focus
of discontent. One of the most energetic of these prisoners, in free
custody, as it was termed, was RICHARD KNIGHTLEY, a gentleman belonging to Northamptonshire, an intimate friend of the leaders of the
Massachusetts Colony, and connected by marriage with JOHN HAMPDEN,
in conjunction with whom he was named as executor to the will of ISAAC
JOHNSON.

Most of the proceedings against the remonstrants were taken in the
Star Chamber, the decree-books of which are unfortunately lost, or we
might readily have traced many, if not all the suits, citations, fines and
censures instituted in, or imposed by, the Court. The Star Chamber
was a tribunal taking cognizance of all kind of delinquencies, and there
still remains in the Record Office an immense mass of documents ap-
pertaining to suits before the Court, in which, when they can be sorted,
arranged, and made available to the public, we may hope to find some
important information respecting the personal histories of some of the
original settlers in New England.

The proceedings, which were taken chiefly against the Nonconformists,
caused many English families to leave their homes. Unfortunately, the
records of the High Court of Commission, which has been not inaptly
called "The English Inquisition," are very imperfect, but enough remains
to show that proceedings were taken in it against many of the ministers
and public men who afterwards became eminent in the New England
States. It was not until the Rev. JOHN COTTON, RICHARD BELLING-
HAM, recorder, and WILLIAM CODDINGTON, a member of the corpo-

ration of the town of Boston (co. Lincoln), had been fined for nonconformity, that they gave up their English preferments and places to join their friends in Massachusetts. Other instances might be adduced of the same result attending prosecutions in that Court.

The imposition of Ship Money was the culminating measure that drove hundreds from England to find homes in America, and among other causes, was that which most of all contributed to bring about the war between the King and the Parliament. Though, after a long and tedious struggle, the levy of ship money was declared to be illegal, enough had been effected to make far-sighted men tremble for impending troubles, and no doubt the stand made by men of great influence and high position, such as HAMPDEN (who was intimately associated with the leaders of the Massachusetts settlement), had an immense weight with persons of an inferior standing in worldly wealth. By the Act of Parliament, which declared the illegality of the tax, it was ordered that all proceedings which had been taken should be cancelled, and in consequence a wholesale destruction of documents must have taken place, which, had they been preserved, would have been of great value to the topographer and genealogist, as the rolls of assessments were very minute. One volume of assessments only appears to have escaped the general fate, and this contains the names of all the persons assessed in the county of Essex (with the exception of four towns), numbering about 18,000, and, without doubt, includes many of the subsequent emigrants who went out from that county to New England, in the years 1637 and 1638. A copy of this very interesting document has been prepared for publication.

In 1860, Mr. SAMUEL GARDNER DRAKE, of Boston (Mass.), published his "*Result of some Researches among the British Archives, for information relative to the Founders of New England.*"

That work first suggested the desirability of making a systematic collection of authentic documents relating to the early settlers in America, not only to those who removed to the New England States but to those also who settled in Virginia, the Summer Islands, Barbadoes, Carolina, Jamaica, and other places. It is impossible to overestimate the value of these records, and it is a matter of the deepest regret that comparatively so few have survived to the present time. Those that we have, therefore, of undoubted authenticity, are all the more to be prized. It is a transcript of some of these documents which is here submitted. The aim of the transcriber has been to present an absolute copy of the originals. He has not even ventured to correct palpable mistakes in the spelling of names, or other clerical errors. Where such occur, and they are by no means infrequent, he has called attention to the fact, either by inserting the correct word in brackets, or by adding a foot-note, but the text is a faithful reproduction of the originals.

There are some papers included in Mr. DRAKE'S volume, which have not been deemed admissible in the body of this work, inasmuch as they are not in themselves official documents, but they may not inaptly be quoted here. The first to be noticed are the following lists, taken from the History of Sandwich, being transcripts of records belonging to the corporations of that port.

A LIST OR REGISTER

Of all such persons as embarked themselves in the good ship called the *Hercules*, of Sandwich, of the burthen of 200 tons, John Witherley, master, and therein transported from Sandwich to the plantation called New England in America; with the certificates from the ministers where they last dwelt of their conversation, and conformity to the orders and discipline of the church, and that they had taken the oath of allegiance and supremacy. (The certificates, all dated February and March, 1634, are here omitted.)

Masters of Families.	Children.	Servants.
NATHANL. TILDEN of Tenterden yeoman and LYDIA his wife	Seven by name	Seven by name
JONAS AUSTEN of Tenterden and CONSTANCE his wife	Four.	
ROB. BROOK of Maidstone mercer and ANNE his wife	Seven.	
THO. HEYWARD of Aylesford taylor and SUSANNAH his wife	Five.	
WILL. WITHERELL of Maidstone schoolmaster and MARY his wife	Three	One

Masters of Families.	Children.	Servants
FANNET ...... of Ashford hemp-dresser.		
THO BONEY and HEN. EWELL of Sandwich, shoe-makers		
WILL. HATCH of Sandwich merchant and JANE his wife	Five	Six
SAM. HINKLEY of Tenterden and SARAH his wife	Four.	
ISAAC COLE of Sandwich carpenter and JOAN his wife	Two.	
		A Servant.
THO. CHAMPION of Ashford		
THO. BESBEECH of Sandwich	Six	three
JNO. LEWIS of Tenterden and SARAH his wife	One	
PARNEL HARRIS of Bow London		
JAMES SAYERS of Northbourn taylor		
COMFORT STARRE of Ashford chirurgion	Three	Three
JOS. ROOTES of Great Chart.		
EM. MASON of Eastwell wid.		
MARGT. wife of Will. Johnes late of Sandwich, now of New England, painter		
JNO. BEST of the said parish taylor.		
THO. BRIDGEN of Faversham husbandman and ...... his wife.		

History of Sandwich, by W. BOYS, 1792, pp. 750-1.

A TRUE ROLL OR LIST

Of the names, surnames, and qualities of all such persons who have taken passage from the town and port of Sandwich for the American plantations, since the last certificate of such passengers returned into the office of Dover Castle.

THOMAS STARR of Canterbury yeoman and SARAH his wife — 1 child

EDWARD JOHNSON of Canterbury joiner and SUSAN his wife — 7 children 3 servants

NICHOLAS BUTLER of Eastwell yeoman and JOICE his wife	3 children	5 serv.
SAMUEL HALL of Canterbury yeoman and JOAN his wife.		3 serv.
HENRY BACHELOR of Dover brewer and MARTHA his wife		4 serv.
JOSEPH BACHELOR of Canterbury taylor and ELIZABETH his wife	1 child	3 serv.
HENRY RICHARDSON of Canterbury carpenter and MARY his wife	5 children	1 serv.
JARVIS BOYKETT of Chanington carpenter		
JOHN BACHELOR of Canterbury taylor		
NATHANIEL OVELL of Dover cordwinder		1 serv.
THOMAS CALLE of Faversham husbandman and BENNET his wife	3 children	
WILLIAM EATON of Staple husbandman and MARTHA his wife	3 children	1 serv
JOSEPH COLEMAN of Sandwich shoemaker and SARA his wife	4 children	
MATTHEW SMITH of Sandwich cordwinder and JANE his wife	4 children	
MARMADUKE PEERCE of Sandwich taylor and MARY his wife		1 serv.

Certified under the seal of office of mayoralty 9th June, 1637.

History of Sandwich, by W. BOYS, 1792, p. 752.

We have next to notice the record compiled by Mr. DANIEL CUSH-ING, first printed in Mr. SOLOMAN LINCOLN'S Centennial Address, at Hingham, September 28, 1835. It contains the names of one hundred and seventy-five emigrants from the county of Norfolk, who emigrated between the years 1633 and 1638, almost wholly from Hingham, Wind-ham, and other neighbouring parishes, and who consequently called their new settlement Hingham. But there is something to be said about this emigration, which it is believed has hitherto escaped notice—that is, that the movement was largely fostered by, if not directly traceable to, the influence of JOHN HAYNES, who was subsequently Governor of Connecticut.

The first name on the list referred to, is that of THEOPHILUS CUSHING, from Hingham, who lived several years upon the farm of Mr. HAINS, as he is described in the original. Hitherto, Governor HAYNES has always been regarded as an Essex man, and he is said to have married MARY, daughter of ROBERT THORNTON, of Nottingham. This is not in accordance with the facts of the case, for JOHN HAYNES was the son of another JOHN HAYNES, who lived at Great Hadham, and afterwards at Codicote, both in the county of Hertford, but inherited an estate in Essex, which had been purchased by his father. He married MARY, one of the three daughters and co-heirs of ROBERT THORNTON, who possessed a good estate in Hingham, Windham, and Wramplingham. Mr. THORNTON died when his daughter, who was afterwards Mrs. HAYNES, was very young, and there are reasons for the belief that after the marriage, JOHN HAYNES went to reside at Hingham, and that their first child, called JOHN (whose name is not recorded by any genealogist either in England or America), was born there. But, before he left England, Mr. HAYNES certainly took up his abode in Essex, on a newly-acquired property, called Copford. Taking then the residence at Hingham of a man of the character of HAYNES, it is easy to account for the emigration from that place, especially as the first portion of the company went out in the same year; indeed, there is every reason to suppose that they sailed in the same ship. There can be but little doubt that THEOPHILUS CUSHING was a trusted servant of JOHN HAYNES, and probably a family connection on his wife's side, her maternal grandmother being the heiress of EDMUND CUSHING, by which marriage the THORNTON family acquired the estates at Hingham, Windham, and Wramplingham, which they enjoyed at the time Mr. HAYNES married into that family.

This list of Mr. CUSHING'S is undoubtedly of great value, tending, as it does, to confirm other statements and unofficial lists, but as it is only a compilation made by a private individual, it is not inserted in this work.

There is another very interesting paper included in Mr. DRAKE'S work, which may be briefly noticed. It consists of extracts from the municipal records of Leyden, in Holland, made by the Hon. HENRY C. MURPHY. Many English families took refuge in Leyden, and the list referred to is a register of the births, marriages, and deaths which occurred there among the exiles. It was from Leyden that many of the first settlers in New England, popularly known as the Pilgrim Fathers, came, and embarking from English ports, sailed on board the ships *Mayflower, Fortune, Ann,* and *Little James.*

Among other notices contained in this list, are the following :—

> WILLIAM BRADFORD, of Austerfield, Eng., m. Nov. 30, 1613, DOROTHY MAY, of Witzbuts, Eng.*
>
> EDWARD WINSLOW, of London, m. 16 May, 1618, ELIZABETH BARKER, of Chetsum, Eng.*
>
> JOHN JENNE, of Norwich, Eng., m. 1 Nov., 1614, SARAH CAREY, of Moncksoon.†

The three places here mentioned may be traced as Wisbeach, in Cambridgeshire ; Chesham, in Buckinghamshire ; and Monk Soham, in Suffolk. A family of the name of MAY certainly lived at Wisbeach at the time referred to, as did one of the name of BARKER at Chesham.

The foregoing extracts sufficiently demonstrate the nature of the Leyden records. Further notices are unnecessary, but the list of those who embarked in the before-mentioned ships is of sufficient value to entitle its insertion in this place, though it must be remembered that it is not absolutely official. It is taken from the interesting work of the Rev. Ashbel Steele, A.M., entitled "*Chief of the Pilgrims, or the Life and Times of William Brewster.*" Philadelphia, 1857, pp. 401—410.

---

* Both Bradford and Winslow sailed in the *Mayflower.*

† His wife probably died shortly afterwards, as the name of John Jenny is given alone in the following list as coming over in the *Ann,* or *Little James.*

LIST OF PASSENGERS IN THE *MAYFLOWER ;*

Being the *names* of those who came over first, in the year 1620, and were the founders of New
 Plymouth, which led to the planting of the other New England Colonies. This list of their
 " names " and families, was preserved by Governor Bradford at the close of his History,
 and is here presented in the order in which he placed them. The value of such an accurate
 list cannot be too highly estimated.

Mr. JOHN CARVER ; who was chosen their first Governor on their arrival
 at Cape Cod. He died the first spring. KATHERINE, his
 wife ; she died a few weeks after her husband, in the beginning
 of summer.

DESIRE MINTER ; afterwards returned to her friends, in poor health, and
 died in England.

JOHN HOWLAND ; man servant, afterwards married the daughter of
 John Tillie, and had ten children.

ROGER WILDER ; man servant, died in the first sickness.

WILLIAM LATHAM ; a boy, after more than twenty years visited England, and died at the Bahama Islands.

A maid servant ; who married, and died one or two years after.

JASPER MOORE ; who died the first season.

Mr. WILLIAM BREWSTER ; their Ruling Elder, lived some twenty-three
 or four years after his arrival. MARY, his wife ; died between
 1623 and 1627. LOVE BREWSTER ; a son, married, lived to
 the year 1650, had four children. WRESTLING BREWSTER ;
 youngest son.

RICHARD MORE and Brother ; two boys placed with the Elder. Richard
 afterwards married, and had four or more children. His brother
 died the first winter.

Mr. EDWARD WINSLOW ; Mr. W. afterwards chosen Governor, died in
 1655, when on a commission to the West Indies. ELIZABETH,
 his wife ; died the first winter. Mr. W. left two children by a
 second marriage.

GEORGE SOULE and ELIAS STORY ; two men in Winslow's family. G.
 Soule married and had eight children. E. Story died in the
 first sickness.

ELLEN MORE; a little girl placed in Mr. Winslow's family, sister of Richard More, died soon after their arrival.

Mr. WILLIAM BRADFORD; their second Governor, author of the history of the Plymouth Colony, lived to the year 1657. DOROTHY, his wife; who died soon after their arrival. Governor Bradford left a son in England to come afterwards—had four children by a second marriage.

Mr. ISAAC ALLERTON; chosen first assistant to the Governor. MARY, his wife; who died in the first sickness. BARTHOLOMEW; son, married in England. REMEMBER and MARY, daughters. Remember married in Salem, had three or four children. Mary married in Plymouth, had four children.

JOHN HOOK; servant boy, died in the first sickness.

Mr. SAMUEL FULLER; their physician. His wife and child remained, and came over afterwards; they had two more children.

WILLIAM BUTTEN; servant, died on the passage.

JOHN CRACKSTON; who died in the first sickness. JOHN CRACKSTON, his son; who died some five or six years after.

Capt. MYLES STANDISH; who lived to the year 1656; chief in military affairs. ROSE, his wife; died in the first sickness. Capt. Standish had four sons living in 1650, by a second marriage.

Mr. CHRISTOPHER MARTIN and his wife; SOLOMON PROWER and JOHN LANGEMORE, servants; all died soon after their arrival.

Mr. WILLIAM MULLINS, his wife, JOSEPH, a son; these three died the first winter. PRISCILLA, a daughter; survived and married John Alden. ROBERT CARTER, servant; died the first winter.

Mr. WILLIAM WHITE; died soon after landing. SUSANNA, his wife; afterwards married to Mr. E. Winslow. RESOLVED, a son; married and had five children. PEREGRINE, a son; was born after their arrival at Cape Cod, he cannot therefore be numbered among the passengers proper; married, and had two children before 1650.

WILLIAM HOLBECK and EDWARD THOMSON, servants; both died soon after landing.

Mr. STEPHEN HOPKINS, and ELIZABETH, his wife; both lived over

d

twenty years after their arrival, and had a son and four daughters born in this country. GILES, and CONSTANTIA, by a former marriage. Giles married ; had four children. Constantia married ; had twelve children. DAMARIS, a son, and OCEANUS, born at sea ; children by the present marriage.

EDWARD DOTY, and EDWARD LITSTER, servants. E. Doty by a second marriage had seven children ; after his term of service went to Virginia.

Mr. RICHARD WARREN ; his wife and five daughters were left, and came over afterwards. They also had two sons ; and the daughters married here.

JOHN BILLINGTON ; he was not from Leyden, or of the Leyden Company, but from London. ELLEN, his wife. JOHN, his son ; who died in a few years. FRANCIS, the second son ; married and had eight children.

EDWARD TILLIE, and ANN, his wife ; both died soon after their arrival. HENRY SAMSON and HUMILITY COOPER, two children, their cousins. Henry lived, married, had seven children. Humility returned to England.

JOHN TILLIE, and his wife ; both died soon after they came on shore. ELIZABETH, their daughter; afterwards married John Howland.

FRANCIS COOKE ; who lived until after 1650 ; his wife and other children came afterwards ; they had six or more children. JOHN, his son ; afterwards married ; had four children.

THOMAS ROGERS ; died in the first sickness. JOSEPH, his son ; was living in 1650, married and had six children. Mr. Rogers' other children came afterwards, and had families.

THOMAS TINKER, wife and son ; all died in the first sickness.

JOHN RIGDALE, ALICE, his wife ; both died in the first sickness.

JAMES CHILTON, his wife ; both died in the first sickness. MARY, their daughter ; lived, married, and had nine children. Another married daughter came afterwards.

EDWARD FULLER, his wife ; both died in the first sickness. SAMUEL, their son ; married ; had four children.

JOHN TURNER, two sons ; names not given ; all three died in the first sickness. A daughter came some years afterwards to Salem and there married.

FRANCIS EATON, SARAH, his wife; she died the first winter; by a third marriage he left three children. SAMUEL, a son; married and had one child.

MOSES FLETCHER, JOHN GOODMAN, THOMAS WILLIAMS, DIGERIE PRIEST, EDMOND MARGESON, RICHARD BRITTERIGE, RICHARD CLARKE; these seven died in the general sickness. The wife of D. Priest, and children, came afterwards, she being the sister of Mr. Allerton.

PETER BROWN; lived some fourteen years after, was twice married, and left four children.

RICHARD GARDINER; became a seaman, and died abroad.

GILBERT WINSLOW; after living here a number of years, returned to England.

JOHN ALDEN; "a hopeful young man," hired at Southampton, married Priscilla Mullens, as mentioned, and had eleven children.

JOHN ALLERTON.

THOMAS ENGLISH.

WILLIAM TREVORE, and — 'ELY; two seamen; are commonly, but incorrectly reckoned in the number of the first company of passengers for the Colony; Bradford himself says: "Two other seamen were hired to stay a year; * * when their time was out they both returned." Accordingly he says of the *Mayflower* company: "These being about a hundred souls, came over in the first ship." Afterwards he adds: "Of these one hundred persons who came over in this first ship together, the greatest half died in the general mortality, and most of them in two or three months' time." Omitting those two hired sailors who returned, and counting the person that died and the child that was born while on the passage as one passenger, we have the exact number—*one hundred* of the Pilgrim Company, "who came over in the first ship." And, as *fifty-one* died the first season, this enumeration makes good those other words of the historian, that, "the greater half died in the general mortality."

LIST OF PASSENGERS THAT ARRIVED, AFTER ONE YEAR, IN THE SECOND SMALL SHIP FORTUNE;

Being parts of families, with others, left in England or Holland the year before. They arrived at New Plymouth, on the 11th of Nov., 1621.

JOHN ADAMS.

WILLIAM BASSITE (Bassett, probably two in his family).

WILLIAM BEALE.

EDWARD BOMPASSE.

JONATHAN BREWSTER ; the oldest son of Elder Brewster.

CLEMENT BRIGGES.

JOHN CANNON.

WILLIAM CONER.

ROBERT CUSHMAN ; for several years the Leyden Company's agent in England. He returned in the *Fortune* to act still further as agent for the Company ; was of great service in various ways ; but died before coming again to settle in the Colony. THOMAS CUSHMAN, son of Robert, about twelve years old ; came with his father in the *Fortune*, became an exemplary man in the Colony, and succeeded Elder Brewster in the eldership, in 1649.

STEPHEN DEAN.

PHILIP DE LA NOYE.

THOMAS FLAVELL and son.

WIDOW FORD and three children, WILLIAM, MARTHA, and JOHN.

ROBERT HICKES.

WILLIAM HILTON.

BENNET MORGAN.

THOMAS MORTON.

AUSTIN NICHOLAS.

WILLIAM PALMER (probably two in his family).

WILLIAM PITT.

THOMAS PRINCE, or. PRENCE ; married the Elder's daughter, Patience ; was afterwards Governor.

MOSES SIMONSON.

HUGH STATIE.

JAMES STEWARD.

WILLIAM TENCH.

JOHN WINSLOW ; brother of Mr. Edward Winslow.

WILLIAM WRIGHT.

LIST OF THOSE WHO CAME OVER IN THE *ANN* AND *LITTLE JAMES.*

The vessels parted company at sea ; the *Ann* arrived the latter part of June, and the *Little James* some week or ten days later ; part of the number were the wives and children of persons already in the Colony.

ANTHONY ANNABAL ; afterwards settled in Scituate.

EDWARD BANGS ; settled in Eastham.

ROBERT BARTLETT.

FEAR BREWSTER and PATIENCE BREWSTER ; daughters of Elder Brewster.

MARY BUCKET.

EDWARD BURCHER.

THOMAS CLARKE. This Thomas Clarke's grave-stone is the oldest on the Plymouth Burial Hill.

CHRISTOPHER CONANT.

CUTHBERT CUTHBERTSON ; was a Hollander.

ANTHONY DIX.

JOHN FAUNCE.

MANASSEH FAUNCE.

GOODWIFE FLAVELL ; probaby the wife of Thomas Flavell, who came in the *Fortune.*

EDMUND FLOOD.

BRIDGET FULLER ; apparently the wife of Samuel Fuller, the physician.

TIMOTHY HATHERLY.

WILLIAM HEARD.

MARGARET HICKES and her children ; the wife of Robert Hickes, who came in the *Fortune.*

William Hilton's wife and two children. He had sent for them before
his death.

EDWARD HOLMAN.

JOHN JENNY; had "liberty, in 1636, to erect a mill for grinding and
beating of corn upon the brook of Plymouth."

ROBERT LONG.

EXPERIENCE MITCHELL.

GEORGE MORTON; he brought with him his son, Nathaniel, and four
other children. NATHANIEL MORTON; son of George Morton,
and afterwards Secretary of the Colony.

THOMAS MORTON, jr.; son of Thomas Morton, who came in the
Fortune.

ELLEN NEWTON.

JOHN OLDHAM; a man of some note afterwards.

FRANCES PALMER; wife of William Palmer, who came in the
Fortune.

CHRISTIAN PENN.

Mr. Perce's two servants.

JOSHUA PRATT.

JAMES RAND.

ROBERT RATTLIFFE.

NICHOLAS SNOW; settled in Eastham.

ALICE SOUTHWORTH; widow, afterwards the second wife of Governor
Bradford.

FRANCIS SPRAGUE; settled in Duxbury..

BARBARA STANDISH; *i.e.,* second wife of Captain Standish, married after
her arrival.

THOMAS TILDEN.

STEPHEN TRACY.

RALPH WALLEN.

It must not be imagined that the following pages furnish by any
means a complete list of the early settlers in America. In 1637 Thomas

Mayhew was appointed, for a term of twenty-one years, to keep a record of all those persons who left England "to passe into forraigne partes," but of Mayhew's lists nothing is to be found but the fragment commencing at page 287, and that continues but for a few months. It cannot be doubted but that other lists were made, but they are either lost, or are among the mass of papers still uncatalogued at the Record Office. We learn incidentally that ships left England almost daily for America, but no records of them, or of their passengers, remain. Thus among the registers of deaths in the parish of Deal, co. Kent, we find that on the 4th of May, 1639, Margaret, wife of Thomas Waldigraue, bound for New England, was buried. Who was Thomas Waldigraue, and with what company did he sail?

We know that many ships sailed from Bristol, among others *The Angel Gabriel* and *The James*, conveying the Revd. Richard Mather and the Revd. Daniel Maude, but no records of departures from that port remain. Again, who were the companions who sailed in 1633 in the *The Griffin*, with John Haynes and the Revd. Thomas Hooker? Where are the lists of *The Arabella*, and other ships, in which John Winthrop and the founders of Massachusetts embarked? Who went out with the Revd. Ezekiel Rogers from Rowley, and with Fenwick, and the Revd. Henry Whitfield? These are but a few instances, to show how very imperfect are our records of the early settlers.

Further, it should be borne in mind that only the names of those were taken who legally left the shores of England. At page 142, for example, and elsewhere throughout the book, we find that the passengers were examined by the minister touching their conformity to the church discipline of England, and that they had taken the oaths of allegiance and supremacy; elsewhere (p. 106, &c.) we find it certified that they are no subsidy men, that is, men liable to the payment of a subsidy to the crown. Among the thousands who emigrated to New England, it cannot be doubted but that a very large number left to avoid payment of the hateful subsidy, and that they would not take the oaths of allegiance and supremacy. These, therefore, must have left secretly, and of such no record would exist.

It is perhaps hardly necessary to say, that where, in the following lists, it is stated that so many people were *transported* to New England, it does not mean that they were sent as felons, as the word, at the present time, usually implies. It simply means that they were conveyed. Those persons, however, who were convicted for upholding the cause of the Duke of Monmouth (pp. 315—342), were undoubtedly *transported*, as we now understand the word.

The Summer Islands, mentioned at pages 301—314, and elsewhere, are now called the Bermudas. In 1609, Sir GEORGE SOMERS, or SUMERS, was driven on the islands in the course of a voyage to Virginia, and from him the islands derived their name. The Virginia Company, who claimed the islands by the right of having discovered them, sold them to a company of a hundred and twenty persons, who, having obtained a charter for their settlement in 1612, sent out sixty settlers, with a governor. During and immediately after the civil war in England, many persons of eminence took refuge in the Bermudas, among others the poet WALLER, who celebrated their beauty in a poem, entitled " *The Battle of the Summer Islands.*"

Enough has been said to show the great value of the lists here given, and I trust that others may be induced to make further search among the documents in the Record Office, to bring to light the treasures there hidden.

J. C. H.

May, 1873.

[Regi]ster of the names
of all y^e Passinger w^{ch}
Passed from y^e Port of
London for on whole
yeare Endinge at
Xp^{mas} 1635.

Passinger wch Passed from y^e Port of London.

Post festum Natalis Christi 1634. vsq^e ad festum Na: Christi 1635

Secundo Januarij 1634

THEIS vnder written are to be transported to Virginea imbarqued in ye Merch^t *bonaventure* JAMES RICROFTE M^r bound thither have taken ye oath of Allegeance.

	yeres		yeres
WiḦm Sayer	58	Andrew Jefferies	24
Bazill Brooke	20	Wm Munday	22
Robert Percy	40	Arthur Howell	20
Charles Hilliard	22	Jo: Abby	22
Edward Clark	30	James Moyser	28
Jo: Ogell	18	Mathew Marshall	30
Richard Hargrave	20	Wm Smith	20
Jo: Anderson	20	Garrett Riley	24
Francis Spencer	23	Miles Riley	20
John Lewes	23	WiḦm Burch	19
Richard Hughes	19	Peter Dole	20
John Clark	19	James Metcalf	22
Wm Guy	18	Jo: Vnderwood	23
John Burd	18	Robert Luck	25
James Redding	19	John Wood	26
Richard Cooper	18	Walter Morgan	23

HENRIE IRISH	16	JOHN FOUNTAINE	18
GEORGE GREENE	20	HENRY REDDING	22
HENRY QUINTON	20	LOUGHTON BOSTOCK	16
JO: BRYAN	25	JOHN RUSSELL	19
ROBERT PAYTON	25	THO: RIDGLEY	23
THO: SYMOND'S	27	ROBERT HARRIS	19
MICHELL BROWNE	*35	WIĦM MASON	19
JO: HODGES	37	VICTOR DERRICK	23
JO: EDMOND'S	16	JOHN BAMFORD	28
GARRET POWNDER	19	GEO: SESSION	40
JO: WISE	†28	JO: COOKE	47
HENRY DUNNELL	23	THO: TOWNSON	26
SYMON KENNEDAY	20	THO: PARSON	30
THO: HYET	22	MICHELL HOPKINSON	27
THO: JAMES	20	WᴹSURGISSON	25
JO SOTTERFOYTH	24	EDWARD FISHER	35
EMANUELL BOMER	18	ROBERT FISHER	34
LEONARD WETHERFIELD	17	RICHARD ELLIS	29
JAMES LICKBURROWE	20	JO: ATKINSON	24
THO: SINGER	18	JO. HICKCOMBOTTOM	24
JESPER WITHY	21	JOSEPH WASHBORN	22
ROBERT KERSLEY	22	RICHARD PITT	19
JO: SPRINGALL	18	EDWARD MAIOR	19
THO: JESOPP	18	JO: FAVOR	18
JAMES PERKYNS	42	HENRY ANMER	16
DANIELL GREENE	24	ELLIN JONES	18
WᴹHUTTON	24	WIĦM RIDGDELL	24
JO: WILKINSON	19	CHRISTOPHER CARNOLL	23
HUGH GARLAND	20	JO: FEELDHOUSE	19
RICHARD SPICER	18	THO: TAYLOR	19
HUMFREY TOPSALL	24	JO: GRIMSCROFT	27
THO: STANTON	20	JESPER WESTON	27
JO: WATSON	28	JOHN LEE	17
THO: MURFIE	20	JOHN SKORIE	16

* [This age is uncertain, the first figure having been altered ; it, however, looks like a 3 followed by two 5's.]
† [It is doubtful whether this age is 18 or 28.]

Jo: Mosely	18	Henry Rogers	30
Jereemy Redding	18	Robert Smithson	23
Richard Ast	30	Nic^a: Harvy	30
John Rolinson	26	James Graston [or Grafton]	22
Richard Glaister	31	Daniell Daniell	18
Protherock Alis	24	Reginoll Hawes	25
John Towse	26	Geo: Burlingham*	20
Richard Cave	28	Jo: Hutchinson	22
Tho: Goodman	25	James Grame †	17
Phillipp Conner	21	Richard Harman	20
Launcelot Pryce	21	Sam: Ashley	19
Vxor Thomazin	18	Geo: Burlingham	20
Kat: Yates	19	Elizabeth Jackson	17
Averyn Cowper	20	Sara Turner	20
Jo: Dunn	26	Mary Ashley	24
Leonard Evans	22	Margerie Furbredd	20
Tho: Anderson	18	Margaret Huntley	20
Edward Cranfield	24	Richard Doll	25
vxor Ann Cranfield	18	Tho: Perry	34
Jo: Baggley	14	vxor Dorothy	26
Tho: Smith	14	Ben: Perry	4
Wiłłm Weston	30	Mary Carlton	23
Tho: Townsend	14	Abram Silvester	40
Edward Davies	25	Tho: Bolton	18
Mary Saund^rs	26	Richard Champion	19
Jane Chambers	23	Richard Champion	18
Margaret Maddock's	21	Abram Silvester	14
Roger Sturdevant	21	Elizabeth Nuñick	20
John Wigg	24	Jo: Atkinson	30
John Greenwood	16	Ric^r Hore	24
Andrew Dunton	38	Ralph Nicholson	20
John Wise	30	Robert More	19
Wm Hudson	32	Joan Nubold	20
Tho: Edenburrow	37	Tho: Hebden	20
John Hill	50		

* [It will be observed that this name is repeated five lines below.]
† [It is possible that this name may be intended for Grand; the last two letters are very badly written.]

vj^o Januarij 1634.

THEIS vnder written names are to be transported to St Christophers
ẽ the Barbadoes, JAMES ROMSEY M^r bound thither have taken
ye oath of Allegeance.

	yeres		
JOHN PHILLIPPS	21	JOHN BOWES	23
JOHN ALLIN	23	HENRY CUPPLEDIKE	20
DAVID JOHNES	24	ROB^T STRATFORD	16
W^M WHITE	30	ROBERT HOLLAND	19
HUMFREY DAVIES	22	THO: BORNE	22
W^M CANNION	21	EDWARD ROBERT'S	25
EDWARD LAMPEUGH	35	JOHN CARTER	26
GEORGE CLIFFE	26	GEORGE SUTTON	19
ABRAM JN^OSON	27	EDWARD JENNOR	24
HENRIE WELLS	23	JOSEPH GLADE	20
JOHN VSHER	26	PETER MONK	29
EDMOND KNIGHT	21	RICHARD COKE	38
THO: RASBOTTOM	23	ISACK PETER	20
W^M GRIGGSON	14	PHILLIPP SQUIER	20
RICHARD JONES	23	BARTHOLMEW FLUDE	24
MICHELL WHITE	18	RICHARD LAWRENCE	20
RICHARD BORNE	24	DANIELL SMITH	20
EDWARD FLETCHER	20	JOHN SYMES	17
FRANCIS SOWTH	19	ROBERT KETT	22
JOHN CONNY	20	SUZAN HUDSON	20
ROBERT SKARVILL	21	MARY SEA	16
EDWARD ROBINSON	18	JOHN SHETTLEWORTH	28
JOHN HOLLAND	15	RICHARD FRYME	26
EDWARD ASH	20	ROB^T HOLME	22
THO: SANDBY	17	JOHN MORE	28
THO: GREENE	24	RICHARD PERCE	45
MARK THEODY	18	EDWARD JONES	21
WILLM BURT	22	MARK ELLVYN	20

HENRY PURSTYNN	18	JOHN HIGGINS	20
RICHARD CHITTING	23	WIᴌᴌM HODGSON	20
THO: MARFUTT	22	THO: JENKYNNS	23
RICHARD EDMOND'S	18	JNᵒ GREENEWOOD	26
WᴹPRICHARD	25	JOHN PLACE	22
THO: ARNOLD	18	WᴹHAYMAN	36
RICHARD CHAMBLIS	19	EDWARD SAVAGE	20
EDWARD BRUNT	25	JO: CONNIERS	21
GEORGE STOKES	23	JOHN MORE	30
HENRY FOOKES	21	ROBᵀ GROUND	22
ROBERT GRANGER	21	WILLIAM BRUTON	22
WᴹWALTER	26	WILLIAM WALTON	22
JOHN RODS	20	WIᴌᴌM SEWARD	26
EZECHELL CLEMENT'S	20	HENRY RYMES	40
THO: CARPENTER	20	HENRY ILES	17
THO: SMITH	17	BRYAN ERLE	21
JOHN WHITE	27	JOHN FOX	19
JOHN WATKINSON	22	ROBERT GILBY	18
JOSEPH PARDY	23	ROBERT BAKER	50
ROBERT LANGRIDGE	20	THO: PECK	20
JNᵒ ETHERINGTON	17	WIᴌᴌM HARRIS	35
GEORGE WHITE	27	JOHN TOWNE	27
THO: COCKEY	25	CHRISTIAN MYNNIKYN	19
ANTᵒ BLACKGROVE	24		

17 *Februarij* 1634.

THEIS vnder-written names are to be transported to the Barbadoes imbarqued in yᵉ *Hopewell* Capten THO: WOOD Mʳ bound thither. the passenges have taken the oath of Allegeance & Supremacie.

	yeres		yeres
WIᴌᴌM VSHER	22	JOHN HILL	19
RICᴿ: HANBY	23	RICHARD CLYNTON	23
RICHARD JACKSON	17	JNᵒ HARRISON	46

James Read	19	Jarvice Dodderidge	21
Dunston Kember	20	John Decborn	22
Wm Owen	23	Wiℏm Seriff	19
J^{no} Free	25	John Offword	24
Richard Gane	19	Tho: Lee	20
Thomas Richard's	19	Robert Richard's	18
John Nicks	23	George Hiter	18
Martin Perkynn	20	John Dreadd	17
Ant^o Bládes*	24	Arthur Wvnd	17
Robert Dymond	29	Richard Osborn	22
Tho: Dayes	20	John Phillipps	37
Wm Walker	21	John Steevens	13
Ralph Harwood	23	John Reddhedd	28
Phillipp Philpott	30	Wm Gibson	18
James Pallister	28	Tho: Waterman	27
Richard Clark	21	Tho: Jones	19
Daniell Baker	20	Jo: Nisom	23
John Tayler	23	Edward Layton	30
Thomas Prosser	20	Wiℏm Benson	28
John Eaton	20	John Whitehedd	23
Tho: Smith	21	Richard Barnard	23
John Johnson	18	Henry Long	21
Richard Holmes	24	John Wilks	22
Ralph Terrett	24	Tho: Wellman	21
Henry Tatnum	20	Tho: Gaton	25
Alexander Smith	18	Wiℏm Allin	25
John Crapp	37	Tho: Letteny	20
John Faux	36	Robert Porter	20
Joseph Bryan	20	John Hughes	20
Nevill Hutchins	20	Henry Atkyns	22
Wm Walters	22	Robert Kember	21
Wiℏm Puttex	20	Robert Mills	19
Archibald Weyer	18	John Davies	25
Nathaniell Cobham	17	Thomas Crowder	21

* [This name is very faintly written, but I do not think there can be any doubt about it.]

RICHARD PURNELL	21	THO: EVERIE	19
ROBERT LYNLEY	20	THO: MEDWELL	31
HENRY HOLMES	44	JO: BASHER	20
JOHN KEY	30	JAMES ELLERTON	18
JOHN WILLIAMS	21	RICHARD HANDS	19
JOHN FOWLER	24	MEDUSALA WATT'S	20
JOHN OWEN	20	THO: HAMES	19
OWEN WILLIAMS	21	PHILLIPP CARTWRITE	20
THO: DREW	26	JOHN LOFTIS	21
Wᴹ BUMSTEDD	21	MICHELL ROCKS	21
EDWARD JNᵒSON	20	JO: LING	45
JOHN BOWND	20	THO: SHERMAN	26
JOHN HAIES	30	Wᴹ JACKSON	30
JOHN LYON	18	JAMES GOLDINGHAM	32
Wiłłм CORSER	24	RICᴿ: RAINOLDS	19
THOMAS TRIGG	21	JO: NOKES	20
ROBERT NISBETT	19	FRANC'S [FRANCIS] SYMOND'S	21
Wiłłм CADDY	21	THOMAS LURTING	21
JOHN CASSEDY	20	JAMES ANDERSON	19
ALEXANDER MORE	24	WALTER JAGO	20
RICHARD WELLYN	25	JOHN BEAD	22
RICHARD GRIFF'S [GRIFFITHS]	24	JOHN YOUNG	19
ARTHUR YEOMANS	24	THO: HUBBARD	20
NICHOLAS HOBSON	23	EDWARD BROWNE	24
Wᴹ MARROW	25	Wᴹ SEERE	22
FRANCIS DENE	21	Wᴹ LEVYNS	22
JOHN PHILPOTT	16	JO: HAMOND	17
JOHN STRATTERGOOD	18	EDWARD PULLIN	27
Wᴹ CANT	19	JAMES CULLIMOR	22
HENRIE SPECKMAN	27	JO: DE PARK	28
JOHN YAT'S	19	RICHARD WALTON	21
Wᴹ RANSE	27	ROBERT COLLIE	20
GEORGE SELMAŃ	16	JOSEPH HEPWORTH	33
NICHOLAS BLADES	21	Wiłłм WALTERS	32
JOHN CLARK	24	DANIELL SMITH	33

6

RICHARD TRUEMAN	24	RANDALL OGDEN	19
W^M MASTERS	21	THO: BROWNE	11
JO: CLERE	26		

xj° *Marcij* 1634

de pochia Sci Egiddij [*Giles*] Cripplegate. } THEIS vnder written names are to be transported to New England having brought Certificate from the Justices of the peace ℓ Minister of the pish the ptie hath taken the oaths of Allegeance ℓ Supremacie.

PETER HOWSON xxxj yeres ℓ his Wife ELLIN HOWSON 39 yeres old.

Turris Londoñ } THEIS vnder written names are are (*sic*) to be transported to New-England having brought attestacoñ ℓ Certific from the Justices of peace ℓ Minister of the pish according to the LLs [Lords] of the Councells order the ptie hath taken the oaths of Allegeance ℓ Supremacie.

	yeres
THOMAS STARES	31
SUZAN JOHNSON	12

16 *Marcij* 1634

Mildred Bredstret } THEIS vnder-written names are to be transported to New-England imbarqued in y^e *Christian* de Lo: JO: WHITE. M^r bound thither, the Men have taken ye oath of Allegeance ℓ Supremacie.

	yeres		yeres
FRANCIS STILES	35	JO: HARRIS	28
THO: BASSETT	37	JAMES HORWOOD	30
THO: STILES	20	JO: REEVES	19
THO: BARBER	21	THO: FOULFOOT	22
JO: DYER	28	JAMES BUSKET	28

Tho: Coop [Cooper]	18	Tho: Haukseworth	23
Edward Preston	13	Jo: Stiles	35
Jo: Cribb	30	Henrie Stiles	40
George Chappell	20	Jane Worden	30
Robert Robinson	45	Joan Stiles	35
Edward Patteson	33	Henry Stiles	3
Francis Marshall	30	Jo: Stiles	9. Mo:
Ricʀ: Heylei	22	Rachell Stiles	28
Tho: Halford	20		

22º *Marcij* 1634

THEIS vnder-written names are to be imbarqued in yᵉ *Planter* Nicᵒ: Trarice Mʳ bound for New-England p Certificat from Stepney pish, and Attestacōn from Sʳ Tho: Jay, ꝑ Mʳ Simon Muskett 2 Justices of the Peace. the Men have taken the oaths of Supremacie ꝑ Allegeance.

	yeres		
Nicholas Davies	40	Wᴹ Lock	6
Sara Davies	48	A Sawyer Jo: Maddox	43
Joseph Davies	13	Glover James Lonnin	26

Robert Stevens	22	A Sawyer
John More	24	A Labourer
James Haieward	22	4 servants
Judith Phippin	16	

26 *Marcij* 1635

THIS vnder written name is to be imbarqued in the *Peter Bonaventure*. Tho: Harman Mʳ bound for yᵉ Barbadoes ꝑ Sᵗ Christophers p Certificate from Sᵗ Androwes pish Holborne: And Attestacōn from Justice Grimston ꝑ Justice Sheppard hath taken the oaths of Allegeance ꝑ Supremacie.

Wɪℍm Banks .... 21 yeeres.

Primo Aprill 1635

■ N the *Hopewell* of Lond m' W^M BUNDOCKE v^rs New Engld

JO^N COOPER............... 41 yers	of oney [Olney]*	theis haue taken	
EDMOND FARRINGTON 47 yers	in Buckingham-	the othe of Alleg	
W^M PARRYER 36	sher	& supremcie	

GEO: GRIGG'S .... 42 — { of Landen [? Lavenden]* }

PHILLIP KYRTLAND ... 21 — } of Sherington { in Bucking-

NA^TH KYRTLAND ...... 19 — } of Sherington — hãsher

THO. GRIGG'S .... 15 yers
W^M GRIGG'S............... 14
ELISA. GRIGG'S .... 10 — } Children of GEO: GRIGGS aforsaid
MARY GRIGG'S 6
JAMES GRIGG'S 2

WIBROE .... 42 y^rs wife of JO^N COOPER
ELIZA: .... 49 yers wife of EDMOND FARRINGTON
ALYCE .... 37 yers wife of W^M PURRYER†
ALYCE .... 42 yers wife of GEO. GRIGG'S

MARY COOPER 13
JO^N COOPER............... 10 — } Children of JO^N COOPER aforsaid
THO. COOPER 7
MARTHA COOPER 5

PHILLIP PHILLIPP .... 15 yers seru^t to JO^N COOPER

SARRA FARRINGTON... 14
MATHEW FARRINGTON 12 — } Children of EDW.‡ FARRINGTON
JO^N FARRINGTON 11
ELIZA. FARRINGTON... 8

---

* [I have no doubt that Olney and Lavenden are meant; both which places, as well as Sherington, are in the Hundred of Newport.]

† [It is probable that this is intended for PARRYER, a name which appears above; it is however, clearly written PURRYER.]

‡ [So in the original; but doubtless intended for EDMOND, which name occurs above.]

MARY PURRYER* .... 7 ⎫
SARRA PURRYER* .... 5 ⎬ Children of W^M PURRYER.*
KATHREN PURRYER* 18 monthes ⎭

27 psons

2° Aprilis 1635

HEIS vnder written names are to be transported to New-England imbarqued in the *Planter* NIC^O: TRARICE M^r bound thither the pties have brought Certificate from the Minister of S^t S^t (*sic*) Albons in Hertfordshier ꝑ Attestacōn from the Justices of peace according to thè Lords order.

	yeres
A Mercer JO: TUTTELL	39
JOAN TUTTELL	42
JOHN LAWRENCE	17
W^M LAWRENCE	12
MARIE LAWRENCE	9
ABIGALL TUTTELL	6
SYMON TUTTELL	4
SARA TUTTELL	2
JO: TUTTELL	I
JOAN ANTROBUSS	65
MARIE WRAST	24
THO: GREENE	15
NATHAN HEFORD†	16
servant to JO: TUTTELL	
MARIE CHITTWOOD	24
Shoemaker. THO: OLNEY	35
MARIE OLNEY....................	30
THO: OLNEY	3
EPENETUS OLNEY	I
Husbandman GEO: GIDDINS ...	25
JANE GIDDINS.....................	20
THO: SAVAGE, a Tayler	27
A Tayl^r RICHARD HARVIE ...	22
Husb:man FRANC'S [FRANCIS] PEBODDY	21
Lynnen wever W^M WILCOCK-SON	34
MARGARET WILCOCKSON	24
JO: WILLCOCKSON	2
ANN HARVIE	22
A Mason W^M BEARDSLEY	30
MARIE BEADSLEY	26
MARIE BEADSLIE	4
JOHN BEADSLIE	2
JOSEPH BEADSLIE .... 6. mo:	
Husbandman ALLIN PERLEY .	27
Shoemaker WItM FELLOE ...	24
A Taylor FRANCIS BAKER ...	24

* [See note † on previous page.]
† [This name is very difficult to decipher.]

THO: CARTER .... 25 ⎫
MICHELL WILLMSON [WIL- ⎬ servant's to GEO: GIDDINS prd
   LIAMSON] .... 30 ⎪
ELIZABETH MORRISON .... 12 ⎭

3ᵈ Aprill 1635

Statinor JAMES WEAUER......... 23 yers ℓ
Husbandman dwelge in ⎫ EDMOND WEAVER ... 28 yers ℓ his wife
Auckstrey in herefordsher ⎭   MARGRETT aged 30 yers.

THEIS vnder written names are to be transported to New-England imbarqued in yᵉ *Hopewell* Mʳ Wᵐ BUNDICK. the pties have brought Certificate from the Minister ℓ Justices of peace, that they are no Subsedy men. they have taken the oath of alleg: ℓ Supremacie.

Husbandman JO: ASTWOOD ... 26
   JO: RUGGELLS 10
   MARTHA CARTER 27
   MARIE ELLIOTT 13

Nazing in Essex.
Shoemaker JO: RUGGELLS...... 44
   uxor BARBARIE RUGGELLS... 30
   JO: RUGGELLS 2
   ELIZABETH ELLIOT 8
   GILES PAYSON.............. 26
   ISACK MORRIS............ .. 9

Husbandman. JO: PEAT 38
   of Duffill* pish
   in Derbieshier.

EDWARD KEELE............ 14
JO: GOADBY 16
JO: BILL 13
THO: GREENE 15

p Cert: from Stanstedd Abbey†
   in com Hert.
Husb:man LAWRENCE WHITTI-
   MOR 63
ELIZABETH WHITTIMOR . 57
ELIZABETH TURNER 20
SARA ELLIOTT 6
ROBERT DAY 30
Wᵐ PEACOCK 12

Husbandman ISACK DISBROUGH 18
   of Ell-Tisley‡ in com
   Cambridge.
ELIZ: ELLIOTT 30
LYDDIA ELLIOT 4
PHILLIP ELLIOT 2

Husbandman ROBERT TITUS
   of St. Katherins 35
   uxor HANNA TITUS 31
   JO: TITUS.................... 8
   EDMOND 5

* [Probably Duffield, in Appletree Hundred.]
† [Stansted Abbot is a Township in the Hundred of Braughin, Herts.]
‡ [Eltisley, a parish in the Hundred of Longstow.]

GEO: WOODWARD .... 35.   ffishmonger.

p Certi from Sʳ GEO: WHITMOR (Sʳ NICᵒ RAYNTON two Justices of yᵉ Peace in London. (from JO: THORP Minister of yᵉ pish of St Buttolphs Billings gate.

T O be Imbarqued In the *Peter Bonavᵗʳ* de Lo. m' Capᵗ HARMAN vʳˢ Barbades.

Theis pties here vnder expressed haue brought Certeficat from two Justices of peace that the toke the oathe of Allegā (Sppremacie (Also certᵗ frō yᵉ Ministr of the pishe this 3ᵈ Aprill 1635

	yers		
THO: HATHORNE ....aged	22	ALCE MACE............	22
Wᴹ MORRISON...................	23	MARGRETT ELLGATE	24
RALPH VAUGHAN .... 22 (½		MARGRETT HARTFORDE	22
JANE MADDOCKES	21		

4ᵗʰ *Aprill* 1635

I N the *Peter Bonavᵗʳ* de Lo. m' Capᵗ HARMAN for Barbades Theis two pties brought Certᵗ from two Justices of peace (the Ministr of their Conformity accordᵈ to order.

Wᴹ CLERKE................. 29 yers. | THO: SERGEANT .... 23 yers.

vjᵒ Aprilis 1635

T HEIS pties heerevnder mencioned are to be transported to New-England : imbarqued in the *Planter* NICᵒ: TRARICE Mʳ bound thither : they have brought Certificate from the Justices of Peace (Ministers of yᵉ pish that they are conformable to the orders of yᵉ Church of England and are no Subsedy Men : they have taken the oath of Supremacie (Allegeance die et Anᵒ prd.

	yeres
A Carrier MARTIN SAUNDERS	40
vxor RACHELL SAUNDERS..............	40

3 children { LEA SAUNDERS 10
Judith Saundr's 8
Martin Saunders 4

3 servant's { Marie Fuller 17
Richard Smith 14
Ric^R : Ridley 16

Husb: Francis Newcom 30

wife ℓ 2 children { Rachell Newcom 20
Rachell Newcom.............. 2⅓
Jo: Newcom .... 9 moneths

A Glover Ant° Stannion..................... 24

Daniell Hanbury ...., 29

Francis Dexter 13

Willm Dawes 15

Marie Saunders 15

A Taylor Clement Bates .... 40 ⎤
Ann Bates .... 40 ⎟
5 children { James Bates .... 14 ⎟ Theis pties imbarqued in
Clement Bates ...... 12 ⎬ the *Eliz.* Mr Wm Stagg
Rachell Bates......... 8 ⎟ bound for New England
Joseph Bates........... 5 ⎟ ℓ Cert: from the Justic's
Ben: Bates .... 2 ⎟ ℓ Ministers of ye pish.
servant's { Jo: Wynchester ...... 19 ⎟
Jarvice Gold* .... 30 ⎦

More for the *Planter*

Husbandman Richard Tuttell.............. 42

Ann Tuttell..................... 41

Anna Tuttell 12

Jo: Tuttell 10

Rabecca Tuttell.............. 6

Isbell Tuttell.................. 70

Marie Wolhouston........... 30

---

* ["The scribe made a brace against Jo: Wynchester, and began to write *servant* against the name, but stopped when he had written *se*, and wrote *servants* against Jervice (Jarvice) Gold."—*Drake.*]

Husbandman Wiᴴᴹ TUTTELL 26
          ELIZABETH TUTTELL 23
          JO: TUTTELL 3½
          ANN TUTTELL .... 2 a qʳ
          THO: TUTTELL .... 3. mo:
          SYCILLIE CLARK 16
          MARIE BILL 11

PHILLIPP ATWOOD .... 12 | MARIE BUSHNELL 26
BARTHOL: FALDOE .... 16 | MARTHA BUSHNELL 1
A Carpenter THO: PELL* ...... 26 | Wiᴴᴹ LEA† 16
MARIE PELL .... 26 | MARIE SMITH 18
MARIE PELL .... 1 | ELIZABETH SWAYNE 20
Wᴹ LFA .... 16 | MARGARET LEACH.............. 15
A Carpenter FRANC'S BUSH- | HANNA SMITH 18
    NELL .... 26 | ANN WELLS 15

N the *Hopewell* Wiᴴᴹ BUNDOCK Mʳ bound for New-England ℮c.

          JAMES BURGIS 14
          ALEXANDER THWAIT'S 20
          JO: ABBOTT 16
          JO: BELLOWES 12
          JO: JOHNES 18
          CHRISTIOM ‡ LUDDINGTON 18
          MARIE ABBOTT 16
          MARIE COKE 14
          MARIE PEAKE 15
A Tayler THO: PELL 22
A Glazier JO: BUSHNELL 21

* [This and the three following names are crossed through in the original MS.]
† [It will be seen that this is a repetition of one of the crossed-out names in the first column.]
‡ [Probably intended for CHRISTIAN. The original, however, is distinctly written.]

N the *Rabecca* of London, M^r   HODGES for New-England

A Husbandman. PETER VNDERWOOD 22
                ISABELL CRADDOCK 30

vij° Aprilis 1635

HIS ptie vnder mencioned is to be imbarqued in the *Planter* bound for New-England, p Cert: from ALDERMAN FENN of his conformitie. he hath taken the oath of Allegeance & Supremacie.

RICHARD FENN 27

3 *Aprilis* 1635 At Gravesend.

HEIS vnder written names are to be transported to St Christophers imbarqued in the *Paul* of London, JO: ACKLIN, M^r bound thither. there was Cert: brought from the Minister of St Katherins of their conformitie of their discipline & orders to ye Church of England the Men did take ye oath of Alleg: and Supremacie.

	yeres		yeres
RALPH REASON	23	THO: WATSON	29
EDWARD MERRIFIELD	19	DAVID EVANS	22
ROBERT WADE	35	STEEVEN GARRET	19
WiħM HAIES	24	W^M BEDDLE	19
GEO: RISHFORD	24	RICHARD LOCK	20
MATHEW MOYSES	17	ABRAM WATSON	19
ROBERT RICHARDSON	20	JAMES CARTER	25
JO: MOUNTAIN	20	W^M SCARSBRICK	23
JO: WILLIS	29	W^M CHURCH	21
JO: FRENCH	18	JOHN REINOI D'S	23

HENRY BAGIN	22	JO: WATT'S	21
Wᴹ LAṁYN	21	EDWARD FISHER	27
HANNA ROPER	23	RICᴿ: CROWDER	28
HENRY LEE..	30	RICᴿ: PRESTON	21
EDWARD SMALLMAN	21	RICᴷ: OLDER	24
ROBERT ATKINSON	23	Wᴹ KING	18
THO: FEARFAX	22	JO: HOLMES	22
MATHEW TURNER	46	NICᵒ SEDEN	20
EDWARD GASS	20	FRA: STOTT	32
HENRY SENTENCE	20	PHILLIPP JEÑING'S	25
EDMOND DAVIES	21	ROBERT SPURR	24
EDWARD BARNES	16	THO: SPENDERGRASS	24
THO: NOTT	18	NICᵒ: HOLLIS	20
JO: ADAMS	16	RICᴿ: DANES	20
EDWARD GRAY	32		
			49

IN the *Peter Bonaventure*. THO: HARMAN Mʳ bound for the Bar-babodoes, theis vnder written names p order : they have taken yᵉ oaths of Supremacie and Allegeance.

	yeres		yeres
THO: BERKYNN	24	RICᴿ: LEECH	22
JO: WESTGARTH	28	RICᴿ: ABBOTT	20
JO: SWEETING	26	AMBROSE HUETT	27
JAMES TOWNSON	29	JO: WHITE	25
RICᴿ: DAWSON	28	JO: WESTON	26
THO: GREENWOOD	15	Wᴹ WESTON	16
THO: IVESON	36	Wᴹ HOWSEMAN	12
THO: HYWOOD	22	RICᴿ: CHAPMAN	40
Wᴹ BANK'S	23	THO: CUTLER	35
JO: GREENLY	20	JAMES JACKSON	33
DANIELL DAVIES	26	JO: SMITHEMAN	23
ROBERT BRABAN	29	ROBERT SAVAGE	21
JO: THOMAS	25	GEO: PENNY	24

Jo Pattman	23	Wi͟llm Beckkitt	26
Tho: Coke	30	Tho: Evans	20
Jo: Symonds	19	Jo: Hynd	24
Jo: Boone	12	Wm Mecham	20
Nic^o: Evans	16	Roger Wills	20
Jo: Wydhouse	15	Tho: Tedder	19
Ric^R: Hollinby	20	Jo: Sessions	22
Wm Lodge	13	Daniell Dennis	22
Isack Pratt	22	Capten Jacob Lake	30
o: Evans	17	Luke Stokes	35
ames Robard's	20	Richard Speed	35
Ric^R: Clark	19	Phillipp Henson	21
Geo: Plunckett	19	Arthur Watkyns	25
Wm Maccowdin	19	Jo: Joyner	25
Jo: Alliday	20	Jo: Dent	30
Walter Gibson	25	Robert Jn^oson	26
Jo: Wynkles	20	Jo: Sawcott	18
Jo: Vynn	17	Jo: Bunce	18
Robert Roe	19	Jo: Robinson	26
Maurice Wi͟llms [Williams].	18	Ric^R: Pell	22
Dennis Mortagh	30	Jo: Disherd	22
Jo: Dukkartii	31	Tho: Lamberd	23
Ric^R: Mansfield	22	Geo: Chapman	17
Gregorie Ogell	15	Wm Aston	17
Wm Whitlock	31	Adrian Coke	27
Jo: Long	20	Robert Philkynn	25
Jo: Thomson	31	Jno Sympson	29
Tho: Farmer	22	Steeven Greenly	16
Ric^R: Brownley	19	Mary Loveley	35
Matiiew Westwood	18	Ann Lovely	10
Jo: Matiier	21	Margaret Lucock's	27
Robert Pendred	40	Annis Percy	24
David Robinson	20		

8 *Aprilis* 1635

HEIS pties herevnder mencioned are to be transported to New-England : imbarqued in the *Elizabeth* of London Wᴹ STAGG Mʳ bound thither : they have taken the oath of Allegeance ℰ Supremacie p Cert: from the pish of St Alphage Cropplegate [Cripplegate] the Minister there.

Tanners Wᴹ HOLDRED 25
ROGER PRESTON 21
DANIELL BRODLEY 20
ISACK STUDMAN*............ 30

That theis 3 ptics prd are no Subsedie men : wee whose names herevnto are written belonging to Blackwell Hall, do averr they are none.

ROBᵀᴱ FARRANDS.
THOMAS SMITH.

HEIS pties herevnder written are to be transported in the *Planter:* prd. p Cert: from the Minister of Kingston vpon Thames in the County of Surrey of their conformitie : ℰ yᵗ they are no Subsedy men.

A Miller PALMER TINGLEY † 21
An ostler Wᴹ BUTTERICK 20
A Miller THO: JEWELL 27

ix° *Aprilis* 1635

N the *Elizabeth* de London prd Mʳ WIꞪM STAGG bound for New-England : Theis vnder-written names have brought Cert: from yᵉ Minister of Hauckust ‡ in Kent : ℰ Attestation from two Justices of

---

* [This fourth name is in a different handwriting from the preceding three, and was doubtless inserted after the succeeding paragraph (in which *three* only are referred to) had been written.]

† [The first letter of this name is very faintly marked ; but, after close examination, I cannot doubt that it is a T.]

‡ [Hawkhurst, in the Lathe of Scray.]

Peace being conformable to the Church of England ⸾ that they are no Subsedy Men.

		yeres
A Clothier JAMES HOSMER	....	28
Vxor ANN HOSMER	......	27
wife ⸾ 2 children { MARIE HOSMER	....	2
ANN HOSSMER	...... 3. mo:	
maidserv^{ts} { MARIE DONNARD	......	24
MARIE MARTIN	....	19
JO: STON	....	40
EDWARD GOLD	....	28
GEO: RUSSELL	....	19
JO: MUSSELL	....	15

Nono die Aprilis 1635

IN the *Rabecca* M^r JO: HODGES bound for New-England.

Husbandman. JACOB WELSH	....	32
GEO: WOODWARD	....	35

THEIS vnder-written names are to be transported to New-England imbarqued in the *Rabecca* prd.

ELIZABETH WINCKOLL	.. 52	W^M SWAYNE aged	 16
JO: WINCKOLL	 13	FRANCIS SWAYNE	 14

17th *Aprill* 1635

IN the *Elisa* ⸾ *Anne* m' RO. COWPER v^rs New England

THOMAS HEDSALL .... 47 yers.

IN the *Encrease* of Lond. m' ROBERT LEA vᵣs New Engłd

    a Mason GEO: BACON* .... 43 yers :

SAMUELL .... 12 yers ⎫
JOⁿ .... 8 ⎬ Children of the Said Mason* [BACON].
SUSAN .... 10 ⎭

    a Husbandman THO: JOSTLIN 43
        REBECCA his wife.................... 43
        ELIZA, WARD a maid serut........... 38

REBECCA ...... 18 ⎫
DOROTHY ...... 11 ⎪
NATHANIELL .. 08 ⎬ Children of the said THO: JOSTLIN
ELIZA. .... 6 ⎪
MARY......... 1 ⎭

xº Aprilis 1635

THEIS vnder written names are to be transported in the *Planter* prd NICº: TRARICE Mʳ bound for New Engl: p Cert: of the Minister of Sudburie in Suffolk ℇ from the Maior of the Towne of his conformitie to the orders ℇ discipline of the Church of England ℇ that he is no Subsedy man. he hath taken the oath of Alleg: ℇ Suprem:

                                          yeres
    Carrier RICHARD HASFELL† 54
       vxor MARTHA 42

5 daughters. ⎧ MARIE HASFELL 17
⎪ SARA HASFELL 14
⎨ MARTHA HASFELL 8
⎪ RACHELL HASFELL........... 6
⎩ RUTH HASFELL 3

* [This name was first written MASON, in mistake, and then altered to BACON ; the correction, however, was not made for the children. I therefore suggest, in their case, what is doubtless the correct reading, within brackets.]

† [With some of the daughters, this name appears to be written HAFFELL; it is, however, evidently intended for HASFELL : in the first name, that of RICHARD HASFELL, it is quite clear.]

ALICE SMITH 40
ELIZABETH Coop [COOPER] 24
JO: SMITH 13
JOB HAWKINS 15

I N the *Planter* prd: Theis vnder names are to be transported to
New-England.

EGLIN HANFORD 46
2 daughters { MARGARET HANFORD 16
ELIZ: HANFORD 14
RODOLPHUS ELMES 15
THO: STANSLEY 16

I N the *Elizabeth* of London : W^M STAGG M^r bound for New-England.

WIĦM WILD... 30
PETER THORNE 20
ALICE WILD 40

xj° die Aprilis 1635

I N the *Eliz:* prd W^M STAGG M^r bound for New-England : the pties
vnder written have brought Certificate according to order

A Carpenter W^M WHITTEREDD 36 | JO: CLUFFE 22
vxor ELIZABETH .... 30 | JO: WILD 17
sonn THO: WHITTREDD .. 10 | SAM̄VEL HAIEWARD 22
| JO: DUKE 20

I N the *Planter* prd : Theis vnder written names are to be transported to New-England p Certificate according to order

SARA PITTNEI .... 22 | MARGARET PITNEY 22
2 children { SARA PITNEI .. 7 | RACHELL DEANE 31
SAMVELL PITNEY 1:½ |

xiij° Aprilis 1635

IN the *Elizabeth & Ann* Mᵘ ROGER Coop [COOPER] bound for New-England p Cert: from the Maior of Evesham in com worcᵘ & from the Minister of yᵉ pish. of their Conformitie.

MARGERIE WASHBORN	49
JO: WASHBORNE	14 } 2 sonns
PHILLIPP WASHBORNE	11

IN the *Elizabeth* de Lo: Wᵖ STAGG Mᵘ prd: theis vnder written names brought Certi. from the Minister of St Savioᵘs Southwark: of their conformitie.

THO: MILLET	30	JOSUA WHEAT	17
vxor MARIE MILLET	29	JO: SMITH	12
VRSULA GREENOWAY	32	RALPH CHAPMAN	20
HENRIE BULL	19	THO: MILLET	2

THIS vnder written name is to be imbarqued in yᵉ *Increase* ROBERT LEA Mᵘ bound for New-England.. p Cert. from Billerecay in Essex, from the Minister of yᵉ pish that he is no Subsedy man.

Husbandmen Wᵖ RUSCO	41
et vxor RABECCA	40
SARA RUSCO	9
MARIE RUSCO	7 } 4 children.
SAMVEL	5
Wᵖ RUSCO	1

N the *Increase* prd. Theis vnder written names are to be transported to New England : p Cert: from All Sᵗ's Stayning's
Mark-lane of their Conformitie to the Church of England.

A Taylor Tᴴᴏ: Page 29
          Elizabeth Page .... 28 ⎫
          Tᴴᴏ: Page .... 2 ⎬ wife ℓ 2 children.
          Katherin Page .... 1 ⎭
          Edward Spark's .... 22 ⎫ 2 servᵗˢ
          Kat: Taylor .... 24 ⎭

N the *Elizabeth ℓ Ann* Roger Coop [Cooper] Mʳ : Theis pties
herevnder expressed are to be imbarqued for New-England
having taken the oaths of Allegeance ℓ Supremacie ℓ likewise brought
Certificate both from the Ministers ℓ Justices where their abiding's were
latlie of their conformitie to the discipline ℓ orders of the Church of
England, ℓ yᵗ they are no Subsedy Men.

Husb: Robert Hawkynns ..	25	Tᴴᴏ: Hubbard	10
Jo: Whitney	35	Tᴴᴏ: Eaton	1
Jo: Palmerley	20	Marie Hawkynns	24
Richard Martin	12	Ellin Whitney	30
Jo: Whitney	11	Abigall Eaton...........	35
Richard Whitney	9	Sara Cartrack	24
Nathaniell Whitney	8	Jane Daṁand	9
Tᴴᴏ: Whitney	6	Mary Eaton	4
Jonathan Whitney	1	Marie Broomer	10
Nicᵒ: Sension............	13	Mildred Cartrack........	2
Henry Jackson...........	29	Joseph Alsopp	14
Wᴹ Hubbard	35		

N the *Suzan & Ellin* EDWARD PAYNE Mʳ for New- England Theis pties herevnder expressed have brought Certificate from the Minister & Justices of their Conformitie & that they are no Subsedy Men

Husbandman JOHN PROCTER .	40	Husb: RICHARD SALTONSTALL	23
MARTHA PROCTER	28	MERRIALL SALTONSTALL	22
JOHN PROCTER	3	MERRIALL SALTONSTALL ..9 Mo:	
MARIE PROCTER............	1	THO: WELLS	30
ALICE STREET	28	PETER COOp [COOPER]	28
Husb: WALTER THORNTON ..	36	Wᴹ LAMBART	26
JOANNA THORNTON	44	SAᴍVEL PODD	25
JOHN NORTH	20	JEREMY BELCHER	22
MARY PYNDER	53	MARIE CLIFFORD	25
FRANCIS PYNDER	20	JANE COE..................	30
MARIE PYNDER	17	MARIE RIDDLESDEN	17
JOANNA PINDER	14	JO: PELLAM	20
ANNA PYNDER	12	MATHEW HITCHCOCK	25
KATHERIN PINDER	10	ELIZABETH NICHOLLS	25
JO: PYNDER	8	TOMAZIN CARPENTER	35
RICHARD SKOFIELD	22	ANN FOWLE	25
EDWARD WEEDEN	22	EDMOND GORDEN	18
GEORGE WILBY	16	THO: SYDLIE	22
RICHARD HAWKINS	15	MARGARET LEACH..........	22
THO: PARKER	30	MARIE SMITH	21
SYMON BURD	20	ELIZABETH SWAYNE	16
JO: MANSFIELD	34	GRACE BEWLIE	30
CLEMENT COLE	30	ANN WELLS	20
JO: JONES...............	20	DYONIS TAYLER	48
Wᴹ BURROW	19	HANNA SMITH	30
PHILLIP ATWOOD	13	JO: BACKLEY	15
Wᴹ SNOWE	18	Wᴹ BATTRICK	18
EDWARD LUᴍUS*	24		

* It is very likely this name may be intended for Lam[m]as ; the second letter is, however, plainly written *u*.

15 *May* 1635

PENELOPY PELLAM 16 yers to passe to her brother plantao͂ [plantation]

---

xiiij° Aprilis 1635

I N the *Increase* of London M^r ROB^{TE} LEA bounde for New England

ROBERT CORDELL	SAMUELL ANDREWES aged 37 y^{rs}		Theis haue taken the oathes of Allegance ℓ Supremacye, and haue brought Certeficat of their conformety wch are this day filed
Gouldsmith in	ROB^{TE} NANEY .... aged 22 yeres		
Limbert Stret*	ROB^{TE} SANKEY .... aged 30 yeres		
sent them a Way	JAMES GIBBONS.... aged 21 yeres		

Also.

JANE the wife of thabouesaid SAM̄ ANDREWES 30 y^{rs}
ELLYN LONGE her s'runte aged 20 yeares........
JANE ANDREWES her daughter aged 3 yeares ....
ELIZABETH ANDROWES her daughter aged 2 yeares

All for newland [New England] in the *Increase* aforesaid

---

xv^{th.} Aprill 1635

I N the *Eliza.* de Lond. m' W^M STAGG vrs New Englād

RICH. WALKER .... 24 yers
JO^N BEAMOND 23
W^M BEAMOND 27
THO: LETTYNE 23
JO^N JOHNSON 23

theis ptis haue taken Oathe of Allegane ℓ of Supremacy before Sr W^M WHITIMOR ℓ Sr NICHO: RANTON

Wiłłm WALKER 15

---

* [Doubtless intended for Lombard Street.]

15ᵗʰ *Aprill* 1635

IN the *Eliza..* ℓ *Anne* de Lon m' ROGER COOPER vᵗˢ New England

PERCY KINGE 24 yers. a Maid seruant to m' RO: CROWLEY:

IN the *Eliza..* de Lo. m' Wᴹ STAGG vrs New England

JAMES WALKER 15 yers ℓ SARRA. WALKER 17 yers: Seruᵗˢ to Joˣ
BROWNE a Baker ℓ to on Wᴹ BRASEY linen drap in Cheapside
Lond p Cert. of their Conformity.

---

xviij° Aprilis 1635

THEIS vnder written names are to be transported to New-England
imbarqued in the *Increase* de Lo: ROBERT LEA Mʳ the ptie prd
having brought Certificat's from the Minister ℓ Justices of yᵉ Peace of
his conformitie to the Church of England

	yeres	
Glover THO: BLOGGETT	30	
uxor SUZAN BLOGGETT	37	
DANIELL BLOGGET.............	4	} 2 children.
SAMVELL BLOGGET	1½	

IN the *Increase* prd. The ptie vnder written hath brought Certificate from the Minister of Wapping ℓ from two Justices of peace,
of his Conformitie to yᵉ Church of England: to passe in yᵉ said Ship
for New-England

Lynnen wever THO: CHITTINGDEN...........	51	
uxor RABECCA CHITTINGDEN	40	
ISACK CHITTINGDEN	10	} 2 children
HEN: CHITTINGDEN	6	

HEIS vnder written names are to be transported to New-England imbarqued in the *Suzan & Ellin* EDWARD PAYNE M^r: the pties have brought Certificates from ye Ministers & Justices of the peace y^t they are no Subsedy Men : & are conformable to ye orders & discipline of the Church of England

A Drap RALPH HUDSON	42
vxor MARIE HUDSON	42
3 children { HANNA HUDSON	14
ELIZ: HUDSON	5
JO: HUDSON	12
THO: BRIGGHAM	32
servant's { BEN: THWING	16
ANN GIBSON	34
JUDITH KIRK	18
JO: MORE	41
HENRY KNOWLES	25

GEO RICHARDSON	30
BEN: THOMLINS	18
EDWARD THOMLINS	30
BARBARA FORD	16
JOAN BROOMER	13
RICHARD BROOKE	24
THO: BROOKE	18
Husbandman SYMON CROSBY	26
vxor ANN CROSBY	25
THO: CROSBY	8 week's } 1 Child
Husbandman RIC^R: ROWTON	36
vxor ANN ROWTON	36
EDMOND ROWTON	6 } 1 child.
A Husb:man PERCIVALL GREENE	32
vxor ELLIN GREENE	32

Jo: Trane	25 } 2 servant's
Margaret Dix	18 }
Jo: Atherson	24
Ann Blason	27

Ben: Buckley	11
Daniell Buckley	9
Jo: Corrington	33
Mary Corrington	33

xiiij° Aprilis 1635

THEIS vnder-written names are to be transported to the Barbadoes imbarqued in the *Faulcon* de London, Tho: Irish Mr p Certificate from the Minister of the pish of their conformity to the orders of the Church of England, The Men have taken the oaths of Allegeance & Supremacie.

Gabriell Bolt	29	Henry Dye	20
Owen Bliss	30	Edward Bull	22
Geo: Say	26	Farford Goldsmith	22
Bassell Terry	22	Tho: Crispin	19
Marmaduke Turner	21	Francis Sheres	26
Jo: Bassett	19	John Bathe	23
Jo: Sheering	26	Smith Baker	28
Henrie Biddleston	17	James Hibbins	17
Tho: Lett	22	Jo: Belton	48
Samvel Stor*	17	Nicolas Flitcroft	16
James Burt	13	Wm Bingham	18
Charles Fall	19	Humfrey Morris	18
Wm Sennott	20	Jo: Dallinger	16
Jo: Browne	20	Jo: Rogers	34
Tho: Webb	18	Jo: Spyer	32
Jo: Hopwood	20	Francis Smith	20
Nico: Wade	19	Abraham Halloway	20
Robert Davers	14	Joseph Drap [Draper]	21

* [The last letter is very indistinctly written : the name *may* be read as Stor, Ston, or Stow.]

THO: BROMBY	59	TOBY HAZELL	20
JO: BROMBY	27	GEO: CLARK	15
JESPER GIGGON	18	THO: ROBERT'S	18
JOHN BRUMWELL	22	MARMADUKE CROSBY	28
RIC^K: DENT	17	GEO: HARRIS	17
THOMAS GUALMAY	22	ROGER SAWTER	17
RICHARD SNATHE	19	MARIE PERRY	18
RICHARD COCKMAN	2C	ELIZABETH ELSON	18
THOMAS ALLIN	22	BRIDGET GERDEN	19
VALENTINE LOVE	18	KATHERIN HILL	20
ROBERT HAXLEY	21	MARIE NEWCOM	17
THO: METCALF	20	BENEDICTER SHERHACK	20
W^M KNIGHT	30	MARIE CREW	19
HENRIE GILDER	18	ELIZABETH LONG	21
GEORGE LEE	16	WINIFRED HAND	20
ANT^O: BOLDSWORTH	18	ELIZABETH CURTIS	22
JOHN CHURCH	21	~~W^M LANGLEY~~ *	14
JOHN SCOTT	16	W^M STURGIS	18
ROBERT JONES	25	THO: KNOWLES	16
NATHANIELL WRITE	32	PETER LOSTELL	14
JOHN JONES	24	WALTER HOLBURD	24
THO: WALLIS	27		

xv° Aprilis 1635.

THEIS pties hereafter expressed are to be transported to New-England imbarqued in y^e *Increase* ROBERT LEA M^r· having taken the oathes of Allegeance & Supremacie : As also being conformable to the Governm^t & discipline of the Church of England whereof they brought testimony p Cert: from ye Justices & Ministers where there abodes have latlie been. (vizt.)

		yeres
Husbandman SAMVELL MORSE		50
vxor ELIZABETH MORSE		48

---

* [Crossed through in the original ; the age is doubtful.]

JOSEPH MORSE................ 20
ELIZABETH DANIELL 2

Alynnen wev' PHILEMON DALTON 45
        vxor HANNA DALTON 35
        SAMVEL DALTON.............. 5½
        W^M WHITE 14

Husbandman MARTHAW MARVYN 35
        vxor ELIZABETH MARVYNN 31
        ELIZABETH MARVINN.......... 31
        MATHEW MARVYNN 8
        MARIE MARVYNN 6
        SARA MARVYNN 3
        HANNA MARVYNN .... ½
        JO: WARNER.................. 20
        ISACK MORE.................. 13

Carpenter SAMVELL IRELAND............ 32
        vxor MARIE IRELAND.............. 30
        MARTHA IRELAND 1½

Plowrite. WIłłM BUCK 50
        ROGER BUCK 18

A joyner. JO: DAVIES 29

A Husbandman. ABRAM FLEMING 40

Husb: JO: FOKAR.................... 21

Clothier. THO: PARISH 22
        JOHN OWDIE 17

Butcher W^M HOUGHTON 22

Husb: WIłłM PAYNE 37
        ANNA PAYNE................. 40
        W^M PAYNE.................... 10
        ANNA PAYNE 5
        JO: PAYNE.................... 3
        DANIELL PAYNE .... 8. week's.

9

JAMES BITTON	27	JO: KILBORNE	10
W^M POTTER	25	JAMES ROGER	20
ELIZABETH WOOD	38	RICHARD NUNN	19
ELIZABETH BEARDS	24	THO: BARRET	16
SUZAN PAYNE	11	JO: HACKWELL	18
AYMES GLADWELL	16		
PHEBE PERCE	18	Chirurgion SYMON AYRES	48
Carpenter HENRY CROSSE	20	*vxor* DOROTHY AYRES	38
Husb: THO: KILBORNE	55	MARIE AYRES	15
vxor FRANCIS KILBORNE	50	THO: AYRES	13
MARGARET KILBORNE	23	SYMON AYRES	11
LYDDIA KILBORNE	22	RABECCA AYRES	9
MARIE KILBORNE	16	JANE RAWLIN	30
FRANCIS KILBORNE	12		

Husbandman SYMON STONE 50

vxor JOAN STONE 38

children
   FRANCIS STONE 16
   ANN STONE 11
   SYMON STONE 4
   MARIE STONE 3
   JO: STONE............ 5 weekes

CHRISTIAN AYRES 7

ANNA AYRES 5

BENIAMIN AYRES 3

SARA AYRES .... 3. mo:

A Sawy^r STEEVEN VPSON 23

JO: WYNDELL 16

seruants
   ISACK WORDEN 18
   NATHANIELL WOOD 12
   ELIZABETH STREATON 19
   MARIE TOLLER 16

16 *Aprilis* 1635

THEIS pties hereafter expressed are to be transported to the Island of Providence imbarqued in yᵉ *Expectacion* CORNELIUS BILLINGE Mʳ, having taken the Ooaths of Allegeance ℘ Supremacie: As likewise being conformable to the Church of England ; whereof they brought testimonie from the Ministers ℘ Justices of Peace, of their Abodes

FRANCIS SMITH	36	MARY BAKER	42
THO: PALMER	18	ELISHA BRIDGES	16
LEONARD SMITH	22	WIĦM THORP	30
MATHEW HAMBLEN	38	ELIZABETH THORP	20
Wᴹ LYNLIE	58	ELIZABETH THORP	2
CHRISTIAN WHETSTON	19	JOAN FELVER	50
Wᴹ CAWDLE	19	MARGARET ROLLRIGHT	45
FLORENCE DICKENSON	19	ELLIN COOPER	24
JO: BAKER	42	ELIZABETH COKE	20
JO: MARTIN	30	MARIE CHADDOCK	20
Wᴹ SMITH	20	ELIZABETH HAMOND	25
ANTᵒ DOWSELL	20	ALICE AWBREY	29
RICHARD SLIE	20	ELIZABETH LAWRENCE	26
FRANCIS DALES	20	ANN NOBLE	21
PETER AWBREY	32	MARIE HARROWIGG	21
THO: FELD	18	MILLICENT LEECH	28
EDWARD HASSARD	24	MARIE GOODWYNN	20
RICHARD BULL	17	KATHERIN WEBB	22
RICHARD REINOLD'S	16	ELIZABETH SCOTT	20
Wᴹ EAKINS	15	MARIE HOWES	18
JO: TOTNELL	16	DOROTHY LAWRENCE	28
EDWARD HORSHAM	14	ELIZAB: HORSHAM	16
RICHARD TRENDALL	16	ALICE GOLDHAM	26
Wᴹ READ	16	RICHARD PRICE	14
MATHEW PIPPIN	20	RICHARD LANE	38

ALICE LANE	30	ELIZABETH OWEN	30
SAMVEL LANE	7	MARIE MILWARD	21
JO: LANE	4	ISACK BARTON	27
OZIELL LANE	3	ABRAM RAY	20
JO: ATKINSON	36	DORCAS HORSHAM	40
LOVE ATKINSON	38	MARIE GRIFFINN	17

17 *Aprilis* 1635

HEIS pties herevnder expressed are to be transported to New-England imbarqued in y^e *Elizabeth* W^M STAGG M^r p Cert: from the Ministers ℓ Justices of the Peace of their Conformitie to the Church of England : they have taken the oaths of Allegeance ℓ Supremacie

	yeres		
Husb: JAMES BATE	53	*filia* MARY SMITH	15
ALICE BATE	52	PETER GARDNER	18
LYDDIA BATE	20	W^M HUBBARD	35
MARIE BATE	17	RACHELL BIGG	6
MARGARET BATE	12	PATIENCE FOSTER	40
JAMES BATES	9	HOPESTILL FOSTER	14
Husbandman EDWARD BUL-		FRANCIS WHITE	24
LOCK	32	JOAN SELLIN	50
ELIZABETH STEDMAN	26	ANN SELLIN	7
NATHANIELL STEDMAN	5	EDWARD LOOMES	27
ISACK STEDMAN	1	JO: HUBBARD	10
ROBERT THORNTON	11	JO: DAVIES	9
MARGARET DAVIES	32	MARIE DAVIES	4
ELIZABETH DAVIES	1	JO: BROWNE	40
DOROTHY SMITH	45		

THE ptie herevnder named with his wife & children is to be transported to New-England imbarqued in the *Elizabeth & Ann* Wᴵᴸᴸᴹ Cooper Mʳ bound thither the ptie hath brought testimony from the Minister of his conformitie to the orders & discipline of the Church of England & from the two Justices of peace yᵗ he hath taken the oaths of Allegeance & Supremacie.

Alexander Baker	....	28
Vxor Elizabeth	....	23
Elizabeth Baker	....	3
Christian Baker	....	1
Clement Chaplin	....	48
Wᴹ Swayne	....	50

Braced 28, 23, 3, 1 : yeres

24 *Aprilis* 1635

THEIS vnder written names are to be transported to the Island of Providence imbarqued in the *Expectacon* aforesaid, the pties have taken yᵉ oath of Alleg:

	yeres		
Nicholas Riskyᴹer	31	Sam: Goodenuff	22
Wᴹ Randall	26	Edward Hasting's	23
Andrew Leay	24	Tho: Hobbs	18
Jo: Leay	25	Jo: Saracole	17
Jo: Bloxsall	28	Tho: Wilson	18

27 *Aprilis* 1635

THEIS vnder written names are to be transported to New-England Roger Cooper Mʳ bound thither, in the *Elizabeth & Ann*. the pties have brought Certificate from the Minister at Westminster : (͠ the Justices of the Peace of his Conformitie. the ṗtie hath taken the oaths of Alleg. (͠ Suprem:

A Carpenter RICHARD BROCKE 31
EDWARD SALL............... 24
DANIELL PRESTOÑ 13

HEIS vnder-written names are to be transported to the Barbadoes (͠ St Christophers, imbarqued in the *Ann* (͠ *Elizabeth* JO: BROOKEHAVEN Capten (͠ M^r having taken the oaths of Allegeance (͠ Supremacie. As also being Conformable to the orders (͠ discipline of the Church of England (͠ no Subsedy Men. whereof they brought test : from the Minister of St Katherins neere ye Tower of London.

	yeres		yeres
JOHN CROFT'S	30	BARTHOLOMEW BENNET	18
NATHANIELL BEDFORD......	19	THOMAS TYLER	21
JO: MASON	20	JOHN PRICHARD	20
JO: ORAM..................	21	GILES BARNES............	19
CHRISTOPHER FISH	24	HUGH SADLER	20
OWEN ANDROWE	18	HARFORD YOUNG	20
ROBERT ANDERSON	22	JOHN WILLIAMS	16
JOHN GREENE..............	25	ANDREW EVANS............	16
JOSEPH WALLINGTON	19	JOHN BARRET.............	16
JOHN HAIEWARD	22	JOSEPH WALKER...........	18
THOMAS MARTIN	16	JAMES TATE..............	17
EDMOND HOLLOWAY........	17	JOHN SMITH	14
THOMAS PIERCE	19	NATHANIELL BOLTON	19
WILLIAM HAYWARD	18	W^M LAYDON	17
EDWARD WILKINSON........	17	THOMAS AVERY	18
RICHARD GALE	16	THO: LEAKE	18
ROBERT TRATT	21	DAVIE WILLIAMS	17
THOMAS REDDMAN..........	16	WIℏM HARRIS	23
WIℏM GRUBB	16	JOHN TURPIN	22
JOHN GOLDING	21	FRANCIS SAIEWELL	18
CLEMENT HUTCHINSON......	20	MATHEW ROGERS	21

Bryan Bourk	19	Robert Laycock	18
Antᵒ Taylor	26	Michell Estplynn	18
Andrew Carr	23	James Bell	19
Owen Garret	20	Frend Picto	20
John Frazill	29	John Whithedd	22
John Porter	24	Jo: Mallion	21
Charles Pollington	26	Tho: Bedlam	24
Charles Jackson	18	Tho: Lone*	19
Edward Bacon	25	Thomas Wazell	21
Thomas Robinson	31	Edward Garrard	26
Patrick Conly [or Couly]	21	John Coke	22
George Goddin	31	Jeremy Hartley	30
Arthur Roker	20	Gilbert Holdsworth	30
Tho: Dale	28		
John Davies	19		
Tho: Burton	19	*Women.*	
Hugh Wynstonly	20	Katherin Lloyd	19
Bartholmew Draper	20	Suzan Greene	20
Robert Brock	25	Margerie Barran	19
Hugh Tawyer	18	Elizabeth Bennïng	18
Wᴹ Greene	17	Elizabeth Bruster	18
Patrick Connyer	20	Joan Smith	27
Richard King	23	Suzan More	21
Wiłłm Barnes	17	Alice Dixon	21
Wiłłm Taylor	23	Jane Stafford	24
Robert Sennodd	23	Alice Hilton	18
Thomas Perkynn	29	Katherin Russell	20
Wiłłm Longwith	26	Mary Powell	23
Tho Gullifer	28	Debora Winke	21
John Davies	18	Rabecca Bedding	18
Richard Cawood	25	Mathew Page	20
Richard Dynley	19	Ann Spicer	26
Dennis Peke	20	Marie Jones	20
Nicholas Greene	18	Margery Harding	20
		Marie Kinderslie	26

* [Perhaps intended for Loue, *i.e.* Love.]

29° *Aprilis* 1635

THEIS vnder written names are to betrans ported to New-England imbarqued in the *Elizabeth & Ann* ROGER COOP [COOPER] M^r the pties have brought Certificate from the Minister of the pish & Justices of Peace of their conformitie to the orders & discipline of the Church of England & y^t they are no Subsedy-men

RIC^R: GOARD	17	THO: POUNT*	21
A Smith THO: LORD	50	ROBERT LORD	9
vxor DOROTHY	46	AYMIE LORD	6
THOMAS LORD	16	DOROTHY LORD	4
ANN. LORD	14		
W^M LORD	12	JOSIAS COBBET	21
JOHN LORD	10	JO: HOLLOWAY	21
JAMES COBBETT	23	JANE BENNET	16
JOSEPH FABERR	26	W^M REEVE	22

eodem 29 *Aprilis* 1635

A Taylor CHRISTOPHER STANLEY............ 32
vxor SUZANNA 31
W^M SAMOND........................ 19

4° *Maij* 1635.

THEIS vnder-written names are to be transported to New-England imbarqued in the *Eliz: & Ann* prd. The pties have brought Certificate from the Minister & Justic's of the Peace of their conformitie & that they are no Subsedy Men.

A Tallow-Chandler HEN: WILKINSON 25
ROBERT HAIES............... 19 A soapeboyler.

* [It is impossible to decide whether this name is PONNT or POUNT; it is so indistinctly written, that it may even be intended for POUND.]

THEIS vnder-written names are to be transported to New-England: imbarqued in the *Abigall* RICHARD HACKWELL Mʳ: The pties have brought Certificate from yᵉ Minister ℘ Justices of their conformitie to the orders ℘ discipline of the Church of England

THO: BUTTOLPH	32	NATHANIELL TYLLY	32
vxor ANN BUTTOLPH	24	PETER KETTELL	10
Wᴹ FULLER	25	THO: STEEVENS	12
JO: FULLER	15	ELIZ: HARDING	12

2° Maij 1635

THEIS vnder-written names are to be transported to yᵉ Barbadoes imbarqued in the *Alexander* Capt: BURCHE and GILBERT GRIMES Mʳ p Certificate from the Minister where they late dwelt the Men tooke the oaths of Alleg. ℘ Supremacie die et Aº prd

	yeres		yeres
Wiłłm RAPEN	29	Wᴹ POWELL	19
LEONARD STAPLES	22	RALPH PROWD	26
JO: STANFORD	24	JO: BULLMAN	40
JAMES MANZER	27	JO: WATT'S	19
JO: WATTS	25	Wᴹ DENCH	16
THO: CLARK	26	FRANCIS PECK	22
MICHELL KIMP	27	JO: BENSTEDD	24
HENRY BROUGHTON	20	SYMON PARLER	24
GEO: VENTIMER	20	RICHARD HOWSEMAN	19
ROBERT HARDY	18	WALTER JONES	20
THO: DABB	25	PHELIX LYNE	25
GEO: NORTON	22	ARTHUR WRITE	21
Wᴹ HUCKLE	20	LEWES Wiłłms [WILLIAMS]	21
EDWARD KEMP	19	Wᴹ POTT	18

yeres		yeres
THOMAS GILSON 21	GEO. RIDGLIE 17	
NIC^o: WATSON...................... 26	DENNIS M^aBRIAN [MACBRIAN] 18	
OLLIVER HOOKHAM 32	JO: BUSSELL...................... 36	
CHRI: BUCKLAND 25	JAMES DRIVER 27	
JO: HILL 23	HUGH JOHNES..................... 22	
ANTHONY SKOOLER 20	THO: GILDINGWATER........... 30	
JO: ANDERSON.................... 21	JOHN ASHURST 24	
W^M PHILLIPPS 17	JAMES PARKINSON 23	
JO: BESFORD 18	WIĦM YOUNG 21	
HENRY YATMAN................. 21	W^M SMITH 18	
ROBERT DUCE..................... 18	MORGAN JONES 31	
OWEN WILLIAMS 18	JO: RICHARD 30	
JO: WRITE 24	PETER FLAMING.................. 16	
WILLIAM CLARK.................. 19	MILES FARRING 24	
EDWARD HALINGWORTH 46	ROBERT ATKINS................. 23	
RICHARD POWELL 32	BENIAMIN MASON 23	
HENRY LONGSHA 23	THO: RUTTER 22	
JO: BUSH 22	JO: HOWSE 41	
JONATHAN FRANKLIN 17	JO: COLE 20	
JO: PHILLIPPS 20	JAMES WATTS 35	
RICHARD CRIBB 19	W^M CROWE†....................... 17	
THO: BROWNE 18	PHILLIPP LOVELL 34	
JO: GREENWICH 21	*vxor* ELIZABETH LOVELL 33	
JO: NEDSOM * 19	ROWLAND MATHEW 27	
EDWARD CHURCH 18	ROBERT SPRITE 30	
ANT^o THRELCATT 19	JO: WESTON...................... 41	
W^M WILLIS 17	JAMES SMITH 19	
CLEMENT HAWKINS 16	JO: SMITH....................... 19	
LEWES HUGHES 19	RICHARD LEE 22	
JOHN GREENE..................... 22	W^M SEELY........................ 29	
RICHARD MARSHALL 36	EDWARD PLUNKET.............. 20	
MATHEW CALLAND.............. 16	THO: PLUNKĿTT................. 28	
LEWES DAVID 28	ROWLAND PLUNKETT 18	
GEO: WHITE 18	TEAGUE NACTON 28	

* [*Might* be read as NEESOM.]   † [Or, perhaps, CROME.]

Dermond ô Bryan	20	Richard Fane	15
Charles Galloway	19	Robert Robert's	18
James Montgomery	19	Wᴹ Lake	14
Jᴺᵒ Mᵃ Conry	28	Richard Iveson	16
Samvell Priday	20	Humfrey Kerby	18
Samvell Farron	30	Edward Cokes	17
Edmond Montgomery	26	Henry Morton	20
Olliver Bassett	14	James Brett	17
Parry Wy	15	Tho: Dennis	18
Daniell Burch	14	Tho: More	33
Richard Stone	13	Jo: Lawrence	17
Thomas Tayler	27	Wᴹ Martin	13
Edmond Nash	21	Richard Philpe	17
Jo: Herring	28		
Wᴹ Beaton	24	*Women.*	
Tho: Roe	22	Barbarie Reason	20
Edward Bank's	35	Jane Marshall	21
Tho: Fludd	21	Diana Drake	19
David Collingworth	22	Mary Inglish	17
Wᴹ Mathews	30	Annis Barrat	20
Tymothie Goodman	27	Marie Lambeth	17
Tho: Penson	20	Ann Mann	17
Wiłłm Anderson	36	Elizabeth Warren	17
Geo: Merriman	41	Ann Skynggle	18
Jo: Dellahay	27	Alice Chump*	20
Robert Lee	33	Mathew May	21
Jo: Jackson	24	Elizabeth Chambers	20
Alexander de la Garde	27	Elizabeth Farmer	20
Francis Marshall	26	Margaret Conway	20
Walter Lutterell	20	Grace Walker	34
Jo: White	15	Edith Jones	21
Jo: Burton	17	Alice Guy	20
Symon Wood	14	Mary Spendley	17
Robert Mussell	14	Ann Gardner	36

* [It is possible this name may be intended for Champ.]

6 *Maij.* 1635

THEIS vnder-written names are to be transported to New-England imbarqued in the *Elizabeth & Ann* ROGER COOP [COOPER] M^r, the pties have brought Cert: from the Ministers where their abodes were: & from the Justices of peace of their conformitie to the orders & discipline of the Church of England, & y^t they are no Subsedy Men, they have taken the oaths of Alleg: & Suprem:

SAMVELL HALL	25	VYNCENT POTTER	21
W^M SWYNDEN	20	RIC^R: GOARD	17
†JO: HALSEY*	24	W^M ADAMS	15
		†HENRY CURTIS*	27

viij° Maij 1635.

IN the *Elizabeth & Ann* prd ROGER COOP [COOPER] M^r. Theis vnder written names are to be transported to New-England imbarqued in the said Shipp: They brought Cert. of their Conformite to the Church of England & y^t they are no Subsedy Men.

JOHN WYLIE	25	GEORGE ORRIS	21
JO: THOMSON	22	†JO: JACKSON*	27
EDMOND WESTON	30	ELIZABETH FABIN	16
GAMALIELL BEOMONT	12	GRACE BULKLEY	33
AWDRY WHITTON	45		

Nono die Maij 1635.

THEIS vnder-written names are to be transported to New-England, imbarqued in y^e *Suzan & Ellin* EDWARD PAYNE M^r. The pties have brought Certificate from the Minister of the pish of their conformitie

---

* [The † is in the original.]

to the Church of England, ƿ that they are no Subsedy Men. the pties
have taken the oaths of Alleg ƿ Suprem:

	yeres		yeres
PETER BULKLEY	50	RICᴿ: BROOKE	24
THO: BROOKE	20	ELIZABETH TAYLOR	10
PRECILLA JARMAN	10	ANN LIEFORD	13

N the *Elizabeth ƿ Ann* prd ROGER COOP [COOPER] Mʳ bound for
New-England.

		yeres
	ROBERT JEOFFERIES	30
	MARIE JEOFFERIES	27
wife ƿ 3	THO: JEFFERIES	7
children	ELIZABETH JEFFERIES	6
	MARY JEFFERIES	3
	HANNA DAY	20 } 2 maidservᵗ's
	SUZAN BROWNE	21
	ROBERT CARR	21 A Tayler
	CALEBB CARR	11
	RICᴿ: WHITE	30 } Carpenters
	THO: DANE	32
	Wᴹ HILLIARD	21

---

xjᵒ Maij 1635.

HEIS vnder-written names are to be transported to New-England
imbarqued in the *Elizabeth ƿ Ann* prd   The pties have brought
Certificate from the Minister ƿ Justices of Peace of their conformitie to
yᵉ orders ƿ discipline of the Church of England, ƿ yᵗ they are no
Subsedy Men.

		yeres
A Shoemaker	Wɪʟʟᴹ COURSER	26 } yeres
A Husbandman	GEO: WYLDE	37
A Carpenter	GEO: PARKER	23

xij° Maij 1635

IN the *Elizabeth & Ann* ROGER COOPER M^r bound to New-England: Theis vnder written names are to be transported p Certificate from ye Minister of *Bennandin** in Kent of their Conformitie to ye orders & discipline of ye Church of England.

JOHN BORDEN	28	JEREMY WHITTON	8
vxor JOAN	23	MATHEW BORDEN	5
NIC°: MORECOCK	14	ELIZ: BORDEN	3
BENNET MORECOCK	16	bro wevert† THOMAS WHITTON	36
MARIE MORECOCK	10	SAMVELL BAKER	30

14 *Maij* 1635

THEIS vnder-written names are to be transported to New-England imbarqued in the *Elizabeth & Ann* ROGER COOPER M^r the pties have brought Certificatt from the Minister of the pish of his conformitie to the orders & discipline of the Church of England.

	yeres		
A Tayler RICHARD SANSOM	28	THO: OLDHAM	10
THO: ALSOPP	20	ROB^T STANDY	22
JOHN OLDHAM	12		

xv° Maij 1635

THEIS vnder-written names are to Virginea: imbarqued in the *Plaine Joan* RICHARD BUCKAM M^r. the pties having brought Attestacōn of their conformitie to the orders & discipline of the Church of England.

* [Benendon is a parish in the Hundred of Rolvenden, in the Lathe of Scray.]
† [Meaning not clear.]

	yeres		yeres
ROBERT BRIERS	21	RICHARD WOLLEY	36
Jᴺᵒ JOHNSON	20	Wi͡lM CLARK	27
ROBERT COKE	25	Wᴹ BALDWINN	24
Jo: ALSOPP	50	Wᴹ COLLINS	20
Wᴹ PIGGOTT	50	THO: PITCHER	20
Wᴹ TOPLISS	30	JOSEPH NELSON	26
THO: ARNOLD	30	FRANCIS GRAY	15
Wᴹ PAULSON	23	SAMVELL YOUNG	14
Jo: NORTHIN	22	ROBERT HUTT	14
THO: TURNER	21	Jo: RADDISH	23
Jo: BEDDELL	22	THO: BULKLEY	32
Jo: BARROWE	26	ROBERT BROOKE	33
Jo: TRENT	27	RICHARD DOWNES	34
Jo: COKER	21	ARTHUR PEACH	20
HENRIE DONOLDSON	25	Wᴹ JAMES	26
Wᴹ LAVOR	22	TYM: BLACKETT	40
CHRI: DAVIES	22	ROGER KOORBE	25
CHRI: TAYLOR	22	ANN PERK'S	27
DANIELL CLARK	33	THO: BRITTON	26
RICHARD DAY	32	Wᴹ COLLINS	34
ROBERT LEWES	23	Jo: RESBURIE	30
LUKE BLAND	20	HENRY JACKSON	24
Jo: WARREN	27	CHARLES Mᵃ CARTIE	27
JAMES WARD	18	OWEN Mᵈ CARTIE	18
THO: STUMP*	32	CHARLES FLANE	18
TOBIAS FRIER	18	RICHARD LAWRENCE	20
WILLM STEDDALL	26	THO: GODBITT	20
CHRI: THOMAS	26	NICᵒ: KENT	16
RICHARD FLEM͡ING	24	THOMAS NEWMAN	15
MATHEW LEM͡	20	PETER SUDBURROWE	20
HENRY PERPOYNT	22	THO: LLOYD	20
THO: HALL	21	Wᴹ HITCHCOCK	27
EDWARD WILSON	22	FRANCIS BARBER	18
Jo: PALLIDAY	23	EDWARD WHEELER	18

* [May, however, be read STAMP.]

JAMES MILLER	18	JO: HUGHES	30
JO: SHAWE	21	GEO: TALBOTT	18
JO: MARSHALL	21	ROBERT GILBERT	18
JO: ARIS	19	JO: BENNET	18
ROBERT WARD	22	JO: ROLLES	22
THO: VIPER	26	JAMES WYND	23
ROB^T SHINGLEWOOD	26	J^{NO} MARSH	26
GEO: SMITH	34	RALPH WRAY	64

21° *Maij* 1635

THEIS vnder-written names are to be transported to St Christo-phers, imbarqued in the *Mathew* of London, RICHARD GOOD-LADD M^r p warrant from ye Earle of Carlisle.

	yeres		yeres
THOMAS KNIGHT	21	ROBERT WENDEVER	25
JO: HILL	18	SAMVEL TRESE	20
JO: RAWLINS	18	EVAN JONES	19
FRANCIS PENN	22	GABRIELL DAVIES	38
GEORGE ALLERTON	23	EDWARD EELES	20
ROWLAND MILLINGTON	24	DAVIE THOMAS	40
RIC^R: THOMAS	40	RICHARD HORRIBYNN	31
ROGER THOMAS	22	CHRISTOPHER WATSON	21
RICHARD GRIGGSON	34	JAMES HUBBARD	27
JO: BRUÑING	20	W^M STOE	18
ROBERT COKE	32	MATHEW TOMLINSON	31
CLINTON CUTLER	20	THO: HALL	25
THO: TURNER	25	W^M MARSH	26
JO: WOOD	22	JO: HATTERTON	38
W^M ROBINSON	26	THO: TERRILL	18
EDWARD BICROFT	22	ROBERT FAUCE [*or* FANCE]	40
JO: STURDY	26	MILES COVENTRIE	18
ANT°. NETBIE	20	JO: THOMAS	14

	yeres		yeres
THO: REEVE	24	PIERCE STAPLETON	22
LEWES AWBREY	30	GEO: EATON	27
JAMES WALKER	30	LEONARD HUNT	38
THO: VENN	27	JO: CAVE	34
GEO: BALL	51	Wᴹ BARBER	22
THO: GOSLING	22	JO: HODDINS	50
JO: PALMER	19	ALEXANDER TADD	38
JAMES COTES	21	ROBᵀ WOODSTOCK	40
Wᴹ HELAWE	21	JOHN OFFLENT	20
MATHEW HELY	21	NICᵒ: WATTS	18
ORIGINALL LOWIS	28	RICHARD BROOKES	16
JO: THOMSON	34	THO: HADBIE	22
Wᴹ BROOKES	25	THO: REINOLDS	18
JO: DOE	22	DARBY HURLIE	18
MATHEW WALKER	19	JO: HILLIARD	35
WALTER COLLINS	18	ROBERT LACIE	21
JO: CLINTON	19	THO: BELL	14
ADAM CHESTERMAN	19	ROWLAND MORTON	17
HUYN HALLOWELL	22	JAMES HIDE	22
Wᴹ SALMON	25	RICHARD NELME	20
JO: LANGE	22	THO: HODGES	20
RICHARD LOVE	28	EDWARD THOMSON	18
JO: GREENE	29	THO: WILLIAMS	18
EDWARD WARREN	28	RICᴿ: LEE	18
JO: PAPLE	21	WALTER ANTONY	23
ROBERT DENTON	26	CHARLES CAVERLIE	17
Wᴹ ELVYN	23	THO: COXSON	21
GEO: TEMS [or TENIS]	20	THO: GOODWVNN	30
GEO: SWALES	19	NICᵒ: WILCOCKS	21
MARMADUKE READ	25	GEO: EEKE	26
JO: KIBE	21	RICᴿ: HUBBARD	18
THO: GARRETT	20	WIꞀꞀM RUSH	20
JO: GOSLINN	20	Wᴹ DONN	22
THO: MILWARD	18	PAUL BOTTELL	32
MORGAN BRINT	19	JO: BOSWELL	17

JO: WOODGREENE	16	ROB^T SANDLEY	20
JO: HARLOWE	16	EDWARD MAWFREY	15
ROBERT WARRINGTON	20	GEO: WADE	16
JO: REINOLDS	20	JO: FULFORD	18
ANT^O. TRUE	18	GEO: SMITH	17
W^M KNIGHT	13	THO: POWELL	24
ANT^O. WILLIAMS	14		
JO: BARLOE	22	*Women.*	
W^M PARKER	17		
JO: WOOD	18	MARGARET PRICHARD	17
JO: PAYNE	18	JANE BURROWE	17
DANIELL LEE	25	KATHERIN ARMSTRONG	20
THO: POWELL	21	MARY BARKER	12
JO: SMITH	22	ELIZ: SPEERE	20
GEO: DODD	17		

28 *Maij* 1635

THEIS vnder-written names are to be transported to Virginea imbarqued in the *Speedwell* of London JO: CHAPPELL M^r being examined by the Minister of Gravesend of their conformitie to the orders ℘ discipline of the Church of England ℘ have taken the oath of Allegeance.

HENRY BEERE	24	WIŁŁM BASFORD	19
JO: WEST	30	JO: WATSON	22
RICHARD MORRIS	19	JO: GILGATE	22
NIC^O: TETLOE	35	ROB^T SPYNK	20
W^M SHIPMAN	22	RICHARD ROWLAND	20
NATHANIELL FAIERBROTHER	21	THO: CHILDS	30
RICHARD BAYLIE	22	JO: CURDEN	22
W^M SPENCER	17	THO: ROMNEY	19
JAMES LOWDER	20	JO: HARRIS	20
CHRI: METCALF	19	CHRISTOPHER PIDDINGTON	18
JEREMY BURR	20	EDMOND CLARK	16

Jonas Smith	22	Tho: Willis	19
Wᴹ Hynton	25	Wᴹ Straughan	22
Jo: Mowser	22	Geo: Sympson	19
Samvell Tyres	21	Richard Phillips	20
Wᴹ Steevens	22	Arthur Saiewell	25
Tho: Busby	19	Melashus Mᵃ Kay	22
Richard Harvy	32	Richard Thomas	20
Tho: Robins	17		
Jo: Beeby	17	Katherin Richard's	19
Jo: Turner	19	Marie Sedgwick	20
Samvell Holmes	20	Elizabeth Biggs	10
Jo: Bever	24	Dorothie Wyncott	40
Jo: Talbott	27	Ann Wyncott	16
Edward Austin	26	Phillipp Biggs	6. mo:
Tho: Greene	24	Elizabeth Pew	20
Richard Browne	19	Francis Langworth	25
Wᴹ Appleby	32	Chri: Reinolds	24
Robert Parker	21	Abram Poore	20
Wᴹ Cunningham	21	Elizabeth Tuttell	25

vjᵒ Junij 1635

THEIS vnder-written names are to be transported to Virginea imbarqued in the *Thomas & John* Richard Lambard Mʳ: being examined by the Minister de Gravesend concerning their conformitie to the orders & discipline of the Church of England: And tooke the oath of Allegeance.

	yeres		yeres
Richard Pew	23	Edward Dix	19
Richard Waynewrite	24	Wᴹ Chaplin	18
Chri: Houghton	19	Jo: Singleton	18
Richard Jones	24	Geo: Dickenson	19
Francis Garret	25	Geo: Hawkins	18
Richard Dally	18	Henry Rastell	30

Fra: Spight	21	Sylus Foster	22
Wm Aymie	26	Edward Mountfort	20
Wm Hynton	20	Henry Newby	24
Jo: Edwardson	22	Jo: Eeden	19
Tho: Mann	23	Tho: Sherly	23
Robt Aldred	24	Jo: Thomson	24
Zachary Taylor	24	Henry Warren	15
Humfrey Grudge	21	Jo: Wilkenson	28
Wm White	22	Ralph Hudson	17
Joseph Monnvs	21	Tho: Allin	33
Wm Yard	21	Wm Jones	17
Christopher Wheatly	28	Tho: Sharples	20
Robert Heed	27	Wm Crooke	23
Edward Coles	20	Wiłłm Bead	15
Morris Jones	28	Lawrence Platt	15
Wardin Fossitt	22	Robert Spencer	21
Tho: Chamberlin	20	Samvell Walden	16
Jo: Shorter	26	Henry Morley	25
Ant^o· Terry	50	Ben: Easy	13
Robert Wiłłms [Williams]	44	Jo: Moss	21
Tho: Rosdell	23	Jane Wilkinson	20
Thomas Terry	25	Ann Brookes	18
Charles Wyngate	22	Katherin Wiseman	'19
Jo: Hampton	30	Jane Scott	19
Jo: Evans	22	Jane Catesby	20
Robert Sewar	23	James Powell	12
Richard Berry	23	Wm Mann	25
Owen Hughes	27	Tho: Warner	26
Jo: Sutton	24	Tho: Ram	19
Wm Stonhouse	43	Griffin Jones	21
Wm Clark	18	Tho: Tollie	17
Jo: Dickenson	22	Wm Jones	21
Tho: Bell	17	Morris Parry	30
Wm Bett	20	Marmaduke Young	24
James Cross	27	Wiłłm White	22

	yeres		yeres
JAMES SHERBONE	15	FRANCIS HUNTER	19
Wᴹ GARDENER	15	FRANCIS ASHBORN	20
JO: ROBINSON	19	Wᴹ DIXON	18
ROBERT TURNER	16	Wᴹ SMART	20
THO: CLARK	16	LAWRENCE PRESTON	21
GILES TERRY	33	Wᴹ WHEATLIE	17
EDWARD CRESSITT	20	Wᴹ LACY	18
THO: WAGGITT	17	JAMES BANK'S	30
MARY FORD	22	GEO: COBCRAFTE	22
KATHERIN WATERMAN	20	GEO: KENNYON	25
SUZAN SHERWOOD	22	JO: KENNYON	21
GRACE BYCROFT	20		

xᵒ Junij 1635

THEIS vnder-written names are to be transported to the Bormoodes or Somer-Islands, imbarqued in the *Truelove* de London, ROBERT DENNIS Mᵣ, being examined by the Minister of Gravesend concerning their conformitie to the orders & discipline of the Church of England as it now stands established: And tooke the oath of Allegeance.

	yeres		yeres
HENRY MORE	19	DAVID HUSWITH	22
Wᴹ HOLT	19	HENRY HILL	24
JO: NORMAN	19	JO: WARREN	19
ANTᵒ GILLIARD	38	ZEVERIN VICCARS	18
ROBᵀ STOCK	26	GEO: NORMAN	25
THO: FOSTER	27	GABRIELL STOCKWELL	16
ROBERT HART	30	THO: TOOLIE	27
Wᴹ PENDLETON	27	EDWARD GODDIN	16
JAMES TAYLER	28	THO: DORRELL	22
CHRI: HART	20	RICHARD CAÑON	24
RICHARD ANDERSON	30	*vxor.* ELIZABETH CAÑON	23
THO: RICHARDS	24	BARNARD COLMAN	26
JO: NORRIS	18	CHRI: TUKE	16

	yeres		yeres
W^M PAUL	20	ROB^T POOLE	20
W^M BATES	17	THO: JONES	17
SAMVELL SHORT	24	THO: EWYNN	16
W^M HOOPER	18	SYMON BARCOTT	16
RICHARD HURT	17	GEO: CALVERLIE	14
WIttM WELLS	17	EDWARD PARNELL	16
THO: DENE	17	W^M LEE	18
JO: A Negroe	18	W^M TAYLER	17
JO: RICHARDS	21	EDWARD GIBBS	17
ANT^O BULLOCK	19	JAMES REASON	27
THOMAS BASSIT	18	JACOB WILSON	18
EDWARD ALEWORTH*	13	BEN: STRANGE	18
EDWARD VYNCENT	18	RALPH VENNABLE	21
JO: TRIPPATT	17	THO: BLOES	10
ANT^O COOPER	17	THO: HEDLEY	11
JO: LAKE	16	THO: THOMSON	17
RIC^R: TAYLER	16	HEN: STONWORD	13
THO: MORDIN	18	SAMVELL HUBBARD	16
EDWARD SELL	18	THOMAS BULL	13
ROGER WIttMS [WILLIAMS]	16	DANIELL HAMOND	12
JO: BAYLIE	18	GEO: MORGAN	12
FRANCIS WOODCOTT	16	JO: BARNES	16
JO: BEE	17	ABRAHAM CLAXSON	17
RIC^R: GREENE	17	JAMES ASTON	22
GEO: PALMER	18	RIC^R DAUGHTON	13
THO: SMITH	14	MATHEW STEEVENS	12
NATHANIEL WIttMSON [WIL-		THO: LARKYNN	15
LIAMSON]	17	DAVID JONES	15
PHILLIPP WHARTON	14	GEORGE HANMER	24
W^M HENRY	18	ROGER HODGES	17
GEO: SAIRES	12	W^M POWELL	15
NIC^O: GAUGHTON	14	SAMPSON MEVERILL	20
EDWARD HEDLEY	13	HENRY CARTER	42
W^M SARES	17	JO: YATES	48

* [May, however, be read as ALDWORTH.]

	yeres		
JO: BROWNE	16	JOSIAS FORSTER	43
FRANCIS RAYNNE [or RAYMIE]	10	THO: HALL	24
FRANCIS HEDGES	13	HUMFREY SMITH	14
DAVIE MORRIS	18	FRANCIS WATSON	16
THO: WEST	17	KATHERIN WHITE	18
HUGH WENTWORTH	44	ELIZABETH CLARK	18
ANN TAYLOR	24	ELLIN BURROWES	30
ELIZABETH GROVES	35		
JO: GROVES	1 q^r	JO: PAGE	33
BLANCH ROBERT'S	20	THO: JENNICOM	21
		SARA PAGE	31
2 Ministers.		SARA PAGE	3
JO: OXENBRIDGE	24	MARY PAGE	3. mo.
HENRY JENNING'S	24	RICHARD HARRIS	17
		JEFFERY WRIGHT	18
BENIAMIN MILLER	30	SAMVELL MAYO	10
HENRY FLETCHER	35	MARIE GOFFE	18
EDWARD STAUGHTON	50	JO: BROOKES	12

xv° Junij 1635

![T]HEIS vnder written names are to be transported to New-England: imbarqued in the *Abigall* de Lo: M^r H: HACKWELL: The ptie having brought Certificate from the Minister of Thisselworth* of his conformitie to the orders & discipline of the Church of England. He hath taken the oaths of Allegeance & Supremacie.

	yeres		
DENNIS GEERE	30	ANNS PANCRUST	16
wife & 2 children { ELIZABETH GEERE	22	ELIZ: TASELIE	55
ELIZABETH GEERE	3	CONSTUNT WOOD	12
SARA GEERE	2		

---

* [Is it possible that this is intended for ISLEWORTH? I can find no THISSELWORTH.]

19 *Junij* 1635

THEIS vnder written names are to be transported to New-England imbarqued in ye *Abigall:*   HACKWELL Mr the pties having brought Certificate from the Minister of the pish of the litle Miniries of his conformitie ℓ opinion of the discipline of the Church of England.

	yeres		
Wᴹ Tɪʟʟʏ	28	Cʜᴀʀʟᴇs Jᴏɴᴇs	21
Rᴏʙᴇʀᴛ Wʜɪᴛᴇᴍᴀɴ	20	Lɪᴅᴅɪᴀ Bʀᴏᴡɴᴇ	16

ABOARD the *James* Jᴏ: Mᴀʏ for N. England.

Tayler Tʜᴏ: Eᴡᴇʀ	40	Sᴀʀᴀ Bᴇᴀʟᴇ	28
Sᴀʀᴀ Eᴡᴇʀ	28	Eʟɪᴢᴀʙᴇᴛʜ Nᴇᴡᴍᴀɴ	24
Eʟɪᴢᴀʙᴇᴛʜ Eᴡᴇʀ	4	Jᴏ: Sᴋᴜᴅᴅᴇʀ	16
Tʜᴏ: Eᴡᴇʀ	1½		

xxth June 1635

THEIS vnder Written names are to be imbarqued in the *Abbigall* de Lnd [London] m'   HACKWELL ℓ bond to New Engld haue taken oathe of Allegance ℓ Supremacie ℓ Conforable [conformable] to ye Ch as p Cert from Two Justices of Peace ℓ minstr of St Lawrence in Essex

Hᴇɴʀʏ Bᴜʟʟᴏᴄᴋᴇ	40 yers	husbandman
ℓ Sᴜsᴀɴ his wife	42	

iij Children { Hᴇɴʀʏ 8
                 Mᴀʀʏ 6
                 Tʜᴏ: 2

more xxᵗʰ 1635

I N the *defence* de Lond m'   PEARCE ꝑ bōd for New Engłd p
   Cert. frō ij Justices of Peace ꝑ Ministr of All Saint's homan.* in
Northapton.

WᴹˑHOEMAN............ 40 yers   husbandman
his wife WINIFRID ... 35
ALCE ASHBEY .... 20 yers   amaid Seruant.
5 Children ⎰ HANNA............ 8
           ⎱ JEREMY............ 6
MARY......... 4
SARRA 2
ABRAHAM .... 1 qʳᵗʳ

xxᵗʰ June 1635

I N the *Abbigall* de Lo. m'   HACKWELL bōd for New Engłd p
   Certꜩ from.† of his Conformity from Justices of Peace ꝑ
Ministr Eaton Bray‡ in Cō Bedford.

JOⁿ HOUGHTON............ 4 [? 40] yers old.

7ᵗʰ Jully 1635

BOSTOCKE‖
I N the *defence* de Lond. m' EDWARD§ ~~PEARCE~~ vrs New Engłd p
   Cert frō ij Justices of peace ꝑ ministr frō Dunstable in Conᵗ·
Bedfordsher:

ROBERT LONGE.................... 45 yers   Inholder
ELIZA: his wife 30

* [There is no place bearing this name in Northampton. Query, is it a misspelling of the name HOEMAN in next line, wrongly written in here, and not afterwards erased?]

† [*Sic*. The word must be omitted, to make sense.]

‡ [Eaton Bray is a Township in the Hundred of Manshead.]

§ [*Or* EDMOND. The word is blotted in the original.]

‖ [So in the original. There would seem to have been more than one ship called the *Defence*, since we find the names of four different commanders to ships so named : EDWARD BOS-TOCKE (as here); — PEARCE (June 20) ; EDWARD BOSWELL (June 22); THOMAS BOSTOCK (July 2).]

x Children {
MICHELL.............. 20
SARRA................. 18
ROBERT 16
ELIZA 12
ANNE 10
MARY 9
REBECCA............. 8
JO^N 6
ZACHERY.. 4
}

JOSHUA.. .... 3 q'trs old.

LUCE MERCER... 18. a seruant

---

xxth *June* 1635

IN the *Defence* de Lond m'   PEARCE vrs New Engld p Cert frō
two Justices of Peace ꝑ Minstr of Towcester in Co^{t.} Northampton

JO^N GOULD............... 25 yers   husbandman
GRACE his wife .... 25 yers

---

xxijth *June* 1635

IN the *Abbigall* de Lond. m'   HACKWELL vrs New Engld p
Cer^t frō Minstr of Crancbroke* in Kent.

EDW. WHITE .... 42 yers   husbandman
ꝑ his wife MARTHA 39
ij Children { MARTHA 10
MARY 08
JO^N ALLEN...................... 30 yers   husbandman
his wife ANNE 30
p Cert hernehil* in Kent

* [Both Cranbrook and Herne-Hill are in the Lathe of Scray.]

N the *Abbigall.*
  p Cert· from Justice peace ꝑ Ministʳ of Stepney.

GEO: HADBORNE	43 yers	Glouer.
his wife ANNE	46	

2 Children { REBECCA 10
            { ANNA 4

JOSEPH BOREBANCKE .... 24 } Seruant's to GEO: HAD-
JOANE JORDEN .... 16 } BORNE.

22ᵗʰ

N the *Defence* de Lo. m' EDW: BOSWELL vrs New England ꝑ Certᵗ·
from Sʳ Henry Mildmay ꝑ Ministr of Baddow* in Essex.

JOˣ BROWNE................ 27 yers. Taylor.

his 3 seruant's { THO: HART 24
                { MARY DENNY .. 24
                { ANNE LEAKE .. 19

---

26 *Jun* ij 1635

N the *Abigall* ROBERT HACKWELL Mʳ to New-England ꝑ Cert:
from Northton Tho. Martin Maior ꝑ 2 Justices

Shoemaker JO: HARBERT................ 23
Bricklayer RICHARD ADAMS 29
           SUZAN ADAMS 26

4ᵗʰ *Jully*

HENRY SOMNER 15
ELISA. SOMNER 18

---

* [There are two Baddows, Great and Little, in the Hundred of Chelmsford.]

17 *Junij* 1635

THEIS vnder written names are to be transported to New-England, imbarqued in the *Abigall* ROBERT HACKWELL M^r p Cert from the Minister ₡ Justices of Peace of their Conformitie, being no Subsedy Men. they have taken ye oaths of Alleg: ₡ Supremacy being all Husbandmen

	yeres		
RALPH WALLIS	40	MARY MONING'S	30
RALPH ROOTE	50	MARY MONNING'S	9
J^{NO} FREEMAN	35	ANNA MONNING'S	6
WALTER GUTSALL	34	MICHELALIELL MONING'S	3
RICHARD GRAVES	23	ELIZABETH ELLIS	16
ROBERT MERE	43	ELLIN JONES	36
SAMVELL MERE	3	ISACK JONES	8
EDMOND MANING	40	HESTER JONES	6
THO: JONES	40	THO: JONES	3
GEO: DREWRIE	19	SARA JONES	3. mo:
W^M MARSHALL	40	CESARA COVELL	15
THOMAS KNORE	33	JOAN WALL	19
JOHN HALLIACK	38	W^M PAYNE	15
GEORGE WALLIS	15	NOLL KNORE	29
RABECCA PRICE	14	SARA KNORE	7
MARIE FREEMAN	50	ROB^T DRIVER	8
JO: FREEMAN	9	ELIZABETH MERE	30
SYCILLIE FREEMAN	4	JOHN MERE	3. mo:
JO: WEST	11		

IN the *Abigall* prd: p Cert: from the Minister of their conformitie ₡ from the Justices, that they are no Subsedy men.

CHRISTOPHER FOSTER ...... 32 | *vxor* FRANCIS FOSTER 25

children	RABECCA FOSTER ..	5	ELIZABETH ROOKMAN	31
	NATHANIELL FOSTER	2	JO: ROOKEMAN	9
	JO: FOSTER	1	HUGH BURT	35
	EDWARD IRESON	32	ANN BURT	32
	W^M ALMOND	34	W^M BASSETT	9
	MARY JONES	30	EDWARD BURT	8
	AWDRY ALMOND	32	THO: FREEMAN	24
	ANNIS ALMY	8	W^M YATES	14
	CHRI: ALMIE	3	ELIZABETH IRESON	27
	JOHN STROWDE	15	JO: FOX................	35
	EDWARD RAINSFORD........	26	RICHARD FOX	15
	ROB^T SHARP	20	JO: PAYNE	14
	JOHN ROOKEMAN	45	EDMOND FREEMAN	45

HEIS vnder-written names are to be transported to New-England imbarqued in the *Blessing* JO₁ LECESTER M^r the pties having brought Cert from the Minister ₽ Justices of their conformitie being no Subsedy Men, tooke ye oaths of Alleg: ₽ Supremacie.

WILłM COPE................	26	ROBERT TURNER	24
RICHARD COPE	24	ELIZA: HOLLY.............	30
THOMAS KING.............	21	ANN VASSALL.............	6
JO: STOCKBRIDGE	27	MARGARET VASSALL	2
ROBERT SAIEWELL..........	30	MARY VASSALL	1
W^M BROOKE................	20	ELIZABETH ROBINSON	32
GILBERT BROOKE	14	SARA ROBINSON............	1.½
NATHANIELL BYHAM........	14	NIC^o: ROBERTSON	30
JO: WASSELL	10	JO: MORY................	19
W^X VASSALL	42	CHARLES STUCBRIDGE	1
RIC^R: MORE	20	JAMES SAIEWELL	1½

Jo: Robinson	5	Sara Tynkler	15
Ann Stocbridge	21	Fra. Vassall	12
Suzan Saiewell	25	Thomazin Munson	14
Ann Vassall	42	Kat: Robinson	12
Suzan King	30	Mary Robinson	7
Judith Vassall	16	Robᵀ Onyon	26

20 *Junij* 1635

THEIS vnder-written names are to be transported to Virginea imbarqued in the *Phillip* Richard Morgan Mʳ the Men have been examined by the Minister of the towne of Gravesend of their conformitie to the orders ℈ discipline of the Church of England: And tooke the oath of Alleg. die et Aᵒ prd.

John Hart	33	John Taylor	16
John Coachman	28	John Gorham	18
John Reddam	32	Richard Wilson	19
John Shawe	30	Robert Morgan	33
George Hill	23	Samvell Milner	18
George Bonham	31	Tymothie Featlie	23
Wᴹ Rogers	35	Wᴹ Arundell	32
Edward Halock	22	Alexander Leake	22
Ricᴿ: Dawson	31	John Mason	16
Peter Johnson	36	Wiłłm Enson	33
Wiłłm Bransby	34	James Habroll	22
Nicholas Rippin	31	Thomas Trumball	22
James Quarrier	22	Richard Jnᵒson	19
Isack Owdell	22	John Lawters	17
Wᴹ Taylor	36	Thomas Edwards	20
James York	21	Robert Davies	28
Thomas Gorham	19	Richard Vppcott	26
Nathaniell Disnall	23	Thomas Poslett	23

		MARCIE LANGFORD	24
Women.		ELIZABETH WILLERTON	18
ELLIN BURGIS...........	45	SARA SHAWE	18
KATHERIN BOWES	20	MARIE BAKER	25
SUZAN TRASH [*or* TRASK] ..	25	ANN: BARNIE	23

23° *Junij* 1635

THEIS vnder-written names are to be transported to Virginea imbarqued in the *America* WItM BARKER Mr: p Cert: from the Minister of the Towne of Gravesend of their conformity to the orders & discipline of the Church of England.

RICHARD SADD	23	RICHARD HERSEY	22
THOMAS WAKEFIELD	17	JOHN ROBINSON	32
THOMAS BENNETT	22	EDMOND CHIPPS	19
STEEVEN READ	24	THO: PRICHARD	32
WItM STANBRIDGE	27	JONATHAN BRONSFORD	21
HENRY BARKER	18	WItM COWLEY	20
JAMES FOSTER..........	21	JOHN SHAWE.	16
THOMAS TALBOTT	20	RICHARD GUMY	21
RICHARD YOUNG	31	BARTHOLMEW HOLTON	25
ROBERT THOMAS	20	JOHN WHITE	21
JOHN FAREPOYNT	20	THOMAS CHAPPELL	*33
ROBERT ASKYN	22	HUGH FOX	24
SAMVELL AWDE	24	DAVIE MORRIS	32
MILES FLETCHER	27	ROWLAND COTTON.........	22
WILLIAM EVANS..........	23	WILLIAM THOMAS	22
LAWRENCE FAREBERN	23	JOHN YATES	20
MATHEW ROBINSON	24	RICHARD WOOD..........	36
ISACK BULL............	27	JAMES SOMERS	22
PHILLIPP REMINGTON	29	DAVIE BROMLEY..........	15
RADULPH SPRAGING	37	WALTER BROOKES	15
GEORGE CHAUNDLER.......	29	SYMON RICHARDSON	23

* [The original has been altered, and is not clear; it is possible the age should be 23.]

THOMAS JNºSON	19	THOMAS BOOMER	13
JO: AVERIE	20	GEORGE DULMARE	8
JOHN CROFTES	20	JOHN VNDERWOOD	19
THOMAS BROUGHTON	19	WIĦM BERNARD	27
BENIAMIN WRAGG	24	CHARLES WALLINGER	24
HENRY EMBRIE	20	THOMAS DYMETT	23
ROBERT SABYN	40	RYCE HOOE	36
GEORGE BROOKES	35	JOHN CARTER	54
THOMAS HOLLAND	34		
HUMFREY BELT	20	*Women.*	
JOHN MACE	20	ELIZABETH REMINGTON	20
WALTER JEWELL	19	KATHERIN HIBBOTT'S	20
WIĦM BUCLAND	19	ELIZABETH WILLIS	18
LAUNCELOT JACKSON	18	JOAN JOBE	18
JOHN WILLIAMSON	12	ANN NASH	22
PHILLIPP PARSONS	10	ELIZABETH PHILLIPS	22
HENRY PARSONS	14	DOROTHY STANDICH	22
ANDREW MORGAN	26	SUZAN DEATH	22
WIĦM BROOKES	17	ELIZABETH DEATH	3
RICHARD HARRISON	15	ALICE REMINGTON	26
THOMAS PRATT	17	DOROTHIE BAKER	18
JOHN EELES	16	ELIZABETH BAKER	18
RICHARD MILLER	12	SARA COLEBANK	20
ROBERT LAMB	16	MARY THURROGOOD	19

29 *Junij* 1635

ABOARD the *Abigall*, ROBᵀ HACKWELL, Mʳ for New-England.

A Baker JOSEPH FLUDD	45	JOSEPH FLUDD	½
vxor JANE FLUDD	35	EDWARD MARTIN	19
ELIZABETH FLUDD	9	SUZAN HATHWAY	34
OBEDIAH FLUDD	4		

vltīo Junij 1635

BOARD the *Abigall* ROBERT HACKEWELL M^r p Cert from the Minister of Stepney pish of their conformitie : ℓ that they are no Subsedy men.

		yeres
Starchmaker HENRY COLLINS	....	29
vxor ANN COLLINS	....	30
3 children { HENRY COLLINS	....	5
JO: COLLINS	....	3
MARGERY COLLINS	....	2
JOSUA GRIFFITH	....	25
HUGH ALLEY	....	27
MARY ROOTE	....	15 } servant's
JO: COKE	....	27
GEO: BURDIN	....	24

N the *Abigall* prd p Cert from the Minister ℓ Justices according to order.

		yeres
EDWARD FOUNTAINE	....	28
		yeres
RALPH SHEPPARD	....	29
THANKES SHEPPARD	....	23 } Wife ℓ Daughter.
SARA SHEPPARD	....	2

Primo die Julij 1635

N the *Abigall* prd.

ANN GILLAM	....	28
sonn BEN: GILLAM	....	1
Husbandman THOMAS BRANE	....	40
THO: LAUNDER	....	22
Husb: WILLIAM POTTER	....	27
vxor FRANCIS POTTER	....	26

13

JOSEPH POTTER ...... 20 week's.	PHILLIP DRINKER 39
RIC_R.: CARR 29	*uxor* ELIZABETH DRINKER .. 32
W^M KING 28	EDWARD DRINKER 13
GEORGE RAM 25	JO: DRINKER 8
JO: STANTLEY 34	MARG_T: TUCKER 23
JAMES DODD 16	ELLNER HILLMAN 33
MATHEW ABDY 15	JO TERRY 32
Husb: EDWARD FREEMAN .. 34	JO: EMERSON 20
uxor ELIZABETH FREEMAN .. 35	RIC^R: WOODMAN............ 9
EDMOND FREEMAN 15	ELIZAB: FREEMAN 12
JOHN FREEMAN 8	ALICE FREEMAN 17
JO: JONES 15	HUGH BURT 15
JOHN COOKE .... 15* ⎫ servant	ANNIS ALDCOCK............ 18
EDWARD BELCHER 18* ⎭	THO: THOMSON 18
ANN WILLIAMS 10	

Secundo die Julij

IN the *Abigall* prd. p Certificate from ye Minister of Shorditch pish ℓ Stepney pish.

JOHN DEYKING .... 25 ⎫
JESPER ARNOLD .... 40 ⎬ yeres. bound to New-England
ALICE DEYKING .... 30 ⎪
ANN ARNOLD .... 39 ⎭
ALICE STEEVENS 22
MARGARET DEVOCION.... 9
RUTH BUSHELL 23

THEIS vnder written names are to be transported to New-England imbarqued in the *Defence* THO: BOSTOCK, M^r the ptie hath brought testimony from the Justices of Peace ℓ Minister in Cambridge

---

* [These figures are not clear in the original.]

of his conformitie to the orders ℓ discipline of the Church of England: he hath taken yᵉ oaths of Alleg: ℓ Suprem:

		yeres
A Taylor	ADAM MOTT	39
vxor	SARA MOTT	31
Mason.	HENRY STEEVENS	24
Husb:	JOHN SHEPPARD	36
	MARGARET SHEPPARD	31
	THO: SHEPPARD	3. mo.
	JO: MOTT	14
	ADAM MOTT	12
	JONATHAN MOTT	9	children.
	ELIZABETH MOTT	6
	MARY MOTT	4

IN the *Defence* prd THO: BOSTOCK Mʳ for New England, p Cert: from the Minister of Fenchurch of his conformitie ℓc.

THO: BOYLSON .... 20 yeres

4ᵗʰ *Jully* 1635

IN the *Abbigall* de Lo: p Certᵗ from the Ministr ℓ Justice of peace of Sᵗ Oliues Southwarke:

RALPH MASON	35 yers	Joyner
his wife ANNE	35 yers	
3 Children { RICHARD	5 yers	
SAMUELL	3 yers	
SUSAN	1 yere	

IN the *Defence* prd:

ELIZABETH FRENCH	30	FRANCIS FRENCH	10
ELIZABETH FRENCH	6	JO: FRENCH	5. mo.
MARIE FRENCH	2½		

iiij^th Jully 1635

I N the *Defence* de Lond m' THOMAS BOSTOCKE vrs New Engłd p
Cer^t: from the Minstr & Justice of Peace, of his Conformity to y^e
Gou'm^t [Government] of Churche of Engłd & No Subsidy man.

ROGER HARLAKENDEN aged 23 toke oathe of Allegance & Supremacie
ELIZA his wife 18
MABLE his sister 21
ANNE WOOD his seru^t 23
SAMUELL SHEPHERD ser^t .. 22
JOSEPH COCKE 27
GEO: COCKE............. 25   Seruant's to ye afore said ROGER
W^ FRENCH 30   HARLAKENDEN.
ELISA. his wife........... 32
ROBERT a Man ser^t:.... —
SARRA SIMES 30

6th Jully.

I N the *Defence* de Lond. m' THO: BOSTOCKE vrs New Engłd

JO^N JACKSON 30 yers whole Sale Man in Burchenlane
p Cer^t from s^r GEO: WHITMORE & Ministr of ye pish

x^o Julij 1635

I N the *Abigall* RICHARD HACKWELL M^r p Cert: from the Minister
& Justice of Peace of his conformitie to the Church of England &
that he is no Subsedy Man

	yeres		
JOHN WYNTHROPP	27	THO: GOAD	15
ELIZABETH WINTHROPP	19	ELIZABETH EPPS	13
DEANE WINTHROPP	11	MARY LYNE.	6

N the *Defence* prd. p Cert from the Justic's ℮ Minister of his conformitie to the Church of England.

A Taylor JAMES FITCH....... 30 | *vxor* ABIGALL FITCH 24

4° *Julij* 1635.

HEIS vnder-written names are to be transported to Virginea Imbarqued in the *Transport* of London EDWARD WALKER Mʳ p
Certificate from the Minister of Gravesend of their conformitie to the
orders ℮ discipline of the Church of England.

	yeres		
OLLIVER VAN HECK	35	JO: GODFREY	21
vxor KATHERIN VAN HECK ..	34	RICHARD CRITCH	27
PETER VAN HECK	7	ELLIS BAKER	21
RICHARD MATON	23	JONATHAN NEALE	12
Wᴹ PAGE	18	JO: BUSH	17
ROBERT KEVYNN	19	Wᴹ NESSE	23
PETER SMITH..............	25	JO: SPREATE	20
BRIAN Mᵃ GAWYN	3	THO: STEEVENS	25
DANIELL SYMPSON..........	17	JO: WATERS...............	29
PATRICK BREDDY	21	ROBᵀ FOSSITT.....	26
HENRY CASTELL	22	WALTER DOWNES	24
STEEVEN BLOCK...........	18	SYMON JONES	40
GOWEN LANCASTER	28	ROBERT JENKINSON	18
ROBERT FARRAR	24	FRANC'S CLARK	28
BRYAN GLYNN	20	FRANCIS BICK.............	23
HUMFREY HADNET	22	THOMAS CRANFIELD	14
JO: WODDALL	18	THO: PAYNE	23
WIℏM WALLINGTON	32	PHILLIP JONES	22
RICHARD SHARP...........	15	JOHN GOODSON	21
MARMADUKE KIDSON	18	STEEVEN BEANE...........	20

Geo: Barber	20	George Johnson	19
Richard Wheatlie	32	John Voss	22
Richard Lloyd	28	Andrew Adams	18
Henrie Barnes	22	John Wilson	32
Tho: More	21	Nathan Anley	28
John Harrison	30	Anthony Grimston	20
Wm Hudson	20	Tho: Hatchet	19
Wm Mason	30	Robert Honniborn	21
Mark Briggoll	21	Jo: Parson	18
Henry Porter	30	Alexander Burlie	18
Patrick Woddall	20	Wm Hart	26
John Gee	18	Nathaniell Patient	16
Richard Cooper	28	Henry Armstrong	22
Richard Eggleston	24		
Wm Harbert	15	*Women.*	
John Wise	18	Katherin Long	34
Thomas Coles	32	Elizabeth Sames	19
Tho: Williams	18	Joan Hardiss	18
George Ashon	22	Elizabeth Riley	18
Peter Sexston	20	Ellin Rogerson	20
Tho: Johnson	23	Elizabeth Lincoln	23
Thomas Saunders	20	Elizabeth Corker	19
John Lee	16	Ann Wandall	18
Robert Farest	20	Sibbell Lakeland	25
Richard Bick	18	Ellin White	26
Willm Hardisse	22	Wm White	7 weekes old
Daniell Rose	25	Ellener Rogers	19
Richard Anderson	17	Dorothie Charles	20
James Phillips	26	Hester Brotherton	18
Robert Tynman	21	Margaret Watson	18
Peter Waller	24	Oliff Sprawe	21
Richard Petley	22	Ann Brisco	22
Roger Hollidge	19	Ann Gudderidge	23
Wm Reddman	18	Rabecca Lane	22
Robert Greene	20	Elizabeth Yore	23
Henry Meddowes	20		

RALPH GOLTHORP	20	JO: SYARD	38
EDWARD THOMSON	24	GEO: MIDLAND	19
Wᴹ WHITE	37	Wᴹ WATSON	24
ROBERT LEWES	38	HARBERT JUDD	16
BARNABIE BARNES	35	JOHN FOX	33
EDWARD ISON	20	HENRY BURKET	34
JOHN SOMERTON	24	BENNET FREEMAN	20
JO: RUSSELL	14	EDWARD SALTER	19
ROBERT BATEMAN	20	ROBERT COVETT	25
Wᴹ COOKE	20	THO: MORE	18
HENRY BANISTER	22	JO: RUSSELL	16
THO: RICHARDSON	26	EDWARD HUNT	19
JO: WALLER	19	ROBERT BECKWITH	21
RICHARD WEVER	27	JO: WITTON	16
JOHN TRUE	26	JOHN HARRIS	28
JO: HORNE	21	JO: BAYLIE	42
ROBERT MEDLEY	16	JO: HATHORN	20
RICHARD ATKINSON	21	EDWARD DRUE	18
JO: POWND	20	JO: ARP	19
EDWARD ROE	17	EDMOND PRYME	16
FRANCIS WEBSTER	27		

vjᵒ Julij 1635

IN the *Paule* of London LEONARD BETTS Mʳ bound to Virginea p Certificate from the Minister of Gravesend of their Conformitie to the Church of England.

ADRIAN FORD	26	THO: GREENE	21
Wᴹ EAST	23	JO: JONES	18
ROBERT CAPLIN	22	THO: BAREFOOTE	19
EDWARD WADE	24	ROBERT TAYLOR	18

JO: RICHARDSON	22	FRANCIS LATTNER	17
RICHARD HUGHES	20	WIłłM BERRY	17
ROBERT MARKCOM	22	DAVID FLUDD	17
PETER PRICE	23	JO: HODGES	17
JOHN DAVIES	23	SAMVELL BURNET	17
NICHOLAS PARKER	23	FRANCIS WODDALL	18
JOHN GILL	19	ABRAM BRUSTER	16
JO AYNIS	21	EDWARD HOBSON	22
ARON EVERETT	20	HENRY JACOB	20
LAUNCELOTT LIMRICK	20	RICHARD CLAYTON	24
WᴹSTRANGE	25	THOMAS WEBB	18
WᴹPALMER	18	HENRY WORLIDGE	18
PHILLIP BAGLEY	19	RICHARD DAVIES	20
CIPRIAN WARNER	21	WᴹJACKSON	26
HENRY DUDMAN	18	THO: DRAPER	26
THO: HITCHCOCK	22	ANT⁰. POTT'S	27
GILES COLLINS	20	MARK WHITE	25
JO: MACHEM	18	WᴹHICKEY	22
ROBERT WILE [*or* WILD]	21	FRANCIS SEARLE	28
JOHN THOMKINS	25	WIłłM RIDDELL	16
SYLVESTER THATCHER	21	JO: POTTER	26
NICHOLAS FOX	20	WILLIAM CAPELL	25
JEREMY WATTS	21	JO: MYNTER	16
JOHN COOP [COOPER]	24	WᴹHAREFINCH	30
HENRY BANK'S	19	SYMON SIMES	15
NATHANIEL DEANE	27	ANTHONY DAY	22
THOMAS LISTER	22	RICHARD EGGLESTON	16
EDWARD WYGON	20	JO: COURTNEY	32
WᴹJACKSON	26	ROBERT VNDERWOOD	30
THO: SIMPSON	17	WᴹQUYÑIE	40
DANIELL COLLIER	30	NICHOLAS CLARK	31
JOHN COOKE	20	SAMVELL SYMONDS	30
ARTHUR PATIENT	22	JO: GILL	34
HUGH HARRISON	22	MATHEW BENNET	18
WᴹPACK	27	WIłłM HIND	35

MARGARET HINDE	30	SAMVELL DAVIES	24
AUGUSTIN HARWOOD	25	THO: WARNER	12
KATHERIN WILSON	28		

2 childr: { ROBERT WILSON ... 6 / RICHARD WILSON ... 5

Women.

LEONARD WOOD	22	GRACE ALDERMAN	22
Wᴹ POSTELL	22	MARY HUSBAND	20
CHARLES FORD	33	ALICE FULLER	22
JOHN SCOTT	26	ELIZABETH RAYNTON	16
THOMAS FLEXNEY	23	ELIZABETH COLLINS	20
JOHN HERON	18	DOROTHIE BRADLIE	18
THO: BAKER	16	GRACE JONES	24
WIHM HUGHES	20	SYBBILL COURTNEY	33
JO: COXSHEDD	14	JOAN BOWDEN	24
PETER PRYER	26	ANNIS SEEDEN	22
BENIAMIN HOOKE	20	JOAN COLCHESTER	23
JO: GIBBS	35	ELIZABETH STACIE	20
GEO: DAWE	23	DOROTHY DAY	17
HUGH BEACON	25	ANN EMMERTON	20
JO: BISHOPP	23	MARTHA HOLLAND	24

---

xjᵒ die Julij 1635

THEIS vnder-written names are to be transported to New-England imbarqued in the *Defence* of Lndon [London], EDWARD BOS-TOCK Mʳ p Certificate of his Conformitie in Religion ꝑ that he is no Subsedy-man.

A Miller RICHARD PERK...... 33 ⎫
         MARGERY PERK ... 40 ⎪
         ISABELL PERK ...... 7 ⎬ yeres | HENRY DUHURST 35
         ELIZABETH PERK... 4 ⎭

14th *Jully* 1635

IN the *Defence* de Lond m' EDMOND BOSTOCKE v^{rs} New England p Cer^t from the Minstr

ROBERT HILL, 20 yers seru^t to m'· CRADDOCKE.

---

xviij° *Julij* 1635

THEIS vnder written name is to be transported to New-England imbarqued in the *Pide-Cowe* p Cert: from the Minister of his conformitee ℓ from Sr EDWARD SPENCER resident neere Branford that he is no Subsedy man. hath taken the oathe of Alleg. ℓ Suprem.

WiḦM HARRISON .... 55 yeres old
JO: BALDIN 13
W^M BALDIN 9

THEIS vnder-written names are to be transported to N. England imbarqued in the *defence* prd p Cert: from the Minist^{rs} ℓ Justic's of their conformitie ℓ y^t they are no Subsedy Men.

SARA JONES	34	W^M SAWKYNN	25
SARA JONES	15	Husb: W^M HUBBARD	40
JO: JONES	11	JUDITH HUBBARD	25
RUTH JONES	7	JOHN HUBBARD	15
THEOPHILUS JONES	3	W^M HUBBARD	13
RABECCA JONES	2	W^M READ	48
ELIZ. JONES	½	MABELL READ	30
THO: DONN	25	GEORGE READ	6
SUZANNA FAREBROTHER	25	RALPH READ	5
ELIZ: FENNICK	25	JUSTICE READ	18 Mo:

DOROTHIE KNIGHT	30	MARTHA BANES	20
NATHANIEL HUBBARD	6	JASPER GONN	29
RICHARD HUBBARD	4	ANN GONN	25
MARTHA HUBBARD	22	FEBE MAULDER	7
MARY HUBBARD	20	SYM: ROGER	20
ROBERT COLBURNE	28	JO: JENKYNN	26
EDWARD COLBORN	17	ROBERT KEYNE	40
DOROTHIE ADAMS	24	ELIZ STEERER	18
FRANCIS NUTBROWNE	16	SARA KNIGHT	50
Wᴹ WILLIAMSON	25	ANN KEYNE	38
MARIE WILLIMSON	23	BEN: KEYNE	16
LUCE MERCER	19	JO: BURLES	27
JO: FITCH	14	MARY BENTLEY	20
PENELOPE DARNO	29		

13 *July* 1635

THEIS vnder-written names are to be transported to N. England imbarqued in the *James* Jɴᵒ MAY Mʳ for N. E. p Cert: from the Ministers of their conformitie in Religion ℘ that they are no Subsedy Men.

Husb: Wᴹ BALLARD	32	Wᴹ HOOPER	18
ELIZABETH BALLARD	26	EDMOND JOHNSON	23
HESTER BALLARD	2	SAMVEL BENNET	24
JO: BALLARD	1	RICᴿ: PALMER	29
ALICE JONES	26	ANTᵒ BESSY	26
ELIZA: GOFFE	26	EDW: GARDNER	25
EDMOND BRIDGES	23	Wᴹ COLBRON	16
MICHELL MILNER	23	HENRY BULL	25
THO: TERRY	28	SALOMON MARTIN	16
ROBERT TERRY	25	wheelewrite. Wᴹ HILL	70
RICᴿ: TERRY	17	NICᵒ BUTTRY	33
THO: MARSHALL	22	MARTHA BUTTRY	28

GRACE BUTTRY 1
Shoemaker JO: HART........... 40
MARY HART 31
Shoemaker HENRY TYBBOT ... 39
ELIZABETH TIBOTT 39
JEREMY TYBBOTT 4
SAMVELL TYBBOT 2
REMEMBRANCE TYBBOTT 28
Cloth Worker NICO: GOODHUE 60
JANE GOODHEW 58

JOHN JOHNSON 26
SUZAN JOHNSON................. 24
ELIZA: JOHNSON................. 2
THO: JOHNSON.............. 18 mo.
Barber RALPH FARMAN......... 32
ALICE FARMAN 28
MARY FARMAN 7
THO: FARMAN................... 4
RALPH FARMAN 2

HEIS vnder written names are to be transported to N. England imbarqued in the *Blessing* JOHN LESTER M^r the pties have brought Cert: from the Minist^rs ℘ Justices of their conformitie in Religion, ℘ that they are no Subsedy Men.

fisherman JO JACKSON 40
MARGARET JACKSON 36
JOHN JACKSON 2
JO: MANIFOLD.................... 17
JOHN BURLES 26
JO: FITCH........................ 14
NICO: LONG 19
CHRISTIAN BUCK 26
BARNABIE DAVIES 36
SUZAN DANES [*or* DAUES] ... 16
ROBERT LEWES 28
ELIZ: LEWES 22
EDWARD INGRAM 18
HENRY BECK 18
JO: HATHOWAY 18
RICHARD SEXTON 14
MARY HUBBARD................. 24

MARY SPRATT.................... 20
RIC^R: HALLINGWORTH 40
SUZAN HALLINGWORTH 30
CHRISTIAN HUNTER 20
ELIZ: HUNTER 18
THO: HUNTER.................... 14
W^M HUNTER 11
W^M HOLLINGWORTH 7
RIC^R: HALLINGWORTH 4
SUZAN HALLINGWORTH 2
ELIZ: HALLINGWORTH 3
THO: TRENTUM 14
THO: BIGG'S..................... 13
JO: BRIGG'S 20
ROB^T LEWES* 28
ELIZ: LEWES* 22

* [It will be observed that these names also appear in the first column.]

THEIS vnder-written names are to be transported to New-England imbarqued in the *Love* JOSEPH YOUNG Mʳ·

Baker Willm CHERRALL	....	26	SARA HARMAN	10
VRSULA CHERRALL	....	40	WALTER PARKER	18
JO: HARMAN	....	12	fisherman Willm BROWNE	26
FRANCIS HARMAN	....	43	MARY BROWNE	26

THEIS vnder-written names are to be transported to Virginea, imbarqued in the *Alice* RICHARD ORCHARD Mʳ the Men have taken the oaths of Allegeance ᵽ Suprem:

EDWARD HUGHES 21	CHRI: HUDSON	30
JAMES MORFY 21	JO: SMITH	20
ROBERT HAGGAR 33	JO: COOP [COOPER]	20
THO: ASKEW 21	EDWARD WAGGITT..........	20
RICᴿ: COOKE 21	JO: VICCARS................	35
MILES ATKINSON 22	THO: ATKINSON	27
ROWLAND VAUGHAN 19	ROWLAND SUDGERNER......	21
RICHARD NATT 18	Wᴹ MASSINGBURD	23
FRA: JENKINSON............. 28	JO: HUTTON	17
Willm KENDRIDD 20	ELIZABETH DEW............	32
JO: WILSON................. 29	ANN DEW .... 9 mo.
ROBᵀ BAXTER 21	RACHELL ADAMS	16
JO: BENTLEY 34	AVIS DEACON	19
JO: HOLDSWORTH 20	HANNA GLIFFORD	20
JO: WRIGHT................ 21	ELIZ: BLANCH.............	20
CHARLES PEACOCK.......... 28	SOPHIA ROTTRIE	16

23 *July*

THIS vnder-written name is to be transported to New-England imbarqued in the *Fide-Cowe*, M^r   ASHLEY: the ptie hath brought Certificate of his conformitie in Religion ℈ Attestacōn from the Justices that he is no Subsedy man.

Husb: ROBERT BILLS........ 32

28 *July* 1635

THEIS psons herevnder expressed are to be transported to New-England, imbarqued in the *Hopewell* of London, THO: BABB, M^r p Certificate, from the Minister of St Giles Cripplegate, that they are conformable to the Church of England.   the Men have taken the oaths of Allegeance, ℈ Supremacie.

	yers		yeres
A Smith THOMAS TREDWELL	30	THO: BLACKLY	20
MARY TREDWELL	30	THO: TREDWELL............	I

[24 *July*]*

THEIS vnder-written names are to be transported to Virginea imbarqued in the *Assurance* de Lo: ISACK BROMWELL ℈ GEO. PEWSIE M^r examined by the Minister of the Towne of Gravesend of their conformitie in o^r Religion.   the men have taken the oaths of Allegeance ℈ Supremacie.

	yeres		
ROBERT BRIAN	27	RICHARD HAMEY [*or* HAMDY]	38
MAUDLIN JONES............	60	W^M HOLLAND..............	35
ANN SHAWE	32	HENRY SNOWE	26
JO: DUNCOMB	46	MARIE SOUTHWOOD	22
SITH HAIEWARD	30	FRANCIS ROWLSON	29

* [There is no date to this list; but a *list of troops to be transported to Flanders*, which precedes it in the original MS., is thus dated.]

JANE SOWTHERN	19	RICᴿ: ROGERS	48
MARGERIE BAKER	39	RICᴿ: LOCKLEY	51
SARA RAYNE	18	JO: JAKES	20
ANDREW VNDERWOOD	22	THO: MORE	19
PHILLIPP JOHNS	22	JO: BAKER	22
HENRIE MARSHALL	35	NEHEMIAH CASON*	21
HENRY HEIDEN'	30	ROBERT MAVES	28
ELIZABETH SHERLOCKE	29	RICHARD BARNES	38
THO: HURLOCK	40	JO: BUTTLER	50
SAm̄VEL HANDY	25	Wᴹ REBBELL	19
JO: GATER	36	ROBERT WYON	22
JOAN GATER	23	MATHEW DIXON	18
Wᴹ LEE	36	JOHN WHEELER	23
JOSUA TITLOE	19	JO: NORTH	24
JO: MIDDLETON	23	MOUNTFORD NEWMAN	27
ROBERT HAIWARD	22	ROBERT STEERE	17
SAm̄VEL POWELL	19	Wᴹ LAKE	35
RICHARD GLOVER	24	HUMFREY WILKINS	19
THO: PAGITT	41	ANTᵒ STILGO	21
MATHEW HOLMES	21	THO: DEACON	19
ELIAS HARRINGTON	22	ROBᵀ RIGGLIE	19
RICHARD SMITH	35	BENIAMIN PILLARD	18
THO: ROBINSON	24	ROBERT DAVIES	28
EVAN AP-EVAN	19	JO: SMITH	20
JO: BROWNE	21	WALTER MERRIDITH	33
ROBERT FRITH	23	THO: PHILLIPS	24
THO: WILKINSON	23	JAMES KINGSMILL	18
DENNIS HOGGIN	24	JO. BOWTON	20
JO: FRICCAR	25	WALTER CHAPMAN	44
RICHARD RIDGES	19	JAMES ARNOLD	37
EDWARD DAVIES	27	RICHARD LEAKE	18
THEODORUS BAKEWELL	21	THO: EDWYNN	13
JO: DERMOT	21	HANDGATE BAKER	22
JO: MORGAN	27	JO: ABROCK	20
THO: BAYCOCK	46	THO: HALL	15

[* Second letter not clearly written : the name *might* be read COSON.]

JAMES EDWIN	18	THO: LEONARD	18
EDWARD COM͞INS	28	THO: BESON	24
JO: GATER	15	CHRI: DIXON	24
NIC° GIBSON	22	ISACK KEMP	23
JO: ROBERT'S	46	JEREMIE SLIE	19
GEO: MOSELY	20	JO: ô MULLIN	18
JAMES RAVISH	20	ANTO PROCTER	16
JO: HALES	21	ROBERT HANDLEY	19
WARRAM TUCK	20	JO: AYMIES	18
JO: JONES	30	JO: TAYLER	21
W͞ COLTURE	19	W͞ ROFFIN	18
ROBERT SILBY	19	RIC^R: HALSEY	13
RIC^R: BRUSTER	26	ANT° OTLAND	18
JO: SWANLEY	21	ROBERT OLDRICK	18
W͞ CHARLES	21	W͞ HALL	21
ANTHONY LEE	21	JO COPELAND	19
WIꝯM WILLIAMS	28	JOHN GOAD	18
HENRY GEORGE	19	JO: POOLY	17
JO: BILLINS	21	FRANCIS GAYER	18
W͞ WRITE	18	THO: CRAVEN	17
ROBERT LOVETT	20	RIC^R: LUCAS	16
JOB JEFFERIE	19	GEO: CULLIDGE	18
HENRIE HALER	22	LAWRENCE BARKER	26
RICHARD SYMONDS	30	JO: BOWES	20
JAMES SPARK'S	57	JO: WOODBRIDGE	32
RICHARD KIRBIE	32	JO: JOHNSON	20
JAMES HINGLE	40	JO: CHAPPELL	38
THO: SAUNDERSON	24	GEO: WHITTAKER	32
W͞ SPICER	20	RICHARD LIVERSIDGE	24
WIꝯM THOMAS	19	HENRIE WOOD	20
HENRY MADIN	30	ROB^T MAX	21
EDWARD EDNALL	21	JO: WARREN	18
THO: JEFFERIES	22	THO: TURNER	18
NIC°: JACKSON	22	JO: GARLAND	19
THO: SPRATT	23	JO: HUMFREY	23

Isack Ambrose	18	Isabell Hakesby	23
Wᴍ Huncote	35	Joan Vallins	17
Tho: Williams	19	Marie Chambney	28
Tho: Foxcrofte	19	Elizabeth Allcott	20
Tho: Hobbs	22	Francis Bakewell	30
Charles Collohon	19	Elizabeth Payne	21
Henry Donn	23	Elizabeth Hughson	22
Roger Quintin	21	Marie Averie	22
Wᴍ Small	18	Sara Alport	25
Wᴍ Coleman	16	Marie Lee	22
Antᵒ Androwe	21	Elizabeth Bateman	23
Jo: Richardson	18	Thomazin Markcom	26
Wᴍ Claddin	17	Ann Goldwell	17
Tho: Gudderidge	17	Ann Griffinn	26
Roger Burley	17	James Brookes	28
Tho: Bard	16	*vxor.* Alice Brookes	18
Henry Butler	14	Dorcas Mercer	30
Jo: Budd	15	Ellin Davies	23
Jnᵒ Marshall	35	Alice Harris	21
Wᴍ Read	30	Eedie Holloway	22
Edward Mitchell	18	Sara Coggin	20
Robert Drewrie	16	Elizabeth Baker	20
Ricᴿ: Wells	17	Dorothie Davies	17
Jo: Cotes	17	Elizabeth Raynard	20
Jo: Stubber	17	Marie Olliver	21
Henry Lee	18	Alice Riall	18
Ricᴿ: Ball	17	Rabecca Parmeton	19
Jo: Cooke	17	Marie Middleton	17
Tho: Syer	14	Kat: Fulder	17
Jo: Partridge	18	Eliz: Dick's	18
Jo: Johnson	24	Sara Greene	20
		Margaret Rickord	20
Women.		Winnifredd Congrave	22
		Mathew Plant	23
Isbell Davies	22	Jo: More	28

ELIZABETH POWELL	17	MARIE LEE	14 weekes
MARIE SHORTER	26	MATHEW CLATWORTHY	25

188

———

33*

———

27° *July* 1635

THEIS vnder-written names are to be transported to Virginea imbarqued in the *Primrose* Capten DOUGLASS, M^r p Certificate vnder ye Ministers hand of Gravesend, being examined by him touching their Conformitie to the Church Discipline of England   The Men have taken the oaths of Allegeance ℓ Supremacie.

WILLIAM SPRAWSON	28	W^M ALDERTON	35
JO: SYMOND'S	18	THO: CLIFTON	25
RICHARD WEBB	36	W^M BROWNE	19
LUKE SNODEN	21	ALEXANDER MASIE	21
W^M STARLING	18	GEO: LEE	16
LAWRENCE WHITHORSE	17	THO: BEANE	21
ROBERT NUTTALL	18	JO: PEW	16
JO: HALL	24	GEORGE COTTINGHAM	20
MATHEW BURR	27	JO: SWIFTE	23
THO: DAGGETT	21	GEO: FOWLER	22
JO: BALDWYNN	27	THO: FARRABY	26
THO: BRUXSTON	20	ROBERT SHARP	21
HENRY BANBRIDGE	18	W^M EVANS	25
NIC^O: PETTING	24	W^M HARRIS	50
ROBERT WILLIAMS	21	THOMAS COKE	24
W^M THORNCOME	19	ABRAM SWIFTE	23
THO: WIGGIN	21	OLIVER FAYRIE	25
CHRI: LEGG	19	OLIVER SYMON	30
HENRIE ROBINSON	26	HENRY MAGGITT	29
JO: SHERRICK	19	THO: BALES	18
JO: PALMER	18	W^M ALLINSON	25

fetch off by M. Secretary Windebanks Warrant.

———

* [There are 221 names in the list. It will be observed that adding these two numbers together, will yield 221.]

WALTER MARSHALL	17	JAMES HALL	18
JO: SHIPLEY	21	ROBERT BENTON	18
THO: SMITH	18	THO: MASON	19
JO: JOHNSON	21	THO: SAKER	16
JO: WICK'S	26	JO: MARSH	33
RIC_R: WEST	21	FRANCIS MURSH*	28
GEO. WADE	19	THO: ADAMS	21
Wᴹ PERCE	19	PHILIP DAVIES	25
JO: BEETELL	20	EDWARD DANNELL	18
FRANCIS RATFORD	20	HENRY CHAPMAN	19
JO: MORFIN	20	JO: NORTH	22
JO: LEE	25	CHARLES WHITE	18
JO: BALME	34	JOHN PARRY	27
JO: STROWDE	17	GODFREY HUNDLEY	24
Wᴹ FOX	21	RICHARD WATT'S	24
THO. PYNCH	32	CLEMENT DONN	22
RICᴿ· GILL	26	RICᴿ STANFORD	25
HENRY DIKES	33	BEN: GREGORIE	24
Wᴹ SHAWE	25	EDWARD MILLS	30
HENRY SMITH	22	ROBERT EELIE	14
RALPH HUNT	22	RICᴿ: KELLUM	16
JO: LUPTON	25	ROBERT PAGE	17
JAMES RYDIE	45	JO: BALDWYN	21
GARRET COOKE	20	ELLIS HARMAN	18
JO: MERIE	17	JO: BOTTOMLY	19
OLLIVER CLIFFORD	18	Wᴹ MORE	16
WiⅡⅿ WHITE	23	SAMVELL BOSWELL	23
THO: MORTIMER	20	Wᴹ SWIFTE	21
JO: RIDGE	16	Wᴹ GRIFFIN	21
THO: VINSON	18	JO: NORMAN	20
FRANCIS DELLICAT	20	RICHARD WARDD	13
THO: RIDGE	23	FRANCIS JARVICE	14
RICHARD CARY	17	THO: THOMAS	20
THO: MANNING'S	16	LUKE RICHARDSON	17
Wᴹ PARRY	16	JO: FLETCHER	18

* [So in the original ; but probably intended for MARSH.]

ROBᵀ HARRIS	20	SICILLIA WESTON	37
ROBERT FEAT'S	25	JANE PRVM̄	18
JO: SAKER	30	ANN VISHER	20
Wᴹ JOHNSON	26	KAT: YORK	19
JO: WEEKES	18	DOROTHY JAKES	29
EDMOND ARDINTON	20	AYMIE HUMFRIE	23
CHRISTO: BANBRIDGE	19	MARGARET JNºSON	20
ELIZ: MAYNARD	22	MARIE SAKER	24
ANN JACKSON	23	ELLIN SUTTON	20
JO: MOLIN	30	JO: SAKER	1
MARGARET CLARK	21	THO: POOLE	43
Wᴹ CLARK	1	JO: WHETSTON	20
ELLIN HALY	55	THOMAZIN MILLS	38
	100		

38

Vltimo Julij 1635

THEIS vnder-written names are to be transported to Virginea, imbarqued in yᵉ *Merchant's Hope* HUGH WESTON Mʳ: p examinacō̄n by the Minister of Gravesend touching their conformitie to the Church discipline of England ꝑ have taken the oaths of Alleg: ꝑ Suprem:

EDWARD TOWERS	26	CHARLES RILSDEN	27
HENRY WOODMAN	22	JO: EXSON	17
RICHARD SEEMES	26	Wᴹ LUCK	14
ALLIN KING	19	JO: THOMAS	19
ROWLAND SADLER	19	JO: ARCHER	21
JO: PHILLIPS	28	RICHARD WILLIAMS	25
VYNCENT WHURTER	17	FRANCIS HUTTON	20
JAMES WHITHEDD	14	SAVILL GASCOYNE	29
JOSIAS WATTS	21	RICᴿ: BULFELL	29
PETER LOE	22	RICᴿ: JONES	26
GEO: BROOKER	17	THO: WYNES	30
HENRY EELES	26	HUMFREY WIᵭMS [WILLIAMS]	22
JO: DENNIS	22	EDWARD ROBERT'S	22
THO: SWAYNE	23	MARTIN ATKINSON	32

EDWARD ATKINSON	28
Wᴹ EDWARD'S	30
NATHAN BRADDOCK	31
JEFFERY GURRISH	23
HENRY CARRELL	16
THO: RYLE	24
GAMALIEL WHITE	24
RICHARD MARK'S	19
THO: CLEVER	16
JO: KITCHIN	16
EDMOND EDWARD'S	20
LEWES MILES	19
JO: KENNEDAY	20
SAᵐ: JACKSON	24
DANIELL ENDICK	16
JO: CHALK	25
JO: VYNALL	20
EDWARD SMITH	20
JO: ROWLIDGE	19
Wᴹ WESTLIE	40
JO: SMITH	18
JO: SAUNDERS	22
THO: BARTCHERD	16
THO: DODDERIDGE	19
RICHARD WILLIAMS	18

JO: BALLANCE	19
Wᴹ BALDIN	21
Wᴹ PEN	26
JO: GEERIE	24
HENRY BAYLIE	18
RICᴿ: ANDERSON	50
ROBERT KELUM	51
RICHARD FANSHAW	22
THO: BRADFORD	40
Wᴹ SPENCER	16
MARMADUKE ELLA	22

Women.

ANN SWAYNE	22
ELIZ: COTE	22
ANN RYCE	23
KAT: WILSON	23
MAUDLIN LLOYD	24
MABELL BUSHER	14
ANNIS HOPKINS	19
ANN MASON	24
BRIDGET CROMPE	18
MARY HAWKES	19
ELLIN HAWKES	18

66
—
9

Primo die Augusti 1635

THEIS vnder-written names are to be transported to Virginea, imbarqued in the *Elizabeth* de Lo: CHRISTOPHER BROWNE Mʳ examined by the Minister of Gravesend touching their conformitie to the ordʳˢ ℯ discipline of the Church of England the Men have taken the oaths of Alleg: ℯ Supremacie.

JO: BENFORD	20	W^M THURROWGOOD	13
LODOWICK FLETCHER	20	SAMVELL MATHEW	14
JO: BAGBIE	17	THO: FRITH	17
ROB^T SALTER	14	JO: AUSTIN	24
EDWARD WHITE	18	PAUL FEARNE	24
STEEVEN PIERCE	30	THOMAS ROYSTON	25
RIC^R: BEAUFORD	18	JO: TAYLER	18
RIC^R: CHAPMAN	18		
ANDREW PARKINS	18	*Women.*	
JO: BAKER	16	KATHERIN JONES	28
JO: WAKERS	16	ELIZ: SANKSTER	24
JO: VAUGHAN	17	ELLIN SHORE	20
YEOMAN GIBSON	16	ALICE PYNDON	19
THO: LEED	16	SARA EVEREDGE	22
GEO: TREVAS	18	MARGARET SMITH	28
W^MR SHILBORN	20	ELIZAB: HOEMAN	20
SAMVEL GROWCE	38	MOULES NAXSTON	19
W^M GLASBROOKE	21	MARIE BURBACK	17
EDWARD DICK'S	30	ELIZ: RUDSTON	40
JO: BENNETT	18	ELIZ: RUDSTON	5
MICHELL SAUNDBY	25		

26
—
13

xj^{th} Aug^{ti} 1635

N the *Batcheler* de Lo: m' THO. WEBB vrs New Engld

LYON GARDNER 36 yers ℓ his wife MARY 34 yers, ℓ ELIZA. COLES 23
yers, their maid Seruant, ℓ W^M JOPE 40 yers, who are to passe to
new England, haue brought Cert. of their Conformity.

vij° Augusti 1635

THEIS vnder-written names are to be transported to Virginea imbarqued in the *Globe* of London JEREMY BLACKMAN M^r, have been examined by the Minister of Gravesend of their Conformitie, ℓ have taken the oaths of Alleg: ℓ Supremacie.

Minister JOHN GOODBARNE	30	GEO: NETTELLFORD	19
EDWARD LEWES	21	THO: PARKER	22
JO: WHITWHAM	26	PHILIP MEREDITH	12
JO: BABINGTON	20	ROBERT COPPYN	11
W^M SATCHILL	22	W^M BROWNE	20
THO: GOWEN	18	ROBERT YATES	25
SYMON MOODY	20	W^M GRIFFITH	18
THOMAS TUCKER	21	OLOUGH BERNE	19
JO: WATTON	20	JAMES COPLEY	22
JO: RAMSEY	30	THO: BLITHE	20
RICHARD BATES	16	W^M HOWARD	16
WIℓℓM BOWLER	14	JO: HALE	14
HENRY HOPES	23	NICHOLAS TAYLER	17
W^M BARNES	22	BENEDICT ROLLS	16
HENRY SMITHICK	26	MARTIN PERKINS	18
THO: GRIGG	16	W^M ENNIS	22
CHRISTOPHER LEGG	18	DAVIE VAUGHAN	18
RANDALL BURNE	20	JO: SEATON	19
HUMFREY BUCKLEY	18	THO: BOWYER	19
HENRY STON	27	ABRAM BENTLEY	20
PHILLIPP SHERRINGHAM	17	RIC^R: ADAMS	22
THO: SHARP	17	JOHN RUSSELL	15
W^M SAVORY	25	W^M BURTON	20
EDWARD KING	21	MATHEW BATEMAN	20
NATHANIEL ROGERS	17	JO: BYNSTEDD	20
MICHELL VICTOR	18	MICHELL HAYNES	21
W^M SHARP	21	THO: JN^OSON	21
W^M OSMOTHERLY	14	JOHN WHITFIELD	20

HENRY MOSTON	23	JOHN PETER	20
ALLIN HAMOCK	32	RICHARD WOLLMAN	22
GEORGE FORTH	27	EDWARD CLEIBORN	20
CHARLES SMITH	22	NICHOLAS BATE	24
MATHEW MORTON	19	W^M BATE	35
W^M LEWES	25	RICHARD WELLS	26
ROBERT ARNOLD	30	RICHARD GUY	23
JO: THATCHER	22	JO: SWANN	18
W^M NASH	22	EDWARD LENE	32
PETER PAYTON	22	THO: SAWELL	29
ROBERT BALDRY	18	THO: WHAPLETT	21
EDWARD LANGSTEDD	18	MABELL EATON	27
JAMES SCOTT	21	SARA CLEYTON	27
W^M ANDROWES	18	ANN LEVYNNS	31
JO: BLAND	26	MARY WILLIS	22
PHILIP WESTLAKE	20	ANN CREEDE	22
JO: MARWOOD	17	JULIAN MERIDETH	38
JO: GRIFFITH	20	LUCIE BUCKLE	18
JO: HOWGATE	17	JOAN JERNEW	30
LUKE HANES [or HAUES]	27	ELIZ: JERNEW	25
JO: STIBBS	19	ROBERT SCRIVEN	18
JEFFERY WYNCH	20	ROBERT ISHAM	14
RICHARD ABBOTT	25	JO: ARMSBY	30
RIC^R: STEEVENSON	19	W^M LENNON*	19
THO: SMITH	30	MICHELL WHITLEY	23
ANT^O: CARTER	22	JO. MANNING'S	20
GEO: MORE	25	W^M BARLOE	19
ROBERT GANNOCK	20	EDWARD HOLLINBRIGG	27
RIC^A: COOKE	46	W^M MANIFOLD	20
RICHARD TOWNSEND	28	GREGORIE ALLIN	17
NICHOLAS JERNEW	28	W^M TALBOTT	14
THO: WALLIS	32	GEO: HAWLEY	17
WIltM SCARFIELD	22	EDWARD HODGSKYNNS	21
SAMVEL STRINGER	17	MARK GILL	22
NIC^O: REINOLD'S	38	THO: HARRWOOD	26

* [Or LEMON. The strokes of the letters are thick and clumsy.]

Abram Watson	17	Francis Townsend	21
Allin Rippin	28	Francis Townsend	2
John Hobson	25	Tho: Needham	13
Tho: Chapman	26	Tho: Axstell	35
Robert Vass	19	Jo: Reddman	46
Richard Ward	23	Robert Mascrie	32
Geo: Aldin	20	Robert Crouch	15
Wᴹ Warner	25	Tho: Owen	23
Geo: Grace	25	Tho: Knibb	23
Christopher Hamond	32	Robert Waltum	26
Jacob Averie	33	Debora Barnie	23
Geo: Averie	23	Jo: Tyler	16
Francis Bullock	26	Tho: Gregorie	15
Richard Vpgate	21	Tho: Tate	22
Ann Willett	23	Tho: Hancock	15
Joyce Robinson	20	Fra: Pepper	16
Margaret Baylie	20	Wᴹ Saundᴿ's	19
Mary Brackley	20		

xᵒ Augᵗⁱ 1635

THEIS vnder-written names are to be transported to Virginea, imbarqued in the *Safety*, John Graunt Mʳ

	yeres		yeres
John Hardon	27	Mary Pitway	4
Richard Haieward	33	Jo: Jones	29
Barthol: Hoskyns	34	Mathew Gough	22
Antᵒ Haies	24	Robert Boddy	19
Jo: Catts	23	Jo: Carter	22
Jo: Wazen	19	Thomas Heath	23
Henry Gadling	16	Jo: Hornwood	21
Richard Hopkins	25	Francis Barker	21
Robert Sutton	17	W Tighton	24
Robert Pitway	27	Christopher Wynn	20

JO: HEMING	25	JAMES BETHELL	27
RALPH SYMPKYNN	28	JO: BROWNE	25
JAMES BARNES	25	JO: GIBSON	30
CHRI: STOPE	24	THO: BELK	37
ROBERT LENDALL	20	GEO: TUCKER	22
DAVID KIFFIN	24	THO: JENNIONS	24
W^M SYMONDS	32	ROBERT PERKINS	25
TYMOTHY TRALLOPP	21	JO: MARTIN	23
HENRY DUGDELL	20	EDMOND FARRELL	20
JOHN LOWND	16	W^M HASSELL	24
JAMES ATKINSON	16	EDWARD GIFFORD	30
NIC^O: WATSON	16	ROGER GILBERT	16
JO: TAYLOR	18	RICHARD ALLIN	22
ARTHUR RAYMOND	20	JO: WILKINSON	14
EDWARD SPICER	21	FRANCIS VYONS	25
ROBERT HARRWOOD	17	WILM DAVIES	27
RICHARD FOSTER	16	RICHARD ALDERLEY	26
JO: BELL	30	HENRY DALLEPER	18
GABRIELL FISHER	36	RICH: HUDSON	30
THO: BROWNE	18	JO: HILL	22
CORNELIUS MAIES	12	EDMOND MULLENEUX	20
STEVEN GORTON	35	HUMFREY BLACKMAN	16
JO: GLOSTER	23	RICHARD COTTON	20
JO: PIGEON	15	JAMES ALLIN	19
THOMAS THORNE	13	MARTIN CHURCH	16
JO: WRITE	15	HENRY GILBERT	34
RICHARD PRESTON	17	W^M Q'NY*	20
ANDREW STRETCHER	14	BRIAN KELLY	20
ALEXANDER HARVIE	15	LEWES SMITH	22
EDMOND JENKINS	15	THO: DOE	33
NIC^O: MORTON	17	THOMAS SAUNDERS	13
JO: BAY	16	EDWARD SAUNDERS	9
JAMES PATTISON	21	THOMAS CARTER	25
W^M LOWTHER	24	THOMAS AP THOMAS	30
EDWARD SAUNDERS	40	RICHARD CAUNT	36

* [Clearly so in the original.]

RICHARD MOSS	20	HANNA WADDINGTON	16
JOHN PERRYN	21	ELIZABETH HOLLOWAY	26
HUGH LE ROY	19	ELIZ: GOLD	17
THOMAS REINOLDS	15	ELIZABETH FRISBY	24
JO: CURTIS	21	ELIZ: SMITH	50
ROBERT GLENESTER	25	MARGARET GARD	24
HENRY BUCKLE	30	MARGERIE SMITH	22
JO: NEWMAN	20	ELIZAB: PISCER	16
THOMAS GARDNER	22	ELIZABETH WARD	25
JO: NEWMAN	24	JOAN GRIFFIGE	35
ROBERT FRISTER	20	ELIZ: TURNER	44
RICHARD FIELD	20	JOAN ALLIN	20
GEO: HABBITTELL	26	MARIE BOOTH	19
WIḤM KARSEWELL	20	JANE CUTTING	17
Wᴹ GRASSON	20	Wᴹ HINDSLEY	23
RICHARD WRIGHT	23	KATHERIN SMITH	18
JO: BUTLER	21	THOMAZIN BROAD	24
JO: HENDRY	24	ANN WATERMAN	18
RICHARD BROOKES	20	JOAN TURNER	21
JO: MARTIN	17	JANE FOXSLEY	25
GEO: CASTELL	21	ROSE HILLS	22
JO: BILLINS	26	ANN CROFT'S	16
THO: WRENN	20	GRACE TUBLEY	20
ROBERT PISCER	44	MARGARET SNALES	22
		ANN HOLLAND	19
MARIE LERRIGO	19	ANN FOSSITT	34
MARGARET HOMES	23	DOROTHY MOYLE	24
ALICE ASHTON	20		

21ᵗʰ Augᵗⁱ 1635

IN the *Hopewell* de Lo: mᵉ   BABB, vᵗˢ New Engld

HENRY MAUDSLEY 24 yers hath brought Certᵗ from the Ministr of his Conformity hath taken the oathe of Allegance.

21 *Aug^{ti}* 1635

THEIS vnder-written names are to be transported to Virginea, imbarqued in the *George* Jo: SEVERNE M^r bound thither p examination of the Minister of Gravesend &c.

	yeres		yeres
MICHELL MASTERS	21	MARY BURTWEZILL	18
THO: MORECOCK	26	ALICE WATSON	30
JO: GILLAM	21	JOAN LUDCOLE	18
THO: GILLAM	18	NATHAN: WILSON	23
HUMFREY HIGGINSON	28	THEODOR ROGERSON	20
MATHEW SILSBY	31	W^M THOMSON	22
THO: BULLARD	32	JO: JONES	17
THO: ROGERS	15	MICHELL HEDLY	24
NOWELL LLOYD	16	EDWARD ABBS	37
ANN HIGGINSON	25	W^M GOLDER	22
FRANCIS FOSTER	18	THO: HAND	20
ROBERT SCOTCHMORE	39	GEORGE FOX	14
JO: EVANS	19	JO: DAYNIE	20
RABECCA PALMER	19	W^M HAWKES	22
ARTH^R BODILIES	19	RALPH CLEYTON	20
PETER MANING	25	THO: BEST	33
DANIELL BOWYER	30	JO: HUNT	23
MICHELL WILLIAMS	18	JO: FELD	20
CHRI: KIRK	23	ELIZ: BRISTOWE	17
RICHARD GENNEY	20	MARY ROBINSON	18
CHRISTOPHER THOMAS	21	ELIZABETH WOODBRIDGE	22
WALTER WALKER	23	BRYAN HARE	27
JO: POPE	28	ROGER CUTTS	20
ANT^O HODGSKINS	22	W^M DICKENSON	21
JOHN BELL	21	W^M MITCHELL	15
ANN LAYFIELD	30	MARIE NEELE	13
JO: HUTCHINSON	47	ANN COOPER	20
ALICE LEVITT	16	GEO: TAYLER	20

HENRY KILBY	27	ALEXANDER GREENE	40
JO: FYNCH	27	JAMES BANKES	35
GEO: QUITHOR	25	OLIFF GIBBINS	13
THO: MOTHROPP	21	CONSTANCE FISTER	23
JAMES HORNER	24	Wᴹ SCOTT	24
JO: RAY	21	RALPH BROWNE	23
RICᴮ: DIXON	20	ROBᵀ MORRISON	21
THO: PEACOCK	19	EDWARD GREENE	6
JO: ROGERS	18	THO: BANK'S	4
GRIFFITH HUGHES	24	ELIZ: BANK'S	9 mo.
ANN WHITE	19	JO: ALLIN	21
JO: QUYLE	15	LEWES JAMES	30
THO: ALLIN	17	THO: WIGGINS	20
JO: BUTLER	13	SARA MERRIMAN	20
THO: PURNELL	16	ARTHUR FIGISS	40
VALENTINE BISHOPP	11	Wᴹ HINSHAWE	20
Wᴹ CLOWDLSLIE*	26	ROGER NEVITT	20
RICHARD VERDIN	24	MATHEW PRICE	20
JO: BADDAM	40	RIC: JAMES	33
ELIAS WIGGMORE	24	Wᴹ NEESAM	21
SUZAN HARE	24	THO: BUCK	17
RICHARD HIDE	24	GEO: SMITH	20
ROBERT DUNHAM	30	JOSEPH MILLS	20
JO: GOODRIDGE	19	THO: ROGERS	16
JO: TIFFING	19	JO: RICHARDS	17
HENRY CUTLING	40	Wᴹ SAIE	17
LEONARD RICHARDSON	43	GEO: CRANWELL	23
JESPER HODGSKYNS	24	JO: WESTON	20
JO: WYNN	25	FRANCIS BLAKE	18
THO: HOWELL	20	THO: MAYNARD	22
LAWRENCE BARWICK	20	JO: PRICE	34
JO: MUSGRAVE	37	PETER STARKIE	22
EDWARD LILLIE	19	JAMES HAWKINS	17
JO: GOODSON	25	JOSEPH WARRWELL	17
MICHELL PRYNN	25	FRANCIS YOUNG	21

* [So in the original: doubtless intended for CLOWDESLIE.]

THO: CONNIER	22	FRANCIS HAVERCAMP	17
THO: PERRY	18	EDMOND JONES	22
JO: STAUNTON	27	HENRY HAWLEY	34
THO: WHITE	16	ROBERT BURR	19
RIC^R: PHILLIPS	14	W^M MILLER	29
JANE SWIFTE	23	W^M CURTIS	19
MARGERY CARTER	23	THO: BEOMONT	29
GRESSAM PARKINS	19	JO: COVELL	18
W^M BLOCK	23	MARY LOVETT	18
THO: GADSBY	19	JOAN VIZARD	18
Minister. RICHARD JAMES	33	W^M STEEVENS	22
VRSULA JAMES	19	THO: HORROCK'S	22
ARTHUR FIGISS	33	MARY SOANES	26

152

THEIS vnder-written names are to be transported to Virginea imbarqued in the *Thomas* HENRY TAVERNER M^r, have been examined by the Minister of Gravesend touching their conformitie in o^r Religion, &c.

JO: LEWES	16	EDWARD ERLE	45
W^M GREENE	18	RICHARD CRANE	32
WALTER SMITH	20	ADAM CROWE	19
W^M BURTON	24	JACOB DENTON	20
JO: HILL	15	HUGH STANLEY	16
JOSEPH BROWNING	20	BENIAMIN SYMES	42
THO: FOUCH	16	MARY JOLLY	21
EDWARD SAWNDERS	20	ELIZ: AYRES	26
W^M JAMES	18	HUMFREY AWDRY	21
JO: TULLIE	20	EDWARD JOHNSON	28
JANE GIBBS	27	JO: COLLOPP	22
MARY CHADD	17	PETER RICARD	19
JANE COLERACK	22	HENRY GEW	20
ALICE WRIGHT	21	W^M ADAMS	24

Robᵀ James	18	Edward Robins	33
Jo: Browton	20	Geo: Dawe	23
Ricᴿ: Wheeler	24	Joseph Preston	20
Robert Wells	30	Ananiah Dyer	24
Jo: Gressam	22	Roger Wilkyns	33
Teague Quillin	20	Jo: Booth	19
Wᴹ Peas	19	Peter Harbynn	21
Bartholm: Furbank	20	Tho: Maltman [or Multman]	17
Robert Johnson	27	Nicᵒ: Folly	16
Mary Johnson	23	Hugh Fouche	17
Alice Jnᵒson	22	Michell Hutchinson	16
Eliz: Johnson	18	Wᴹ Pallmer	17
Mary Lucie	20	Wᴹ Chamberlin	16
Joan Looker	20	Nathan: Tooly	19
Suzan Jennoway	26	Henry Wilson	12

58

Secundo die Septembris 1635

THEIS vnder-written names are to be transported to Sᵗ Christophers: imbarqued in the *William & John* Rowland Langram Mʳ. have been examined by the Minister of Gravesend & tooke the oaths of Alleg: & Supreͫ: die et Aᵒ pd

James Lampley	19	W Williams	21
Wᴹ Greene	18	Christopher Steevenson	19
Henry Daniell	20	Tho: Barnes	20
Rowland Davies	20	Robert Watler	20
Wᴹ Reddish	20	Andrew Young	40
Edward Broomish	20	Francis Hudson	36
Robert Fitt	18	Jo: Parr	19
Richard Lewes	26	Wᴹ Morley	24
Richard Corie	18	Ricᴿ: Gavyn	21
Richard Cristie	20	Tho: Phillipps	35
Jo: Brunt	24	Jo: Willard	16

THO: HANMER	14	THO: HAMES [or HAINES]	16
W^M BURNHAM	21	JOHN PINKLEY	30
WALTER WALL	16	ROBERT THOMSON	22
W^M BATHOE	18	W^M DAVIES	30
THO: TAPPER	21	RICHARD BEARE	28
W^M BAYLIE	23	GEO: FORD	19
THO: BROOKES	21	THO: LOWYNN	20
NATHANIELL BERNARD	22	JO: DRAKE	18
THO: PRICE	20	ROBERT OUTMORE	38
GEO: FRIE	19	HUGH HILTON	23
THO: HART	25	THO: KING	27
MATHEW ADDISON	17	LAWRENCE ADDERFORD	26
THEOBALD WALL	18	JAMES DOCKKIE	17
ROBERT RICHARDSON	33	EZECHELL RENNAM	*13
ROBERT LEAKE	38	THO: HAIDEN	15
BARNABIE BROOKE	20	EDWARD BRUNT	26
JO: COCK	18	THO: REINOLDS	16
NIC^O: COBB	24	W^M BENN	24
JO: HINSON	21	PHILLIP SKORIER	26
THO: EKKERSOE	24	W^M WORRALL	23
GEO: CARTER	28	JO: BENSON	27
RIC^B: HARRIS	26	HENRY BUGLAND	21
HENRIE NOKES	27	JO: MORTON	24
THO: THOMSON	28	JO: DITCHFIELD	22
SAM͠VEL KNIPE	23	NATHANIELL SIMPKINS	26
JO: WATTON	25	W^M PROCTER	26
JO: BYRALL	29	EDWARD GRESSAM	17
MORRIS PARRY	30	W^M STEEVENS	21
JO: NAYLER	20	THO: WHITHEDD	24
EDWARD NAYLER	21	THO: CLARK	25
GEO: NOBLE	22	W^M STIFFCHYNN	16
W^M COCK'S	20	JO: BONN	18
MARTIN SOWTH	19	W^M DUNBARR	15
W^M GREENELEFE	26	JO: MORRISH	18
JO: SAWNDERS	17	ALEXANDER GLOVER	37

* [Originally written 15, but afterwards altered.]

EDWARD KING	25	RICHARD MASON	29
JO: KENT	23	MANLEY RICHARDSON	21
ROBERT LYNT	21	ISACK BELT	23
EDWARD BELLIS	21	JOHN PICKERING	25
THO: GILL	30	THO: ARCHBOLD	19
Wᴹ GROVE	32	MATHEW WELLS	28
			*103

THEIS vnder written names are to be transported to Virginea imbarqued in the *David* JO: HOGG Mʳ· have been examined by the Minister of Gravesend, &c.

EDWARD BROWNE	25	JO: MORRIS	26
SAMVEL TROOPE	17	RICHARD BROOKES	30
Wᴹ HATTON	23	ROBERT BARRON	18
DANIELL BACON	30	JONATHAN BARNES	22
ROBERT ALSOPE	18	HENRY KENDALL	17
TEDDER JONES	30	THO: POULTER	31
THO: SIGGINS	18	JO: LAMB	22
ABELL DEXTER	25	THO: NUNN	22
RICᴿ: CATON	26	JO: STEEVENS	19
HENRY SPICER	28	EDWARD CRABBTREE	20
THO: GRANGER	19	Wᴹ BARBER	17
JO: BONFOLLY†	21	ANN BEEFORD [*or* BEDFORD]	25
ROGER MANNINGTON	14	MARTHA PORTER	20
JOSUA CHAMBERS	17	GURTRED LOVETT	18
HENRY MELTON	23	JANE JENNING'S	25
DAVID LLOYD	30	MARGARET BOLD	30
DONOUGH GORHIE	27	MARY ROGERS	20
GER: BUTLER	27	MARGARET WALKER	20
ADDAM NUNNICK	25	FREESE BROOMAN	20
JO: STANN	27	ELIZ: JONES	20
EDWARD SPICER	18		
JO: FEELDING	19		41

* [It will be observed that these totals are not always correct; there are 104 names in this list. The next, too, is wrong.]
† [Possibly BONFILLY. The fifth letter is indistinctly written; it looks like an *o*, but has a *dot* above it.]

xj^{o} Sept: 1635

THEIS vnder-written names are to be transported to New-England imbarqued in the *Hopewell* THO: BABB, m^{r} p Cert from the Ministers & Justices of their conformitie in Religion to o^{r} Church of England: & y^{t} they are no Subsedy Men. they have taken ye oaths of Alleg: & Suprem.

	yeres
Husb: Willm Wood	27
Elizabeth Wood	24
Jo: Wood	26
Robert Chambers	13
Tho: Jn°son	25
Marie Hubbard	24
Jo: Kerbie	12
Jo: Thomas	14
Isack Robinson	15
Ann Williamson	18
Tanner. Jo: Weekes	26
Marie Weekes	28
Anna Weekes	1
Suzan Withie	18
Robert Baylie	23
Marie Withie	16
Sam̄vel Younglove	30
Margaret Younglove	28
Samvel Younglove	1
Andrew Hulls	29
Anthony Freeman	22
Twiford West	19
Roger Toothaker	23
Margaret Toothaker	28
Roger Toothaker	1
Robert Withie	20
Henrie Ticknall	15
Harnis maker Isack Heath	50
Elizabeth Heath	40
Elizabeth Heath	5
Martha Heath	30
W^{M} Lyon	14
Grace Stokes	20
Tho: Bull	25
Joseph Miller	15
Jo: Prier	15
Richard Hutley	15
Daniell Pryer	13
Katherin Hull	23
Mary Clark	16
Jo: Marshall	14
Joan Grave	30
Mary Grave	26
Joan Cleven	18
Edmond Chippfield [Chipperfield]	20
Mary With	62
Robert Edward's	22
Robert Edge	25
Walter Lloyd	27

ELLIN LEAVES	17	JO: FORTEN	14
ALICE ALBON	25	GABRIELL RELD	18
BARBARY ROFE	20		—
			54

xix Sept: 1635

THEIS vnder-written names are to, be transported to New-England imbarqued in the *Truelove* JO: GIBBS Mʳ. the Men have taken the oaths of Alleg: ℮ Suprem.

	yeres		
Labouring man. THOMAS BURCHARD	40	RABECCA FENNER	25
MARY BURCHARD	38	THO: TIBBALD'S	20
ELIZABETH BURCHARD	13	THOMAS STREME	15
MARIE BURCHARD	12	JO: STREME	14
SARA BURCHARD	9	Husb: RALPH TOMKINS	50
SUZAN BURCHARD	8	*vxor* KAT. TOMKINS	58
JO: BURCHARD	7	ELIZABETH TOMKINS	18
ANN BURCHARD	18 mo.	MARIE TOMKINS	14
PETER PLACE	20	SAM̄VEL TOMKINS	22
Wᴹ BEERESTO	23	RICHARD HAWES	29
GEO: BEERESTO	21	ANN HAWES	26
Husbandmon EDWARD HOWE.	60	ANNA HAWES	2½
ELIZABETH HOWE	50	OBEDIAH HAWES	6. mo
JEREMIE HOWE	21	RALPH ELLWOOD	28
SARA HOWE	12	GEO: TAYLER	31
EPHRAIM HOWE	9	ELIZABETH JENKINS	27
ISACK HOWE	7	Wᴹ PRESTON	44
Wᴹ HOWE	6	MARIE PRESTON	34
JO: SEDGWICK	24	ELIZ: PRESTON	11
JEREMY BLACKWELL	18	SARA PRESTON	8
LESTER GANTER [or GUNTER].	13	MARIE PRESTON	6
ZACHARIA WHITMAN	40	JO: PRESTON	3
SARA WHITMAN	25	Wᴹ JOES*	28
ZACHA: WHITMAN	2½	WILLIÀM BENTLEY	47
		ALICE BENTLEY	15

* [This name *may* be read as IVES.]

MARGARET KILLINGHALL	20	JOHN DONE	16
JO: BENTLEY	17	ROGER BROOME	17
THO: STOCKTON	21	DOROTHIE LOWE	13
GEO: MORREY	23	JO: SIMPSON	30
RICHARD SRAYNE	34	THO: BRIGHTON	31
SARAH HAILE	11	THO: RUMBALL	22
SAMVEL GROVER	16	EDWARD PARRIE	24
ROBERT BROWNE	24	JANE WALSTON	19
THO: BLOWER	50		—
EDWARD JEOFFERIES	24		*66
			—

Tricessimo die Septembris 1635

ABOARD the *Dors^t* JOHN FLOWER M^r bound for ye Bormodos.

JOHN REDFORD [*or* REEFORD]	16	JO: HETH	21
ROBERT RAMSEY	15	NATHANIELL BONNICK	16
JOHN WILLIAMS	16	JO: DENMAN	14
WIḦM ELLISTON	13	THO: MORE	18
LUBAS WRIGHT	16	W^M BRUISTER	17
HUMFREY HOLT	18	GEORGE HUBBARD	16
THO: JOYNER	16	EDW: MIDDLETON	15
RIC^R: TREGAGELL	18	FRANCIS RUSSELL	23
JO: LOE	18	JAMES RISING	18
JOSUA WOODCOCK	11	GEO: ABSOLON	16
ROBERT FISHER	10	JO: MOSDELL	24
THO: SHARP	17	W^M STOKER	19
JO: ROWLAND	21	EDWARD MORRIS	18
W^N WHEELER	22	W^M THOMAS	17
W^M PENNINGTON	18	RIC^R: BUNTING	17
JO: MATHEWS	16	THO: STOKES	30
ROBERT VARDELL	20	W^M ROSDEN	16

* [So in the original. But there are 67 names in the list.]

NATHANIELL WEST	15	EDWARD GRUBTHORN	14
JO: DONN	14	JONAS GOLDENHAM	16
EDWARD EDWYNN	15	JUDITH BAGLEY	58
JO: SELL	15	JOHN GLASSENDEN	14
THO: IRELAND	10	Wᴹ HARDING	30
EDWARD DAVIES	17	uxor SARA HARDING	30
EDWARD SIMPSON	13	HENRY ROSSE	31
EDWARD ALDIN*	17	TYMOTHIE PYNDER	26
THO: ATKINS	16	MARGARET PYNDER	41
THO: RILEY	16	JANE DART	17
Wᴹ BARNES	15	Minister GEO: TURK	40
JO: DAY	16	EZIA VYNCENT	30
Wᴹ BARRITH	16	uxor MARTHEW	30
JO: TUSTIN	16	Minister DANIELL WITE	30
JO: NICKLIN	17	SAMPSON LORT	30
JO: HARKWOOD	20	JO: MILLER	47
HUMFREY KEMP	16	JOHN JOHNSON	23
DAVID THOMAS	26	RICHARD JENNING'S	35
WILLM ALBURIE	15	uxor SARA JENNING'S	18
ARTHUR THORNE	33	RICHARD PALMER	30
Wᴹ CHEESEMAN	20	uxor ELLIS PALMER	21
JOHN MITCHELL	20	THO: GRIFFIN	32
JOHN CASSON	18	ANN GRIFFIN	35
ALEXANDER BRABANT	30	ROBERT RIDLEY	23
HENRY FULCOCK	15	ELIZABETH RIDLEY	30
JO: MANSFIELD	19	EDWARD CHAPLIN	20
WILLM EAST	15	Wᴹ CASSE	19
RICHARD HALDIN	14	PETERNELL NOWELL	46
GEO: PALMER	27	CHRISTIAN WELLMAN	43
Wᴹ SIMPSON	17	ELIZ: ALDWORTH	15
EDWARD SIMPSON	13		
			—
			95

* [Originally written ALLIN, afterwards altered to ALDIN.]

2° *die Octobris* 1635

BOARD the *John* of London JAMES WAYMOTH M^r bound to
St Christophers

JOHN BATCHELLER	26	THO: WALKER	19
SAṁVEL PARKER	19	JO: MULLENEUX	24
THO: JAMES	25	OSWELL METCALF	22
CHRI: THOMSON	21	EDWARD COOKE	22
ALEXANDER FLEETWOOD	19	JO: SHERLOCK	20
WALTER LEE	21	THO: FROST	28
EDWARD DODSON	21	LEWES EVANS	25
GILBERT CLARK	19	JO THOMSON	19
GEO: HEELIS	19	RICHARD TOWNSEND	19
RICHARD ELMES	21		—
RICHARD SMITH	22	MARY GOODWINN	18
WIḦM RICHARDSON	24	JANE GOODWYNN	20
EDWARD MEKINS	18	MARTHA LILLIOT	20
JO: CLYMER	30	ELIZABETH MURRIN	21
RICHARD EVANS	21	JOAN HILL	21
HENRIE FEELD	25	ELIZABETH FREEMAN	18
HENRIE RADFORD	20		—
JO: HENMAN	19		33

13° *die octobris* 1635

BOARD the *Amitie* GEORGE DOWNES M^r bound to St Christo-
ph^{rs}

ISACK DRAKE	25	EDWARD FARR	28
RICHARD IVESON	24	W^M BURROWE	19
ROBERT BARNE	33	THO: BREWYNN	24
THO: HERNDEN	23	MARMADUKE BORNE	21

Wiꟼm Creswell 22	Jo: Goddin 20
Henrie Hodgskynns 19	Richard Larkynn 32
Robert Payne 21	Richard Boeman 23
George Hatrell 32	Tho: Molton 20
Jo: Hippsley 19	David Owen 26
Wiꟼm Stanley 22	Henrie Rowles 22
John Snape 22	Nicᵒ: Alford 28
Isack Buck............... 33	Samvell Sakell 23
Walter Ellitt 20	Robert Jones 30
Aymies Halfyard 19	Jo: Browne............... 33
Oliver Johnes 25	Peter Salmon 20
John Smith 23	Jo: Saunderson 23
Hamblet Sankey.......... 22	Robert Rolfe 23
Edward Porter 21	John Jack 27
Tho: Galley 20	Tho: Yott 24
Tho: Pitt's 24	John Teirrer 24
Jo: Thomson 25	John Farmer............. 24
Richard Webster 24	Wᴹ Daughton 20
Lewes Jones 20	Ricᴿ: Skynner 20
John Coombes 26	Wᴹ Egerton 20
George Coop [Cooper] 20	James Makynn 20
Mathew Preston.......... 22	Wᴹ Harris............... 20
John Pynkston........... 27	Bastian Petite.......... 23
Wᴹ Geies................. 18	John Warren 20
Wiꟼm Vbank 20	Ricᴿ: Phinnei............ 30
Charles Parker 18	James Brigg's............ 25
James Leachman 22	John Musick 19
Wᴹ Cartwrite 18	Jo: Griddick 16
Richard West-Garrett .. 20	Wᴹ Davies 40
Wᴹ Harris............... 16	Robᵀ Heath 30
Jer: Nicholls 16	Tho: Baggelay 24
Tho: Rodes 20	William Yateman 25
Jo: Boughei 21	Richard Grind........... 11
Edward Grindall 21	Wᴹ Galler................ 20
Jo: Vaughan 23	Robert Downe 35

JOHN HYE	36	MARY WYND	18
EDWARD WEBB	17	MARGARET COLES	21
JAMES JOHNSON	28	MARIE MERRITON	21
JOHN AVERY	22	KAT: BREWETT	16
DANIELL CANNELLY	20	ELLIN CHAUNCE [*or* CHANNCE]	21
RICE POKE	30	ANN PALMER	29
ROGER JAMES	29	ALICE BARKER	30
JAMES CURTIS	18	PATIENT WHITE	44
CLEMENT HAMES	22	ISACK }	
JOHN FYNN	22	JACOB... } Twynns	2
WIĦM GOFF	30	JUDITH LLOYD	18
ANDREW WHITE	11	MARIE MAXWELL	21
JOHN BILLINGHURST	24		
MORRICE DAVIE	24		105
W^M RULE	20		

24° *Octobris* 1635

ABOARD the *Constance*, CLEMENT CAMPION M^r bound to Virginia.

	yeres		yeres
JOHN WADE	21	GEO: ATKINSON	16
GARRET NICHOLSON	23	ROBT SEXSTON	24
JOHN BURROWES	18	THO: PURSELL	26
W^M BETT	21	DAVIE LUPTON	23
THOMAS SIMPSON	24	HENRIE MORE	20
THO: PATRICK	22	MICHELL SUCKLIFF	18
JOHN TILL	20	GEORGE ATTERBORN	20
JOSEPH PRICHARD	17	RIC^R: STEERE	24
W^M BENNERMAN	18	THO: LEER	18
RIC^R: TAYLER	18	W^M PRICHARD	34
JOHN GRIFFIN	26	JAMES COTES	22
SAM̃VEL JACKSON	21	JAMES REVELL	20

	yeres		
Wᴹ Androwes	20	Jo: Palmer	12
Symon Garr	14	Griffin Maymor	21
Wᴹ Hunt	21	Francis Marsden	19
Tho: Jackson	23	Steephen Pack	22
Miles Coke	23	Geo: Davie	22
Chri: Chambers	24	Henrie Johnson	27
Davie Williams	24	Jo: Ashcrofte	33
Nicᵒ: Huggins	24	Mathew Gowgh*	28
Jo: Davies	20	Tho: Digglin	22
Wiłłm Jones	25	Robert Baskervile	22
Henrie Richardson	21	Nathaniell Young	20
Roger Williams	19	Tho: Hodson	20
Jo: Wythins	24	Sampson Alkynn	24
Tho: Jay	25	Jo: Coke	24
Elizabeth Brewer	17	John de Cane	20
Isack Bever	24	Jo: Elliott	36
Alice Brass	15	Wᴹ Gillam	27
Tho: More	26	Tho: Smith	24
Wᴹ King	21	Antᵒ Miles	11
Jo: Mitchell	22	Chri: Boyce	38
Tho: Hall	21	Tho: Saddock	17
Robert Ellis	22	Mary Parker	15
James Haies	28	Wᴹ Hulett	19
John Hancock	17	Walter Jenkyns	30
Ricᴿ: Gray	21	Edmond Porter	35
Wᴹ Tyse	20	Edward Herrott	35
Tho: Wathin	35	Hugh Douglas	22
Charles Hughes	50	Walter Colly	19
James Symonds	20	Joan Carraway	22
Jo: Clark	38	Tho: Hart	18
Geo: Dyos	38		—
			85

* [There is a *flourish* at the end of this name in the original ; I do not think it is intended for a final *e*.]

18

BOARD the *Abraham* of London JOHN BARKER M^r bound to
Virginea.

TOBIE SYLBIE	20	HENRY DOBELL	20
ROBERT HARRISON	32	GEORGE BREWETT	18
WiĦM LAWRENCE	22	FRANCIS STANLEY	23
JOHN JOHNSON	35	WiĦM FREEMAN	46
W^M FISHER	25	EDWARD GRIFFITH	33
STEEVEN TAYLER	17	WiĦM MANTON	30
THO: PENFORD	30	OWEN WILLIAMS	40
W^M SMITH	25	THO: FLOWER	32
THO: ARCHDIN	18	JO: BULLAR	32
RIC^R: MORRICE	17	JO: CLANTON	26
WALTER PIGGOTT	19	ALEXANDER SYMES	19
RICHARD WATKYNS	20	ANT^{O.} PARKHURST	42
JO: BRAUNCH	13	JO: HILL	36
JO: CLARK	20	ALEXANDER GREGORIE	24
GABRIELL THOMAS	30	MARTIN WESTERLINK	20
DAVIE JONES	21	PATRICK WOOD	24
ALEXANDER MADDOX	22	THO: KEDBY	25
FRANCIS TIPPSLEY	17	ROGER GREENE	24
EMANUELL DAVIES	19	WiĦM DOWNES	24
W^M WILLIAMS	25	JO: BURNETT	24
ROGER MATHEWS	28	THO: ALLIN	31
JO: MASTERS	23	SIMON FARRELL	19
WILLM MATHEWS	18	THO: CLEMENT'S	30
JO: BRITTEN	18	W^M HUNT	20
GEORGE PRESTON	20	KATHERIN ALDWELL	33
ROBERT TOULBAN	23		
			51

20 *Novembris* 1635

THEIS vnder-written names are to be transported to the Barbadoes imbarqued in the *Expedition* PETER BLACKLER Mr. The Men have taken the oaths of Allegeance ℘ Supremacie : And have been examined by the Minister of the Towne of Gravesend touching their Conformitie to the ord^{rs} ℘ discipline of the Church of England die et A^o prd

	yeres		yeres
Minister NICHOLAS BLOXĀ [BLOXAM] aℓs INGLES	31	BRIAN ASTON	21
ABRAM HOLLAND	19	NICHOLAS COLLON	19
THOMAS HUDSON	16	HENRIE FIELD	24
BLACKWELL LAWRENCE	16	RICHARD SMITH	20
LEONARD BRIGGINS	17	JOHN KNOWLES	27
THOMAS CLARK	27	JOHN DICKENSON	24
MORGAN JENKINS	32	JOHN MANN	21
RIC^R: PRATT	18	THO: PEACOCK	17
THO: FREEMAN	19	EDWARD STEEVENS	53
WIℓℓM GREEFESON	26	THOMAS WEEKES	23
RICHARD WARTUMBEE	21	HUGH CHESWOOD	21
HENRY BRYAN	21	JO: COERT	21
HUGH DAWSON	18	JOHN PIKE	30
MATHEW BEADS	19	GEORGE BLACKLOCK	32
CHARLES LAMBERT	23	JOHN COLEMAN	40
JO: LAKE	18	W^x WATTS	28
JO: SMITH	18	JOHN BONNER	18
ANTHONY HUTCHINS	32	WIℓℓM SINGNELL	18
WIℓℓM GIBSON	19	THO: HOBIN	20
JO: WILLIAMS	17	FRANCIS BARNIT	23
WILLIAM STEWARD	21	WIℓℓM BUCKLEY	26
JOHN PIERCE	18	JOHN CLARK	16
HUGH EVANS	18	PHILLIPP MORLIN	21
		HENRY RAWLINS	25

Jo: Rudge	42	Wiłłm Warr	19
Edward Evans	22	Mathew Wilkinson	18
John Hownsefield	20	Mathew Gibbons	20
Tho: Davie	20	W^M Awdley	19
Henry Gowde	19	James Kingston	22
W^M Mellison	25	Ric^R: Smart	20
John York	26	W^M Walters	26
W^M Carpenter	19	Tho: Davies	23
John Wynter	23	Nathaniell Nordin	46
Jo: Waller	17	W^M Pitt	25
John Sumes	20	Jo: Chater	17
John Heron	20	Jo: Chapman	24
Wiłłm Tayler	26	Geo: Sterry	24
John Parlin	21	Abram Cheynei	22
W^M Jackson	33	Jo: Sturton	18
John Medgley	21	Jo: Edens	19
W^M Wrench	21	Lawrence Brock	18
Robert Hurt	19	Ric^R: Best	18
James Farebank	26	Robert Hobbs	26
Henrie Berrisford	32	Peter Jones	30
James Nettleton	22	W^M Topleife	18
Thomas Armetage	24	Jo: Robinson	19
Francis Mann	19	Morrice Jones	21
John Felkynn	20	Henry Stint	18
John Jones	20	Josias Weston	25
Richard Lightbound	22	Francis Birkenhedd	24
Christopher Hartlie	19	Edward Jones	29
Tho: Wood	23	Ellis Williams	18
Henrie Godfrie	36	W^M Tayler	40
Tho: Palmer	19	Tho: Burnham	18
Jo: Humfrey	20	Joseph Boyce	24
John Smith	22	Jo: Rainsecrofte	23
Ambrose Greene	23	Henrie Bostock	19
Jo: Hilliard	18	Jefferie Ship	24
Jo: Browne	26	W^M Brooke	26

LAUNCELOTT LACON	32	MARY LUPTON	30
Wᴹ PLOMER	23	RICᴿ: HORNE	22
Wᴹ SHEICROFTE*	17	JOHN NEWTON	29
Wᴹ COKE	18	THOMAS COWDELL	17
JO: JENNING'S	18	RICHARD GIBSON	25
THO: OSSEBROOKE	27	NICHOLAS NEVELL	19
JO: DAVENPORT	30	GEORGE TAYLER	20
GEO: BURTON	23	Wᴹ GOAD	21
Wᴹ MORGAN	20	Wᴹ MARRITT	26
DAVIE THOMAS	20	ROGER ERITAGE	22
RICᴿ: HANNIS	21	DAVIE DODDERIDGE	20
PETER CRONINGBURK	20	GEORGE FULLWOOD	19
JO: HALL	29	RICᴿ: HAMIS	21
JO: COMPTON	26	RALPH WEBSTER	20
CLEMENT BACKFORD	30	THO: ROBINSON	15
ROBERT BROWNE	18	JOSEPH THOMLINSON	26
JOHN KEY	32	BALTAZAR DEDERIX	26
HOWELL PRYCE	25	JAMES SMITH	24
EDWARD ASTON	32	NICᵒ: FLATTER	27
ROBᵀ EDWARDS	38	NICᵒ: WHITHEDD	24
RICHARD ASH	24	Wᴹ HINKYNN	26
JOHN MEDLEY	26	THOMAS GILBERT	26
THOMAS KING	24	RICHARD SEABRIGHT	21
RICHARD SNOWE	28	ROBERT GREENEWOOD	18
ROBERT FILBORNE	18	ANTHONY ASHMORE	33
PIERCE MORGAN	23	LAUNCELOTT BROMLEY	44
JO: WILLIAMS	17	PETER SPENCER	15
NICᵒ: BROGAN	28	THOMAS PHIPPS	15
ANTᵒ: SMITH	18	DAVIE THOMAS	20
JOHN SPENCELEY	24	Wɪꜰꜰᴹ GREENE	23
MATHEW SHORE	46	JO: WATTS	20
THOMAS SPARLIN†	19	Wᴹ LOCK	21
DOROTHY SYMONDS	40	GEORGE LEAS	20

* [Or SHERCROFTE. The fourth letter is not clear.]

† [The first two letters are capitals in the original; possibly the name is intended for S[T] PARLIN.]

John Spencer	19	John Chesting	21
Henry Antony	19	Roger Sanford	35
James Fassitt	34	Wiłłm Cornwell	20
Henry Ellotts	23	Wm Gosselin	21
Henrie Çoke	28	Jo: Coop [Cooper]	21
Richard Benes	25	Wm Price	22
Wm Cosson	20	Sam: Skynner	22
Wm Thomson	20	Robt Dunstarr	34
Thomas Vsherwood	28	Richard Buck	24
Wm Haning	30	Nic^o: Lynton	22
John Goad	22		
Richard Moncaster	32		205

19 *Dec:* 1635

HEIS vnder-written names are to be transported to the Barbadoes imbarqued in the *Falcon* Tho: Irish M^r the Men have been examined by the Minister of the Towne of Gravesend touching their conformitie to the Church Discipline of England : And also have taken the oaths of Alleg. ¿ Suprem. Die et A^o prd̃

	yeres		yeres
Arnold Ownstedd	30	Jo: Barnet	20
Tho: Skyddell	28	James Spencer	25
Ant^o Cadwold	23	Jo Chubnell	21
Phillipp Miller	21	Wm Gunter	22
Maximillian Prichard	20	Jo: Thurrogood	20
Tho: Tiffin	28	Tho: Greene	16
Jo: Butler	21	Richard Richardson	36
Phines Trusedell	18	Rabecca Burgis	17
Bryan Cowly	30	Richard Panke	19
Jo: Mason	19	Leonard Robinson	20
Robert Harris	42	Francis Buck	20
Abram Shawe	20	John Hogg	21
Geo: Sabyn	21	Robert Symper	20
Wm Cartwrite	23	Tho: Page	20
Nathan: Murfitt	23	Dennis Brittin [*or* Brittøn]	20

Jo: Rogers	18	Jo: Scott	42
James Wolton	22	Tho: Evans	23
Jo: Burkitt	21	Wᵐ Phillips	28
Tho: Harrwell	29	James Cotesworth	21
Gregorie Booth	18	Ellinn Robb	27
Edward Howe	19	*filia* Elizabeth Robb	7
Robᵀ Clark	18	Tho: Clark	27
Francis Martin	18		—
Tho: Webb	22		46

25 *Decembris* 1635

THEIS vnder-written names passed in a Catch to the Downes : and were put aboard the aforesaid Shipp.

Wᵐ Rofe	20	Jane Hickles	25
Jo: Lawnder	16	Henry Van Luccom	24
Wᵐ Atwell	21	Jo: King	30
Hugh Perry	27	Wᵐ Flatter	18
Jo: Stotter	26	Jo: Weston	27
Ricᴿ: Hughes	28	Tho: Clark	28
Tho: Davies	17	Wᵐ Conisby	31
Henry Benson	19	Robert Tissall	30
Jo: Welsh	35	Tho: Vnyon [*i.e.* Unyon]	19
Henry Southward	20	Tristram Ford	21
Ricᴿ: Newbolt	28	Elias Carpenter	20
Lawrence Keysie	28	Richard Hames	18
James Robinson	15	Thomas Streter	21
Antᵒ Pope	28	James Lee	28
Jo: Lee	30		—
Griffinn Evans	40		32
James Terrill	20		—
Elizabeth Cossen	25	In all ..	78

21° *July*

JANE GIBBS of age. 25 yeeres resident in Virginea to passe to
Flushing about certen her affares.

---

29 *Augusti* 1635

WILLIAM NORTON xxv yeres old is to transport himself to
New-England ℓ to imbarque himself in the *Hopewell* p Cert:
from the Minister of his conformitie to the Church discipline of England:
he hath taken the oaths of Allegeance ℓ Suprem. die et A° prd

---

iiij^{th} Sep^{tr} 1635

ROBERT EDWARD'S. 27 yers who is to passe to Virginia hath
taken the oathe of Allegance

ROBERT EDWARDS:

---

v^{to} die Septembris

THOMAS TURNER of age xlij yeres to passe to New England
imbarqued in the *Hopewell* hath brought Certificate of his Conformitie, ℓ tooke the oaths of Allegeance ℓ Supremacie.

THOMAS TURNER

---

viij° die Sept.

A Turner ROBERT PENNAIRD of age 21 yeres ℓ THO: PEN-
NAIRD x yeres old are to [be] imbarqued in* Mr BABB bound to
New-England have brought Certificate from Doctor DENISON of his
conformitie. he hath taken the oaths of Alleg ℓ Suprem̄

---

* [So in the original ; name of ship omitted.]

HESE men Whose names are heere vnder written belonginge **vnto** the *Friendshipe* of London, nowe ridinge att An Ankere in the reuer of Themes bound for Vergenia: March 1636

LEONARD BETTS Master

JOHN GOODWENE Masters Mat

JOHN CHAMBERS yᵉ other Mate

SAMVELL LAWSONE gunner

DAUEY SLAWCOME Carpenter

JOHN YONGES botsman

RICHARD DAUES Cooper

LARENCE WILLKISSON q': Master

JOHN HUCHENS Carpenters Mate

JOHN LEE

WILLIAM BLORKE

JOHN POLLEN

RICHARD BONNER

THOMAS REEUES

NICHOLAS PORTE

RICHARD FRYE

BENIAMONE WILLKISSON

JOHN BLAKE

THOMAS GRIBELL Cooke

HENERY JOYCE

and A boye

A Booke of Entrie for Passengers by yᵉ Comission, ℯ Souldiers according to the Statute passing beyond the seas begun at Christmas 1631, and ending at Christmas 1632*

---

* [This is the title on the cover of the original. It really refers only to the book from which the matter in the next two pages has been extracted; but for convenience the lists, pp. 151—154, have been arranged under it. The "souldiers" were not for America, and their names are therefore not reprinted.]

A Booke of Entrie for Passengers, &c.

vij° Marcij 1631

THE names of such Men as are to be tr be [*sic*] transported New-England to be resident there vppon a plantacōn ha tendred ℔ taken the oath of allegeance according to the Statute

vizt:

THOMAS THOMAS	JOHN LEVINS
THOMAS WOODFORD.	THOMAS OLLIVER.
JOHN SMALLIE.	JOHN OLLIVER.
JOHN WHETSTON.	THOMAS HAEWARD
W^M HILL.	EDMOND WYNSLOE
WIℍM PERKINS	JOHN HART
WALTER HARRIS	WIℍM NORTON.
JOSEPH MANNERING	ROBERT GAMLIN

xij° Aprilis 1632

THE names of such Men women and children wch are to passe to New-England to be resident there vppon a Plantacōn have tendred ℓ taken the oath of allegeance according to ye Statute.

JOHN BARCROFTE.

JANE BARCROFTE.

HUGH MOIER.

HENRIE SHERBORN

JOHN GREENE

PERSEVERANCE GREENE.

JOHN GREENE.

JACOB GREENE.

ABIGALL GREENE.

SARA. JOHNES madserv^t.

JOSEPH GREENE.

xxij Junij 1632

THE names of such Men transported to New-England to the Plantacōn there p Cert: from Capten MASON have tendred and taken the oath of allegeance according to the Statute

WILLIAM WADSWORTH

JOHN TALLCOTT

JOSEPH ROBERT'S.

JOHN COXSALL

JOHN WATSON.

ROBERT SHELLEY.

WIłłM HEATH.

RICHARD ALLIS

THOMAS VSFITT

ISACK MURRILL.

JOHN WITCHFIELD

JONATHAN WADE

ROBERT BARTLETT

JO: BROWNE.

JOHN CHURCHMAN.

TOBIE WILLET

WILLIAM CURTIS

NIC°: CLARK.

DANIELL BREWER

JO: BENIAMIN.

RICHARD BENIAMIN.

WILLIAM JAMES.

THOMAS CARRINGTON.

WILLIAM GOODWYNN.

JOHN WHITE.

JAMES OLMSTEDD.

WILLIAM LEWES

ZETH GRAUNT

NATHANIELL RICHARD'S.

EDWARD ELLMER.

EDWARD HOLMAR.

JO: TOTMAN.

CHARLES GLOWER.

HE Names of those psons that went from Dartmouth to the Barbadoes beinge sworne before me ALLEXANDER STAPLEHILL
Maio^r of Dartmouth the 15th day of Aprill Año Dñi 1634

Impris DANIELL POWELL of Curmer.

LIST of the names and surnames of those psons wch are bound for
St Christoph^{rs} ℓ haue taken the oath of Allegeance before M^r
WILLIAM GOURNEY Maio^r: of Dartmouth they beinge brought befor me
the Twentyeth day of February in ye Yeare of o^r lord god 1634

Inprimis WILLIAM HAUKINS of Exōn A Glover Aged 25 years or there
  abouts
JAMES COURTNEY of Exōn A Blacksmith Aged 23 Years or there-
  abouts
RICHARD SKOSE of Newton Abbot A Seafaringe man 37 Years or
  thereabouts
FRANCIS BOYCE of London a Button hole maker aged 25 Yeares or
  thereabouts
WILLIAM CARKILLE of Plimouth A Saylemaker aged 21 Years or
  thereabouts
WILLIAM GURGE of Exōn a Shoemaker aged 20 Yeares or thereabouts
ALCE WHITMORE of Huniton in Devon Spinster Aged 25 Years or
  thereabouts
PHILIPP* STEPHENS of Ashberton in Devon Spinster Aged 28 Yeares or
  therabouts
SARA COOSE of Exon Spinster aged 18 Years or therabouts
JUDETH STEVENS of Exon Spinter [Spinster] aged 19 Years or therabouts
MARGARETT HARWOOD of Stoke-gabriell in Devon spinster Aged 22
  Years or therabouts
EDWARD MORRIS of Exōn a' Locker aged 21 years or therabouts
THOMAS BRYANT of Bampton in Devonshire a husbandman aged 23
  Years or therabouts

---

* [Probably intended for PHILIPPA.]

WILLYAM MAY of Myniard in Somersett a sea man aged 32 Yeares or therabouts

HUTINNE OWETH of St Steevens in Cornwall a husbandman Aged 24

JOHN WILLS in Barnstable in Devon a Feltmaker Aged 35 Years or thereabouts

SYMON WEEKS of Exōn a Worsted weaver aged 16 years or thereabouts

THOMAS JERMAYNE of Exōn an Ostler aged 30 Years

JOHN FRENCH of Washford in Ireland a seaman 26 years

WILL^M HILL of great Torington in Devonshire a husbandman Aged 28 Years

JOHN HOCKSLEY of Stoke Cannon in Devon a Tayler aged 28 Years

JAMES ROSMAN of London a husbandman aged 21 years.

ELIZABETH REED of Exon a Spinster aged 19 Years or thercabouts

MARY HARTE of Lyme a Spinster aged 18 Years or there abouts

MARY HOPPINE of Exmister a spinster aged 20 Yeares

MARYES HARRIES of Stoke Pommeroy in Devon aged 23 Years or therabouts

ELIZABETH QUICKE of Barnstable in Devon aged 18 Years

ELIZABETH HILL of Brixam in Devon aged 24 Years

JOANE SHORTE of Exon Aged 20 Yeares

JOANE LANERS [*or* LAUERS] of Modbury in Devon aged 19 Years

JANE GOULDINGE of St Thom. the Apostle in Devon aged 16 years or therabouts

JAMES WORTHY

Deputy.

for Mr THOROUGHGOOD

The Name of such as passed out of the Poart of Plimworth
Ano Dnie 1634

Plymouth
Febr: 1633.   PASSENGERS.

IN the *Robert Bonaventure* for St Christophers.

GEORGE FORD of Exon aged 30 yeares.

STEPHEN WHITTINGTON of Lincolne 20 yeares.

JOHN THOMAS of St Tissey 26 yeares.

JOHN LIDDICOTT of St Cullum 22 yeares.

W^M CLARKE of Truro 20 yeares.

THO: FRETHY of Perintho 24 yeares.

MICHAELL BOWDEN of Helston 27 yeares.

JOHN BADLAND of Northill 22 yeares.

RICHARD SLAVELIE of Stonehowse 40 yeares.

RICHARD COCKE of Wincklye 33 yeares.

HENRY RENSBY [*or* REUSBY] of St Stephens 28 yeares.

ANTHONY WEBB of Lanceston 20 yeares.

GREGORY SAM of Chidleigh 15 yeares.

CHRISTOPHER CARTER of St Gilt 45 yeares.

MARTIN ROOBY of Guindiron 23 yeares.

W$_M$ CURKE of Monteratt 24 yeares.

HENRY THOMAS of Luxulian 15 yeares.

STEPHEN SYMON of Plimpton 18. yeares.

MATHEW ARTHUR of Plimpton 18. yeares.

JANE TREWIN of Plimpton 26 yeares.

W^M JOHNSON of London 32 yeares.

REIGNOLD FROST of Tottnes 15 yeares.

JOHN FARREN of Peter Tany 2 yeares.

W^M WADE of Bodmin 33 yeares.

NICHAS DABBIN of St Stephens 40 yeares.

ANDREW PICKE of Great Dalby 34 yeares.

JOHN PENINGTON of Symon Ward 40 yeares.

THO: POLLARD of Paraneuth 23 yeares.

ELLIN NANCARRO of Penryn 20 yeares.

RAWLEIGH EDYE of Bodmyn 15 ycares.

W^M DUN of Truro. 16 yeares.

ANTH: PEARSE of St Breage 16 yeares.

EDWARD TREMINEERE of Helston 18. yeares.

ROB^T TRENEIGHAN of Helston 34 ycares.

TEGO LEANE [*or* LEAUE] of Corke in Ireland 30 y^{rs}

Rec. for these ——

All husbandmen bound to serve there some 3 and some 4 ycares.

1633. 1° m'cij [*March*].

N the *Margarett* for St Christophers.

THOMAS ROSETER of Washford 20 yeares.

THO: MARTIN of Cardinham 24 yeares.

JOHN DUSTON of St Cullom 26 yeares.

RICHARD WILLIAMS of St Cullom 30 yeares.

JOHN NEWDON of St Tue 28. yeares.

JOHN HEWBRAYNE of Josias Newton 20 y^{rs}

ANTH: BURROWES of Jacobstow 20 yeares.

ROBERT OLIVER of Crediton 20 yeares.

BARTH: CORNEW, of Crediton 18. yeares.

CLEMENT BARRY of Exon 22 yeares.

FRANCIS PEDLER of St Breage 28 yeares.

ROB^T PEDLER of St Breage 22 yeares.

JOHN MERRY of Withiell 28. yeares.

WALTER BURLACY of Luggan 22 yeares.

SAMUELL FORGIUE of Wallen Lizard 26: y^{rs}

RICHARD EDWARD of St Vivian 28. yeares.

RICHARD SYMOND'S of Wantage 28 yeares.

ROB^T PAINE of Marrozion. 29 yeares.

W^M BADCOCKE of St Hillary. 20 yeares.

SIMON MARTIN of St Ives. 18 yeares.

JOHN MARTIN of St Ives. 18. yeares.

GEORGE GRIFFIN of Marozion 18 yeares.

THO: SLEMAN of St Hillary 18 yeares.

JOHN SANDERS of Marozion 18. yeares.

THOMAS BORINTHON of Helston 22 yeares.

W^M WIETT of Marozion. 17 yeares.

NICHAS. WATERMAN or [of] Marozion 15 y^{rs}

SAMUELL PUREFOY of St Ives 13 yeares.

GEORGE MATHEW. of Ludswan 23 y^{rs}

TEAGE WILLIAMS Irishman 18. yeares

	li	s	d
recd. for them ——	0.	15	0

All husbandmen for the most pt as the former.

JOSEPH BOOLE

is Debutie ther

[ENTRIES RELATING TO AMERICA, &c.,

TAKEN FROM THE

INDEXES TO THE PATENT ROLLS,

COMMENCING 4 JAMES I. (1606),

AND ENDING 14 WILLIAM III. (1702).]

[The following entries, (pp. 155—168*), relating to Proclamations, Commissions, and Grants of Offices, Land, &c., in different parts of America and elsewhere, are taken from the Indexes to the Patent Rolls in the Public Record Office, commencing in 1606 (4 James I.), and ending in 1702 (14 William III.). There are several entries of the appointment of Commissioners to administer oaths to persons desirous of passing beyond the seas, (officers being stationed for this purpose at the ports of London, Harwich, Weymouth, Kingston-upon-Hull, the Cinque Ports, &c.) ; and the student will find among them valuable hints upon which to base more detailed researches. These entries must embody very many memoranda throwing light upon questions of settlement in America. We may add, that licenses were necessary, on leaving England, not only for civilians, but also for soldiers, whether under command, or going singly to join their regiments. Reference to *Roll* and *Part* is given at the end of each paragraph.]

[ENTRIES RELATING TO AMERICA, &c.]

OMMISSION granted to Sir HENRY BILLINGSLEY and Sir WILLIAM ROMNEY, Knights, and others, to minister an oath to all women and persons under the age of One-and-twenty years, that shall desire to go over the seas, at our port of London, &c. (Pat. 4 Jac. I. part 12.)

Commissions granted to the Mayor of Kingston-upon-Hull; the Customer and Comptroller of the Haven of Harwich; the port or haven of Weymouth; to administer an oath to all persons under the age of One-and-twenty who are desirous to pass the Seas from the said ports; also to HENRY, EARL OF NORTHAMPTON, to appoint Deputies to administer an oath to all persons of convenient age who pass the seas at the Cinque Ports. (4 Jac. I. p. 12.)

Proclamation licensing all manner of persons under the age of One-and-twenty years upon due examination of them to pass beyond the Seas. (Pat. 4 Jac. I. p. 12.)

10 April. Grant to Sir THOMAS GATES, Sir GEORGE SOMERS, Knts. and others, special license to make habitation and plantation, and to deduce a Colony of people into that part of America called Virginia. (Pat. 4 Jac. I. p. 19.)

Commission granted to THOMAS, LORD ELLESMERE, Lord Chancellor of England, to award Commissions to divers men for examination of all such persons as go out of the kingdom at any of the Ports of London, Harwich, Weymouth, and Kingston-upon-Hull. (Pat. 4 Jac. I. p. 24.)

20 July. Grant to THOMAS, LORD ELLESMERE, Lord Chancellor of England, of a special Warrant for licensing such as go beyond the Seas. (5 Jac. I. p. 22.)

29 July. Grant to HENRY, EARL OF NORTHAMPTON, of a special license to appoint deputies for ministering the oath of Allegiance to such as pass beyond the Seas. (5 Jac. I. p. 22.)

21 May. Grant to HENRY, EARL OF NORTHAMPTON, Commission special, by his Deputies, to examine all such as shall pass from the Cinque Ports beyond the Seas, &c. (6 Jac. I. p. 20.) Another of the 10th Oct. (same year), p. 30.

7 October. Grant to THOMAS, LORD ELLESMERE, Commission special, to seal several Commissions directed to several persons for the Port of London, licensing persons going beyond the Seas. (6 Jac. I. p. 30.)

1 May. Grant to Sir THOMAS CROMPTON, Sir THOMAS SMYTH, Knts., and others, Commission special, to minister an oath to all passengers that desire to pass over the Seas at the Port of London, and to examine them. (6 Jac. I. p. 37.)

23 May. Grant to ROBERT, EARL OF SALISBURY, THOMAS, EARL OF SUFFOLK, HENRY, EARL OF SOUTHAMPTON, WILLIAM, EARL OF PEMBROKE, and divers others, to plant and inhabit in Virginia, and to incorporate by the name of Treasurer and Company of Adventurers and Planters of the City of London, for the first Colony in Virginia. (7 Jac. I. p. 8.)

2 May. Grant of Incorporation, by the name of the Treasurer and Company of Adventurers and Planters of the City of London and Bristol, for the Colony and Plantation in Newfoundland. (8 Jac. I. p. 8.)

12 March. Grant to the Treasurer and Company of Adventurers and Planters of the City of London, for the first Colony in Virginia, all the Islands in any part of the Ocean, bordering upon the Coast of the Colony in Virginia, &c., to their heirs and successors ; with full power for keeping a Lottery. (9 Jac. I. p. 14.)

28 August. Grant to ROBERT HARECOURT, Esq., Sir THOMAS CHALLONER, Knt., and JOHN ROVENSON, Esq., and to the heirs of the said ROBERT, all that part of Guiana or continent of America lying between the River of Amazons and the River of Dessequebe, et alia. (11 Jac. I. p. 9.)

9 Aug. Commission to EDWARD LORD ZOUCH, Lord Warden of the Cinque Ports, concerning the examining and licensing of passengers, with Instructions touching the same. (13 Jac. I. p. 16.)

29 June. Incorporation of the Governor and Society of the City of London, for planting of the Summer Islands, &c. (13 Jac. I. p. 19.)

3 November. The King grants, ordains, establishes and confirms that LODOWICK, DUKE OF LENOX, GEORGE, MARQUIS OF BUCKINGHAM, and divers others, be the first modern and present Council established at Plymouth in the county of Devon, for the plant-

ing, ruling and governing of New England in America, and that they shall elect and choose others to the number of forty persons, and no more, to be of that Council, and that they shall be incorporated by the name of the Council established at Plymouth for the governing of New England in America. (18 Jac. I. p. 16.)

24 January. Grant to FRANCIS, LORD VERULAM, Warrant special, to make out divers Commissions to such Justices, Officers and Ministers, and to such ports of this Realm as he shall think convenient, for the taking of an oath of all such as shall pass beyond the Seas. (The form of oath is recited in this patent.) (18 Jac. I. p. 16.)

31 Dec. Grant to Sir GEORGE CALVERT, Knt., of Newfoundland. (20 Jac. I. p. 14.) Similar grant made to the said Sir GEORGE CALVERT, on the 7th April. (21 Jac. I. p. 19).

Proclamation against irregular and disobedient persons and disorderly trading into New England, in America. (20 Jac. I. p. 16.)

Commission directed to the Supervisor General of the Customs in the port of London, to examine such persons as pass beyond the Seas, and to minister unto them an Oath. A similar Warrant granted to JOHN, Bishop of Lincoln. (21 Jac. I. p. 19, *in dorso*.)

Commission directed to Sir WILLIAM JONES, Sir NICHOLAS FORTESCUE, Knts., and others, to view, peruse and consider all Charters, Letters Patent, Proclamations and Commissions concerning the Colonies or Plantations in Virginia. (21 Jac. I. p. 19.)

Commission directed to HENRY, VISCOUNT MANDEVILLE, WILLIAM, LORD PAGET, and divers others, giving them power and authority to take into their considerations the state of the Colony and Plantation in Virginia, and to consider of all matters concerning the people's safety, their strength and government. (22 Jac. I. p. 1.)

20 December. Grant to GEORGE, DUKE OF BUCKINGHAM, Lord Warden of the Cinque Ports, Commission special, for him, or his deputies, to examine upon oath all passengers going beyond the Seas from those Ports, and to grant them licences; with instructions. (22 Jac. I. p. 14.)

26 August. Grant to Sir FRANCIS WYATT, Knt., FRANCIS WEST, Sir GEORGE YARDLEY, Knt., and others, Commission special, for the better government of the people in Virginia. (22 Jac. I. p. 17.)

18 September. Commission, appointing Sir GEORGE YARDLEY, Knt., Governor in Virginia. (22 Jac. I. p. 17.)

9 November. The King constitutes EDWARD DICHFEILD and others to be his officers to search and see that no Tobacco be brought

into this Kingdom from foreign parts, except from Virginia and the Summer Islands. (22 Jac. I. p. 4.)

Proclamation for the settling the Plantation of Virginia. (1 Chas. I. p. 4.)

13 September. Grant to THOMAS WARNER, and others, the Custody of the Islands of St. Christophers, the Barbadoes and "Moncerat" [Mountserrat] in the Continent of America. (1 Chas. I. p. 6.)

19 May. Grant to GEORGE, DUKE OF BUCKINGHAM, WILLIAM, EARL OF PEMBROKE, PHILLIP, EARL OF MONTGOMERY, JAMES, EARL OF CARLISLE, and divers others, that they shall be one body politic and corporate of themselves, by the name of Governor and Company of Noblemen and Gentlemen of England, for the Plantation of Guiana; and that they shall have perpetual succession. (3 Chas. I. p. 5.)

26 March. Grant to JOHN HARVEY, FRANCIS WEST, and divers others, Commission special, to be the present Governor and Council for the Colony and Plantation in Virginia. (3 Chas. I. p. 3.)

4 March. Grant to SAMUEL ALDERSEY, THOMAS ADAMS, and others, all that part of New England, in America, lying and extending between the bounds and limits in an Indenture expressed, with divers liberties, jurisdictions and royalties, to them and their heirs for ever.—(4 Chas. I. p. 11.)

20 September. Grant to GEORGE ARCHBISHOP OF CANTERBURY, and others, Commission special, to reprieve and stay from execution such persons as stand convicted, or hereafter shall be convicted, for small offences, who for strength of body or other ability shall be thought fit to be employed in foreign discoveries, or other services beyond the Seas. (4 Chas. I. p. 23.)

4 Feb. Grant to Sir WILLIAM ALEXANDER, Knt., and others of a Commission special, to make a voyage into the Gulf and River of Canada and the parts adjacent for the sole trade of Beaver Wools, Beaver Skins, Furs, Hides and Skins of Wild Beasts. (4 Chas. I. p. 34.)

25 May. Grant to PATRICK CRAFORD and MATHEW BYRKENHEAD, the office of clerks for the writing and entering of licences and passes granted by any Commissioners to persons going beyond the seas from the ports of Bristol, Beaumaris, Chester and Liverpool. (6 Chas. I. p. 5.)

19 Nov. Commission special directed to all Mayors, Recorders, Customers and other Officers within all port towns, ports and havens to examine and minister an oath to all passengers beyond the seas, except merchants and their factors. (6 Chas. I. p. 6, *in dorso*.)

4 December. Grant to ROBERT, LORD BROOKE, and others, to incorporate by the name of the Governor and Company of Adventurers of the City of Westminster, for the plantation of the Island of Providence, Henrietta, and the adjacent Islands lying upon the Coast of America. (6. Chas. I. p. 1.)

Proclamation forbidding the disorderly trading with the "Salvages" in New England in America, especially the furnishing of the Navies in those and other ports of America, by the English, with weapons and habiliments of war. (6 Chas. I. p. 11.)

19 Nov. Grant to EDWARD THOROWGOOD, the office of Clerk for writing of licences and passes to be granted by Commissioners to any person going out of this Realm, for 21 years. (6 Chas. I. p. 6.)

22 June. Grant to ROBERT, EARL OF WARWICK, and others, Governor and Company of Adventurers of the City of Westminster, for the plantation of the Islands of Providence, Henrietta, and the adjacent Islands, lying upon the coasts of America ; all other Islands not formerly granted unto them, beginning at 6 degrees from the Equinoctial line towards the North, and extending from thence to 24 in Latitude towards the Tropic of Cancer, and between the degrees of 290 and 310 of Longitude, and Meridian distance through all the said Latitude, as the said degrees are in common computation reckoned and accompted in this Kingdom, to their heirs and successors. (7 Chas. I. p. 14.)

27 June. Grant to EDWARD, EARL OF DORSET, HENRY, EARL OF DEN· BIGH, and others, Commission special, to consider how the Virginia Plantation now standeth, and to consider what commodity may be raised in those parts. (7 Chas. I. p. 20.)

11 May. Grant to SIR WILLIAM ALEXANDER, and others, to collect Beaver Skins, &c., similar to the Grant made 4 Feb., 4 Chas. I. p. 34, (which see). (9 Chas. I. p. 7.)

23 September. Grant to THOMAS YOUNGE, gent., Commission special, to discover, find out, and search what parts are not yet inhabited in Virginia and America, and other parts thereunto adjoining. (9 Chas. I. p. 1.)

3 April. Grant to ROBERT, EARL OF WARWICK, HENRY, EARL OF HOLLAND, WILLIAM, LORD SAY AND SELE, ROBERT, LORD BROOKE, and others, Merchants Adventurers of the City of London, trading into the parts of America. (11 Chas. I. p. 8.)

Commission Special, directed to the Recorder of the City of London, SIR PAUL PYNDER, Knt., and others, for the taking of oaths of such persons as shall desire to go beyond the seas, and for the doing of many other things, such as in discretion shall seem meet to them. (11 Chas. I. p. 9.)

2 April.   Grant to Sir JOHN HARVYE, Knt., Commission special, to be
the present Governor of the Colony and Plantation in Virginia,
with several powers and authorities therein mentioned.   (12
Chas. I. p. 21, *in dorso.*)

10 April.   Grant to WILLIAM, ARCHBP. OF CANTERBURY, THOMAS,
LORD COVENTRY, Keeper of the Great Seal, and others, Commission special, for the government of all persons within the
Colonies and Plantations beyond the seas, according to the
Laws and Constitutions there; and to constitute Courts as
well Ecclesiastical as Civil for the determining of Causes there.
(12 Chas. I. p. 21, *in dorso.*)

10 May.   Grant to THOMAS MAHEWE, the office of clerk of the passes
and licences in the Outports, and the writing and registering of
the same, and of the names of all those that shall go out of this
Kingdom beyond the Seas, for 21 years in reversion.   (12
Chas. I. p. 14.)

13 November.   Grant to JAMES, MARQUIS OF HAMILTON, HENRY,
EARL OF HOLLAND, and others, all that whole Continent,
Island or Region commonly called Newfoundland, bordering
upon the Continent of America, to them and their heirs.   (13
Chas. I. p. 32.)

Proclamation against the disorderly transporting his Majesty's subjects
to the plantations within the parts of America.   (13 Chas. I.
p. 15.)

11 January.   Grant to Sir FRANCIS WYATT, Knt., Commission special,
to be Governor of the Colony and plantation in Virginia during
pleasure.   (14 Chas. I. p. 29.)

29 March.   Grant to RICHARD MORISON, Esq., the office of Captain or
Keeper of the Castle of "Poynte Comfort," within the Lordship of Virginia, during pleasure, in reversion.   (14 Chas. I.
p. 38.)

Proclamation to restrain the transporting of passengers and provisions
to New England without licence.   (14 Chas. I. p. 6, *in dorso.*)

16 December.   Grant to HENRY ASHTON, Esq., PETER HAY, Esq., and
others, Commission special, to declare in his Majesty's name, in
all public assemblies and places of the Islands and province
of Barbadoes, against HENRY HAWLEY, to be Governor or
Lieutenant General of the said Island; and to charge and
require him and his Deputy or Agents, under his and their
Allegiance, forthwith to yield up the said office and place of
government, and all the incidents thereunto, unto HENRY
HUNCKES, or to such person or persons as the EARL OF CAR-
LISLE shall appoint.   (15 Chas. I. p. 23, *in dorso.*)

3 April. Grant to Sir FERDINAND GORGES, Knt., all that part, purpart and portion of the main land or country, now commonly called or known by the name of New England in America, to him and to his heirs. (15 Chas. I. p. 25.)

6 August. ROGER WINGATE, Esq., appointed King's Treasurer within the Lordship of Virginia for life. (15 Chas. I. p. 23.)

Commission to JAMES, DUKE OF LENNOX, and others, for the tendering of an Oath to all persons that go beyond the seas, except women, and children, and sailors. (16 Chas. I. p. 13.)

9 August. Grant to Sir WILLIAM BERKELEY, Knt., and divers others, Commission special, to be the present Council of and for the colony and plantation in Virginia, and to perform and execute the places, powers, and authorities incident to a Governor there. (17 Chas. I. p. 6.)

31 July. Grant to Sir WILLIAM BERKELEY, Knt., and others, Commission special, to be present Governor and Council of and for the colony and plantation in Virginia, and for the managing of affairs there, during pleasure. (12 Chas. II. p. 26, *in dorso.*)

22 December. Grant to all Mayors, Recorders, Customers, Comptrollers, Surveyors, and Searchers in all ports of England and Wales, a special Commission to minister an Oath to all and every person or persons that shall be licensed to go beyond the seas. (12 Chas. II. p. 31, *in dorso.*)

2 August. FRANCIS CRADDOCK, Esq., appointed Provost Marshal General of the Barbadoes for life. (12 Chas. II. p. 32.)

17 August. JOHN DAWES appointed Secretary of the Islands of Barbadoes, and to the Governor and Council there: also clerk of the several Courts there, during life. (12 Chas. II. p. 23.)

8 January. THOMAS LINCH appointed Provost Marshal of Jamaica for life. (12 Chas. II. p. 30.)

22 September. Grant to THOMAS MAYHEW, Esq., of the office of clerk and clerkship of all Licences or passes in the Outports made, and to be made, to any person or persons, to go unto any foreign parts or places beyond the sea ; and also the office of Register [Registrar] of the names of all the said persons for the term of 21 years in reversion. (12 Chas. II. p. 24.)

26 January. Confirmation of several Laws, concerning the people in Newfoundland, and upon the sea adjoining, and the bays, creeks and fresh rivers there. (12 Chas. II. p. 17.)

10 January. RICHARD POVEY appointed Secretary of and for Jamaica for life. (12 Chas. II. p. 30.)

12 September.   Major JAMES RUSSELL appointed Governor of Nevis, during pleasure. (12 Chas. II. p. 35.)

21 November.   Grant to FRANCIS, LORD WILLOUGHBY, all and singular prize ships, vessels, ordnance, furniture, ammunition, tackle and apparel, goods, chattels, merchandize, and lading whatsoever in the late Wars between this nation and the Dutch taken and seized at sea, in harbour, and at land, in or near the Islands of Barbadoes, St. Christophers, and other Islands in the parts of America, not sold or disposed of, accompted for, and discharged by sufficient discharges or acquaintances, or not pardoned, and discharged by his Majesty, or authority of Parliament, without any accompt whatsoever to be rendered or made for the same. (12 Chas. II. p. 27.)

13 March.   ELIE ASHMOLE, Esq., appointed Secretary of Suranam [Surinam] and clerk of the King's Courts there. (13 Chas. II. p. 44.)

27 Sept.   THOMAS BREEDON appointed Governor of Laccady and Nova Scotia, during life. (13 Chas. II. p. 16.)

13 May.   Grant to JOHN, EARL OF BATH, of 200 acres of land in the parish of St. George, Barbadoes, to him and his heirs. (13 Chas. II. p. 40.)

8 February.   Commission appointing EDWARD DOYLEY to be Governor of Jamaica, with instructions. (13 Chas. II. p. 4.)

1 February.   JOHN MANNE, gent., appointed Chief Surveyor of Jamaica during pleasure. (13 Chas. II. p. 8.)

Proclamation for the encouraging of Planters in Jamaica. (13 Chas. II. p. 17, *in derso.*)

2 August.   THOMAS, LORD WINDSOR, appointed Governor of Jamaica. (13 Chas. II. p. 46.)

10 June.   Revocation of Letters Patent appointing THOMAS BREEDON Governor of Laccady and Nova Scotia. (14 Chas. II. p. 6.)

15 March.   Grant to WILLIAM DAVIDSON and others, licence special to dig for all mines of gold and other metals in Jamaica, for two years. (14 Chas. II. p. 11.)

17 Feb.   JAMES, DUKE OF YORK, appointed High Admiral of Dunkirk, New England, Virginia, &c. (14 Chas. II. p. 12.)

23 April.   Grant to the Governor, &c., of the English Colony of Connecticut in New England, of an Incorporation with divers privileges. (14 Chas. II. p. 11.)

7 Feb.   Grant to the Company for propagating of the Gospel in New England, an Incorporation with divers privileges. (14 Chas. II. p. 11.)

17 July.   THOMAS TEMPLE, Esq., appointed Governor of Laccady, and other the territories in America, for life.   (14 Chas. II. p. 5.)

18 November.   Grant to FRANCIS, LORD WILLOUGHBY, all those Islands called the Caribee Islands, containing in them the Islands of St. Christopher's alias St. Aristooall, Granado alias Greinada, St. Vincent, St. Lucy alias St. Lucre, Barbidas alias Barbadoes, Mittalania alias Martenico, Domenico, and others, to hold the same for 7 years.   (14 Chas. II. p. 20.)

24 March.   Grant to GEORGE, DUKE OF ALBEMARLE, ANTHONY, LORD ASHLEY, and others, all that territory or track [tract] of land called Carolina.   (15 Chas. II. p. 2.)

17 July.   Commission to THOMAS TEMPLE, Esq., to be Governor of several places in America.   (15 Chas. II. p. 18.)

Grant to JOHN CLARKE and others, Inhabitants of New England, of divers liberties, &c.   (15 Chas. II. p. 15.)

9 April.   Grant to THOMAS ROSSE and others, the office of Receiver General, of all sums of money due and payable from the several plantations in Africa and America, for life.   (15 Chas. II. p. 11.)

Grant to the Governor and Company of Rhode Island of divers privileges.   (15 Chas. II. p. 15.)

2 June.   Grant to FRANCIS, LORD WILLOUGHBY, and others, of the main tract of land, being part of the continent of Guiana in America, called Surinam.   (15 Chas. II. p. 10.)

13 August.   Grant to JOHN COLLINS, of a moiety of the profits of the Isle of Barbada, alias Barbuda [Barbadoes], reserved to the King for 7 years, and after the expiration of the said 7 years, then grants it to the said JOHN for 31 years.   (16 Chas. II. p. 11.)

26 April.   JAMES DREBBLE appointed Escheator of the Isles of Barbadoes and Caribee, for life.   (16 Chas. II. p. 3.)

12 March.   Grant to JAMES, DUKE OF YORK, and his heirs, all that part of the main land of New England, and several Islands adjacent.   (16 Chas. II. p. 8.)

17 Feb.   Grant to THOMAS ELLIOTT, of certain Copper Mines and other metals in Nova Scotia, for 31 years.   (16 Chas. II. p. 17.)

29 May.   Grant to Sir GEORGE CARTERET, Knt., and JOHN TRETHEWY, one annuity of 500l. per annum, to be paid out of one moiety of the profits arising out of the Caribee Islands, and due or payable to the Crown during the lives of WILLIAM LEY and JAMES CARTERETT.   (17 Chas. II. p. 5.)

3 April.   Declaration that the commodities of Jamaica shall pay no customs for the space of five years.   (17 Chas. II. p. 3.)

20 December.　Grant to Sir JAMES MODYFORD, Knt., licence to distinguish the Island of Providence alias St. Katherine, into counties, towns, manors, lordships and other privileges. (18 Chas. II. p. 4.)

4 February.　WILLIAM WILLOUGHBY, Esq., appointed Captain General of the Caribee Islands for three years. (18 Chas. II. p. 4.)

19 March.　EDWARD SCARBURGH appointed Surveyor General of Virginia during life. (19 Chas. II. p. 8.)

8 May.　Grant to HENRY, EARL OF ST. ALBANS, JOHN, LORD BERKELEY, Sir WILLIAM MORETON, and JOHN TRETHEWEY, all that entire tract, territory, or parcel of land in America, and bounded by and within the head of the rivers Tappahanocke, alias Rappahanocke, and Quiriough or Patawomack rivers, to them and their heirs. (21 Chas. II. p. 4.)

1 November.　Grant to CHRISTOPHER, DUKE OF ALBEMARLE, WILLIAM, EARL OF CRAVEN, JOHN, LORD BERKELEY, ANTHONY, LORD ASHLEY, Sir GEORGE CARTERET, Sir PETER COLLITON, &c., all those Islands called the Bahama Islands or the Islands of Lucayos, lying in the degrees of 22 to 27, and all ports, havens, creeks, &c., to their heirs and assigns. (22 Chas. II. p. 9.)

11 January.　Grant to EDWARD, EARL OF SANDWICH, RICHARD, LORD GORGES, WILLIAM, LORD ALLINGTON, THOMAS GREY, and HENRY BLOUNCKER, Esquires, Sir HUMPHRY WINCH, Sir JOHN FINCH, and EDMOND WALLER, several yearly salaries, viz¹: to the EARL OF SANDWICH, 700*l.* per annum, and to the rest (to each) 500*l.* per annum, they being of the Council for Foreign Plantations. (22 Chas. II. p. 8.)

6 August.　Grant to FRANCIS RAYNES, all the lands and estates of one HENRY EDLYN, lying and being in the Island of Barbados, escheated to the Crown by his being executed for the murder of his wife. (22 Chas. II. p. 1.)

8 July.　EDWYN STEED appointed Provost Marshal General of the Barbadoes, for life. (22 Chas. II. p. 1.)

9 Sept.　Grant to JOHN STRODE to farm the Imposts upon the growth of the Leeward Islands, for 7 years. (22 Chas. II. p. 5.)

23 March.　Sir ERNEST BRYAN, Knt., appointed Escheator in the Barbadoes and the Caribee Islands, for life. (23 Chas. II. p. 3.)

4 April.　Commission for JAMES, DUKE OF YORK, and others, to be of the Council for Foreign Plantations. (23 Chas. II. p. 2.)

7 March.　CHARLES WHEELER appointed Captain General of the Caribee Islands. (23 Chas. II. p. 2.)

19 June. Commission appointing Sir RICHARD TEMPLE, Knt., to be of the Council of Foreign Plantations. (23 Chas. II. p. 2, *in dorso.*) Another Commission (same part) dated 15 Aug.

17 November. ALEXANDER CULPEPER appointed Surveyor in Virginia, during pleasure. (23 Chas. II. p. 8.)

16 September. ROBERT CLOWES appointed Chief Clerk to attend the Supreme Council in the town of St. Iago, in Jamaica, during life. (24 Chas. II. p. 3.)

27 September. Commission granting to ANTHONY, EARL OF SHAFTES-BURY, and others, a standing Council for Trade and Traffic both at home and for the Foreign Plantations. (24 Chas. II. p. 4.)

19 July. Grant to WILLIAM, EARL OF KINNOUL, in consideration of a surrender by him made of his interest in the Caribee Islands, one annuity of 600*l.* per annum for five years, to be paid out of the four and a half per cent. Customs from those Islands, and after the expiration of five years the like annuity of 1000*l.* per annum to be paid for ever. (24 Chas. II. p. 1.)

10 February. . Revocation of the Grant formerly made to Sir CHARLES WHEELER, of the Government of the Leeward Islands. (24 Chas. II. p. 2.)

10 February. WILLIAM STAPLETON appointed Governor of the Leeward Islands during pleasure. (24 Chas. II. p. 2.)

6 July. WILLIAM, LORD WILLOUGHBY, appointed Captain General, and Governor in Chief, of the Barbadoes and Caribee Islands, during pleasure. (24 Chas. II. p. 2.)

13 April. Grant to LEONARD COMPEARE and THOMAS MARTYN, Esq., the office of Receiver of the Duties upon all Wines, Brandies, &c., imported into Jamaica, for life. (26 Chas. II. p. 2.)

29 June. Grant to JAMES, DUKE OF YORK, of several Islands and main land, near New England, particularly bounded, to him and his heirs, &c. (26 Chas. II. p. 5.)

28 March. RICHARD MORLEY, Esq., appointed Secretary of Barbadoes, and Clerk of the Courts there, during life. (26 Chas. II. p. 2.)

8 July. THOMAS, LORD CULPEPER, appointed Lieutenant and Governor General of Virginia, during life. (27 Chas. II. p. 7.)

18 March. Grant to GEORGE GOSSELYNG, of all the lands, tenements, goods, and chattels of his brother JAMES GOSSELYNG, in the Island of Jamaica, forfeited by his being an alien. (27 Chas. II. p. 2.)

27 January. The King declares and confirms several Laws concerning his people in Newfoundland, and upon the sea adjoining, &c. (27 Chas. II. p. 11.)

Proclamation to prohibit commodities into Foreign Plantations, but from England only. (27 Chas. II. p. 10.)

11 March. JOHN RICHARDS appointed Secretary of the Barbadoes, for life. (27 Chas. II. p. 2.)

25 June. ROBERT THORNTON, gent., appointed Provost Marshal of Jamaica, for life. (27 Chas. II. p. 7.)

3 September. HARBOTTLE WINGFIELD, gent., appointed Clerk of the Court of Common Pleas at Port Royal, Jamaica. (27 Chas. II. p. 3.)

27 January. RALPH WYATT appointed Clerk of the Market in Barbadoes, during pleasure. (27 Chas. II. p. 11.)

10 October. Commission granted to Sir WILLIAM BERKELEY, to pardon the Rebels in Virginia upon their submission. (28 Chas. II. p. 1.)

10 October. HERBERT JEFFERY, and others, Commissioners appointed to enquire and report the grievances of the Inhabitants of Virginia. (28 Chas. II. p. 1.)

10 October. Captain ROBERT WALTER, Commissioner, appointed Governor of Virginia, in the absence of HERBERT JEFFERY. (28 Chas. II. p. 1.)

9 October. HERBERT JEFFERY appointed Governor of Virginia in the place of Sir WILLIAM BERKELEY. (28 Chas. II. p. 1.)

11 November. Commission granted for HERBERT JEFFERYES to be Lieutenant Governor of Virginia. (28 Chas. II. p. 3.)

9 March. GARRETT COTTER appointed Secretary and Marshal of the Islands of Nevis, Teago, and Mountserrat, for three lives. (28 Chas. II. p. 5.)

10 October. Grant to the Governor and Council of Virginia; a special pardon for passing Acts of State to the Rebels. (28 Chas. II. p. 1.)

Same date and part, the King confirms and grants to the Inhabitants of Virginia, privileges, &c.

Commission to JOHN WILLOUGHBY, and others, to administer an oath to Sir JONATHAN ATKINS, appointed Captain General of the Caribee Islands; another, to RANDOLPH RUSSELL, and others, to administer an oath to WILLIAM STAPLETON, appointed Captain General of the Caribee Islands, lying leeward of Guadaloup, and for WILLIAM STAPLETON to administer an oath to the Deputy Governors of the same. (29 Chas. II. p. 10.)

27 April. CHARLES HERBERT appointed Chief Clerk in the town of St. Iago de la Vaga, in Jamaica. (29 Chas. II. p. 4.)

1 March. CHARLES, EARL OF CARLISLE, appointed Governor and Captain General of Jamaica. (30 Chas. II. p. 6.)

13 April. The King confirms divers Laws made in Jamaica. (30 Chas. II. p. 7.) The heads of the Bills are forty in number.

26 September. Grant to EDWARD RANDOLPH, Esq., and others, Commission to administer an oath to JOSIAS WINSLOW, Governor of New Plymouth; also to BENEDICT ARNOLD, Esq., Governor of Rhode Island and Providence Plantation; to JOHN LEVERETT, Esq., Governor of Massachusetts Bay; and to WILLIAM LEET, Esq., Governor of the Corporation of Connecticut. (30 Chas. II. p. 1.)

20 April. Indenture between the King and ROBERT SPENCER, JOHN STRODE, CHARLES TUCKER, and HENRY DANIEL, Esquires, as to the Imposts and Customs due to the King, of four and a half per cent. in the Islands of Barbadoes, Nevis, Antegua, Mountserrat, and St. Christopher's for seven years. (30 Chas. II. p. 4.)

21 June. JOHN BINDLOSS and SIMON WINSLOW appointed Chief Clerk, Register [Registrar], and Sole Examiner in the Court of Chancery in Barbadoes for their lives. (31 Chas. II. p. 5.)

6 December. THOMAS, LORD CULPEPER, appointed Lieutenant and Governor General of Virginia, for life. (31 Chas. II. p. 2.)

2 August. GARRETT COTTER appointed Secretary and Marshal of the Islands of Nevis, St. Christopher's, Antegua, and Mountserrat, for three lives. (31 Chas. II. p. 6.)

Commission to JOHN CUTTS, and others, for governing the Colony of New Hampshire, in America. (31 Chas. II. p. 6.)

8 May. CHARLES JONES appointed Postmaster and Register of the Admiralty in Barbadoes. (31 Chas. II. p. 5.)

5 April. THOMAS ROBSON appointed Clerk of the Market in Bridgtown, in Barbadoes, during pleasure. (31 Chas. II. p. 5.)

20 March. NICHOLAS SPENCER appointed Secretary in Virginia, during pleasure. (31 Chas. II. p. 6.)

8 December. Concerning Laws to be made in Virginia: the confirmation of Tithes, &c. (31 Chas. II. p. 2.)

24 February. JOHN BINDLOSSE appointed Clerk of the Markets in Jamaica. (32 Chas. II. p. 2.)

6 March. JOSEPH CRISPE appointed Escheator in the Leeward Islands. (32 Chas. II. p. 2.)

19 May. WILLIAM BLATHWAITE, Esq., appointed Surveyor and Auditor General of all the Revenues in America. (32 Chas. II. p. 2.)

28 October. RICHARD SUTTON appointed Governor of Barbadoes, &c· (32 Chas. II. p. 3.)

28 February. Grant made to WILLIAM PENN, Esq., of a tract of land,

21*

with the Islands belonging to it, in America, bounded on the east by Delaware, &c.   (33 Chas. II. p. 2.)

2 September.   Sir THOMAS LYNCH appointed Governor of Jamaica. (33 Chas. II. p. 2.)

21 April.   OBEDIAH CLAYTON and SAMUEL TRAVEL appointed Clerks of the Passes, for 21 years.   (33 Chas. II. p. 3.)

9 May.   EDWARD CRANFEILD, Esq., appointed Governor of New Hampshire. (34 Chas. II. p. 1.)

14 Nov.   CORNWALL SOMERS, gent., appointed Postmaster in Barbadoes, vice CHARLES JONES, deceased.   (34 Chas. II. p. 8.)

14 December.   TIMOTHY THORNHILL, of Barbadoes, created a Baronet. (34 Chas. II. p. 9.)

22 March.   The King doth give and grant to JAMES, DUKE OF YORK, his heirs and assigns, the town of Newcastle, alias Delaware, and fort thereunto belonging, situate between Maryland and New Jersey; and all that tract of land within the circle of twelve miles about the said town situate upon the river Delaware; and all Islands in the said river; and the said river and soil thereof, lying north of the said circle; and all that tract of land upon Delaware river, beginning 12 miles south from the said town of Newcastle, alias Delaware, and extending south to Cape Lopin.   To be holden of the manor of East Greenwich, co. Kent, in free and common socage, and not in capite or by knight's service, yielding and rendering therefore every year four beaver skins, when the same shall be demanded, or within ninety days after such demand made—with several powers and authorities, amongst others to exercise Martial Law.   (35 Chas. II. p. 1.)

23 Nov.   GEORGE HANNAH, Esq., appointed Provost Marshal General of Barbadoes.   (35 Chas. II. p. 2.)

28 Sept.   FRANCIS, LORD HOWARD of Effingham, appointed Lieutenant and Governor General of Virginia, during pleasure.   (35 Chas. II. p. 2.)

1 January.   RICHARD CONY, Esq., appointed Lieutenant Governor and Commander in Chief of the Bermuda or Summer Islands, during pleasure, with power of constituting officers; the places of Sheriff, Provost Marshal, and Secretary of the said Islands always excepted.   (36 Chas. II. p. 7.)

11 December.   JOHN MOUNTSTEVEN, Esq., appointed Provost Marshal General of Jamaica, during pleasure; to execute by deputy, first approved by the Governor, or some of the Council there, for the time being.   (36 Chas. II. p. 8.)

17 December. JOHN TUCKER, gent., appointed Provost Marshal General, or Sheriff, and Secretary of Bermuda, alias the Summer Islands, to exercise by himself or deputy, during pleasure. (36 Chas. II. p. 8.)

2 July. THOMAS ROBSON, gent., appointed Clerk of the Markets of St Michael's, alias Bridge Town, Spikes Town, and all the Towns in the Barbadoes. (1 Jac. II. p. 1.)

11 April. JOHN MOUNTSTEVENS, Esq., appointed Provost Marshal General of Jamaica. (1 Jac. II. p. 4.)

17 October. GEORGE HANNAY, Esq., appointed Provost Marshal General of Barbadoes. (1 Jac. II. p. 8.)

15 October. EDWARD RANDOLPH, Esq., appointed Collector, Surveyor, and Searcher of the Customs, within the colonies of New England, which office was erected the 15 Oct., 33 Chas. II., with a salary of 100*l.* per ann. (1 Jac. II. p. 8.)

8 October. The King doth erect, constitute, and appoint a President and Council to take care of the territory and dominion of New England, commonly called Massachusetts Bay ; and appoints JOSEPH DUDLEY, Esq., to be the first president. (1 Jac. II. p. 8.)

28 October. FRANCIS, LORD HOWARD, of Effingham, appointed Lieutenant and Governor General of Virginia. (1 Jac. II. p. 8.)

21 October. NICHOLAS SPENCER, Esq., appointed Secretary in Virginia. (1 Jac. II. p. 9.)

21 October. ALEXANDER CULPEPER, Esq., appointed Surveyor General in Virginia. (1 Jac. II. p. 9.)

17 October. REGINALD WILSON, of Jamaica, gent., appointed Clerk of the Naval or Navy Office in Jamaica. (1 Jac. II. p. 9.)

28 October. Sir PHILIP HOWARD, Knt., appointed Captain General and Governor in Chief, in and over Jamaica, and the other territories depending thereon. (1 Jac. II. p. 10.)

5 December. Grant to HUGH NODEN, Merchant Taylor of London, of five shares of land, with the edifices thereupon, situate in the Summer Islands alias Bermuda, to him and his heirs for ever. To be held in free and common socage, by fealty only. (1 Jac. II. p. 10.)

8 January. ARCHIBALD CARMICHAEL appointed Clerk of the Navy in Barbadoes. (2 Jac. II. p. 2.)

30 April. RICHARD CONY, Esq., is constituted Lieutenant Governor and Commander in Chief of Bermuda or Summer Island : a Quo Warranto being issued, and Judgment thereon entered against the Bermuda Company. (2 Jac. II. p. 6, *in dorso.*)

9 June.   Grant to Colonel JOHN LEGG, CHRISTOPHER GUISE, and JOHN ROBINS, (upon the surrender of ROGER WHALEY,) the office of Master or Registrar, for the taking cognizance of the free consents of such persons as shall go into the plantations in America or elsewhere. (2 Jac. II. p. 7.)

29 June.   JOHN TUCKER appointed Secretary and Provost Marshal General of the Bermuda or Summer Islands. (2 Jac. II. p. 9.)

3 June.   Sir EDMUND ANDROS appointed Governor of New England. (2 Jac. II. p. 9.)

10 June.   THOMAS DUNGAN, Esq., appointed Governor of New York. (2 Jac. II. p. 9.)

9 Sept.   THOMAS MONTGOMERY appointed Attorney General of Barbadoes. (2 Jac. II. p. 10.)

9 Sept.   Sir ROBERT ROBINSON appointed Governor of Bermuda. (2 Jac. II. p. 10, *in dorso.*)

28 Sept.   Sir NATHANIEL JOHNSON to be Governor in and over the Islands of Nevis, &c., known by the name of the Caribee Islands. (2 Jac. II. p. 10, *in dorso.*)

25 Nov.   Commission for the DUKE OF ALBEMARLE to be Governor of Jamaica. (2 Jac. II. p. 11.)

28 Dec.   WILLIAM TYACK, gent., appointed Escheator of the Leeward Islands. (2 Jac. II. p. 12.)

4 March.   Grant to CHRISTOPHER, DUKE OF ALBEMARLE, of all Wrecks of plate, gold, silver, &c., on the north side of Hispaniola, or about the Islands of Bahama and Florida. (3 Jac. II. p. 1.)

2 March.   Grant to CHRISTOPHER, DUKE OF ALBEMARLE, of all Mines of Gold, &c., in the Colonies of America. (3 Jac. II. p. 2.)

12 August.   Ratification of the Letters Patent made to the DUKE OF ALBEMARLE on the 4th March. (3 Jac. II. p. 7.)

23 August.   Grant to the DUKE OF ALBEMARLE, the sole use of saw mills in the plantations of America, (New England excepted), for the term of 14 years. (3 Jac. II. p. 8.)

13 August.   The King erects the office of Provost Marshal General of New England, and grants the same to Sir WILLIAM PHIPPS. (3 Jac. II. p. 8.)

12 November.   HENRY HORDESNELL, Esq., appointed Justice, or Chief Judge of the Bermuda or Summer Islands. (3 Jac. II. p. 9.)

January 20.   Proclamation for the more effectual reducing and suppressing pirates or privateers in America. (3 Jac. II. p. 9.)

4 November. MATHEW PLOWMAN appointed Collector and Receiver of New York, with a salary of 200*l.* per annum, vice LUCAS SANTEN. (3 Jac. II. p. 10.)

20 October. Grant to the EARL OF FEVERSHAM, of all Wrecks, &c., on the north side of the main land of America. (3 Jac. II. p. 10.)

28 February. Grant to ROBERT BRENT, all Wrecks, &c., in or upon any of the rocks, shelves, seas, or banks, on or near the coast of America, between the Bermudas and Porto Rico, or between Cartagena and the Havanna. (4 Jac. II. p. 3.)

5 May. The King authorises the DUKE OF ALBEMARLE, (during his being Governor of Jamaica), to confer knighthood upon any six deserving persons, according to his own discretion, in that Island. (4 Jac. II. p. 4.)

20 April. The King erects and establishes the office of Secretary and sole Register [Registrar] in New England, and grant the said office to EDWARD RANDOLPH, Esq. (4 Jac. II. p. 4.)

27 September. The King confirms to THOMAS, LORD CULPEPER, an entire tract of land in Virginia, bounded within the springs of the rivers of Tapphannock and Quiriough, to him, his heirs and assigns for ever—yielding and paying therefore, 6*l.* 13*s.* 4*d.* (4 Jac. II. p. 7.)

5 September. Grant to JOHN, EARL OF BATH, ANTHONY, LORD FALKLAND, and others, the use of the ship *Forsight,* to take up and recover Gold near Hispaniola. (4 Jac. II. p. 7.)

25 September. HENRY FIFIELD, gent., appointed Secretary and Provost Marshal General of the Summer Islands, alias the Bermudas. (4 Jac. II. p. 8.)

7 April. Sir EDMUND ANDROS appointed Captain General and Governor over the Massachusetts Bay, &c. (Pennsylvania and the county of Delaware only excepted, vide Pat. 3 June, 2 Jac. II.) (4 Jac. II. p. 8.)

6 April. Major HENRY CARRE appointed Provost Marshal General of Jamaica. (1 Will. & Mary, p. 1.)

19 July. HENDER MOLESWORTH, of Jamaica, Esq., created a Baronet. (1 Will. & Mary, p. 2.)

8 August. ARCHIBALD CARMICHAELL appointed Clerk of the Navy in the Barbadoes. (1 Will. & Mary, p. 4.)

25 July. Sir HENDER MOLESWORTH appointed Captain General of Jamaica. (1 Will. & Mary, p. 4.)

3 August. JAMES KENDALL, Esq., appointed Captain General of Barbadoes, St. Lucca, &c. (1 Will. & Mary, p. 4.)

14 September.   CHIDLEY BROOKE appointed Collector and Receiver of New York.   (1 Will. & Mary, p. 5.)

8 August.   REGINALD WILSON appointed Clerk of the Navy in Jamaica.   (1 Will. & Mary, p. 5.)

3 October.   Grant to JAMES KENDALL, (who was made Governor of Barbadoes on the 3d of August last), a salary of 1200*l.* a year.   (1 Will. & Mary, p. 6.)

3 October.   Grant of a large Commission to JAMES KENDALL, lately made Governor of Barbadoes.   (1 Will. & Mary, p. 6.)

26 October.   CHRISTOPHER CODRINGTON, Esq., appointed Governor of the Islands of Nevis, &c.   (1 Will. & Mary, p. 6.)

15 November.   HENRY FIFEILD* appointed Secretary and Provost Marshal of Bermuda.   (1 Will. & Mary, p. 7.)

8 November.   ISAAC RICHIER appointed Governor of Bermuda, &c.   (1 Will. & Mary, p. 7.)

23 December.   WILLIAM, EARL OF INCHIQUIN, Lieutenant General of Jamaica, appointed Vice Admiral of the said Island.   (1 Will. & Mary, p. 8.)

12 December.   RICHARD LLOYD appointed Clerk of the Crown in Jamaica.   (1 Will. & Mary, p. 8.)

6 November.   The King erects an office to be called the Secretary of New York, and appoints MATHEW CLARKSON to the same.   (1 Will. & Mary, p. 8.)

25 November.   JOHN STEDE appointed Clerk of the Markets of St. Michael, alias Bridge-town, &c., in Barbadoes.   (1 Will. & Mary, p. 8.)

4 January.   HENRY SLATER appointed Governor of New York.   (1 Will. & Mary, p. 8.)

7 October.   WILLIAM, EARL OF INCHIQUIN, appointed Lieutenant or Governor General of Jamaica.   (1 Will. & Mary, p. 8.)

13 December.   THOMAS FERNELEY, Esq., appointed Secretary of the Islands of St. Christopher's, &c.   (1 Will. & Mary, p. 9.)

12 December.   EPAPHRODITUS HOUGHTON appointed Provost Marshal General of the Islands of St. Christopher's.   (1 Will. & Mary, p. 9.)

17 January.   Colonel WILLIAM COLE appointed Secretary in Virginia.   (1 Will. & Mary, p. 9.)

31 December.   CHRISTOPHER CODRINGTON, Captain General of Nevis, appointed Vice Admiral of the said Island.   (1 Will. & Mary, p. 9.)

---

* [See 25 Sept., 4 Jac. II.]

25 February. GEORGE HANWAY appointed Provost Marshal General of Barbadoes. (2 Will. & Mary, p. 2.)

5 November. FRANCIS, LORD HOWARD of Effingham, appointed Governor General of Virginia. (2 Will. & Mary, p. 5.)

4 December. JOSEPH BATHURST and RICHARD DODINGTON, appointed Clerk of the Court of Common Pleas of Jamaica. (2 Will. & Mary, p. 6.)

25 November. Grant to THOMAS NEALE, Esq., of all Wrecks, &c., within twenty leagues of the Bermudas. (2 Will. & Mary, p. 6.)

27 June. LIONEL COPLEY, Esq., appointed Governor of Maryland. (3 Will. & Mary, p. 2.)

4 June. ROWLAND WILLIAMS, Esq., appointed Clerk of the Navy of the Leeward Caribee Islands. (3 Will. & Mary, p. 3.)

5 September. Sir THOMAS LAWRANCE appointed Secretary of Maryland. (3 Will. & Mary, p. 6.)

7 October. The King incorporates the inhabitants of Massachusetts Bay in New England, &c. (3 Will. & Mary, p. 7.)

1 October. THOMAS BELCHAMBER appointed Provost Marshal General of the Islands of St. Christophers, &c., vice EPAPHRODITUS HAUGHTON. (3 Will. & Mary, p. 7.)

30 November. JAMES VERNON, Esq., appointed Chief Clerk of St. Iago de la Vaga, Jamaica. (3 Will. & Mary, p. 8.)

11 January. JOHN PALMER, Esq., appointed Secretary of St. Christophers, &c. (3 Will. & Mary, p. 9.)

12 December. Sir WILLIAM PHIPPS appointed Captain of Massachusetts Bay. (3 Will. & Mary, p. 9.)

1 March. Sir EDMOND ANDROS appointed Lieutenant and Governor General of Virginia. (4 Will. & Mary, p. 1.)

18 March. BENJAMIN FLETCHER appointed Captain General and Governor of New York. (4 Will. & Mary, p. 2.)

1 March. SAMUEL ALLEN, Esq., appointed Governor of New Hampshire. (4 Will. & Mary, p. 2.)

5 July. Grant to THOMAS NEALE of all Wrecks, &c., on the Coast of Bermudas, or within 20 Leagues. (4 Will. & Mary, p. 5.)

16 July. Grant to THOMAS NEALE, of all Treasure Trove in the little Island called Ireland, near the Bermudas. (4 Will. & Mary, p. 5.)

20 September. WILLIAM BRODRICKE appointed Attorney General in Jamaica. (4 Will. & Mary, p. 6.)

20 September. WILLIAM BEESTON, Esq., appointed Governor of Jamaica. (4 Will. & Mary, p. 6.)

22 August. Grant to THOMAS NEALE of all mines of gold within their Majesties' plantations in America, for 51 years; yielding and paying a sixth part. (4 Will. & Mary, p. 6.)

19 August. The King and Queen, in consideration of 400*l.*, do give unto THOMAS NEALE, Esq., all Wrecks, &c., between Cartagena and Jamaica; and between either of those two places and the Havanna. (4 Will. & Mary, p. 6.)

16 January. CHRISTOPHER ROBINSON, Esq., appointed Secretary in Virginia. (4 Will. & Mary, p. 8.)

8 February. Licence granted to found a College in the West part of Virginia. (4 Will. & Mary, p. 9.)

21 October. BENJAMIN FLETCHER (lately made Governor of New York), appointed Governor of Pennsylvania. (6 Will. & Mary, p. 10.)

1 March. JOHN GODDARD, Esq., appointed Governor and Commander of the Bermuda or Summer Islands. (5 Will. & Mary, p. 1.)

20 February. The King pardons GEERRARD BEECKMAN, MYNDERT COARTEN, THOMAS WILLIAMS, JOHN VERNNILLIE, ABRAHAM BRASIER, and ABRAHAM GOVERNEUR, all of New York; all treasons and murders for the death of JOSIAH BROWN, of New York (is particularly mentioned). (5 Will. & Mary, p. 1.)

10 March. Grant to MAINHARDT, DUKE OF LEINSTER, of all Wrecks, &c., &c., between the Latitudes of 12 Degrees South and 40 Degrees North, by him to be recovered at any time within 20 years after the date hereof, (the Bermudas, Cartagena, and Jamaica excepted) for several terms of years, one full tenth of the premises reserved to the King and Queen. (5 Will. & Mary, p. 1.)

10 February. FRANCIS NICHOLSON, Esq., appointed Captain General and Governor of Maryland. (5 Will. & Mary, p. 2.)

27 January. WILLIAM BARNES, Esq., appointed Provost Marshal General of the Islands of St. Christopher's, Nevis, Mountserrat and Antegua, during pleasure. (5 Will. & Mary, p. 2.)

25 April. Grant to THOMAS NEALE, Esq., and JOHN TYZACKE, gent., all Wrecks, &c., &c., within 30 Leagues of the Isle of Stables, and betwixt 40 and 50 Degrees of North Latitude, to be gotten and recovered by them within seven years after the date hereof. (5 Will. & Mary, p. 3.)

15 April. Grant to the Widows and Children of JACOB LEISLER and JACOB MILBURNE, of New York, all the real and personal estates of the said LEISLER and MILBURNE, executed for

treason or supposed treason, in the Colony of New York. (5 Will. & Mary, p. 4.)

13 December. Grant to Sir JOHN HOSKYNS, of Harewood, co. Hereford, Knt. & Bart., all those Islands called Ascension, Trinidad, and Martin Vaz, to him, his heirs and assigns, for ever—yielding and paying the fourth part of the profits of all mines of gold and silver wrought in the said Islands on the 5th Nov. yearly. To be holden of the manor of East Greenwich, in socage, and not in capite, nor by knight s service. (5 Will. & Mary, p. 5.)

26 December. FRANCIS RUSSELL, Esq., appointed Captain General and Governor in Chief of the Islands of Barbadoes, Sta. Lucia, Dominico, St. Vincent's, &c., commonly called the Caribee Islands, lying and being to windward from Guadaloupe. (5 Will. & Mary, p. 5.)

26 June. Colonel RALPH WORMLEY appointed Secretary of Virginia, (vice CHRISTOPHER ROBINSON, Esq., deceased,) to hold the same by himself or deputy, during pleasure. (5 Will. & Mary, p. 6.)

10 June. BENJAMIN FLETCHER, Esq., Governor of New York and Pennsylvania, to be Commander of the Militia of Connecticutt. (5 Will. & Mary, p. 7, *in dorso*.)

8 March. EDWARD CRANFEILD, Esq., appointed Clerk of the Navy in Barbadoes, vice ARCHIBALD CARMICHAEL, Esq., deceased, during pleasure. (6 Will. & Mary, p. 1.)

17 January. Revocation of the appointment of GEORGE HANNAH to the office of Provost Marshal of Barbadoes, and appoints JAMES HANNAH, Esq., to the said office. (7 Will. III. p. 4.)

16 April. JOHN PERRIE, Esq., appointed Provost Marshal General of the Islands of St. Christopher's, Nevis, Mountserrat, and Antegua, during pleasure, vice WILLIAM BARNES, Esq., deceased. (8 Will. III. p. 4.)

1 May. WILLIAM BRODERICK, Esq., appointed Attorney General of Jamaica. (8 Will. III. p. 6.)

26 June. WILLIAM PARTRIDGE, Esq., appointed Lieutenant Governor of New Hampshire, during pleasure. (8 Will. III. p. 8.)

4 January. SAMUEL DAY, Esq., appointed Lieutenant Governor and Commander in Chief of the Bermudas or Summer Islands. (9 Will. III. p. 3.)

22 February. EDWARD PARSONS, Esq., appointed Secretary of St. Christopher's, Nevis, Mountserrat, and Antegua, and other Leeward Caribee Islands, during pleasure. (9 Will. III. p. 4.)

18 June.   RICHARD, EARL of BELLOMONT, appointed Captain General and Governor in Chief of Massachusetts Bay ; also Governor and Commander in Chief of all that province of New Hampshire within New England, extending from three miles northward of Merrimac River unto the province of Main.   (9 Will. III. p. 6, *in dorso.*)

18 June.   RICHARD, EARL OF BELLOMONT, appointed Captain General and Governor in Chief of New York,   (9 Will. III. p. 7.)

24 July.   RALPH GREY, Esq., appointed Captain General and Governor in Chief of the Islands of Barbadoes, Sta. Lucia, Dominico, St. Vincent's, &c., and the rest of the Islands, &c., commonly called the Caribee Islands.   (9 Will. III. p. 7.)

17 July.   JOHN BABER, Esq., appointed Secretary of Jamaica, and Commissary of the Stores and Clerk of the Enrolment of Deeds, &c., during pleasure.   (9 Will. III. p. 7.)

18 August.   The King releaseth unto Sir WILLIAM BEESTON, Knt., Lieutenant Governor of Jamaica, all offences and neglects committed for his not taking the oaths, appointed to be taken by the Governors of Colonies in Asia, Africa, or America. (10 Will. III. p. 5.)

12 August.   GEORGE GOLDING, Esq., appointed Provost Marshal General of Jamaica, during pleasure.   (10 Will. III. p. 7.)

20 July.   FRANCIS NICHOLSON, Esq., appointed Lieutenant and Governor General of Virginia. (He succeeded Sir EDWARD ANDROS, Knt., who obtained leave to return home for the recovery of his health.)   (10 Will. III. p. 8.)

19 October.   NATHANIEL BLAKESTON, Esq., appointed Captain General and Governor in Chief of Maryland.   (10 Will. III. p. 9.)

20 September.   THOMAS LAWRENCE, Esq., appointed Secretary of Maryland, during pleasure.   (Letters Patent appointing Sir THOMAS LAWRENCE, Bart., of the 5th Sept., 3 Will. & Mary, are revoked.)   (10 Will. III. p. 10.)

6 May.   WILLIAM NEEDHAM, gent., appointed Clerk of the Crown and Clerk of the Peace of Jamaica, during pleasure.   (11 Will. III. p. 1.)

25 March.   WILLIAM WELBY, Esq., appointed Secretary of Barbadoes, during pleasure.   (11 Will. III. p. 1.)

7 June.   EDWARD JONES, gent., appointed Secretary and Provost Marshal General of the Bermudas, alias Summer Islands.   (11 Will. III. p. 2.)

18 May.   EDWARD CHILTON, of the Middle Temple, Barrister, appointed
Attorney General of Barbadoes.   (11 Will. III. p. 2.)

5 January.   Sir WILLIAM BEESTON appointed Captain General and
Governor in Chief of Jamaica, during pleasure.   (11 Will. III.
p. 4.)

17 March.   ALLEN BRODERICK, Esq., appointed Attorney General of
Jamaica, during pleasure.   (11 Will. III. p. 5.)

29 August.   ALEXANDER SKENE appointed Secretary of, and Clerk of
the several Courts in Barbadoes, during pleasure.   (11 Will. III.
p. 6.)

13 May.   CHRISTOPHER CODRINGTON, Esq., appointed Captain General
and Governor in Chief over the Islands of Nevis, St. Christopher's, Mountserrat, Antegua, Barbadoes, Anquilla, &c.   (11
Will. III. p. 6, *in dorso.*)

23 Nov.   RALPH GREY, Esq., and others, appointed Commissioners at
Barbadoes, Sta. Lucia, Dominico, St. Vincent's, &c., for examining of Piracies.   Similar Commissions to STAFFORD FAIRBORE,
and others, for Newfoundland; to BENJAMIN BENNET, Esq.,
and others, for the Bermudas or Summer Islands; to NATHAN
BLACKSTON, Esq., for Maryland and Pennsylvania; to CHRIS-
TOPHER CODRINGTON, Esq., for St. Christopher's, Mountserrat,
Antigua, Barbouda, [Barbadoes] Anguilla, &c., commonly called
the Caribee Islands; to FRANCIS NICHOLSON, Esq., for Virginia and Carolina; and to RICHARD, EARL OF BELLOMONT,
for Massachusetts Bay, New Hampshire, and Rhode Island.
(12 Will. III. p. 1.)

13 December.   SAMUEL COX, Esq., appointed Clerk of the Navy Office
in Barbadoes, during pleasure.   (12 Will. III. p. 1.)

23 November.   RICHARD, EARL OF BELLOMONT, and others, appointed
Commissioners for examining of Piracies at New York, East
and West, New Jersey, and Connecticut; also to Sir WILLIAM
BEESTON, Knt., for Jamaica and the Bahama Islands.   (12
Will. III. p. 1, *in dorso.*)

24 September.   BENJAMIN BENNETT, Esq., appointed Lieutenant Governor and Commander in Chief of the Bermuda or Summer
Islands, during pleasure.   (12 Will. III. p. 2.)

4 March.   THOMAS WEAVOR, Esq., appointed Collector and Receiver
of New York (during pleasure), with a salary of 200*l.*, vice
CHIDLEY BROOK, who was appointed 14 Dec., 1 Will. & Mary.
(12 Will. III. p. 4.)

11 July.   Sir THOMAS LAWRENCE, Bart., appointed Secretary of Maryland, during pleasure.   (13 Will. III. p. 1.)

31 July. WILLIAM SELWYN, Esq., appointed Captain General and Commander in Chief of Jamaica, during pleasure. (13 Will. III. p. 1, *in dorso.*)

9 September. EDWARD HYDE, Esq., commonly called LORD CORNBURY, appointed Captain General and Governor in Chief of New York, during pleasure. (13 Will. III. p. 2.)

27 November. HENRY CARPENTER, Esq., appointed Secretary of the Islands of St. Christopher's, Nevis, Mountserrat, and Antegua, and other the Leeward and Caribee Islands, during pleasure, &c. (13 Will. III. p. 3.)

13 February. MITFORD CROWE, Esq., appointed Captain General and Governor in Chief over the Islands of Barbadoes, Sta. Lucia, Dominico, St. Vincent, &c. (14 Will. III. p. 1.)

13 February. JOSEPH DUDLEY, Esq., appointed Captain General and Governor in Chief of Massachusetts Bay, (14 Will. III. p. 1); also Governor and Commander in Chief of New Hampshire, during pleasure. (14 Will. III. p. 1, *in dorso.*)

Lists of the
Livinge and
Dead in Virginia
Febr: 16th 1623.*

A List of Names; of the Living in Virginia
february the 16 1623

Att y^e Colledg Land.

THOMAS MARLETT
CHRISTOPHER BRANCH
FRANCIS BOOT.
WILLIAM BROWĪNG [BROWNING]
WALTER COOp [COOPER]
WILLIAM WELDER
LEONARD MORE
DANIELL SHURLEY
PEETER JORDEN
NICHOLAS PERSE
WILLIAM DALBIE
ESAIAS RAWTON
THEODER MOISES
ROBERT CHAMPER
THOMAS JONES
DAVID WILLIAMS
WILLIAM WALKER
EDWARD HOBSON
THOMAS HOBSON
JOHN DAY

WILLIAM COOKSEY
ROBERT FARNELL
NICHOLAS CHAPMAN
MATHEW EDLOW
WILLIAM PRICE
GABRIELL HOLLAND
JOHN WATTSON
EBEDMELECH GASTRELL
THOMAS OSBORNE

Att ye Neck of Land.

LUKE BOYS
Mrs BOYS
ROBERT HALAM
JOSEPH ROYALL
JOHN DOD'S
M^{rs} DOD'S
ELIZABETH PERKINSON
WILLIAM VINCENT
Mrs VINCENT

Living

ALLEXANDER BRADWAYE
his wife BRADWAYE
JOHN PRICE
his wife PRICE
ROBERT TURNER
NATHANIELL REEUE* [REEVE]
Seriant Wᴹ SHARP
Mʳˢ SHARP.
RICHARD RAWSE
THOMAS SHEPPY
WILLIAM CLEMENS
THOMAS HARRIS
his Wife HARRIS
ANN WOODLEY
MARGRETT BERMAN
THOMAS FARMER
HUGH HILTON
RICHARD TAYLOR
vx. TAYLOR
JOSUA CHARD
CHRISTOPHER BROWNE
THOMAS OAGE
Vx: OAGE
infans OAGE
HENRY COLTMAN
HUGH PRICE
Vx PRICE
infans PRICE
Mʳˢ COLTMAN
ROBERT GREENE
vx. GREENE
infans GREENE.

Living

Att West and Sherlow hundred

JOHN HARRIS
DORITHE HARRIS
infants { HARRIS / HARRIS
THOMAS FLOYD
ELLIAS LONGE
WILLIAM NICHOLLAS
ROGER RATCLIFE
ROBERT MILNER
ROBERT PARTTIN
MARGRETT PARTTIN
infantes { PARTTIN / PARTTIN
HENRY BENSON
NICHOLAS BLACKMAN
NATHANELL TATTAM
MATHEW GLOSTER
SYMON TURGIS
NICHOLAS BALEY
ANN BAYLEY
ELMER PHILLIPS
THOMAS PAULETT
THOMAS BAUGH.
THOMAS PACKER
JONAS RAYLEY
JOHN TRUSSELL
CHRISTOPHER BEANE
JOHN CARTTER
HENRY BAGWELL
THOMAS BAGWELL
EDWARD GARDINER
RICHARD BIGGS

* [Might possibly be read as REENE.]

Living

Mrs BIGGS

WILLIAM BIGGS ⎫
THOMAS BIGGS ⎬ fil
RICHARD BIGGS ⎭

WILLIAM ASKEW

HENRY CARMAN

ANDREW DUDLEY

JAMES GAY

ANTHONY BURROWS

REBECCA ROSSE

fil: { ROSSE
      { ROSSE

PETTERS, a maid.

———

At Jordans Jorney

SISLYE JORDAN

TEMPERANCE BAYLIFE

MARY JORDAN

MARGERY JORDAN

WILLIAM FARRAR

THOMAS WILLIAMS

ROGER PRESTON

THOMAS BROOKES

JOHN PEEDE

JOHN FREME

RICHARD JOHNSON

WILLIAM DAWSON

JOHN HELY

ROBERT MANUELL [*or* MANNELL]

ANN LINKON

WILLIAM BASSE

Mrs· BASSE

CHRISTOPHER SAFORD

vx SAFORD

JOHN CAMINGE

THOMAS PALMER

Living

Mrs· PALMER

filia PALMER

RICHARD ENGLISH

NATHANIEL CAUSEY

Mrs CAUSEY

LAWRANCE EVANS

EDWARD CLARKE

vx CLARKE

infans CLARKE

JOHN GIBBS

JOHN DAVIES

WILLIAM EMERSON

HENRY WILLIAMS

vx WILLIAMS

HENRY FISHER

vx FISHER

infans FISHER

THOMAS CHAPMAN

vx CHAPMAN

infans CHAPMAN

EDITH HOLLIS

———

At flourdien hundred

RICHARD GREGORY

EDWARD ALBORN

THOMAS DILLIMAGER

THOMAS HACH

ANTHONY JONES

ROBERT GUY

WILLIAM STRACHEY

JOHN BROWNE

ANNIS BOULT

WILLIAM BAKER

THEODER BERISTON

WALTER BLAKE

THOMAS WATTS   22

Living

THOMAS DOUGHTY
GEORGE DEVERELL
RICHARD SPURLING
JOHN WOODSON
WILLIAM STRAUNGE*
THOMAS DUNE
JOHN LANDMAN
LEONARD YEATS
GEORGE LEVET
THOMAS HAWAY
THOMAS FILENST
ROBERT SMITH
THOMAS GRINDER
THOMAS GASKO
JOHN OLIUES [OLIVES]
CHRISTOPHER PUGETT
ROBERT PEAKE
EDWARD TRAMORDEN
HENRY LINGE
GIBERT PEPPET
THOMAS MIMES
JOHN LINGE
JOHN GALE
THOMAS BARNETT
ROGER TOMPSON
ANN TOMPSON
ANN DOUGHTY
SARA WOODSON

— ⎰ Negors
— ⎪ Negors
— ⎪ Negors
— vj ⎱ Negors
— ⎪ Negors
— ⎱ Negors

Living

GRIVELL POOLEY minister
———
SAMUELL SHARP
JOHN VPTON
JOHN WILSON
HENRY ROWNIGE [*or* ROWINGE]
NATHANIELL THOMAS
WILLIAM BARRETT
ROBERT OKLEY
RICHARD BRADSHAW
THOMAS SAWELL
JOHN BAMFORD
ANTHONY ⎫
WILLIAM ⎪
JOHN ⎬ Negors men
ANTHONY ⎭
an Negors woman
———
the rest at West and Sherlow hundred Iland

CAP: ISACKE MADDESON
MARY MADDESON
THOMAS WATTSON
JAMES WATTSON
FRANCIS WEST
ROGER LEWIS
RICHARD DOMELOW
WILLIAN HATFEILD
THOMAS FOSSETT
ANN FOSSETT
JENKIN OSBORNE
WILLIAM SISMORE
MARTHA SISMORE
STEPHEN BRABY
ELIZABETH BRABY

* [I believe this is correct ; but the third letter is blotted in the original ; and there is, besides, a dot near the end of the word, which makes it possible to read it as STRAMIGE.]

Living

EDWARD TEMPLE
DANIELL VERGO
WILLIAM TATHILL boy
THOMAS HAILE boy
RICHARD MOREWOOD
EDWARD SPARSHOTT
BARNARD JACKSON
WILLIAM BROCKE
· JAMES MAYRO

At Chaplains choise

ISACKE CHAPLAINE
Mrs CHAPLAINE
JOHN CHAPLAINE
WALTER PRIEST
WILLIAM WESTON
JOHN DUFFY
ANN MICHAELL
THOMAS PHILLIPS
HENRY THORNE
ROBERT HUDSON
ISACKE BANGTON [*or* BAUGTON]
NICHOLAS SUTTON
WILLIAM WHITT
EDWARD BUTTLER
HENRY TURNER ·
THOMAS LEY
JOHN BROWNE
JOHN TRACHERN
HENRY WILLSON
THOMAS BALDWYNE
ALLEXANDER SANDERSON
DAVID ELLIS
SARA MORE
ANN a Maid.

Living

At James Cittye and wth the Corporacon therof.

Sr FRANCES WYATT Goveno':
MARGRETT LADY WYATT
HANT WYATT Minister
KATHREN SPENCER
THOMAS HOOKER
JOHN GATHER
JOHN MATHEMAN
EDWARD COOKE
GEORGE NELSON
GEORGE HALL
JANE BURTT
ELIZABETH POMELL
MARY WOODWARD

Sr GEORGE YEARDLEY Knight
TEMPERANCE LADY YEARDLY
ARGALL YARDLEY
FRANCES YEARDLEY
ELIZABETH YEARDLEY
KILIBETT HICHCOCKE
AUSTEN COMBES
JOHN FOSTER
RICHARD ARRUNDELL
SUSAN HALL
ANN GRIMES
ELIZABETH LYON
— YOUNGE
— Negro } women
— Negro

ALICE DAVISON vid:
EDWARD SHARPLES

22—2

Living

JONE DAVIES

———

GEORGE SANDS Trasu'
Cap: Wᴹ PERCE
JONE PERCE
ROBERT HEDGES
HUGH Wᴹ [WILLIAMS]
THOMAS MOULSTON
HENRY FARMOR
JOHN LIGHTFOOTE
THOMAS SMITH
ROGER RUESE
ALLEXANDER GILL
JOHN CARTWRIGHT
ROBERT AUSTINE
EDWARD BRICKE
WILLIAM RAVENETT
JOCOMB ANDREWS
vx ANDREWS
RICHARD ALDER
ESTER EVERE
ANGELO a Negar

———

Doc: JOHN POTT
ELIZABETH POTT
RICHARD TOWNSEND
THOMAS LEISTER
JOHN KULLAWAY
RANDALL HOWLETT
JANE DICKINSON
FORTUNE TAYLOR

———

Cap: ROGER SMITH
Mʳˢ SMITH

Living

ELIZABETH SALTER
SARA MACOCKE
ELIZABETH ROLFE
CHRI: LAWSON
vxor eius LAWSON
FRANCES FOULLER
CHARLES WALLER
HENRY BOOTH

———

Cap: RAPH HAMOR
Mʳˢ HAMOR
JEREME CLEMENT
ELIZABETH CLEMENT
SARA LANGLEY
SISLEY GREENE
ANN ADDAMS
ELKINTON RATCLIFE
FRANCIS GIBSON
JAMES YEMANSON

———

JOHN POÑTES
CHRISTOPHER BEST.
THOMAS CLARKE
Mʳ REIGNOLD'S
Mʳ HICKMORE
vx HICKMORE
SARA RIDDALL

———

EDWARD BLANEY
EDWARD HUDSON
vx HUDSON
WILLIAM HARTLEY
JOHN SHELLEY
ROBERT BEW
WILLIAM WARD

Living

THOMAS MENTIS [*or* MEUTIS]
ROBERT WHITMORE
ROBERT CHAUNTREE
ROBERT SHEPPARD
WILLIAM SAWIER
LANSLOTT DAMPORT
MATH: LOYD
THOMAS OTTWAY
THOMAS CROUCH
ELIZABETH STARKEY
ELINOR

———

Mrs PERRY
infans PERRY
FRANCES CHAPMAN
GEORGE GRAUES* [GRAVES]
vx GRAUES*
REBECCA SNOWE
SARA SNOWE
JOHN ISGRAUE [ISGRAVE]
MARY ASCOMBE vid
BENAMY BUCKE
GERCYON BUCKE
PELEG BUCKE
MARA BUCKE
ABRAM PORTER
BRIGETT CLARKE
ABIGALL ASCOMBE
JOHN JACKSON
vx JACKSON
EPHRAIM JACKSON

———

Mr JOHN BURROWS
Mrs BURROWS

Living

ANTHONY BURROWS
JOHN COOKE
NICHOLAS GOULDSMITH
ELIAS GAILE
ANDREW HOWELL
ANN ASHLEY

———

JOHN SOUTHERN
THOMAS PASMORE
ANDREW RALYE

———

NATH: JEFFERYS
vx JEFFERYS
THOMAS HEBBS

———

CLEM^T DILKE
Mrs DILKE
JOHN HINTON

———

RICHARD STEPHENS
WASSELL RAYNER
vx RAYNER
JOHN JACKSON
EDWARD PRICE
OSTEN SMITH
THOMAS SPILMAN
BRYAN CAWT

———

GEORGE MINIFY
MOYES STON

———

Capt: HOLMES
Mr CALCKER
Mrs CALCKER
infans CALCKER

---

* [Might be read as GRANES.]

Living

PECEABLE SHERWOOD
ANTHONY WEST
HENRY BARKER
HENRY SCOTT
MARGERY DAWSE

———

Mʳ CANN
Cap: HARTT
EDWARD SPALDING
vx SPALDING
puer SPALDING
Puella SPALDING
JOHN HELIN
vx HELIN
puer HELIN
infans HELIN

———

THOMAS GRAYE *et vx*
JONE GRAVE
WILLIAM GRAYE
RICHARD YOUNGE
vx YOUNGE
JONE YOUNGE

———

RANDALL SMALWOOD
JOHN GREENE
WILLIAM MUDGE

———

Mʳˢ SOTHEY
ANN SOTHEY
ELIN PAINTER

———

GOODMAN WEBB

Living

———

in the maine

RICHARD ATKINS
vx ATKINS
WILLIAM BAKER
EDWARD OLIVER
SAMWELL MORRIS
ROBERT DAVIS
ROBERT LUNTHORNE
JOHN VERNIE
THOMAS WOOD
THOMAS REES

———

MICHEALL BATT
vx BATT
vid's TINDALL
Mʳ STAFFERTON
vx STAFFERTON
JOHN FISHER
JOHN ROSE
THOMAS THORNEGOOD
JOHN BADSTON
SUSAN BLACKWOOD

———

THOMAS KINSTON
ROBERT SCOTTESMORE
ROGER KID
NICHOLAS BULLINGTON
NICHOLAS MARTTIN

———

JOHN CARTER
CHRISTOPHER HALL
DAVID ELLIS
vx ELLIS
JOHN FROGMORTON
ROBERT MARSHALL

———

Living

THOMAS SWNOW*

JOHN SMITH

LAWRANCE SMALPAGE

THOMAS CROSSE

THOMAS PRICHARD

RICHARD CROUCH

———

CHRISTOPHER REDHEAD

HENRY BOOTH

———

RICHARD CARVEN

vx CARVEN

JOHN HOWELL

WILLIAM BURTT

WILLIAM STOCKER

NICHOLAS ROOTE

———

SARA KIDDALL

infans { KIDDALL
         { KIDDALL

EDWARD FISHER

RICHARD SMITH

JOHN WOLRICH

Mrs WOLRICH

JONATHIN GILES

CHRISTOPH: RIPEN

THOMAS BANKS

FRANCES BUCHER

HENRY DAWLEN

ARTHUR CHANDLER

RICHARD SANDERS

THOMAS HELCOTT

THOMAS HICHCOCKE

Living

GRIFFINE GUNIE†

THOMAS OSBOURN

RICHARD DOWNES

WILLIAM LAWRELL

———

THOMAS JORDAN

EDWARD BUSBEE

HENRY TURNER

JOSUA CREW

ROBERT HUTCHINSON

THOMAS JONES

vx JONES

REIGNOLD MORECOCKE *et vx*

RICHARD BRIDGWATTER *et* [*vx*]

———

Mr THO: BUN

Mrs BUN

THOMAS SMITH

ELIZABETH HODGES

———

WILLIAM KEMP

vx KEMP

———

HUGH BALDWINE

vx BALDWINE

JOHN WILMOSE

———

THOMAS DOE

vx DOE

———

GEORGE FRYER

vx FRYER

STEPHEN WEBB

* [Clearly so in the original.]

† [Apparently so ; but it might also be read as GUME, or GUINE.]

Living
—
in Jams iland

JOHN OSBOURN
vx OSBOVRN [OSBOURN]
GEORGE POPE
ROBERT CUNSTABLE

WILLIAM JONES
vx JONES
JOHN JOHNSON
vx JOHNSON
infans { JOHNSON
         { JOHNSON
JOHN HALL
vx HALL
WILLIAM COOKSEY
vx COOKSEY
infans COOKSEY
ALICE KEAN

ROBERT FITTS
vx FITTS
JOHN REDDISH

JOHN GREVETT
vx GREVETT
JOHN WEST
THOMAS WEST
HENRY GLOVER

GOODMAN STOIKS*
vx STOIKS
infans STOIKS
Mr ADAMS
Mr LEET

Living
WILLIAM SPENCE
vx SPENCE
infans SPENCE
JAMES TOOKE
JAMES ROBERTS
ANTHONY HARLOW

SARA SPENCE
GEORGE SHURKE
JOHN BOOTH
ROBERT BENNETT

ye neck of land.

Mr KINGSMEALE
vx KINGSMEALE
infans { KINGSMEALE
         { KINGSMEALE
RAPH GRIPHIN
FRANCES COMPTON
JOHN SMITH
JOHN FILMER
EDWARD a Negro
THOMAS SULLEY
vx SULLEY
THOMAS HARWOOD
GEORGE FEDAM
PETER STABER
THOMAS POPKIN
THOMAS SIDES
RICHARD PERSE
vx PERSE
ALLEN his man
ISABELL PRATT

---

* [First written STOCKS, then altered.]

Living

THOMAS ALNUTT
vx ALNUTT
JOHN PAINE
ROGER REDES
ELINOR SPRAD

Ouer the River

JOHN SMITH
vx SMITH
infans SMITH
JOHN VERGO
RICHARD FENN
WILLIAM RICHARDSON
ROBERT LINDSEY
RICHARD DOLFEMB
JOHN BOTTAM
JOHN ELLIOTT
SUSAN BARBER
THOMAS GATES
vx GATES
PERCIVALL WOOD
ANTHONY BURRIN
WILLIAM BEDFORD
WILLIAM SAND'S
JOHN PROCTOR
Mrs PROCTOR
PHETTIPLACE CLOSE
HENRY HORNE
RICHARD HORNN
THOMAS FLOWER
WILLIAM BULLOCKE
ELLIAS HINTON
JOHN FOXEN
EDWARD SMITH

Living

JOHN SKINNER
MARTINE DE MOONE
WILLIAM NAILE
THOMAS FITTS
ELIZABETH ABBITT
ALICE FITTS

At y^· Plantacōn ouer ag^t James Cittie

Capt: SAM: MATHEWS
BENIAMIN OWIN
RICE AP WILLIAMS
JIRO a Negro
WALTER PARNELL
WILLIAM PARNELL
MARGREAT ROADES
JOHN WEST
FRANCIS WEST *Vid*
THOMAS DAYHURST
ROBERT MATHEWS
ARTHUR GOULDSMITH
ROBERT WILLIAMS
MORICE LOYD
ARON CONWAY
WILLIAM SUTTON^·
RICHARD GREENE
MATHEW HAMAN
SAMWELL DAVIES
JOHN THOMAS
JOHN DOCKER
ABRAM WOOD
MICHEALL LUPWORTH
JOHN DAVIES
LEWIS BALY

23

Living	*Living*
James Daries	George Gurr
Alice Holmes	Henry Wood
Henry Barlow	John Baldwine
Thomas Button	John Needome
Edmond Whitt	William Bincks
Zacharia Crispe	Nicholas Tompson
John Burland	John Dency [*or* Deucy]
Thomas Hawkins	Erasmus Cartter
Thomas Phillips	John Edward's
Paule Reinold's	George Bayley
Nich: Smith	George Sparke
Elizabeth Williams	Nicholas Comin
Hugh Cruder	Nicholas Arras
Edward Hudson	Marttin Tvrner
Robert Sheppard	John Stone *infans*
Thomas Ottawell	Davy Mansfield
Thomas Crouch	John Denmarke
Robert Bew	Elizabeth Rutten
John Russell	Goodwife Bincks
Robert Chantry	a servant of mr Morewood's
George Rodgers	
Lanslott Damportt	*the glase howse*
John Shule	Vincencio ———
Nath: Loyd	Bernardo ———
William Sawyer	ould Sheppard his sonn
William Ward	Richard Tarborer
William Hartly	Mrs Barnardo
Jerime Whitt	
Liuetennt Purfrey	*At Archurs hdop.*
Edward Grindall	Leftennat Harris
Mr Swift	Rowland Lottis
Willian Hames*	vx Lottis

* [There is a *dot* above this word, but I fancy it is of later date than the original writing If it *be* part of the word, we must read the name as Haines.]

Living

JOHN ELISON
vx ELISON
GEORGE SANDERS
THOMAS CORDER
JOSEPH JOHNSON
GEORG PRAN
JOHN BOTTOM
THOMAS FARLY
vx FARLEY
a Child
NICHOLAS SHOTTON

At Hogg Iland

DAVID SAND^{rs} mñster [minister]
JOHN VTIE [UTIE]
Mrs VTIE
JOHN VTIE *infnas* [*infans*]
WILLIAM TYLER
ELIZABETH TYLER
RICHARD WHITBY
WILLIAM RAMSHAW
RICE WATKINS
THOMAS FOSKEW lost
HENER ELSWORD
THOMAS CAUSEY
GEORGE VNION* [UNION]
HENRY WOODWARD
ROGER WEBSTER
JOHN DOUSTON
JOSEPH JOHNSON
RICHARD CROCKER Child
WILLIAM HICHCOCKE, lost
GEORGE PROWSE
ROBERT PARRAMORE

Living

JOHN JARVICE, als, GLOVER
JOHN BROWNE
WILLIAM BURCHER
JOHN BURCHER
JOHN FULWOOD
THOMAS BRANSBY
THOMAS COLLY
THOMAS SIMPSON
THOMAS POWELL
NICHOLAS LONGE

At martins hundred

WILLIAM HARWOOD
SAMWELL MARCH
HUGH HUES
JOHN JACKSON
THOMAS WARD
JOHN STEVANS
HUMPHRY WALDEN
THOMAS DOUGHTIE
JOHN HASLEY
SAMWELL WEAVER
Vid's JACKSON
filia JACKSON
Mrs TAYLOR }
ANN WINDOR
ELIZABETH BYGRAUE
Mr LAKE
Mr BURREN
JOHN STONE
SAMWELL CULLEY·
JOHN HELLINE
vx HELLIN

---

* [I am not quite sure as to this name; it certainly *might* be read as VINON.]

Living

a french man *et vx*
THOMAS SIBERY

At Warwick Squeake

JOHN BATT
HENRY PINFFE
WASSELL WEBLIN
ANTHONY READ
FRANCES WOODSON
HENRY PHILLIPS
PETTER COLLINS
CHR: REINOLD'S
EDWARD MABIN
JOHN MALDMAN
THOMAS COLLINS
GEORGE RUSHMORE
THOMAS SPENCER
GEORGE CLARKE
RICH: BARTLETT
FRANCS̄ BANKS
JOHN JENKINS
THOMAS JONES
WILLIAM DENHAM
PETER
ANTHONY
FRANC'S   } negres
MARGRETT
JOHN BENNETT
NICHOLAS SKINNER
JOHN ATKINS
JOHN POLLENTIN
RACHELL POLLENTIN
MARGRETT POLLENTIN
MARY a maid

Living

HENRY WOODWARD
THOMAS SAWYER
THOMAS a boye

At the Indian thickett

HENRY WOODALL
GREGORY DORY
JOHN FOSTER
JOHN GREENE
JOHN WARD
CHRISTÔ: WINDMILE
RICHARD RAPIER
CUTBERT PEIRSON
ADAM RUMELL
RICHARD ROBINSON
JAMES a french mā

At Elizabeth Cittye

Cap ISACKE WHITTAKERS
MARY WHITTAKERS
CHARLES ATKINSON
CHARLES CALTHROP
JOHN LANKFEILD
BRIDG'S FREEMAN
NICHOLAS WESELL
EDWARD LOYD
THOMAS NORTH
ANTHONY MIDDLETON
RICHARD POPELY
THOMAS HARDING
WILLIAM JOY
RAPH OSBORNE
EDWARD BARNES
THOMAS THORNGOOD

Living	*Living*
ANN ATTKINSON	OSBORNE SMITH
LANKFEILD	*vx* MORE
MEDCLALFE*	*vx* WRIGHT
GEORGE NUCE	*vx* WRIGHT
ELIZABETH WHITTAKERS	*filia* WRIGHT
GEORGE ROADS	THOMAS DOWSE
EDWARD JOHNSON	SAMWELL BENNETT
WILLIAM FOULLER	WILLIAM BROWNE
REINOLD GOODWYN	WILLIAM ALLEN
JAMES LARMOUNT	LEWIS WELCHMAN
JOHN JACKSON	ROBERT MORE
vid's JOHNSON	Mrs DOWSE
vid's FOWLER	*vx* BENNETT
2 french men	*pue* { BENNETT / BENNETT
GEORGE MEDCALFE	
WALTER ELY	*At Bucke Row*
THOMAS LANE	THOMAS FLINT
BARTHELMEW HOPKINS	JOHN HAMPTON
JOHN JEFFERSON	RICHARD PEIRSBY
ROBERT THRESHER	WILLIAM ROOKINS
JOHN ROWES	ROWLAND WILLIAMS
Mr YATES	STEVEN DIXON
ROBERT GOODMAN	THOMAS RISBY
vx ELY	HENRY WHEELER
infans ELY	JAMES BROOKS
Cap RAWLEIGH CRASHAW	SAMWELL KENNELL
ROBERT WRIGHT	JOHN CARNING
JAMES SLEIGHT	THOMAS NEARES
JOHN WELCHMAN	ROBERT SALVADGE
JOHN MORE	WILLIAM BARRY
HENRY POTTER	JOSEPH HATFIELD
Mr ROSWELL	EDWARD MARSHALL
WILLIAM GAWNTLETT	AMBROSE GRIFFITH

* [Query MEDCALFE. See twelve lines below.]

Living

PETTER ARRUNDELL

ANTHONY BONALL } french men
   LA GAURD

JAMES BONALL

JOHN ARRUNDELL

JOHN HANIE [*or* HAINE]

NICH: ROW

RICHARD ALTHROP

JOHN LOYD

vx HAME*

vx HAMPTON

ELIZABETH ARRUNDELL

MARGREAT ARRUNDELL

At Basse Choise

Cap: NETHANIEL BASSE

SAMWELL BASSE

BENIAMIN SIMES

THOMAS SHEWORD

BENIAMINE HANDCLEARE

WILLIAM BARNARD

JOHN SHELLEY

NATHANIELL MOPER

NATHA: GAUMON

MARGRETT GILES

RICHARD LONGE

vx LONGE

infans LONGE

RICHARD EVANS

WILLIAM NEWMAN

JOHN ARMY

PETER LANGDEN

Living

HENRY

ANDREW RAWLEY

PETTER

more at Elizabeth Cittie

Liuetennat SHEPPARD

JOHN POWELL

JOHN WOOLFY

CATHREN POWELL

JOHN BRADSTON

FRANC'S PITTS

GILBERTT WHITFEILD

PETER HEREFORD

THOMAS FAULKNER

ESAW DE LA WARE

WILLIAM CORNIE

THOMAS CURTISE

ROBERT BRITTAINE

ROGER WALKER

HENRY KERSLEY

EDWARD MORGAINE

ANTHONY EBSWORTH

AGNES EBSWORTH

ELINOR HARRIS

THOMAS ADDISON

WILLIAM LONGE

WILLIAM SMITH

WILLIAM PINSEN

———

Cap W^M TUCKER

Cap NICH: MARTEAW

Leftennt ED: BARKLY

---

* [It is possible that a *dot* may have been omitted from this word, and that the lady's name should be read HANIE or HAINE ; she may have been wife to the man mentioned four lines above.]

Living	*Living*
DANIELL TANNER	ANN LAYDON
JOHN MORRIS	VIRGINIA LAYDON
GEORG THOMSON	ALICE LAYDON
PAULE THOMSON	KATHERNE LAYDON
WILLIAM THOMSON	WILLIAM EVANS
PASTA CHAMPIN	WILLIAM JULIAN
STEPHEN SHERE	WILLIAM KEMP
JEFFERY HALL	RICHARD WITH'E [WITHERE]
RICH: JONES	JOHN JORNALL
WILLIAM HUTCHINSON	WALTER MASON
RICHARD APLETON	SARA JULIAN
THOMAS EVANS	SARA GOULDOCKE
WESTON BROWNE	JOHN SALTER
ROBERT MOUNDAY	WILLIAM COALE
STEVEN CVLLOE	JERENY DICKENSON
RAPH ADAMS	LAWRANCE PEELE
THOMAS PHILLIPS	JOHN EVANS
FRANCIS BARRETT	MARKE EVANS
MARY TUCKER	GEORGE EVANS
JANE BRAKLEY	JOHN DOWNEMAN
ELIZABETH HIGGINS	ELIZABETH DOWNEMAN
MARY MOUNDAY	WILLIAM BALDWIN
CHOUPOUKE an Indian	JOHN SIBSEY
ANTHONY ⎱ Negres	WILLIAM CLARKE
ISSABELLA ⎰	RICE GRIFFINE
Leftennt LUPO	JOSEPH MOSLEY
PHILLIP LUPO	ROBERT SMITH
BARTHOLMEW WETHERSBY*	JOHN CHEESMAN
HENRY DRAPER	THOMAS CHEESMAN
JOSEPH HAMAN	EDWARD CHEESMAN
ELIZABETH LUPO	PETTER DICKSON
ALBIANO WETHERSLY*	JOHN BAYNAN
JOHN LAYDON	ROBERT SWEET

---

* [Sic in orig.]

Living	*Living*
JOHN PARRETT	ELIZABETH BOOTH child
WILLIAM FOUKS	Cap: THO: DAVIES
JOHN CLACKSON	JOHN DAVIES
JOHN HILL	THOMAS HUGES
WILLIAM MORTEN	WILLIAM KILDRIDGE
WILLIAM CLARKE	ALEXAND^R MOUNTNEY
EDWARD STOCKDELL	EDWARD BRYAN
ELIZABETH BAYNAM	PERSIVALL IBOTSON
GEORGE DAVIES	JOHN PENRICE
ELIZABETH DAVIES	ROBERT LOCKE
ANN HARRISON	ELIZABETH IBOTSON
JOHN CURTISE	ANN IBOTSON
JOHN WALTON	EDWARD HILL
EDWARD ASTON	THOMAS BEST
TOBY HURT	HANNA HILL
CORNELIUS MAY	ELIZABETH HILL
ELIZABETH MAY	ROBERT SALFORD
HENRY MAY. child	JOHN SALFORD
THOMAS WILLOWBEY	PHILLIP CHAPMAN
OLIUER JENKINSON	THOMAS PARTER
JOHN CHANDELER	MARY SALFORD
NICHOLAS DAVIES	FRANCIS CHAMBERLIN
JONE JENKINS	WILLIAM HILL
MARY JENKINS	WILLIAM HARRIS
HENRY GOULDWELL	WILLIAM WORLIDGE
HENRY PRICHARD	JOHN FORTH
HENRY BARBER	THOMAS SPILMAN
ANN BARBER	REBECCA CHAMBERLIN
JOHN HUTTON	ALICE HARRIS
ELIZABETH HUTTON	PHAROW PHLINTON
THOMAS BALDWIN	ARTHUR SMITH
JOHN BILLIARD	HUGH HALL
REYNOLD BOOTH	ROBERT SABIN
MARY	JOHN COOKER

Living	*Living*
HUGH DICKEN	WILLIAM WATTERS
WILLIAM GAYNE	WILLIAM GANEY
RICHARD MINTREN Junior	HENRY GANEY
JOANE FLINTON	JOHN ROBINSON
ELIZABETH FLINTON	ROBERT BROWNE
REBECCA COUBBER	THOMAS PARRISH
RICHARD MINTREN senior	EDMOND SPALDEN
JOHN FRYE	ROGER FARBRACKE
WILLIAM BROOKS	THEODER JONES
SIBILE BROOKS	WILLIAM BALDWIN
WILLIAM BROOKS	LUKE ADEN
THOMAS CRISPE	ANNA GANY
RICHARD PACKE	ANNA GANY *fillia*
MILES PRICHETT	ELIZABETH POPE
THOMAS GODBY	REBECCA HATCH
MARGERY PRICHETT	THOMASIN LOXMORE
JONE GOODBY	THOMAS GARNETT
JONE GRINDRY	ELIZABETH GARNETT
JOHN JUIMAN	SUSSAN GARNETT
MARY GRINDRY	FRANCES MICHELL
JOHN GRINDRY child	JONAS STOCKTON
JOHN WAINE	THIMOTHEE STOCKTON
ANN WAINE	WILLIAM COOKE
MARY ACKLAND	RICHARD BOULTEN
GEORGE ACKLAND	FRANCES HILL
JOHN HARLOW	JOHN JACKSON
WILLIAM CAPP'S	RICHARD DAVIES
EDWARD WATTERS	ANN COOKE
PAULE HARWOOD	DICTRAS CHRISMUS
NICH: BROWNE	THOMAS HILL
ADAM THROUGOOD	ARTHUR DAVIES
RICHARD EAST	WILLIAM NEWCOME
STEPHEN READ	ELIZABETH CHRISMUS
GRACE WATTERS	JOANE DAVIES

24

Living	*Living*
THOMAS HETHERSALL	THOMAS CORNISH
WILLIAM DOUGLAS	JOHN FISHER
THOMAS DOUTHORN	WILLIAM DRY
ELIZABETH DOUTHORN	HENRY WILSON
SAMWELL DOUTHORN a bo[y]	PETTER PORTER
THOMAS an Indian	CHRISTO: CARTTER
JOHN HAZARD	JOHN SUM̄FILL
JOANE HAZARD	NICHOLAS GRAUNGER
HENRY	JAMES vocat PIPER
FRANCES MASON	EDWARD
MICHEALL WILCOCKS	JOHN
WILLIAM QUERKE	THOMAS
MARY MASON	GEORGE
MAUDLIN WILCOCKS	CHARLES FARMER
Mr KETH mīster	JAMES KNOTT
JOHN BUSH	JOHN ASCOMB
JOHN COOp [COOPER]	ROBERT FENNELL
JONADAB ILLETT	PHILLIP
JOHN BARNABY	DANIELL COGLEY
JOHN SEAWARD	WILLIAM ANDREWS
ROBERT NEWMAN	THOMAS GRAUES
WILLIAM PARKER	JOHN WILCOCKS
THOMAS SNAPP	THOMAS CRAMPE
CLEMENT EVANS	WILLIAM COOMES
THOMAS SPILMAN	JOHN PARSONS
THOMAS PARRISH	JOHN ÇOOMES
	JAMES CHAMBERS
At the Eastern Shore	ROBERTT BALL
Cap WILLIAM EPPS	GOODWIFE BALL
Mrs EPPS	THOMAS HALL
PETTER EPPS	ISMALE HILLS
WILLIAM —	JOHN TYERS
EDMOND CLOAKE	WALTER SCOTT
WILLIAM BIBBY	GOODWIFE SCOTT

Living	*Living*
ROBERT EDMOND'S	WILLIAM SMITH
THOMAS HICHCOCKE	EDWARD DREW
JOHN EVANS	NICHOLAS HOSKINS
HENRY WATTKINS	and his Child
PEREGREE WATTKINS	WILLIAM WILLIAMS
DANIELL WATTKINS	Mrs WILLIAMS
JOHN BLOWER	JOHN THROGMORTON
GODY BLOWER	BENNANINE* KNIGHT
JOHN	CHAD GUNSTON
a boy of Mr CANS [*or* CAUS]	ABRAM ANALIN [*or* AUALIN,
JOHN HOW	*i.e.* AVALIN]
JOHN BUTTERFEILD	THOMAS BLACKLOCKE
WILLIAM DAVIES	JOHN BARNETT
PETTER LONGMAN	THOMAS SAVADGE
JOHN WILKINS	WILLIAM BEANE
GOODWIFE WILKINS	SALOMAN GREENE
THOMAS POWELL	JOHN WASBORNE
GODY POWELL	WILLIAM OUILLS.
THOMAS PARKE	

* [Evidently a misspelling for BENJAMINE.]

A List of the names of the Dead in Virgnᵃ since Aprill last

february 16: 1623

Colledg

JOHN WOOD
WILLIAM MORE
THOMAS NAYLOR   }kild
JOHN HUNTER
JAMES HOWELL

WILLIAM LAMBERTT

At the neck of land

MOSES CONYERS
GEORGE GRIMES
WILLIAM CLEMENTS
THOMAS FERNLEY kid [killed]
EDWARD —

At Jurdains Jorney

ROGER MUCH
MARY REEFE
ROBERT WINTER
ROBERT WOOD'S
RICHARD SHREIFE
THOMAS BULL
JOHN KINTON
DANIELL —

At west and Sherlow hundred

SAMWELL FOREMAN
ZOROBABELL

2 Indians
one Negar
THOMAS ROBERTS
JOHN EDMONDS
JOHN LASEY
DANIELL FRANCKE
Cap: NATH WEST
CHRISTOPHER HARDING kild

At flower de hundred

JOHN MAYOR
WILLIAM WAYCOME
THOMAS PRISE
ROBERT WALKIN
JOHN FETHERSTON
JOHN AP ROBERTS
RICHARD JONES
RICHARD GRIFFIN
RICHARD RANKE [*or* RAUKE]
WILLIAM EDGER
JOHN FRY
DIXI CARPENTER
WILLIAM SMITH
JAMES CINDUARE*
EDWARD TEMPLE
SARA SALFORD

---

* [Spelling not very clear; *may* be read CINDNAKE or CINDVARE.]

Dead	*Dead*
JOHN STANSON	ROBERT RAFFE
CHRISTO: EVANS	AMBROSE FRESEY
	HENRY FRY
At James Cittie	JOHN DINSE
Mʳ SOTHEY	THOMAS TINDALL
JOHN DUMPONT	RICHARD KNIGHT*
THOMAS BROWNE	JOHN JEFFEREYS*
HENRY SOTHEY	JOHN HAMUN*
THOMAS SOTHEY	JOHN MERIDIEN*
MARY SOTHEY	JOHN COUNTWANE*
ELIZABETH SOTHEY	THOMAS GUINE [*or* GUNIE]*
THOMAS CLARKE	THOMAS SOMERSALL
MARGRETT SHRAWLEY	WILLIAM ROWSLEY
RICHARD WALKER	ELIZABETH ROWSLEY
VALLENTYN GENTLER	a maid of thers
PETTER BRISHITT	ROBERT BENNETT
HUMPHRY BOYSE	THOMAS ROPER
JOHN WATTON	Mʳ FITZIEFFERYS
ARTHUR EDWARD'S	Mʳˢ SMITH
THOMAS FISHER	PETTER MARTTIN
WILLIAM SPENCE ⎫ lost	JAMES JAKINS
Mʳˢ SPENCE ⎭	Mʳ CRAPPLACE
GEORGE SHARKS	JOHN LULLETT
JOHN BUTH	ANN DIXON
Mʳ COLLINS	WILLIAM HOWLETT
vx	Mʳ FURLOWˢ child
Mʳ PEGDEN	JACOB PROPHETT.
PETTER DE MAINE	JOHN REDING
GOODMAN ASCOMB	RICHARD ATKINS his child
GOODMAN WITTS	JOHN BAYLY
WILLIAM KERTON	WILLIAM JONES his sʳvant
Mʳ ATKINS	JOHN Mʳ PEARNS servant
THOMAS HAKES	JOSIAS HARTT
PETTER GOULD	JUDITH SHARP

* [See next page, where these names are repeated.]

Dead

Ann Ouaile
   Reignold's
William Dier
Mary Dier
Thomas Sexton
Mary Bawdrye
Edward Normansell
Henry Fell
     Enims [*or* Euims]
Roger Turnor
Thomas Guine [*or* Gunie]*
John Countway*
John Meriday*
Beniamine Vsher†
John Haman*
John Jefferyes*
Richard Knight*
John Walker
     Hosier
William Jackson
William Apleby
John Manby
Arthur Cooke
Stephen —

At ye Plantacōn ouer against
James Cittie

Humphry Clough
Morris Chaloner
Samwell Betton
John Gruffin
William Edwards
William Salsbury

Dead

Mathew Griffine
Robert Adward's
John Jones
Thomas Prichard
Thomas Morgaine
Thomas Biggs
Nicholas Bushell
Robert Williams
Robert Reynold's
Edward Huies
Thomas Foulke
Nathew Jenings
Richard Morris
Frances Barke
John Ewins†
Samwell Fisher
John Ewis
James Cartter
Edward Fletcher
Aderton Greene
Morice Baker
Robert Mr Ewins man
Robert Pidgion
Thomas Triggs
James Thursby
Nicholas Thimbleby
Frances Millett
John Hooks
Thomas Lawson
William Miller
Nicholas Fatrice
John Champ
John Maning

---

* [It will be noticed that these names, although in some cases with different spellings, are given above (see previous page).]   † [Repeated on next page.]

Dead

RICHARD EDMONDS
DAVID COLLINS
THOMAS GUINE [*or* GUNIE]*
JOHN VICARS
JOHN MERIDIE*
BENY VSHER*
JOHN CANTWELL
RICHARD KNIGHT*
ROBERT HELLUE
THOMAS BARROW
JOHN EUINES*
EDWARD PRICE
ROBERT TAYLOR
RICHARD BUTTEREY
MARY LACON
ROBERT BAINES

JOSEPH ARCHER
THOMAS MASON
JOHN BEMAN
CHRISTO: PITTMAN
THOMAS WILLER
SAMWELL FULSHAW
JOHN WAMSLEY
ABRAM COLMAN
JOHN HODGES
NAAMY BOYLE

At Hog̃ Iland
WILLIAM BRAKLEY
PETTER DUN
JOHN LONG

At martins hundfed
HENRY BAGFORD
NICHOLAS GLEADSTON

Dead

NICHOLAS DORINGTON
RAPH ROGERS
RICHARD FRETHRAM
JOHN BROGDEN
JOHN BEANAM
FRANCES ATKINSON
ROBERT ATKINSON
JOHN KERILL
EDWARD DAVIES
PERCIVALL MAN
MATHEW STAUELING
THOMAS NICHOLLS
2 Childrens of yᵉ french men
JOHN PATTISON
vx PATTISON } kild
EDWARD WINDOR
THOMAS HORNER
JOHN WALKER
THOMAS POPE
RICHARD STON
JOHN CATESBY
RICHARD STEPHENS
WILLIAM HARRIS
CHRISTOPHER WOODWARD
JOSEPH TURNER

At Warwicke Squeak
JOSIAS COLLINS
CLEMENT WILSON
WILLIAM ROBINSON
CHR: RAWSON
THOMAS WINSLOW
vx WINSLOW
infans WINSLOW

* [Again repetitions. See previous page.]

Dead	*Dead*
ALEXANDER SUSSAMES	JAMES COLLIS
THOMAS PRICKETT	RAPH ROCKLY
THOMAS MADDOX	WILLIAM GEALES
JOHN GREENE	GEORGE JONES
NATHANEL STANBRIDG	ANDREW ALLINSON
JOHN LITTON	WILLIAM DOWNES
CHRISTO: ASH	RICHARD GILLETT
vx ASH	GOODWIFE NONN [*or* NOUN]
infans ASH	HUGO SMALE
NETHANIEL LAME [*or* LAINE] } kild	THOMAS WINTERSALL
JANE FISHER	JOHN WRIGHT
PHILLIP JONES	JAMES FENTON
EDWARD BANKS	CISELY a Maid
JOHN SYMONS	JOHN GAVETT
THOMAS SMITH	JAMES } Irishmen
THOMAS GRIFFIN	JOHN
GEORGE CANE	
ROBERT WHITT	JOCKY ARMESTRONGE
SYMON an Italian	WOLSTON PELSANT
	SAMPSON PELSANT
At Elizabeth Cittie	CATHRIN CAPPS
CHARLE MARSHALL	WILLIAM ELBRIDG
WILLIAM HOPKICKE	JOHN SANDERSON
DORITHIE PARKINSON	JOHN BENBRICKE
WILLIAM ROBERTTS	JOHN BAKER kild
JOHN FARRAR	WILLIAM LUPO
MARTIN CUFFE	TIMOTHY BURLEY
THOMAS HALL	MARGERY FRISLE
THOMAS SMITH	HENRY WEST
CHRISTOPH' ROBERTTS	JASPER TAYLER
THOMAS BROWNE	BRIGETT SEARLE
HENRY FEARNE	ANTHONY ANDREW
THOMAS PARKINS	EDMOND CARTTER
Mr HUSSY	THOMAS ———

Dead	*Dead*
WILLIAM GAUNTLETT	INNOCENT POORE
GILBERT —— kild	EDWARD DUPPER
CHRISTO: Welchman	ELIZABETH DAVIES
JOHN HILLIARD*	THOMAS BUWEN
GREGORY HILLIARD	ANN BARBER
JOHN HILLIARD*	WILLIAM LUCOTT
WILLIAM RICHARDS	NICHOLAS —— kild
ELIZABETH a maid	HENRY BRIDGES
Cap: HITCHCOCKE	HENRY PAYTON
THOMAS KENINSTON	RICHARD GRIFFIN
Cap: LINCOLNE	RAPHE HARRISON
CHAD: GULSTONS	SAMWELL HARVIE
vx GULSTONS	JOHN BOX
infans GULSTONS	BENIANINE BOX
GEORGE COOKE	THOMAS servant
RICHARD GOODCHILD	FRANCES CHAMBERLINE
CHRISMUS his child	BRIDGETT DAMERON.
ELIZABETH MASON	ISARELL KNOWLES
SYMON WITH	EDWARD BENDIGE
WHITNEY GUY	WILLIAM DAVIES
THOMAS BRODBANKE	JOHN PHILLIPS
WILLIAM BURNHOUSE	DANIELL SAUEWELL
JOHN SPARKS	——
ROBERT MORGAINE]	WILLIAM JONES
JOHN LOCKE	ROBERT BALLS wife
WILLIAM THOMPSON	ROBERT LEAUER
THOMAS FULHAM	HUCH NICHCOTT
CUTBERD BROOKS	JOHN ‚KNIGHT.

* [Sic in orig.]

UT of the Ship cald the *Furtherance*

JOHN WALKER	JOHN MANBY
HOSIER	ARTHUR COOKE
WILLIAM JACKSON	STEVEN
WILLIAM APLEBY	

UT of the *Gods gift*

Mr CLARE master
WILLIAM BENNETT

UT of the *Margrett and John.*

Mr LANGLEY
Mr WRIGHT
the gunner of the *William and John.*

[1621? *Promise of certain "WALLOONS and FRENCH" to Emigrate to VIRGINIA.*]

[IN the centre of a large sheet of paper is written in French, " *We promise my Lord Ambassador of the Most Serene King of Great Britain to go and inhabit in Virginia, a land under His Majesty's obedience, as soon as conveniently may be, and this under the conditions to be carried out in the articles we have communicated to the said Ambassador, and not otherwise, on the faith of which we have unanimously signed this present with our sign manual."*

[The signatures and the calling of each are appended in the form of a round robin, and in an outer circle the person signing states whether he is married, and the number of his children. *Endorsed by Sir Dudley Carleton,* " Signature of such Wallons and French as offer themselfs to goe into Verginia." The names with an * have only signed their marks. Total 227, including 55 men, 41 women, 129 children, and two servants. As stated above, the original document is in French. The version here given has the authority of Mr. Sainsbury, of Her Majesty's Public Record Office. *The signatures are very indistinctly written.*]*

MOUSNIER DE LA MONTAGNE, medical student ; marrying man.
MOUSNIER DE LA MONTAGNE, apothecary and surgeon ; marrying man.
JACQUE CONNE, tiller of the earth ; wife and two children.

---

* [The Answer of the Virginia Company is dated Aug. 11, 1621, and a contemporary copy is preserved in the State Paper Department of Her Majesty's Public Record Office. It is signed by JOHN FERRAR, Deputy. The substance is to the effect that the Company do not conceive any inconvenience, provided the number does not exceed 300, and they take the oath of allegiance to the King and conform to the rules of government established in the Church of England. Cannot recommend the King to aid them with shipping ; the exhausted stock of the Company prevents them from affording any help. Land will be granted to them in convenient numbers in the principal cities, boroughs, and corporations in Virginia.]

Henry Lambert, woollen draper ; wife.

*George Béava, porter ; wife and one child.

Michel Du Pon, hatter ; wife and two children.

Jan Bullt, labourer ; wife and four children.

Paul de Pasar, weaver ; wife and two children.

Antoine Grenier, gardener ; wife.

Jean Gourdeman, labourer ; wife and five children.

Jean Campion, wool carder ; wife and four children.

*Jan De la Met, labourer ; young man.

*Antoine Martin ; wife and one child.

François Fourdrin, leather dresser ; young man.

*Jan Leca, labourer ; wife and five children.

Theodore Dufour, draper ; wife and two children.

*Gillain Broque, labourer ; young man.

George Wautre, musician ; wife and four children.

*Jan Sage, serge maker ; wife and six children.

*Marie Flit, in the name of her husband, a miller ; wife and two
    children.

P. Gantois, student in theology ; young man.

Jacques de Lecheilles, brewer ; marrying man.

*Jan Le Rou, printer ; wife and six children.

*Jan de Croy, sawyer ; wife and five children.

*Charles Chancy, labourer ; wife and two children.

*François Clitdeu, labourer ; wife and five children.

*Philippe Campion, draper ; wife and one child.

*Robert Broque, labourer ; young man.

Philippe De le Mer, carpenter ; young man.

*Jeanne Martin ; young girl.

Pierre Cornille, vine dresser ; young man.

Jan de Carpentry, labourer ; wife and two children.

*Martin de Carpentier, brass founder ; young man.

Thomas Farnarcque, locksmith ; wife and seven children.

Pierre Gaspar.

*Gregoire Le Jeune, shoemaker ; wife and four children.

Martin Framerie, musician ; wife and one child.

PIERRE QUESNÉE, brewer; marrying man.

PONTUS LE GEAN, bolting-cloth weaver; wife and three children.

*BARTHELEMY DIGAUD, sawyer; wife and eight children.

JESSE DE FOREST, dyer; wife and five children.

*NICOLAS DE LE MARLIER, dyer; wife and two children.

*JAN DAMONT, labourer; wife.

*JAN GILLE, labourer; wife and three children.

*JAN DE TROU, wool carder; wife and five children.

PHILIPPE MATON, dyer, and two servants; wife and five children.

ANTHOINE DE LIELATE, vinedresser; wife and four children.

ERNOU CATOIR, wool carder; wife and five children.

ANTHOIN DESENDRE, labourer; wife and one child.

ABEL DE CREPY, shuttle worker; wife and four children.

*ADRIAN BARBE, dyer; wife and four children.

*MICHEL LEUSIER, cloth weaver; wife and one child.

*JEROME LE ROY, cloth weaver; wife and four children.

*CLAUDE GHISELIN, tailor; young man.

*JAN DE CRENNE, glass maker? [fritteur]; wife and one child.

*LOUIS BROQUE, labourer; wife and two children.

[MUSTERS

OF THE

INHABITANTS IN VIRGINIA.

162$\frac{4}{5}$.]

[MUSTERS

INHABITANTS IN VIRGINIA.

1624/5.]

Colledg
Land
Henrico **T**HE MUSTER of the Inhabitant's of the Colledge: Land in Virginia taken the 23th of January 1624.

Liuetennt THOMAS OSBORNE arived in the *Bona Nova* November 1619

Servant's

DANIELL SHERLEY aged 30 yeres came in the *Bona Nova* 1619

PEETER JORDEN aged 22 in the *London Marchannt* 1620

RICHARD DAVIS aged 16 yeres in the *Jonathan* 1620*

ROBERT LAPWORTH came in the *Abigaile*

JOHN WATSON came in the *William & Thomas*

EDWARD HOBSON came in the *Bona Nova* 1619

CHRISTOPHER BRANCH came in the *London Marchannt*

MARY his wife in the same Shipp

THOMAS his sonne aged 9 Month's

WILLIAM BROWINGE came in the *Bona Nova*

MATHEW EDLOW came in the *Neptune* 1618

WILLIAM WELDON came in the *Bona Nova* 1619

---

* [The *short rules* here and hereafter in these "Musters," indicate the emission of lists of the stores brought by passengers, given in the original, but omitted here as of no general interest.]

Colledge Land.

FRANCIS WILTON came in the *Jonathan*

EZEKIAH RAUGHTON came in the *Bona Nova*.
MARGRETT his wife in the *Warwick*.

WILLIAM PRICE came in the *Starr*

ROBERT CAMPION came in the *Bona Nova*

LEONARD MOORE came in the *Bona Nova*

THOMAS BAUGH came in the *Supply*

THOMAS PARKER came in the *Neptune*

THEODER MOYSES came in the *London Marchannt*

Neck-of-Land.
Corporation of
Charles Citty.

The MUSTER of the Inhabitant's of the Neck-of-Land in the Corporation of Charles Cittie in Virginia taken the 24th of January 1624.

LUKE BOYSE aged 44 yeares arived in the *Edwine* in May 1619
ALLICE his wife arived in the *Bona-Noua* in Aprill 1622
Servant's
ROBERT HOLLAM aged 23 yeares in the *Bonaventure* August 1620
JOSEPH ROYALL aged 22 yeares in the *Charitie* July 1622

The MUSTER of JOSUAH CHARD

JOSUAII CHARD aged 36 yeares in the *Seaventure* May 1607
ANN his wife aged 33 yeares in the *Bony besse* August 1623

The MUSTER of JOHN DOD's

JOHN DOD's aged 36 yeares in the *Susan Constant* Aprill 1607
JANE his wife aged 40 yeares

The MUSTER of WILLIAM VINCENE

WILLIAM VINCENE aged 39 yeares in the *Mary & James*
JOANE his wife aged 42 yeares

Neck-of-Land
Charles Cittie

The MUSTER of Thomas Harris

Thomas Harris aged 38 yeares in the *Prosperous* in May
Adria his wife aged 23 yeares in the *Marmaduke* in November 1621
Ann Woodlase theire kinswoman aged 7 yeares

Servant's
Elizabeth   aged 15 yeares in the *Margrett & John* 1620

The MUSTER of John Price

John Price aged 40 yeares in the *Starr* in May
Ann his wife aged 21 yeares in the *Francis Bonaventure* August 1620
Mary a Child aged 3 Months

The MUSTER of Hugh Hilton.

Hugh Hilton aged 36 yeares in the *Edwine* in May 1619

The MUSTER of Richard Taylo{r}

Richard Taylor aged 50 yeares in the *Mary Margrett* September 1608
Dorothy his wife aged 21 yeares in the *London Marchannt* May 1620
Mary theire Child aged 3 months.
Servant's
Christopher Browne aged 18 yeares in the *Dutie* in May 1620

The MUSTER of Thomas Oage

Thomas Oage aged 40 yeares in the *Starr* in May
Ann his wife in the *Neptune* in August 1618
Edward theire sonn aged 2 yeares,

The MUSTER of ROBERT GREENLEAFE

ROBERT GREENLEAFE aged 43 yeres in the *Tryall* August 1610
SUSAN his wife aged 23 yeres in the *Jonathan* May 1620
THOMAS theire sonn aged 3 yeres
ANN a daughter aged 22 week's

The MUSTER of HENERY COLTMAN

HENERY COLTMAN aged 30 yeres in the *Noah* August 1610
ANN his wife aged 26 yeres in the *London Marchannt* May 1620

The MUSTER of HUGH PRICE

HUGH PRICE aged 35 years in the *William & John* January 1618
JUDITH his wife aged 24 yeres in the *Marygold* May 1619
JOHN his sonn aged 2 yeres.

The MUSTER of THOMAS FARMER

THOMAS FARMER aged 30 yeres in the *Tryall* 1616

The MUSTER of THOMAS SHEPPEY

THOMAS SHEPPEY aged 22 yeres in the *Supply* January 1620

The MUSTER of ALLEXANDER BRADWAY

ALLEXANDER BRADWAY aged 31 yeres in the *Supply* January 1620
SISLEY his wife aged 28 yeres in the *Jonathan* May 1620
ADRIA theire daughter aged 9 Months.

Neck-of-Land.
Charles Cittie
The MUSTER of William Sharp

WILLIAM SHARP aged 40 yeres in the *Starr* in May
ELIZABETH his wife aged 25 yeres in the *Bonaventure* August 1620
ISACK his sonn aged 2 yeres
SAMUELL his sonn aged 2 Months
Servant's

RICHARD VAUSE aged 20 yeres in the *Jonathan* May 1620

West & Sherley
hundred.
Charles Cittie
The MUSTER of the Inhabitant's of West and Sherley Hundred taken the 22th of January 1624.

RICHARD BIGG's his MUSTER

RICHARD BIGG'S aged 41 yeres arived in the *Swann* in August 1610
SARAH his wife aged 35 yeres in the *Marygold* May 1618
RICHARD theire Sonn aged 3 yeres
THOMAS TURNER his Cozen aged 11 yeres in y^e *Marygold* 1616
SUSAN OLD his Cozen aged 10 yeres in the *Marygold* 1616
Servant's

JAMES GUY aged 20 yeares in the *Marygold* 1622
WILLIAM BROCK aged 26 yeres in the *Margrett* in May 1622
EDWARD TEMPLE age 20 yeres in the *Margrett* May 1622
MARY PEETERS aged 16 yeres in the *London Marchant* May 1620

WILLIAM BAYLEYS MUSTER

WILLIAM BALEY aged 41 yeares in the *Prosperous* in May 1610
MARY his wife aged 24 yeres in the *George* 1617
THOMAS his Sonn aged 4 yeares

West &
Sherley
hundred.

ROBERT PARTINS MUSTER

ROBERT PARTIN aged 36 yeares in the *Blessinge* in June 1609
MARGRETT his wife aged 36 in the *George* 1617

ROBERT ⎫   ⎧ aged 4 Months.
AVIS   ⎬ theire Children ⎨ aged 5 yeares.
REBECCA ⎭   ⎩ aged 2 yeares.

Servant's

THOMAS HALE aged 20 yeares in the *George* 1623 in October
ELLIN COOKE aged 25 yeares in the *London Marchannt* June 1620

CHRISTOPHER WOODWARD'S MUSTER

CHRISTOPHER WOODWARD aged 30 yeares in the *Tryall* in June 1620

JOHN HIGGINS ⎫ his ptn's ⎧ aged 21 yeres in the *George* 1616
RICE HOWE   ⎭   ⎩ aged 26 yeres in the *Gifte* 1618

Servant's

MATHEW GLOSTER aged 20 yeres in the *Warwick* 1621
WILLIAM TOTLE aged 18 yeres in the *George* 1623
JOHN CANON aged 20 yeres in the *Abigaile* 1622

The MUSTER of AMIAS BOLTE]

AMIAS BOLTE aged 23 yeares in the *Neptune* in August 1618

The MUSTER of JOHN COLLINS

JOHN COLLINS aged 30 yeares in the *Suply* 1620
SUSAN his wife aged 40 yeres in the *Treasuror* 1613
ANN VSHER aged 8 yeares born heare

West &
Sherley
hundred.

The MUSTER of HENERY BENSON

HENERY BENSON aged 40 yeares in the *Francis Bonaventure* August
1620
NICHOLAS BLACKMAN his ptner aged 40 in the same Shipp

West & Sherley
hundred.
Charles Cittie

m' THOMAS PAWLETT's MUSTER

THOMAS PAWLETT aged 40 yeares in the *Neptune* in August 1618

Servant's

JOHN TRUSSELL aged 19 yeres in the *Southampton* 1622

The MUSTER of WILLIAM ASKEW

WILLIAM ASKEW aged 30 yeres in the *Prosperous* in May 1610

The MUSTER of REBECCA ROSE Widdow

REBECCA ROSE aged 50 yeares in the *Marygold* in May 1619
MARMADUKE HILL } Children { aged 11 yeres } in the same Shipp
JANE HILL } { aged 14 yeres }

The MUSTER of m's MARY MADDISON Widdow

MARY MADDISON aged 30 yeares in the *Treasuror* 1618
KATHERIN LAYDEN a Child. aged 7 yeares

Servant's

JAMES WATSON aged 20 yeares in the *George* 1623
ROGER LEWES aged 19 yeares in the *Edwin* in May 1617

West & Sherley
hundred.
Charles Cittie

The MUSTER of ROBERT* BAGWELL $\rho^{\bar{c}}$

HENERY* BAGWELL aged 35 yeares in the *Deliuerance* 1608
SYMON TURGIS aged 30 yeares in the *William & Thomas* 1618

Servant's

RANDALL BAWDE aged 30 ycares in the *Due Returne* 1623
CHARLES   aged 19 ycares in the *Jacob* 1624

Sherley hundred.
Charles Cittie

The MUSTER of ROBERT MILNER $\rho^{\bar{c}}$

ROBERT MILNER aged 24 yeares in the *Francis Bonaventure* August 1620
JOHN PASSEMAN aged 29 yeres in the *Jonathan* May 1620
JENKIN OSBORN aged 24 yeres in the *George* 1617
WILLIAM WESTON aged 25 yeres in the *Jonathan* May 1620

The MUSTER of JOHN THROGMORTON $\rho^{\bar{c}}$.

JOHN THROGMORTON aged 24 yeares in ye *William & Thomas* 1618
CHYNA BOYSE aged 26 yeres in the *Georg* in May 1617

Servant's

EDWARD SPARSHOTT aged 31 ycares in the *Scafloure* 1621
FRANCIS DOWNING aged 24 yeres in the *Returne* March 1624
ELLIS RIPPING aged 23 yeares in the *Returne* 1624

The MUSTER of ROGER RATLIFE

ROGER RATLIFE aged 44 yeares in the *Georg* in May 1619
ANN his wife aged 40 in the *George* in May 1619
ISACK his Sonn aged 9 Months

* [So in the original. It will have been observed, that generally the name in the *heading* is the same as the first name in the list.]

Sherley hundred.
Charles Cittie

The MUSTER of NATHANIELL TATAM

NATHANIELL TATAM aged 20 yeares in the *George* May 1619

The MUSTER of m.'s KATHERINE BENETT Widdow

KATHERINE BENETT aged 24 yeres in the *Abigall* 1622
WILLIAM BENETT her sonn aged 3 week's

Servant's

RANDALL CREW aged 20 yeres in the *Charles* 1621

DEAD at WEST & SHERLEY. and at SHERLEY HUNDRED. 1624.

ANDREW DUDLEY, came in the *Trueloue* 1622
RAPH FREEMAN. in the *Margett and John* 1622
m' WILLIAM BENET Minister in the *Seafloure* 1621
Capt ISACK MADDESON
JAMES CROWDER in the *Returne* 1623
DANIELL VIERO in the *George* 1623
BARNARD JACKSON in the *Margrett & John* 1623
THOMAS WESTON in the *George* 1623
JAMES ROLFE Liuetennt GIBB'S Man ⎫
JOHN MICHAELL   ⎬ slaine by the Indians.
FRANCIS   Capt MADISONS Man.   ⎭

Jordans
Jorney.
Charles
Cittie

The MUSTER of the Inhabitant's of JORDANS JORNEY taken the 21th of January 1624

The MUSTER of m' WILLIAM FERRAR & m's JORDAN

WILLIAM FERRAR aged 31 yeares in the *Neptune* in August 1618
SISLEY JORDAN aged 24 yeres in the *Swan* in August 1610

27

Jordans Jorney.
  Charles Cittie

MARY JORDAN her daughter aged 3 yeares ⎫
MARGRETT JORDAN aged 1 yeare   ⎬ borne heare.
TEMPERANCE BALEY aged 7 yeares   ⎭

Servant's

WILLIAM DAWSON aged 25 yeres in the *Discouery* March 1621
ROBERT TURNER aged 26 yeres in the *Tryall* June 1619
JOHN HELY aged 24 yeares in the *Charles* November 1621
ROGER PRESTON aged 21 yeares in the *Discouerie* March 1621
ROBERT MANUELL aged 25 yeres in the *Charles* November 1621
THOMAS WILLIAMS aged 24 yeares in the *Dutie* May 1618
RICHARD JOHNSON aged 22 yeares in the *Southampton* 1622
WILLIAM HATFEILD aged   in the *Southampton* 1622
JOHN PEAD 35 yeares old in the same Shipp
JOHN FREAME aged 16 yeares in the same Shipp

The MUSTER of THOMAS PALMER

THOMAS PALMER arived in the *Tyger* November 1621
JOANE his wife in the same Shipp
PRISILLA her daughter aged xj yeares

Servant's

RICHARD ENGLISH aged xj yeares in the *James* 1622

The MUSTER of ROBERT FISHER

ROBERT FISHER arived in the *Elsabeth* May 1611
KATHERINE his wife in the *Marmaduk* October 1621
SISLY theire daughter aged 1 yeare

Servant's

IDYE HALLIERS a Maid servant aged 30 yeares in ye *Jonathan* 1619

Jordans Jorney
Charles Cittie

The MUSTER of JOHN CLAYE

JOHN CLAYE arived in the *Treasuror* February 1613
ANN his wife in the *Ann* August 1623

Servant's

WILLIAM NICHOLL'S aged 26 yeres in the *Dutie* in May 1619

The MUSTER of CHRISTOPHER SAFFORD

CHRISTOPHER SAFFORD arived in the *Treasuror* 1613
JOHN GIBB'S his ptner in the *Supply* 1619

Servant's

HENERY LANE aged 20 yeres in the *Southampton* 1623

The MUSTER of HENERY WILLIAMS

HENERY WILLIAMS arived in the *Treasuror* 1613
SUSAN his wife in the *William & Thomas* 1618

The MUSTER of WILLIAM BRANLIN

WILLIAM BRANLIN arived in the *Margrett & John* 1620
ANN his wife in the *Trueloue* 1622

The MUSTER of JOHN FLUDD

JOHN FLUDD arived in the *Swan* 1610
MARGETT his wife in the *Supply* 1620
FRANCES FINCH her daughter in the *Suply* 1620
WILLIAM FLUDD his sonn aged 3 week's.

The MUSTER of THOMAS CHAPMAN*

THOMAS CHAPMAN arived in the *Tryall* 1610
ANN his wife in the *George* 1617
THOMAS his sonn aged 2 yeare
ANN theire daughter aged 6 week's

The MUSTER of JOSEPH BULL

JOSEPH BULL arived in the *Abigaile* 1622

The MUSTER of JOHN DAVIES &c.

JOHN DAVIES arived in the *George* 1617
WILLIAM EMERSON his ptner in the *Sampson* 1618

Servant's
WILLIAM POPLETON aged   in the *James* 1622
EUSTICE DOWNES aged 25 yeares in the *Abigall* 1622

The MUSTER of THOMAS CAWSEY.

THOMAS CAWSEY arived in the *Francis Bonaventure* 1620

The MUSTER of THOMAS IRONMONGER

THOMAS IRONMONGER arived in the

The MUSTER of RICHARD MILTON

RICHARD MILTON arived in the *Suply* 1620

* [The fifth letter of this name is not clear; the word begins with an ascending letter, and *might* be read as CHAPLAIN; but it is certainly CHAPMAN in the next line.]

Jordans Jorney.
Charles Cittie   The MUSTER of Nathaniell Cawsey

Nathaniell Cawsey arived in the *Phœnix* 1607
Thomasine his wife in the *Lyon* 1609

Servant's

Edward Denison aged 22 yeares ⎱ arived in the *Trueloue* 1623
James Bonner aged 20 yeares ⎰
James Dore age 19 ycares in the *Bona Nova* 1621
Laurance Evans aged 15 yeares in the *James* 1622
Joane Winscomb aged 20 yeares in the *George* 1618

DEAD at Jordans Jorney 1624

Lidia Sherley came in the *George* 1623
Susan Sherley an Infant.

Chaplains
Choise.   The MUSTER of the Inhabitant's of Chaplains
Charles   Choyse and the *Trueloues* Company taken the
Cittie   21th January 1624

The MUSTER of Ensigne Isack Chaplaine

Isack Chaplaine arived in the *Starr* 1610
Mary his wife in the *James* 1622
John Chaplaine his kinsman aged 15 yeares in the *James* 1622

Servant's

Robert Hudson aged 30 yeares ⎫
Henery Thorne aged 18 yeares ⎬ arived in the *James* 1622
John Duffill aged 14 yeares ⎪
Ivie Banton a Maid servant   ⎭
Ann Mighill a Maid servant arived in the *George* 1619

Chaplains Choise.
  Charles Cittie

The MUSTER of WALTER PRICE &c.

WALTER PRICE arived in the *Willm & Thomas* 1618
HENERY TURNER arived in the *John & Francis* 1615

Servant's

EDWARD FALLOWES aged 30 yeares in the *Hopewell* 1623

The MUSTER of THOMAS KEIE

THOMAS KEIE aged 30 ariued in the *Prosperous* June 1619
SARAH his wife in the *Trueloue* 1622

The MUSTER of JOHN BROWNE

JOHN BROWNE aged 28 yeares in the *Bona Nova* Aprill 1621

The MUSTER of JOHN TREHEARNE

JOHN TREHEARNE aged 33 yeares in the *Trueloue* 1622

The MUSTER of DAVID JONES

DAVID JONES aged 22 yeares in the *Trueloue* 1622

The MUSTER of JOHN BOX

JOHN BOX aged 23 yeares in the *Trueloue* 1622

Murderers for the forte........... 3

DEAD at CHAPLINS CHOISE 1624.

HENERY WILSON came in the *Trueloue* 1622 slaine by yᵉ Indians
NICHOLAS SUTTON in the *James* 1622 slaine by the Indians
NICHOLAS BALDWIN in the *Trueloue* 1622 slaine by the Indians
WILLIAM BARNETT in the *Trueloue* 1623.

Pierseys
hundred.

The MUSTER of the Inhabitant's of PEIRSEYS HUNDRED taken the 20ᵗʰ of January 1624.

SAMUELL SHARPE arived in the *Seaventure* 1609
ELIZABETH his wife in the *Margrett and John* 1621

Servant's

HENERY CARMAN aged 23 yeares in the *Duty* 1620

The MUSTER of m' GRIVELL POOLEY Minister

GRIVELL POOLEY arived in the *James* 1622

Servant's

JOHN CHAMBERS aged 21 yeares in the *Bona Nova* 1622
CHARLES MAGNER aged 16 yeres in the *George* 1623

The MUSTER of HUMFREY KENT

HUMFREY KENT arived in the *George* 1619
JOANE his wife in the *Tyger* 1621
MARGRETT ARRUNDELL aged 9 yeares in the *Abigaile* 1621

Servant's

CHRISTOPHER BEANE aged 40 yeares in the *Neptune* 1618

Pierseys
hundred.

The MUSTER of Thomas Doughtie

Thomas Doughtie arived in the *Marigold* 1619
Ann his wife in the *Marmaduke* 1621

The MUSTER of Edward Auborn

Edward Auborn arived in the *Jonathan* 1620

The MUSTER of William Baker

William Baker arived in the *Jonathan* 1609

The MUSTER of John Woodson

John Woodson ⎫
Sarah his wife ⎭ in the *George* 1619

The MUSTER of Edward Threnorden

Edward Threnorden arived in the *Diana* 1619
Elizabeth his wife in the *George* 1619

The MUSTER of Nicholas Baly

Nicholas Baly arived in the *Jonathan* 1620
Ann his wife in the *Marmaduk* 1621

The MUSTER of John Lipps

John Lipps arived in the *London Marchannt* 1621

Pierseys hundred.

The MUSTER of m' ABRAHAM PEIRSEYS Servant's.

ycres.

THOMAS LEA ....aged 50
ANTHONY PAGITT 35
SALOMAN JACKMAN 30
JOHN DAVIES aged 45
CLEMENT ROPER 25
JOHN BATES aged 24
THOMAS ABBE.................... 20
THOMAS BROOK'S 23
WILLIAM JONES 23
PEETER JONES.................... 24 } arived in the *Southampton* 1623
PIERCE WILLIAMS 23
ROBERT GRAUES................. 30
EDWARD HUBBERSTEAD 26
JOHN LATHROP 25
THOMAS CHAMBERS 24
WALTER JACKSON 24
HENERY SANDERS.............. 20
WILLIAM ALLEN 22
GEORG DAWSON 24

JOHN VPTON aged 26 in the *Bona noua* 1622
JOHN BAMFORD aged 23 yeares in the *James* 1622
WILLIAM GARRETT aged 22 in the *George* 1619
THOMAS SAWELL aged 26 in the *George* 1619
HENERY ROWINGE aged 25 yeares in the *Temperance* 1621
NATHANIELL THOMAS aged 23 ycres in the *Temperance* 1621
RICHARD BROADSHAW aged 20 yeares in the same Shipp
ROBERT OKLEY aged 19 yeares in the *William & Thomas* 1618

Negro
Negro
Negro } 4 Men .
Negro

Pierseys hundred.

ALLICE THOROWDEN ⎫ maid servant's arived in the *Southampton* 1623
KATHERINE LEMAN ⎭

Negro Woman.

Negro Woman and a yong Child of hers.

S' SAMUELL ARGALL'S Cattell

DEAD   at PEIRSEYS HUNDRED   Anno Dñi 1624

JOHN LINICKER.	JOHN ENGLISH.
EDWARD CARLOWE.	CHRISTOPHER LEES Wife.
ROBERT HUSSYE.	ELIZABETH JONES.
JACOB LARBEE.	

Pasbehayghs Corporation of James Citty

The MUSTER of the Inhabitant's of PASBEHAYS & the MAINE taken the 30th of January 1624 belonging to the Corporation of James Citty

ADAM DIXON arived in the *Margrett & John*

JOSEPH RYALE arived in the *William & Thomas*

GEORGE FRIER arived in the *William & Thomas*
VRSULA his wife in the *London Marchant*

ALLEN KENISTON arived in the *Margrett & John*

ROBERT PARAMOUR arived in the *Swan*

WILLIAM KEMP arived in the *George*
MARGRETT his wife in the *George*
ANTHONY his Sonn aged 7 week's

RICHARD BRIDGWATTER arived in the *London Marchannt*
ISBELL his wife in the same Shipp

HUGH HAWARD arived in the *Starr*
SUSAN his wife in the *George.*

Pasbehaighs
James Citty

HENERY TURNER arived in the *London Marchannt*

JOSEPH CREW arived in the *London Marchannt*

THOMAS JONES arived in the *London Marchannt*
MARGRETT his wife in the same Shipp

EDWARD BOURBICTH in the *London Marchannt*

REVOLL MORCOCK arived in the *Jonathan*
ELIZABETH his wife
THOMAS his Sonne aged 1 yeare.

EDWARD FISHER arived in the *Jonathan*
SARAH his wife in the *Warwick*
EDWARD KILDALE her sonn aged 6 yeares
CLARE REN a girle aged 10 yeares.

JOHN MOONE arived in the *Returne* 1623
                    Servant's.
JULIAN HALLERS aged 19 yeares ⎫
GILES MARTIN aged 23 yeares   ⎬ in the *Trueloue* 1623
CLINION RUSH aged 13 yeares   ⎭

RICHARD SMITH arived in the *London Marchannt*

The MUSTER of the Governors Men at Pasbehaighs

THOMAS JORDEN aged 24 came in the *Diana.*
JOHN MILNHOUSE aged 36 in the *London Marchannt*
RICHARD SANDERS aged 25 in the *Francis Bonaventure.*
GRIFFIN WINNE aged 28 in the *Francis Bonaventure.*
ARTHURE CHANDLER aged 19 in the *Jonathan.*
WILLIAM DORRELL aged 18 in the *Trueloue.*
CHRISTOPHER RIPPING 22 in the *Francis Bonaventure.*
THOMAS OSBORN aged 18 in the *Francis Bonaventure.*
GEORGE NELSON aged 19 in the *Francis Bonaventure.*
FRANCIS BUTLER aged 18 in the *Francis Bonaventure.*

Pasbehaighs
James Citty

THOMAS BLANCK'S aged 17 in the *Francis Bonaventure.*
HENERY DOWTIE aged 19 in the *Jonathan.*

JOHN SWARBECK came in the

the Maine.
James Citty.
THOMAS MARLOE came in the *Bona Nova.*

THOMAS BUNN
BRIDGITT his wife
THOMAS his sonn aged 1 yeare
Servant's

JOHN SMITH aged 30 yeares } in the *Abigaile*
THOMAS SMITH aged 16 yeres }
THOMAS JONES aged 35 in the *Bona Nova*
JAMES ROBESONN aged 35 in the *Swan.*
ELIZABETH HODGES a Maid servant in the *Abigaile*

THOMAS SWINHOW came in the *Diana.*
Servant's
LAWRANCE SMALEPAGE aged 20 yeres in the *Abigaile*

JOHN CARTER came in the *Prosperous.*

DAVID ELLIS in the *Mary Margrett*
MARGRETT his wife in the *Margrett & John*

JAMES TOOKE arived in the

WILLIAM BINK'S came in the *George*
ANN his wife in the *George*

MICHAELL BATT came in the *Hercules.*
ELLIN his wife in the *Warwick.*

ROBERT LINCE came in the *Treasuror.*

HUGH BALDWINE came in the *Tryall*
SUSAN his wife in the

the Maine.
James City

ROBERT SCOTCHMORE came in the *George* 1623

THOMAS KNISTON cane [KENISTON came] in the *George* 1623

Servant's

ROGER KIDD aged 24 yeares in the *George* 1623

ROBERT CHOLMLE .... ⎫ came in the *Charitie*
JAMES STANDISH.................... ⎭

The MUSTER of DOCTO' POTT's Men in the MAINE

THOMAS LEISTER aged 33 yeares
ROGER STANLEY aged 27
THOMAS PRITCHARD aged 28
HENERY CROCKER aged 34 ⎬ came in the *Abigaile* 1620
THOMAS CROSSE aged 22
JOHN TRYE aged 20
WALTER BEARE aged 28
RANDALL HOLT aged 18 yeares in the *George* 1620
   The rest of his servant's, Provisions, Amunition &ct. at JAMES CITTY.

DEAD at PASBEHAIGHS & in the MAINE 1624.

JOACHIM ANNDREWS.
HENERY SCOTT.
RICHARD ⎫ 2 Men of m' BUNNS.
RICHARD ⎭

James City **The MUSTER of the Inhabitant's of JAMES CITTIE taken the 24th of January 1624**

The MUSTER of Sr FRANCIS WYATT Kt &ct.

Sr FRANCIS WYATT Kt Governo' &c· came in the *George* 1621

Servant's

CHRISTOPHER COOKE aged 25 in the *George* 1621

James Citty.

GEORG HALL aged 13 in the *Suply* 1620
JONATHAN GILES 21 in the *Triall* 1619
JOHN MATHEMAN 19 in the *Jonathan* 1619
JANE DAVIS 24 in the *Abigaile* 1622

The MUSTER of Sr GEORGE YEARLEY K^t &ct.

Sr GEORGE YEARLLEY K^t &c. came in the *Deliuerance* 1609
TEMPERANCE LADY YEARLLEY came in the *Faulcon* 1608
m' ARGALL YEARLLEY aged 4 yeares ⎫
m' FRANCIS YEARLLEY aged 1 yeare ⎬ Children borne heare
m's ELIZABETH YEARLLEY aged 6 yeres ⎭

Servant's at JAMES CITTY

RICHARD GREGORY aged 40 ⎫
ANTHONY JONES 26 ⎬ came in the *Temperannce* 1620
THOMAS DUNN 14 ⎪
THOMAS PHILDUST 15 ⎭
THOMAS HATCH 17 in the *Duty* 1619
ROBERT PEAKE 22 in the *Margrett & John* 1623
WILLIAM STRANGE 18 in the *George* 1619
ROGER THOMPSON 40 in *London Marchaunt* 1620
ANN his wife
RICHARD ARRUNDELL in the *Abigall* 1620
GEORG DEVERILL 18 in the *Temperannce* 1620
THOMAS BARNETT 16 in the *Elsabeth* 1620
THEOPHILUS BERISTON 23 in the *Treasuror* 1614
Negro Men. 3
Negro Woemen. 5.
SUSAN HALL in the *William & Thomas* 1618
ANN WILLIS in the *Temperance* 1620
ELIZABETH ARRUNDELL in the *Abigall* 1620.
The rest of his servant's at HOG ILAND.

James Citty.   ## The MUSTER of Docto' John Pott

Docto' John Pott .... } arived in the *George* 1620
m's Elizabeth Pott .... }

Servant's.

Richard Townshend aged 19 yeares in the *Abigaile* 1620
Thomas Wilson aged 27 yeares in the *Abigaile* 1620
Osmond Smith aged 17 yeares in the *Bona Nova* 1620
Susan Blackwood a Maid servant in the *Abigaile* 1622

The MUSTER of Cap\ Roger Smith

Cap\ Roger Smith came in the *Abigaile* 1620
m's Joane Smith came in the *Blessinge*
Elizabeth Salter aged 7 yeares came in the *Seafloure*
Elizabeth Rolfe aged 4 yeares } borne in Virginia.
Sarah Macock aged 2 yeares. }

Servant's

Charles Waller aged 22 came in the *Abigaile* 1620
Christopher Bankus aged 19 yeares in the *Abigaile* 1622
Henery Booth aged 20 in the *Dutie*
Henery Lacton aged 18 yeares in the *Hopwell* 1623

The rest of his men theire Provisions Armes &ct. Over the Watter.

The MUSTER of Cap\ Raph Hamor

Cap\ Raph Hamor
m's Elizabeth Hamor
Jeremy Clement } her Children.
Elizabeth Clement }

Servant's

John Lightfoote in the *Seaventure*
Francis Gibb's a boy in the *Seaflower*.
Ann Addams a Maid servant.

The rest of his servant's, Provisions Armes e^c. at Hog-Iland.

James Citty   The MUSTER of Cap^T WILLIAM PIERCE

Capt WILLIAM PIERCE came in the *Sea-venture*
m^s JONE PIERCE his wife in the *Blessinge*
Servant's
THOMAS SMITH aged 17 yeares in the *Abigaile*
HENERY BRADFORD aged 35 yeres in the *Abigaile*
ESTER EDERIFE a maid servant in the *Jonathan*
ANGELO a Negro Woman in the *Treasuror.*

The rest of his servant's ; Provisions, Armes, Munition &ct at
MULBERY ILAND.

The MUSTER of m' ABRAHAM PEIRSEY Marchannt

m' ABRAHAM PEIRSEY came in the *Susan* 1616
ELIZABETH his daughter aged 15 yeres } came in the *Southampton* 1623
MARY his daughter aged 11 yeres
Servant's.
CHRISTOPHER LEE aged 30 yeres
RICHARD SERIEANT aged 36 yeres } came in the *Southampton* 1623.
ALICE CHAMBERS } maid servant's.
ANNIS SHAW

The rest at Peirseys Hundred.

The MUSTER of m' EDWARD BLANEY.

m' EDWARD BLANEY came in the *Francis Bonaventure*
Servant's
ROBERT BEW aged 20 came in the *Dutic.*
JOHN RUSSELL aged 19 in the *Bona Nova.*

The rest of his Servant's Armes &ct at his Plantacon Over ye Watter.

ROBERT POOLE came in the

JAMES HICMOTT came in the *Bonaventure*
his wife in the

James Cittie.

JOHN SOUTHERN came in the *George* 1620

Servant's.

THOMAS CRUST aged   came in the *George* 1620

RANDALL SMALEWOOD came in the

GEORGE GRAUE came in the *Seaventure*
ELNOR his wife in the *Susan*
JOHN GRAUE theire sonne aged 10 yeares
REBECCA SNOW ⎫
             ⎬ her daughters.
SARA SNOW   ⎭

EDWARD CADGE came in the *Marmaduke*
NATHANIELL JEFFREYS came in the *Gift.*

JOHN JACKSON came in the
JOHN JACKSON his sonn aged 9 yeares
GERCIAN BUCK aged 10 yeares

THOMAS ALNUTT came in the *Gifte*
his wife in the *Marygold*

Servant's.

ROGER ROED'S aged 20 yeares in the *Bony bess.*

PEETER LANGMAN came in the *William & Thomas.*
MARY his wife came in the
PEETER ASCAM her sonn aged 1 yeares
ABIGAILE ASCAM her daughter aged 4 yeres.
BENOMY BUCK aged 8 yeres
PELEG BUCK aged 4 yeres

Servant's

ABRAHAM PORTER aged 36 yeares in the
THOMAS SAWIER aged 23 yeares in the

m' JOHN BURROWES came in the
BRIDGETT his wife
MARA BUCK aged 13 yeares

29

James Citty.

Servant's

JOHN COOKE aged 27 yeares
NICHOLAS GOULDFINCH aged 19 yeres
JOHN BRADSTON aged 18 yeres*
THOMAS THOROWGOOD aged 17 yeres
ELLIAS GAILE agèd 14 yeares
ANDREW HOWELL aged 13 yeres
ANN ASHLEY aged 19 ycres

———

The Cattell belonging to m' BUCKS Children

ELIZABETH SOOTHEY came in the *Southampton*
ANN SOOTHEY her daughter

———

JOHN JEFFERSON came in the *Bona Nova*
WALGRAUE MARK'S in the *Margrett & John.*

———

WILLIAM MUTCH came in the *Jonathan*
MARGERY his wife in the *George* 1623

———

RICHARD STEEPHENS came in the *George* 1623

Servant's.

WASSELL RAYNER aged 28 yeres came in the
THOMAS SPILLMAN aged 28 yeres in the *George* 1623
EDWARD PRISE aged 29 yeres in the *George* 1623
JOANE RAYNER wife of WASSELL RAYNER

———

GEORGE MINIFIE arived in the *Samuell* July 1623

Servant's

JOHN GRIFFIN aged 26 yeares in the *William & John* 1624
EDWARD WILLIAMS aged 26 yeres came in the same Shipp.

———

JOHN BARNETT aged 26 yeres came in the *Jonathan* 1620

———

* [Thus erased in the original.]

James Ileand

JOHN STOAK'S } came in the *Warwick.*
ANN his wife }

RICHARD TREE came in the *George*
JOHN his Sonne aged 12 yeres

              Servant's
SILVESTER BULLEN aged 28 yeres came in the

WiᵗᵗM LASEY } came in the *Southampton* 1624
SUSAN his wife }

JOHN WEST came in the *Bony bess*
THOMAS CROMPE came in the

JOHN GREEVETT came in the
ELLIN his wife in the

THOMAS PASSMORE } came in the *George.*
JANE his wife }

              Servant's.
THOMAS KERFITT aged 24 yeares in the *Hopwell*
ROBERT JULIAN aged 20 yeares in the *Jacob.*
JOHN BUCKMUSTER aged 20 yeres in the *Hopwell.*

CHRISTOPHER HALL came in the

ROBERT FITT came in the *George.*
ANN his wife in the *Abigaile*

GEORGE ONION came in the *Francis bona venture.*
ELIZABETH his wife in the same Shipp.
FRANCIS PALL a boy aged 6 yeares
THOMAS PALL a boy aged 4 yeres

JOHN HALL came in the *John & Francis.*
SUSAN his wife in the *London Marchant*

James Iland.

ROBERT MARSHALL came in the *George*
ANN his wife in the same Shipp

———

THOMAS GRUBB came in the *George*

———

JOHN OSBORN came in the
MARY his wife in the

———

WILLIAM SPENCER came in the *Sarah.*
ALLICE his wife in the
ALLICE theire daughter aged 4 yeres.

———

THOMAS GRAVE came in the
MARGRETT his wife in the
WILLIAM theire Sonn aged 3 yeres
JONE theire daughter aged 6 yeres.

———

GABRIELL HOLLAND came in the *John & Francis.*
REBECCA his wife in the same Shipp

———

JOSIAS TANNER aged 24 yeres came in the
ANDREW RAILEY came in the
WILLIAM COOKSEY
THOMAS BAGLEN
WILLIAM CARTER

JOHN JOHNSON
ANN his wife
JOHN his sonn aged 1 yeare
ANN his daughter aged 4 yeres
ALICE KEAN a Maid servant.

JOHN HITCHY
THOMAS DE LA MAIOR.

DEAD at James Cittie & in the Iland 1624

  Richard Mumford
  George Clarke
  Bartlomew Blake
  William Wañerton
  Sibill Royall
  Goodwife Jeffereys
  Thomas Popkin
  Thomas Sides
  Thomas West
  Wm Spencer a Child
     a servant of m' Keths
  m's Peirse
  John Gee
     a servant of Peeter Langman
    Phinloe
  m's Susan Keth.

Neck of Land nere James Citty. The MUSTER of the Inhabitant's of the Neck-of-Land neare James Citty taken Feb_r the 4th 1624.

Richard Kingsmell came in the *Delaware*
Jane his wife in the *Susan*
Nathaniell his sonne aged 5 yeares.
Susan his Daughter aged 1 yeare.

     Servant's

Horten Wright aged 20 yeres came in the *Susan*
John Jackson aged came in the *Abigall.*
Edward a Negro
Isbell Pratt came in the *Jonathan*

John Smith came in the *Bonaventure.*

Thomas Bagwell came in the

Neck of Land neare
   James Citty

THOMAS BENETT came in the *Bona Nova*

MARGERY his wife in the *Guift*

SARAH BROMEDG a Child of 2 yeares old.

JOHN REDDISH came in the

----

m' ALNUTT and his servant here Planted reconed before in the Muster
   of JAMES CITTIE.

DEAD in this Plantacon 1624

a Man servant of m' KINGSMELL'S.

LIUING

RICHARD PIERCE ⎫ came in the *Neptune.*
ELIZABETH his wife ⎭

Archers Hope
   James Citty

THOMAS BRANSBY came in the *Charitie*
              Servant's

NICHOLAS GREENHILL aged 24 yeres ⎫
CHADWALLADER JONES aged 22 yeres ⎬ came in the *Marmaduk* 1623
ROBERT CREW aged 23 yeares ⎭

JOHN ELLISON came in the *Prosperous*
ELLIN his wife in the *Charitie*
              Servant's
JOHN BADELEY aged 24.yeres came in the *Hopwell* 1623

THOMAS FARLEY came in the *Ann* 1623
JANE his wife in the same Shipp.
ANN a Child
              Servant's
NICHOLAS SHOTTEN aged 40 yeres in the *Ann* 1623

Archers Hope.
James Citty

JOSEPH JOHNSON came in the *William & Thomas*
MARGRETT his wife in the *Abigaile*
GEORGE PROUSE came in the *Diana*

DEAD at ARCHERS HOPE 1624
GEORGE ELLISON a Child
    a Maid servant of m' BRANSBYES.
WILLIAM BROWNE.

Burrows Hill
James Citty

m' BURROWES and six of his men wch are planted heare are recoñed,
   wth theire Armes Provisions ℯ^{c,} at JAMES CITTIE
JOHN SMITH came in the *Elizabeth* 1611
SUSANNA his wife in the *Bona Nova* 1619
FRANCIS SMITH his sonne aged 1 yeare
      Servant's
JOHN ELLATT aged 15 yeres in the *Margrett & John* 1621

GEORGE PELTON came in the *Furtherance* 1622

RICHARD RICHARD'S came in the *London Marchant* 1620
RICHARD DOLPHINBE came in the *Guift* 1618

Paces Paines
James Citty

JOHN PROCTOR came in the *Seaventure* 1607
ALLIS his wife in the *George* 1621
      Servant's
RICHARD GROUE aged 30 yeres in the *George* 1623
EDWARD SMITH aged 20 in the *George* 1621
WILLIAM NAYLE aged 15 in the *Ann* 1623

PHETTIPLACE CLOSE came in the *Starr* 1608
DANIELL WATTKINS in the *Charles* 1621
      Servant's
MARTIN DEMON aged 15 yeres in the *George* 1617
JOHN SKINNER in the *Marmaduk* 1621

Paces Paines
James Citty

THOMAS GATES came in the *Swan* 1609
ELIZABETH his wife in the *Warwick.* 1620
WILLIAM BEDFORD in the *James* 1621

FRANCIS CHAPMAN came in the *Starr* 1608

[C]apt Smiths Plant.   The MUSTER of CAPT ROGER SMITHS men
  James Citty
                        Over ye Watter

FRANCIS FOWLER aged 23 yeres

CHRISTOPHER LAWSON
ALCE his wife

CHRISTOPHER REDHEAD aged 24

STEPHEN WEBB aged 25 yeres

JOHN BUTTERFEILD aged 23 yeres

WILLIAM BAKER aged 24 yeres

RICHARD ALFORD aged 26 yeres

THOMAS HARVIE aged 24 yeres

THOMAS MOLTON aged 25 yeres

mr Blaneys Plant.   The MUSTER of mr EDWARD BLANEYS Men
  James Citty
                       Ouer ye Watter.

RICE WATKINS aged 30 yeres came in the *Francis bonaventure.*
NATHANIELL FLOID aged 24 in the *Bona Nova.*
GEORG ROGERS 23 ....
JOHN SHELLEY 23 ....
THOMAS OTTOWELL 40 .... } in the *Bona Nova.*
THOMAS CROUCH 40 ....
ROBERT SHEPPEARD 20 in the *Hopwell.*
WILLIAM SAWIER 18 in the *Hopwell.*
ROBERT CHAUNTRIE 19 in the *George*

mᵣ Blaneys Plant.
  James Citty

WILLIAM HARTLEY 23 in the *Charles*
LAWLEY DAMPORT 29 in the *Duty*
WILLIAM WARD 20 in the *Jonathan*
JEREMY WHITE 20 in the *Tyger*
JOHN HACKER 17 in the *Hopwell*
ROBERT WHITMORE 22 in the *Duty*

Capᵗ Mathews Plant
  James Citty

Capᵗ SAMUELL MATHEWS came in the *Southampton* 1622
mᵣ DAVID SAND'S Minister came in the *Bonaventure* 1620

Servant's.

ROBERT MATHEWS aged 24 ⎫ cam
ROGER WILLIAMS......... 20 ⎪
SAMUELL DAVIES......... 18 ⎪
HENERY JONES........... 25 ⎬ came in the *Southampto* 1622
AARON CONAWAY ...... 20 ⎪
JOHN THOMAS .... 18 ⎪
MICHAELL LAPWORTH... 16 ⎭
WILLIAM LUSAM .... 27 ⎫
WILLIAM FEILD .... 23 ⎬ in the *Charles* 1621
PEETER MONTECUE...... 21 ⎭
ROBERT FERNALL 31 in the *London Marchant* 1619
WALTER COOP [COOPER] 33 in the *Jonathan* 1619
WILLIAM WALTERS 27 in the *Bona Nova* 1618
NICHOLAS CHAPMAN 31 in the *Jonathan* 1619
GREGORY SPICER 22 in the *Triall* 1618
NICHOLAS PEIRSE 23 in the *Falcon* 1619
ROBERT PENN 22 in the *Abigaile* 1620
WILLIAM DALBY 28 in the *Furtherance* 1622
THOMAS HOPSON 12 in the *Bona Nova* 1618
ABRAHAM WOOD 10 in the *Margrett & John* 1620

Capt Mathews Plant
   James Citty

WILLIAM KINGSLEY 24 ...... }
THOMAS BRIDGES 12 .... } in the *Marmaduk* 1623

ARTHURE GOLDSMITH 26 came in the *Diana* 1618

Crowders Plant.
   James Citty

m.' HUGH CROWDER came in the *Bona Nova* 1619

Servant's

RICHARD BALL in the *George* 1617

THOMAS HAWKINS in the *James* 1622

PAULE RENALLES in the *Tryall* 1619

NICHOLAS SMITH a boy of 18 yeres in the *Bona Nova* 1621

JOHN VERIN a boy of 14 yeares in the *George* 1623

---

m.^r Treasurors Plant.

The MUSTER of m.' GEORG SAND's Esquire

m.' GEORG SANDIS Esquire Treasuro' &c came in the *George* 1621

Servant's

MARTIN TURNER
GEORGE BAILIFE
JOHN SPARK'S
JOHN DANCY
JOHN EDWARD'S } came in the *George* 1621
NICHOLAS TOMPSON
ROSAMUS CARTER
JOHN STONE a boy

NICHOLAS COMON
NICHOLAS EYRES a boy } in the *Guifte* 1622

DAVID MANSFEILD
JOHN CLAXON } in the *Bona Nova* 1619 hired servant's

THOMAS SWIFTE
JOHN BALDWINF } in the *Tyger* freemen. 1622

mr Treasurors Plant.

hired. DANIELL POOLE a french man
his wife
a yong Child of theires

mr Treasurors Plant.
  James Citty

The MUSTER of those that Liue in ye TREASURORS Plant.

ROBERT SHEAPERD came in the *George* 1621
JAMES CHAMBERS in the *Dutie* 1620
JOHN PARSONS ⎱
WILLIAM BENGE ⎰
JOHN EVENS ⎬ in the *Marygold* 1619
ROBERT EDMUND'S ⎰
JOHN COMES ⎭
JOHN TYOS ⎱
WILLIAM PILKINTON ⎬ in the *Bona Nova* 1620
ELIAS LONGE ⎰
THOMAS HALL ⎭
MARGRETT PILKINTON ⎱ weomen
JANE LONG ⎰
m' VINCENCIO the Italian
m' BERNARDO
his wife
a Child

ZACHARY CRIPP'S came in the *Margrett & John* 1621
EDWARD WHITE in the *Bona Nova* 1620
MATHEW HAMON in the *Southampton* 1622
PHILLIP KITHLY in the *Furtherance* 1622
ANTHONY WEST in the *James* 1622

mʳ Treasurors Plant.
　James Citty

DEAD at all these PLANTATIONS Over the Watter 1624

JOHN PHILMOTT

WILLIAM PLANT

THOMAS ROWLSON

EDWARD JONES

JOHN DIMSDALE

JOHN DOCKER

ROBERT ALDRIDGE

RICHARD GREENE

JAMES DAVIS

DAVID WILLIAMS

JOHN FOXEN

ELIAS HENTON

THO: FITCH

ENECHA FITCH

JOHN SERE

WILLIAM SAND'S

GEORG GURR ⎫ slaine by the

WILLIAM COMES ⎬ Indians

ROBERT EVARS.

PEACEABLE SHEREWOOD.

WILLIAM HALL

Hog Iland

The MUSTER of CAPᵀ RAPH HAMORS servant's

JEFFEREY HULL came in the *George*

MORDECAY KNIGHT in the *William & John*

THOMAS DOLEMAN in the *Returne*

ELKINTON RATLIFFE in the *Seafloure*

THOMAS POWELL in the *Seafloure.*

THOMAS COOPER in the *Returne*

JOHN DAVIES in the *Guifte.*

The MUSTER of LIUETENNT BARKLEY.

Liuetennt EDWARD BARKLEY in the *Vnitie.*

mˢ JANE BARKLEY in the *Seafloure.*

JANE BARKLEY his daughter.

Servant's

THOMAS PHILLIP'S ⎫ in the *Bona Nova*
FRANCIS BARRETT ⎭

Hog Iland

ROBERT MARTIN in the *George*.
KATHERIN DAVIES in the *Southampton*.

——

JOHN VTY came in the *Francis Bonaventure*
ANN his wife in the *Seafloure*.
JOHN his Sonn in the *Seafloure*.

Servant's

WILLIAM BURT ⎱
WILLIAM STOCKER ⎰ in the *Bony besse*
RICHARD BICKLEY in the *Returne*.

——

JOHN CHEW came in the *Charitie*.
SARAH his wife in the *Seafloure*.

Servant's.

ROGER DELK in the *Southampton*.
SAMUELL PARSON in the *Hopewell*.
WALTER HASLEWOOD in the *Due Returne*.

——

HENERY ELWOOD ⎱
WILLIAM RAMSHAW ⎰ in the *Francis Bonaventure*.
JOHN STONE in the *Swann*
SISLY his wife in the *Seafloure*.
HENERY CROCKER in the *Marygold*
JONE his wife in the *Swan*.
HENERY WOODWARD in the *Diana*.
JANE his wife
THOMAS HITCKOCK in the *Marygold*
ALICE his wife
ROGER WEBSTER
JOANE his wife
JOANE D'AVIS.

Hog Iland.

The MUSTER of Sᵣ Georg Yearlleys Men

Maximillian Stone aged 36 came in the *Temperance* 1620

Elizabeth his wife in the same Shipp.

Maximillian his sonn aged 9 months.

Robert Guy 22 in the *Swann* 1619

Edward Yates 18 in the *Duty* 1619

Cesar Puggett 20 in the *Diana* 1619

Allexander Sanders 24 in the *Trueloue* 1623

William Strachey 17 in the *Temperance* 1620

George Whitehand 24 in the *Temperance* 1620

Henery King 22 in the *Jonathan* 1620

John Day 24 in the *London Marchannt* 1620

The wife of John Day in the same Shipp

John Root in the *Guift* .... ⎫
Walter Blake in the *Swan* ...... ⎬ Dwellers.
Thomas Watt's in the *Treasuror.* ⎭

    David Dutton...... ⎫ Dead
    Rich: Baker......... ⎭

The rest of his servant's. Provisions
Armes &ct reconed at James Citty

Martins Hundred.

The MUSTER of the Inhabitant's of Martins Hundred taken the 4ᵗʰ of February 1624.

m' William Harwood came in the *Francis Bonaventure*

Servant's

Hugh Hughs came in the *Guifte.*

Ann his wife........................ ⎫
Thomas Doughtie aged 26...... ⎬ came in the *Abigall.*
John Hasley aged 22 yeres...... ⎭

Samuell Weaver 20 in the *Bony bess*

Elizabeth Bygraue 12 came in the *Warwick.*

Martins Hundred

ELLIS EMERSON ....
ANN his wife......................... } came in the *George* 1623.
THOMAS his sonn aged 11 ....

Servant's.

THOMAS GOULDING aged 26 yeres came in the *George* 1623

MARTIN SLATIER aged 20 cam frō Canada in the *Swan* 1624

ROBERT ADDAMS..................... }
AUGUSTINE LEAK .... } came in the *Bona Nova*.

WINIFRED LEAK his wife came in the *George* 1623

Servant's

RICHARD SMITH aged 24 yeres came in the *George* 1623.

STEEPHEN BARKER came in the *James*
HUMPHREY WALDEN in the *Warwick*

JOHN JACKSON .... }
ANN his Wife.............. } came in the *Warwick*.
A Child aged 20 week's

Servant's.

THOMAS WARD aged 47 yeres ... }
JOHN STEEPHENS 35 yeres ...... } came in the *Warwick*

SAMUELL MARCH came in the *William & Thomas*.
COLLICE his wife in the *Ann* 1623
SAMUELL CULLEY came in the *London Marchant*

ROBERT SCOTCHMORE and his Company now planted heare are reconned before in the MAINE

DEAD at MARTINS HUNDRED this yeare

ALLICE EMERSON a girle
ROBERT   a boy of m' EMARSONS
                a girle of JOHN JACKSONS
                a Child of SAMUELL MARCH.

Mulburie Iland.

The MUSTER of the Inhabitant's att MULBURY ILAND taken the 25th of January 1624.

The MUSTER of Capt WILLIAM PIERCES servant's

RICHARD ATTKINS aged 24 came in the *London Marchannt*

ABIGALL his wife ....⎫
WILLIAM BAKER aged 20 . ⎭ came in the *Abigall*

ROBERT ASTON 29 in the *Treasuror*

HUGH WING 30 ⎫
ROBERT LATHOM 20 ⎪
RICHARD ALDON 19 ⎬ came in the *George* 1620
THOMAS WOOD 35 ⎭

ROGER RUCE came in the *Charles*

ALLEXANDER GILL 20 in the *Bony bess*

SAMUELL MORRIS 20 in the *Abigall*

THOMAS ROSE 35 in the *Jonathan*

ROBERT HEDGES aged 40 yeres in the

———

JOHN VIRGO came in the *Treasuror*
SUSAN his wife in the same Shipp

———

JOHN GATTER came in the *George* 1620

———

WILLIAM RICHARDSON came in the *Edwine*

———

RICHARD FINE came in the *Neptune*

———

JOHN NOWELL came in the *Margrett & John*

———

RICHARD DOWNES came in the *Jonathan*

———

JOHN CRANICH came in the *Marygold*

———

PERCEVALL WOOD came in the *George*
ANN his wife in the *George.*

———

WILLIAM RAYMONT came in the *Neptune*

———

WILLIAM BULLOCK came in the *Jonathan*

Mulbury Iland

ANTHONY BARAM came in the *Abigall*
ELLIZABETH his wife in the *William & Thomas*

THOMAS HARWOOD came in the *Margrett & John* 1622
GRACE his wife in the *George*

Servant's.

THOMAS READ aged 65 yeres

Wariscoyack.

The MUSTER of the Inhabitant's at WARISCOYACK taken the 7th of Febr 1624.

The MUSTER of m' EDWARD BENNETT's servant's

HENERY PINKE came in the *London Marchannt* 1619
JOHN BATE in the *Addam* 1621
PEETER COLLINS in the *Addam* 1621
WASSELL WEBLING } in the *James* 1621
ANTONIO a Negro
CHRISTOPHER REYNOLD'S
LUKE CHAPPMAN } in the *John & Francis* 1622
EDWARD MAYBANK
JOHN ATTKINS
WILLIAM DENUM } in the *Guifte* 1623
FRANCIS BANK'S
MARY a Nergro Woman in the *Margrett & John* 1622

[Basses Choyse]

A MUSTER of the Inhabitance of BASSES CHOYSE

CAP^T NATHANIELL BASSE his MUSTER

NATHANIELL BASSE aged 35 in the *furtherance* 1622
WILLIAM BARNARD aged 21 in the *furtherance* 1622
EDWARD WIGGE aged 22 in the *Abigall* 1621

31

Basses Choyse

The MUSTER of Thomas Phillipes

Thomas Phillipes aged 26 in the *William and Thomas* 1618
Elzabeth Phillipes aged 23 in the *sea Flower* 1621

The MUSTER of Thomas Bennett

Thomas Bennett aged 38 in the *Neptune* 1618
Mary Bennett aged 18 in the *Southampton* 1622
Roger Heford aged 22 in the *Returne* 1623
Beniamine Simes aged 33 in the

Richard Longe his MUSTER

Richard Longe aged 33 in the
Alice Longe aged 23 in the *London Marchant* 1620
Robart Longe a Child borne in Virginia

Wariscoyack

Richard Evand's his MUSTER

Richard Evand's aged 35 in the *Neptune* 1618

William Newman his MUSTER

William Newman aged 35 in the *Furtherance* 1622
John Army aged 35 in the *Furtherance* 1622

Henrie Woodward his MUSTER

Henrie Woodward aged 30 in the
John Browninge aged 22 in the *Abigall* 1621

Servant's

Ambrose   aged 25 in the *Marmiducke* 1621
Peeter   aged 19 in the *Margett and John* 1620

Wariscoyack

A list of the DEAD in WARISCOYACKE 1624.

JOHN SELLEY

NATHANIELL HAUKWORTH [*or* HANKWORTH]

THOMAS SHEWOUD

BENIAMIN HANDCLEARE

MARGRETT SYMES

NATHANIELL
THOMAS
} Servant's

of M' BENNET's men
slayne by the Indianes
} 5

Newportes newes

Mr DANNIELL GOOKINES MUSTER

Servantes

WILLIAM WADSWORTH aged: 26

WILLIAM FOOCKES aged: 24

THOMAS CURTIS aged: 24

PEETER SHERWOOD aged: 21

GILBERT WHITFILD aged: 23

RISE GRIFFIN aged: 24

WILLIAM SMITH aged: 23

ANTHONIE EBSWORTH aged: 26

} All wch Came in the *Flyinge Harte.* 1621:

ISAYE DELYWARR aged 22

HENRIE CARSLEY aged: 23

ROGER WALKER aged: 22

EDMOND MORGON aged: 22

WILLIAM CLARKE aged: 25

JOSEPH MOSLEY aged: 21

JOHN PARRATT aged: 36

ROBART SMITH aged: 22

WILLIAM CRONEY aged: 24

WILLIAM LONGE aged: 19

ANNE EBSWORTH aged: 44

ELLNOR HARRIS aged: 21

in the *Prouidence* 1623*

DEAD in this Plantatō

one ARMESTRONGE

---

* [I suppose this refers to the whole of the names from DELYWARR to HARRIS; but there is no " brace " in the original.]

Elizabeth Cittie

Capt William Tucker his MUSTER

Capt WILLIAM TUCKER: aged: 36: in the *Mary and James:* 1610
Mrs MARY TUCKER aged: 26: in the *George:* 1623.
ELZABETH TUCKER borne in Virginia in August:
GEORGE TOMSON aged: 17 .... ⎫
PAULE TOMSON aged: 14............. ⎬ in the *George* 1623:
WILLIAM THOMSON — 11 .... ⎭
PASCOE CHAMPION aged 23......... ⎫ in the *Ellonor* 1621:
STRENGHT SHEERE aged: 23 ...... ⎬
THOMAS EVAND'S aged: 23 .... ⎫
STEPHEN COLLOWE aged: 23 ...... ⎬ in the *George:* 1623.
ROBART MUNDAY aged: 18 .... ⎭
MATHEWE ROBINSONN aged: 24 in the *greate hopewell* 1623:
RICHARD APPLETON aged: 19: in the *James* 1622.
JOHN MORRIS aged 24: in the *Bona Noua:* 1619.
MARY MORRIS aged 22: in the *George* 1623
WILLIAM HUTCHINSON aged 21: in the *Diana* 1618
PEETER PORTER aged 20 in the *Tyger* 1621.
WILLIAM CRAWSHAW an Indean Baptised.
ANTONEY Negro: ISABELL Negro: and WILLIAM theire Child Baptised

---

John Downeman his MUSTER

JOHN DOWNEMAN aged: 33: in the *John and Francis:* 1611:
ELZABETH DOWNEMAN aged: 22: in the *Warwicke* 1621.
MOYSES STONES aged: 16: in the *Bone Bes* 1623

John Laydon his MUSTER

JOHN LAYDON aged 44: in the *Susan* 1606
ANNE LAYDON aged 30: in the *Mary Margett* 1608

Elzabeth Cittie

VIRGINIA LAYDON ....
ALCE LAYDON .... } borne in Virginia.
KATHERIN LAYDON...... ....
MARGERETT LAYDON ....

WILLIAM COLE his MUSTER

WILLIAM COLE aged 26 in the *Neptune* 1618
FRANCIS COLE aged 27 in the *Susan* 1616
ROGER FARBRASE aged 26 in the *Elzabeth* 1621

MILES PRICKETT and FRANCIS MITCHELL their MUSTERS.

MILES PRICKETT aged 36 in the *Starr:* 1610
FRANCIS MITCHELL aged 38 in the *Neptune* 1618
MAUDLIN MITCHELL aged 21 in the *Bona Noua* 1620
JOHN MITCHELL borne in Virginia 1624

RICHARD YONGE his MUSTER

RICHARD YONGE aged 31 in the *George* 1616
JOANE YONGE aged 26 in the *Guifte* 1618
JOANE YONGE aged 2 borne in Virginia
SUSAN   aged 12 in the *Swan* 1624

LEIUETEN: ALBIANO LUPO his MUSTER

ALBIANO LUPO aged 40 in the *Swan* 1610
ELIZABETH LUPO aged 28 in the *George* 1616
TEMPERANCE LUPO aged 4 borne in Virginia

Servant's

HENRIE DRAPER aged 14 in the *George* 1621
JOSEPH HAM aged 16 in the *Warwicke* 1621

Elzabeth Cittie

JOHN POWELL his MUSTER

JOHN POWELL aged 29 in the *Swallowe* 1609
KATHREN POWELL aged 22 in the *flyinge Hart* 1622
JOHN POWELL borne in virginia

Servant's

THOMAS PRATER aged 20 in the *Marie Prouidence* 1622

LARENCE PEALE his MUSTER

LARENCE PEALE aged 23 in the *Margett and John* 1620
WILLIAM SMITH aged 30 in the *Jacob* 1624

ROBART BRITTIN his MUSTER

ROBART BRITTIN aged 30: in the *Edwin* 1618

MIHELL WILCOCKES and JOHN SLATER their MUSTER

MIHELL WILCOCKES aged 31 in the *Prosporouse* 1610
ELZABETH WILLCOCKES aged 23 in the *Concord* 1621
JOHN SLATER aged 22 in the *George* 1617
ANNE SLATER aged 17 in the *Guyft* 1622

Servant's

JAMES FEILD aged 20 in the *Swan* 1624
JOHN JORNALL aged 20 in the *Ann* 1623
THEODORE JOONES aged 16 in the *Margett and John* 1620

JOSEPH COBB his MUSTER

JOSEPH COBB aged 25 in the *Treasoror* 1613
ELZABETH COBB aged 25 in the *Bone Bes* 1623
JOHN SNOWOOD aged 25 in the

Elzabeth Cittie

CORNELIUS MAY his MUSTER

CORNELIUS MAYE aged 25 in the *Prouidence* 1616

WILLIAM MORGAN als BROOCKES his MUSTER

WILLIAM MORGAN aged 30 in the *Starr* 1610
WILLIAM MORGAN aged 2 borne in Virginia

Mr WILLIAM JULIAN his MUSTER.

WILLIAM JULIAN aged: 43: in the *Hercules* 1609
SARA JULIAN aged 25 in the *Neptune* 1618
WILLIAM KEMP aged 33 in the *William and Thomas* 1618
THOMAS SULLY aged 36 in the *Sara* 1611
MAUDLYN SULLY aged 30 in the *London Marchant* 1620

Servant's

THOMAS FLOWER aged 22 in the *George* 1623
WYATT MASONN aged 16 in the *Ann* 1623

LEIUETEN̄ THOMAS PURFRAY his MUSTER

THOMAS PURFRY aged 43 in the *George* 1621
CHRISTOPHER COLETHORPE aged 18: in the *Furtherance* 1622
DANNIELL TANNER aged 40 in the *Sampson* 1618

Servant's

HENRIE FEELDES aged 26 in the *Jacob* 1624
WILLIAM BAULDWIN

JOHN BARNABE his MUSTER

JOHN BARNABIE aged 21: in the *London Marchant* 1620

Elzabeth Cittie

JOHN HAZARD his MUSTER

JOHN HAZARD aged 40 in the *William and Thomas* 1618

Servant's

ABRAHAM PELTEARE aged 14 in the *Swan* 1624.

JERIMIAH DICKINSON his MUSTER.

JERIMIAH DICKINSON aged 26 in the *Margett and John* 1620
ELZABETH DICKINSON aged 38 in the *Margett and John* 1623

PHILLIP LUPO his MUSTER

PHILLIP LUPO aged 42 in the *George* 1621

ENSIGNE THOMAS WILLOBY his MUSTER

THOMAS WILLOBY aged 23 in the *Prosporouse* 1610

Servant's

JOHN CHAUNDLER aged 24 in the *Hercules* 1609
THOMAS aged 20 in the *greate hopewell* 1623
ROBERT BENNETT aged 24 In the *Jacob* 1624
NICCOLAS DAVIS aged 13 in the *Mariegould* 1618

JOHN HATTON his MUSTER

JOHN HATTON aged 26 in the *Tresorer* 1613
OLIUE HATTON aged 32 in the *Abigall* 1620

Mr CISSE Minister his MUSTER

Mr GEORGE KETH aged 40 ....⎫
JAMES WHITINGE aged 16 .... ⎬ in the *George* 1617
JOHN KETH aged 11   ....⎭

Elzabeth Cittie

Susan Bush her MUSTER

Susan Bush aged 20 in the *George* 1617
Sara spence aged 4 borne in virginia

Servant's

Clement Evand's aged 30 in the *Edwin* 1616
William Parker aged 20 in the *Charles* 1616
John Seward aged 30 in the *Gcife* 1622
Gilbert Marburie aged 32 in the *Southampton* 1622
Thomas Killson aged 21 in the *Trueloue* 1623

Capt Niccolas Martue his MUSTER

Niccolas Martue aged 33 in the *Francis Bonaventure*
Peter Eccallowe aged 30 in the *Southampton*
William Stafford aged 17 in the *furtherance*

M' John Banum and Robart Sweete theire MUSTER

John Banum aged 54 in the *Susan* 1616
Elzabeth Banum aged 43 in the *Bona Noua,* 1620
Robart Sweete aged 42 in the *Neptune* 1618

Servant's

Niccolas Thredder aged 30 in the *Katherin* 1623
Richard Robisonn aged 22 in the *Bona noua* 1620
John Hill aged 26 in the *Bona Noua* 1620
William Morton aged 20 in the *Margett and John* 1620
James Pascoll aged 20 in the *Warwicke* 1621
Robart Draper aged 16 in the *Jacob* 1624
Sara Gouldinge aged 20 in the *Ann* 1623

Elzabeth Cittie

RICHARD MINTRENE his MUSTER

RICHARD MINTRENE aged 40 in the *Margett and John* 1620
WILLIAM BEANE aged 25 in the *Diana* 1618
EDWARD MINTRENE aged 12 in the *Margett and John* 1620
JOHN INMAN aged 26 in the *falcon* 1619
WILLIAM BROWNE aged 14 in the *Southamton* 1622

ANTHONEY BURROES his MUSTER

ANTHONEY BURROES aged 44 in the *George* 1617

JOHN WAINE his MUSTER

JOHN WAINE aged 30 in the *Neptune* 1618
AMYTE WAINE aged 30 in the *Swan* 1610
GEORGE ACKLAND aged 7 } borne in Virginia
MARY ACKLAND aged 4 }
JOHN HARLOW aged 28 in the *Sampson* 1619
ROBART SABYN aged 30 in the *marget and John* 1622
PHILLIP CHAPMAN aged 23 in the *flyinge Hart* 1621

M' ROBART SALFORD his MUSTER and JOHN SALFORD.

M' ROBART SALFORD aged 56 in the *John and Francis* 1611
JOHN SALFORD aged 24 in the *George* 1616
MARY SALFORD aged 24 in the *Bona Noua* 1620

Servant's
WILLIAM ELLISON aged 44 in the *Swan* 1624
THOMAS FAULKNER aged 28 in the *Mary Prouidense* 1622

Elzabeth Cittie

BARTHOLEMEW WETHERSBIE and RICHARD BOULTON their MUSTERS

BARTHOLEMEW WETHERSBIE aged 30 in the *Providence* 1616
DORYTHIE WETHERSBIE aged 30 in the *London Marchant* 1620
RICHARD BOULTON aged 28 in the *Mary and James* 1610
RICHARD   aged 15 in the *Swan* 1624

JOHN GUNDRIE his MUSTER

JOHN GUNDRIE aged 33 in the *Starr* 1610
MARIE GUNDRIE aged 20 in the *George* 1618
JOHN GUNDRIE aged 2 borne in Virginia

FRANCIS MASON his MUSTER

FRANCIS MASON aged 40 in the *John and Francis* 1613
ALICE MASON aged 26 in the *Margett and John* 1622
FRANCIS MASON borne in Virginia

Servant's
WILLIAM QUERKE aged 30 in the *Marmaducke* 1621
THOMAS WORTHALL aged 14 in the *Marmaducke* 1621
WILLIAM STAFFORD aged 16 in the *furtherance* 1622
HENRIE GANY aged 21 in the *Dutie* 1619
JOHN ROBINSON aged 21 in the *Margett and John* 1622

FARRAR FLINTON his MUSTER

FARRAR FLINTON aged 36 in the *Elzabeth* 1612
JOANE FLINTON aged 38 in the *Elzabeth* 1612
WILLIAM BENTLIE aged 36 In the *Jacob* 1624

32—2

Elzabeth Cittie

Servant's

ARTHUR SMYTH aged 25 } in the *Marget and John* 1622
HUGH HALL aged 13

MATHEW HARDCASTELL aged 20 in the *Jacob* 1624
HENRIE NASFEILD aged 19 in the *Swan* 1624

JAMES SLEIGHT and FRANCIS HUFF theire MUSTER

FRANCIS HUFF aged 20 in the *Swan* 1624
JAMES SLEIGHT aged 42 in the *Tryall* 1610

LEIUETEN JOHN CHISMAN his MUSTER

JOHN CHISMAN aged 27 in the *flyinge hart* 1621
EDWARD CHISMAN aged 22 in the *Prouidence* 1623

M' THOMAS SPILMAN his MUSTER

THOMAS SPILMAN aged 24 in the *George* 1616
HANNA SPILMAN aged 23 in the *Bona Noua* 1620
ELIZABETH HILL borne in Virginia

Servant's

ROBART BROWNE aged 25 in the *Mary gould* 1618
REBECCA BROWNE aged 24 in the *Southampton* 1623
THOMAS PARRISH aged 26 in the *Charity* 1622
JOHN HARRIS aged 21 in the *Jacob* 1624.

OLIVER JINKINES his MUSTER

OLIVER JINKINES aged 30, in the *mary James* 1610
JOANE JINKINES aged 26 in the *George* 1617
ALLEXAND' JINKINES borne in Virginia

Elzabeth Cittie

WILLIAME GAYNE and ROBART NEWMAN theire MUSTER

ROBART NEWMAN aged 25 in the *Neptune* 1618
WILLIAM GAYNE aged 36 in the *Bona Noua* 1620
JOHN TAYLOR aged 34 in the *Swan* 1610
REBECCA TAYLOR aged 22 in the *Margett and John* 1623
JOHN COKER aged 20
RICHARD PACKE aged 23 in the *Warwicke* 1621
ABRAHAM AVELIN aged 23 } in the *Elzabeth* 1620
ARTHUR AVELIN aged 26 }

THOMAS GODBY his MUSTER

THOMAS GODBY aged 38 in the *Deliu'ance* 1608
JOANE GODBY aged 42 in the *Flyinge Hart* 1621
JOHN CURTIS aged 22 in the *Flyinge Harte* 1621
CHRISTOPHER SMITH aged 23 in the *Returne* 1624

M' EDWARD WATERS his MUSTER

EDWARD WATERS aged 40 in the *Patience* 1608
GRACE WATERS aged 21 in the *Diana* 1618
WILLIAM WATERS } borne in Virginia
MARGERETT WATERS }
WILLIAM HAMPTON aged 40 in the *Bona Noua* 1620
JOANE HAMPTON aged 25 in the *Abigall* 1621
THOMAS LANE aged 30 in the *Treasorer* 1613
ALICE LANE aged 24 in the *Bona Noua* 1620
THOMAS THORNEBURY aged 20 in the *George* 1616

Servant's

ADAM THOROGOOD aged 18 } in the *Charles* 1621
NICCOLAS BROWNE aged 18 }
PAULE HARWOOD aged 20 in the *Bona Noua* 1622
STEPHEN REEDE aged 17 in the *George* 1618

Elzabeth Cittie

MATHIAS FRANCISCO aged 18 in the *Jacob* 1624

ROBART PENRISE aged 12 in the *Bona noua* 1620

CAP^T THOMAS DAVIS his MUSTER

Capt THOMAS DAVIS aged 40 in the *John and Francis* 1623

THOMAS HEWES aged 40 in the *John and Francis* 1623

M' FRANCIS CHAMBERLIN his MUSTER

FRANCIS CHAMBERLIN aged 45 in the *Marmaducke* 1621

REBECCA CHAMBERLIN aged 37 in the *Bona Noua* 1622

FRANCIS CHAMBERLIN aged 3 borne in Virginia.

Servant's

JOHN FORTH aged 16 ⎱

WILLIAM WORLIDGE aged 18 ⎰ in the *Bona Noua* 1622

SIONELL* ROWLSTON aged 30 in the *God's Guifte* 1623

RICHARD BURTON aged 28 in the *Swan* 1624

PERCIVALL IBOTTSON his MUSTER

PERCIVALL IBOTTSON aged 24 in the *Neptune* 1618

ELZABETH IBOTTSON aged 23 in the *Flyinge Hart* 1621

JOHN DAVIS aged 24 in the *John and Francis* 1623

Servant's

WILLIAM GREENE aged 28 in the *Hopewell* 1623

ROBART LOCKE aged 18 in the *Warwicke* 1621

M' DANNIELL COOKINS his MUSTER

| WILLIAM WADSWORTH aged 26 | THOMAS CURTIS aged 24 |
| WILLIAM FOULKE aged 24 | PEETER SHEREWOOD aged 21 |

---

* [So in the original : probably intended for LIONEL

Elzabeth Cittie   THOMAS BOULDINGE his MUSTER

THOMAS BOULDINGE aged 40 in the *Swan* 1610
WILLIAM BOULDINGE borne in Virginia.
WILLIAM COXE aged 26 in the *Godspeede* 1610
RICHARD EDWARD'S aged 23 } in the *Jacob* 1624.
NICCOLAS DALE aged 20

REYNOLD BOOTH his MUSTER

REYNOLD BOOTH aged 32 in the *Hercules* 1609
ELIZABETH BOOTH aged 24 in the *Ann* 1623

Servant's
GEORGE LEVETT aged 29 in the *Bona Noua* 1619
THOMAS SEYWELL aged 20 in the *Tyger* 1623

THOMAS GARNETT his MUSTER

THOMAS GARNETT aged 40 in the *Swan* 1610
ELZABETH GARNETT aged 26 in the *Neptune* 1618
SUSAN GARNETT aged 3 borne in Virginia
AMBROSE GYFFITH aged 33 in the *Bona Noua* 1619
JOYSE GYFFITH aged 20 in the *Jacob* 1624

THOMAS DUNTHORNE his MUSTER

THOMAS DUNTHORNE aged 27 in the *Margett and John* 1620
ELZABETH DUNTHORNE aged 38 in the *Tryall* 1610

Servant's
WILLIAM TOMSON aged 22 ᔩ
GEORGE TURNOR aged 27 ᔥ in the *Swan* 1624
GEORGE BANCKES aged 15 ᔧ
THOMAS an Indian Boaye
ELZABETH JOONES aged 30 in the *Patience* 1609
SARA JOONES aged 5 borne in Virginia

Elzabeth Cittie

THOMAS STEPNEY his MUSTER

THOMAS STEPNEY aged 35 in the *Swan* 1610

M' STOCKTON his MUSTER

JONAS STOCKTON aged 40 in the *bona Noua* 1620
RICHARD POPELEY aged 26
RICHARD DAVIS aged 22
WALTER BARRETT aged 26   } in the *Bona Noua* 1620
TIMOTHEY STOCKTON aged 14

Servant's

WILLIAM DUGLAS aged 16 in the *Margett and John* 1621
JOHN WATSON aged 24 in the *Swan* 1624

TOBIAS HURST his MUSTER

TOBIAS HURST aged 22 in the *Treasurer* 1618

M' WILLIAM GANY his MUSTER

WILLIAM GANY aged 33 in the *George* 1616
ANNA GANY aged 24 in the *Bona Noua* 1620

Servant's

ANNA GANY borne in Virginia
THOMASIN EESTER aged 26 in the *Falcon* 1617
ELIZABETH POPE aged 8 in the *Abbigall* 1621
JOHN WRIGHT aged 20
WILLIAM CLARKE aged 20   } in the *Ambrose* 1623
HATHER TOMSON aged 18
THOMAS SAVADGE aged 18

Elzabeth Cittie

ALLEXANDER MOUNTNEY his MUSTER

ALLEXAND' MOUNTNEY aged 33 in the *Mary James* 1610.
LENORD MOUNTNEY aged 21 in the *Bona Noua* 1620
JOHN WALTON aged 28 in the *Elzabeth* 1621
BRYAN ROGERS aged 18 in the *Elzabeth* 1621
JOHN WASHBORNE aged 25 in the *Jonathan* 1619

A list of the BURIALLES in ELZABETH CITTY 1624.

WESTON BROWNE Aprill. 20.
RICHARD WIFFE Aprell 26
JOHN MILEMAN Aprell 28
JOHN JACKSON Maye 12
EDWARD HILL Maye 15
PEETER   Maye 16
JAMES MORE June 24
M' TOMSON
PHILLIP COOCKE   July 8
THOMAS EBES July 12
M' CHAMBERLINS Man July 17
SIBILL MORGON July 18
          WETHERSBY August 8
JAMES CHAMBERLIN August 11

M' FENTON Minister Septemb' 5.
WILLIAM WHITE Septemb' 12.
JAMES CHAMBERLIN Septemb' 22
MARY DOWNEMAN a Child Nouemb' 23.
JOHN STAMFORD Septemb' 30
THOMAS DAVIS
PEETER DICKENSON
RICHARD EASTE
THOMAS HUNTER
JOHN SIMNELL*
HENRIE MIDDELLTON
SAMMUELL LAMBERT
JOHN BUSH.

A MUSTER of the Inhabitente of ELIZABETH CITTIE beyond Hampton River.   Beinge the Companyes land.

CAP^t FRANCIS WEST his MUSTER

Capt FRANCIS WEST Counseler aged 36 in the *Mary Ann Margett* 1610
Mrs FRANCIS WEST Widdowe in the *Supply* 1620
NATHANIELL WEST borne in Virginia

---

* [This name has been altered from some previous spelling : but it is doubtless correct as printed.]

Elzabeth Cittie   Servant's
JOANE FAIRECHILD aged 20 in the *George* 1618
BENIAMIN OWIN aged 18 in the *Swan* 1623
WILLIAM PARNELL aged 18 in the *Southampton* 1622
WALTER COUPER aged 22 in the *Neptune* 1618
REINOULD GODWIN aged 30 in the *Abigall* 1620
JOHN PEDRO a Neger aged 30 in the *Swan* 1623

CAP^T JOHN MARTIN his MUSTER

Capt JOHN MARTIN
SACKFORD WETHERELL aged 21
JOHN SMITH aged 31   }in the *Swan* 1624
JOHN HOWARD aged 24
JOHN ANTHONIE aged 23

GEORGE MEDCALFE his MUSTER

GEORGE MEDCALFE aged 46
SARA MEDCALFE aged 30 in the *Hopewell* 1624
JOANE A Child.

EDWARD JOHNSON his MUSTER

EDWARD JOHNSON aged 26 in the *Abigall* 1621
                         in the *Bona Noua* 1621
A Child borne in Virginia

JOHN LAUCKFILD his MUSTER

JOHN LAUCKFILD aged 24 in the *Bona Noua* 1621
ALICE LAUCKFILD aged 24 in the *Abbigall* 1621
SAMMUELL KENNELL aged 30 in the *Abigall* 1621

Elzabeth Cittie

WILLIAM FOWLER his MUSTER

WILLIAM FOWLER aged 30 in the *Abigall* 1621
MARGRETT FOWLER aged 30 in the *Abigall* 1621

WALTER ELY his MUSTER

WALTER ELY
ELZABETH ELY aged 30 in the *Warwicke* 1622
ANN ELY borne in Virginia

WILLIAM TILER his MUSTER

WILLIAM TILER in the *Francis Bonaventure* 1620
ELIZABETH TILER in the *Francis Bonaventure* 1620

Servant's

ROBART MORE aged 50 in the *Prouidence* 1622
WILLIAM BROWNE aged 26 in the *Prouidence* 1622
ROBART TODD aged 20 in the *Hopewell* 1622
ANTHONIE BURT aged 18 in the *Hopwell* 1622
SAMIELL BENNETT aged 40 in the *Prouidence* 1622
JOANE BENNETT in the *prouidence* 1622

THOMAS FLYNT his MUSTER

THOMAS FLYNT in the *Diana* 1618
THOMAS MERRES aged 21 in the *Francis Bona Venture* 1620
HENRIE WHEELER aged 20 in the *Tryall* 1620.
JOHN BROCKE aged 19 in the *Bona Noua* 1619
JAMES BROOKES aged 19 in the *Jonathan* 1619
ROBART SAVADGE aged 18 in the *Elzabeth* 1621

Elzabeth Cittie

John Ward his MUSTER

John Ward in the *Elzabeth* 1621
Adam Rimwell aged 24 in the *Bona noua* 1619
Christopher Wynwill aged 26 in the *Bona Noua* 1619
Oliuer Jenkin aged 40
Joane Jenkin ℮ a littell Child
Henrie Potter aged 50
Ann Potter in the *London Marchant*
Robart Goodman aged 24 in the *Bona Noua* 1619

Gregorie Dorie his MUSTER

Gregorie Dorie aged 36 in the *Bona Noua* 1620.
his wiffe ℮ a littell Child borne in Virginia

John More his MUSTER

John More adge 36 in the *Bona Noua* 1620
Elzabeth More in the *Abigall* 1622.

Sargent William Barry his MUSTER

William Barry in the *Bona Noua* 1619

Servant's
Richard Frisbie aged 34 in the *Jonathan* 1619
William Rookines aged 26 in the *Bona Noua* 1619
Joseph Hattfild aged 24 in the *Bona Noua* 1619
Cutbert Seirson aged 22 in the *Bona Noua* 1619
John Gibbes aged 24 in the *Abigall* 1621
Francis Hill aged 22 in the *Bona Noua* 1619
John Vaghan aged 23 in the *Bona Noua* 1619
Edward Marshall aged 26 in the *Abigall* 1621

Elzabeth Cittie

WILLIAM JOYCE aged 26 in the *Abigall* 1621
WILLIAM EVAND'S aged 23 in the *Bona Noua* 1619
RALPH OSBORNE aged 22 in the *Bona Noua* 1619
MORRIS STANLEY aged 26 in the *hopewell* 1624
NICCOLAS WEASELL aged 28 in the *Abigall* 1621
STEPHEN DICKSON aged 25 in the *Bona Noua* 1619
THOMAS CALDER aged 24 in the *Bona Noua* 1619

WILLIAM HAMPTON his MUSTER

WILLIAM HAMPTON age 34 in the *Bona Noua* 1621.
JOANE HAMPTON
JOHN ARNDELL age 22 in the *Abigall* 1621

ANTHONIE BONALL his MUSTER

ANTHONIE BONALL age 42 ⎱ in the *Abigall* 1621
ELIAS LEGARDO age 38 ⎰
ROBART WRIGHT age 45 in the *Swan* 1608
JOANE WRIGHT and two Children borne in virginia
WILLIAM BINSLEY age 18 in the *Jacob* 1624
ROBART GODWIN age 19 in the *Swan* 1624

VIKBRITT ⎱ two frenchmen in the *Abigall* 1622
OBLE HERO ⎰

ROBART THRASHER his MUSTER

ROBART THRASHER age 22 in the *Bona Noua* 1620
ROLAND WILLIAMES age 20 in the *Jonathan* 1623.

Servant
JOHN SACKER age 20 in the *Marget and John* 1623

JOHN HANEY age 27 in the *Margett and John* 1621

Elezabeth Cittie

ELZABETH HANIE in the *Abigall* 1622

NICHOLAS ROWE in the *Elzabeth* 1621

MARY ROWE in the *London Marchant* 1620

Servant's

THOMAS MORELAND } age 19 in the *Abigall* 1621
RALPH HOOLE ......

A list of the DEAD beyond Hampton River

of M' BONALES Servant......... 1

M' DOWSE his men.............. 2

M' PEETER ARNDELL

The Easterne Shore.

A MUSTER of the Inhabitance of the Easterne Shore ouer the Baye.

CAPᵀ WILLIAM EPES his MUSTER. (in the *William and Thomas*

MARGRETT EPES in the *George* 1621

Servant's

NICCHOLAS RAYNBERD age 22 in the *Swan* 1624

WILLIAM BURDITT age 25 in the *Susan* 1615

THOMAS CORNISH age 25 in the *Dutie* 1620

PEETER PORTER age 19 in the *Tiger* 1621

JOHN BAKER age 20 in the *Ann* 1623

EDWARD ROGERS age 26 in the *Ann* 1623

THOMAS WARDEN age 24 in the *Ann* 1623

BENIAMINE KNIGHT age 28 in the *Bona Noua* 1620

NICCOLAS GRANGER age 15 in the *George* 1618

WILLIAM MUNNES age 25 in the *Sampson* 1619

HENRIE WILSON age 24 in the *Sampson* 1619

JAMES BLACKBORNE age 20 in the *Sampson* 1619

NICHOLAS SUMERFILD age 15 in the *Sampson* 1619

Capᵀ JOHN WILLCOCKES his MUSTER

Capᵗ JOHN WILLCOCKES in the *Bona Noua* 1620
HENRIE CHARLTON age 19 in the *George* 1623

Ancient THOMAS SAUAGE his MUSTER

THOMAS SAVAGE in the *John and Francis* 1607
ANN SAVAGE in the *Sea Flower* 1621

Servant's

JOHN WASHBORNE age 30 in the *Jonathan* 1620
THOMAS BELSON age 12

Capᵀ THō: GRAUES his MUSTER

Capᵗ THOMAS GRAUES in the *Mary and Margrett* 1607

WALTER SCOTT his MUSTER

WALTER SCOTT in the *Hercules* 1618
APPHIA SCOTT in the *Gift* 1618
PERCIS SCOTT borne in Virginia

THOMAS POWELL his MUSTER

THOMAS POWELL in the *Sampson* 1618

WILLIAM SMITH his MUSTER

WILLIAM SMITH age 26 in the *Sampson* 1618

EDWARD DREWE his MUSTER

EDWARD DREWE age 22 in the *Sampson* 1618

Easterne shore   CHARLES HARMAN his MUSTER

CHARLES HARMAN age 24 in the *Furtherance* 1622
JOHN ASKUME age 22 in the ⎫
ROBERT FENNELL age 20 in the ⎬ *Charles* 1624
JAMES KNOTT age 23 in the *George* 1617

NICHOLAS HODGSKINS his MUSTER

NICHOLAS HODGSKINES age 27 in the *Edwin* 1616
TEMPORANCE HODGSKINES in the *Jonathan* 1620
MARGRETT HODGSKINS borne in virginia

SOLLOMAN GREENE his MUSTER

SOLLOMAN GREENE age 27 in the *Diana* 1618

THOMAS GASKOYNE his MUSTER

THOMAS GASKOYNE age 34 in the *Bona Noua* 1619

WILLIAM ANDROS at the age 25 in the *Treasuror* 1617
DANNIELL CUGLEY age 28 in the *London Marchant* 1620

JOHN BLORE his MUSTER

JOHN BLORE age 27 in the *Star* 1610
FRANCIS BLORE age 25 in the *London Marchant* 1620
Servant's
JOHN PARRAMORE age 17 in the *Bona Venture* 1622
JOHN WILKINES

Easterne shore

ROBART BALL his MUSTER

ROBART BALL age 27 in the *London Marchant* 1619

WILLIAM BIBBIE his MUSTER

WILLIAM BIBBIE age 22 in the *Swan* 1621*
THOMAS SPARKES age 24 in the *Susan* 1616

JOHN HOME his MUSTER

JOHN HOME age 25 in the *Margerett and John* 1621

JOHN WILKINES his MUSTER

JOHN WILKINES age 26 in the *Mary gould* 1618
BRIGGETT WILKINES age 20 in the *Warwicke* 1621

PERREGRIM WATKINES his MUSTER

PERREGRIN WATKINES age 24 in the *George* 1621

WILLIAM DAVIS his MUSTER

WILLIAM DAVIS age 33 in the *William and Thomas* 1618

DEAD in this Plantation 1624

THOMAS HELCOTT.
JOHN WILKINES.

* [Not quite clear : may be 1620, blotted.]

[PATENTS GRANTED, &c.]

THE CORPORAĈON OF HENERICO*
[1626.]

ON the Northerly side of James River, from the Falles downe to
Henerico. Contayning about x Miles in length, are yᵉ publique
Land's, reserved ℓ laid out, wherof 10,000: Acres, for the
Vniuersitie Lands, 3000 Acres for the Companys Lands, wᵗʰ
other Land belonging to the Colledge; the Coṁon Land for
the Corporaĉon 1500 Acres.

On the Southerley side begining from the Falles, their are these
PATTENTS graunted (vizt.

JOHN PETERSON	100: Acres	
ANTHONY EDWARD'S	100:	
NATHANELL WORTON	100:	
JOHN PROCTER	100:	
THOMAS TRACY..................	100:	
JOHN BILLIARD..................	100:	
FRANCIS WESTON...............	300:	
PHETTIPLACE CLOSSE	100:	} By Pattent.
JOHN PRICE	150:	
PETTER NEVMART†	120:‡	
WILLIAM PERRY	100:	
JOHN BLOWER	100: Surrendred	
for the vse of the Iron Workes.		
EDWARD HUDSON	100:	
THOMAS MORGAN..............	150:	
THOMAS SHEFFIELD............	150:	

* [There is a duplicate of this list, but it agrees in the main : we have indicated in notes
all differences of any importance in the spelling of names.]

† [NEWMART in the duplicate list.]

‡ [Apparently 120, though blotted ; but in the duplicate list it is 100.]

In COXENDALE, wthin the same Corporacon of HENERICO.

EDWARD BARKLEY..............	12 Acres	
RICHARD BOLTON	100	
ROBERT AUKLAND*	200	
JOHN GRIFFIN	50	By Pattent.
PETTER NEINNEART†	40	
THOMAS TINDALL	100	
THOMAS READE	100	
JOHN LAYDEN	200	

THE CORPORACON OF CHARLES CITTIE

GEORGE GRINES‡	30 Acres	planted	
WILLIAM VINCENT	100	planted	
RICHARD TAYLOR	100	planted	
ROBERT PARTTEN	50		
THOMAS DOUSE	400		
GEORGE CAWCOTT..............	100		
ISACKE CHAPLINE	50		
THOMAS ROSSE	100		
JOHN OWLYE	50		By Pattent.
JOSUAH CHARDE	100		
JOHN DODD'S	50		
WILLIAM SHARPES	40		
JAMES VSHUR.............	100		
WILLIAM CRADOUKE	100		
JOHN OWLY	150		
THEOPHILUS BERISTON	100		

* [ACKLAND in the duplicate list.] † [NEIMART in the duplicate list.]
‡ [GRIMES in the duplicate list.]

JOHN HARRIS......................	200 Acres	planted
ROBERT PARTTIN	100	planted
NATHANIELL CAUSEY	200	
JOHN CARTTER	40	
Captaine MADDISON	250	planted
RICHARD BIGGS	150	planted
FRANCIS MASON	50	
HENRY BAGWELL	50	
SAMUELL JARRATT*	100	
JOHN DADE........................	100	
THOMAS SWINHOW	300	
THOMAS HOBSON	150	
SYMON FORTESCUE	100	
THOMAS OAGUE..................	100	
WILLIAM BALY	100	
JOHN WRITTERS	100	
Leift: RICH: CRUDGE.............	250	
JOHN CARR........................	100	
RICHARD TAYLOR	100	
ROBERT BOURNE	250	planted

} By Pattent.

Laid out for the Company Land belowe SHERLEY HUNDRED Iland 3000 Acres

Claimed by CAPTAINE FRANCIS WEST, att WESTOUER 500 Acres

Vppon APMATUCKE RIVER

WILLIAM FARRAR	100 Acres	
HENRY MILWARD	250	
CHARLES MAGNOR	650	
SAMUELL SHARPE	100	
HUMPHERY KENT...............	50	

} By Pattent.

* [JERRATT in the duplicate list.]

Mr ABRA: PERSEY .... 1150 Acres		
RICHARD SYMONS 100		
ARTHUR ANTONYE .... 150 Acres	} By Pattent	
WILLIAM SIZEMORE .... 100 Acres		
WILLIAM DOWGLAS .... 250 Acres		

Here is Land laid out for CHARLES CITTIE, and the Comon Land.

The Territory of GREATE WEYONOKE.

CHRISTOPHER HARDING ...... 100 Acres		
WILLIAM BAILY 50		
RICHARD PRATT 150		
WILLIAM JARRET* 200		
Capt JO: WOODLIFFE 550		
TEMPERANCE BAILY 200	} By Pattent	
SAMUELL JORDAN .... 450 planted		
TEMPERANCE BAILY .... 200 planted		
ISACKE CHAPLIN .... 200 planted		
Capt: NATHANIELL POWLE ... 600 Acres		

Mr SAMUELL MAICOCKES Diuident.

PERSEYS hundred .... 1000 Acres planted

TANKS WAYONOKE ouer against } 2200 Acres.
    PERSEYS hundred

Captaine SPILLMANS Diuident.

MARTTIN BRANDON belonging to Captaine JOHN MARTTIN by Pattent out of England (planted).

Vppon the easterly Side of Chapokes Creeke, is appointed 500 Acres, belonging to ye place of Treasure by order of Courtt

JOHN MARTTIN .... 100 Acres		
GEORGE HARRISON 200	} By Pattent	
SAMUELL EACH 500		

---

* [JERRATT in the duplicate list.]

On the Northerly Side, is the land belonging to Southampton hundred Containeing 100000: Acres, extending from Tanks Wayonoke downe to the mouth of Chicahomny River.

THE CORPORACŌN OF JAMES CITTIE

Adioyneing to the mouth of Chicohominy River ther are 3000 Acres of Land, laid out for yᵉ Company 3000 Acres, laid out for the place of the Gouerner (planted) in wᶜʰ are Some smale parcells, graunted by Sir THOMAS DALE and Sir SAMUELL ARGALL (planted)

Mʳ RICHARD BUCKE .... 750 Acres planted ⎫ By Pattent
The GEABE [GLEABE] LAND......... 100 .... ⎭ By Pattent

In the Iland of James Cittie, are many parcells of land, graunted to the inhabitant's by Pattent, and order of Courtt

The Territory of TAPPAHANNA ouer against JAMES CITTIE.

JOHN DODD'S.....................	150 Acres		⎫
JOHN BURROWS	150	planted	
RICHARD PACE	200	planted	
FRANCIS CHAPMAN	100		⎬ By Pattent
THOMAS GATES	100		
Mʳ JOHN ROLFE	400	planted	
Capt Wᴹ POWELL*	200	planted	⎭

Capt SAMUELL MATHEWS Diuident planted
Captaine JOHN HURLESTONS Diuident planted

JOHN BAINHAM..................	200 Acres	planted	⎫
Mʳ GEORGE SANDYS	300	planted	
EDWARD GRINDON	150	planted	
WILLIAM EWENS	1000	planted	⎬ By Pattent
Capt Wᴹ POWELL*	550	planted	
Ensigne JO: VTIE	100		
ROBERT EUERS......	100 Acres		⎭

* [POWLE, in each case, in the duplicate list.]

In Hog Iland MARY BAILY 500 Acres planted (by pattent

Southāpton hundred in Hog Iland planted

Captaine RAPHE HAMAR* by Clame in Hog Iland. 250 Acres
planted

ARCHERS HOPE

Capt ROGER SMITH............	100 Acres planted	} byorder of Courtt.
RICHARD KINGSMELL	200	
Mʳ Wᴹ CLAYBOURNE...........	250	
Ensigne Wᴹ SPENCE ....} ℓ JOHN FOWLER ....}	300 Acres planted	
JOHN JOHNSON	100	
RICHARD KINGSMELL	300	
WILLIAM FAIRFAX	200	
JOAKIN ANDREWES	100	} By Pattent.
JOHN GRUBB	100	
JOHN JEFFERSON	250	
GEORGE PERRY	100	
RICHARD STAPLES.............	150	
RICHARD BREWSTER...........	100	

MARTTINS HUNDRED Containeing as is Alledged 80000 Acres part
planted

Nere MULBERY ILAND

NATHANILL HUATT†	200 Acres	
Capt Wᴹ PEERCE ....} Mʳ JOHN ROLFE with some } others ....}	1700: Acres planted	} By Pattent

---

* [HAMOR in the duplicate list.]

† [Apparently so, though the second and third letters are blotted; but it is clearly HUTT
in the duplicate list.]

WAROSQUOIACKE Plantacōn Contayneing downe ward's, from Hog
   Iland xiiij[ten] miles by the River side, in w[ch] are these pattents
   following (vizt) :

JOHN CARTER	100 Acres		
CHRISTOPHER DANIELL	100		
ADAM DIXSON	100		
JOHN BERRY	100		
THOMAS WINTER	100		By Pattent
JOHN POLLINGTON	600		
THOMAS POOLE	100		
ANTHONY BARHAM	100		
Capt NETHA: BASSE	300	planted	
GILES JONES	150	planted	

BLUNT POINTE

Mr Wm CLAYBOURNE	500 Acres by orde' of Court	
JOHN BAINHAM	300 Acres by pattent	
Capt RAPHE HAMER*	500 Acres by order of Court	
GILBERT PEPPETT	50 Acres planted	By pattent
FRANCIS GIFFORD	50 Acres planted	
Captaine SAMUELL MATHEWS his Diuedent by order of Court. planted.		
THOMAS HETHERSALL	200 Acres	
CORNELIUS MAY	100	
RICHARD CRAUEN	150	
RICHARD TREE	50	By Pattent.
RICHARD DOMELAWE	150	
PERSIUALL IBBISON	50	
EDWARD WATTERS	100 Acres	

---

* [HAMOR in the duplicate list.]

Belowe BLUNT POINT

Capt JOHN HURLESTONE ...	100 Acres	} by pattent
ROBERT HUTCHINS	100 Acres	
JOHN SOUTHERNE	40 Acres	} by Order of Courtt
Sʳ FRANCIS WYATT	500 Acers	
MORRIS THOMSON	150 Acres	
JOHN SALFORD	100	
PHARAOH FLINTON	150	
LEIFT GILES ALINGTON	100	} by pattent
WILLIAM BENTLEY	50	
THOMAS GODBY.................	100 Acres	

THE CORPORACON OF ELIZABETH CITTIE

NEWPORTS NEWES	1300 Acres	plantd	
The GLEAB LAND	100	planted	
Mʳ KEYTH*	100	planted	
THOMAS TAYLOR	50	planted	} by pattent
JOHN POWELL	150	planted	
Capt Wᴹ TUCKER	150	......	
RICHARD BOULTON	50 Acres	Claimed ℓ planted	
JOHN SALFORD	50 Acres	planted	
ROBERT SALFORD†	100	planted	
ROBERT SALFORD†	100		
MILES PRICKETT	150	planted	
JOHN BUSH	300	planted	
WILLIAM JULIAN	150	planted	
LEIFT: LUPO	350	planted	} by pattent
ELIZABETH LUPO	50		
THOMAS SPILMAN..............	50	planted	
EDWARD HILL	100	planted	
ALEXANDER MOUNTNEY......	100	planted	
WILLIAM COLE	50	planted	
WILLIAM BROOKS..............	100	planted	
The GLEAB LAND	100	planted	
ELIZA: DONTHORNE‡	100	planted	} by pattent
WILLIAM GANY.................	200	planted	

* [KETH in the duplicate list.]   † [Thus repeated in the original.
‡ [DUNTHORNE in the duplicate list.]

WILLIAM CAPPS divident planted

WILLIAM LANDSDELL ....   100 Acres plantd ⎫
Mr Wm CLAYBOURNE   150   planted |
JOHN GUNNERY   150   planted |
MARY BOULDIN................   100   planted |
THOMAS BOULDIN   200   planted ⎬by Pattent.
Mr PETTER ARUNDELL ......   200 |
BARTHOLMEW HOSKINS ......   100 |
Capt RAUGHLY CROSHAW betweene Fox hill & Pemonkey River.............. } 500 ⎭

THO: WILLOWSABY about 2 miles w^{thin} the mouth of Pemonkey River } 200 Acres, by order of Court

On the Easterly Side of Southampton River, their are 3000 Acres, belonging to the Company at Elizabeth Cittie, planted, And 1500* Acres Comon Land,

---

On ye South Side of the maine River against ELIZABETH CITTIE

THOMAS WILLOUGHBYE......   100 Acres ⎫
THOMAS CHAPMAN ....   100 |
THOMAS BREWOOD ....   200 |
JOHN DOWNMAN† ....   100 ⎬ by pattent
Capt Wm TUCKER ....   650 |
JOHN SIPSEY....................   250 |
LEIFT: JO: CHEESMAN‡ ......   200 ⎭

The Easterne shore Ouer the Bay

JOHN BLOWER ....   140 Acres
Ensigne SALVADGE his Diuident
Sir GEORGE YARDLY at Hangers 3700 Acres by Order of Court

Certaine others haue planted their, but no Pattents haue bene graunted them, the Companyes and the Secretaryes Tennants, were alsoe their Seated but no land ordered, to bee laid out for them, as in the other 4 Corporacons.

---

* [150 in the duplicate list.]   † [DOWNEMAN in the duplicate list.]
‡ [CHESMAN in the duplicate list.]

[PORTS OF IPSWICH AND WEYMOUTH,

RETURNS OF THOSE WHO EMBARKED

FOR NEW ENGLAND.

1634—1635.]

[RETURNS OF THOSE WHO EMBARKED
FOR NEW ENGLAND.
1634—1635.]

To the right honno^{ble} the Lords & others of his Ma^{t's} moste honno^{ble}
privie Councell.

The humble peticon ℯ Certificates of JOHN CUTTINGE
Ma^r of the Shipp called the *Francis*, and WILLIAM
ANDREWES Ma^r of the *Elizabeth*, both of Ipsw^{ch}

Right honno^{ble} according to yo' Lopps order, wee doe heerewth presente
vnto yo' Lopps, the names of all the Passengers that wente for Newe-
England in the said Shipps the Tenth daye of Aprill laste paste.

Humblie intreatinge yo' Lopps (they havinge pforemed yo'
honno's order) that the bond's in that behalfe given may
bee delivered back to yo' peticon's.

And they as in dutie bound will daylie praye for yo'
honno's healthes ℯ happynes

IPSWICH   A Note of all the names and ages of all those which
did not take the Oath of Allegiance or Supremacy being vnder
age shipped in our Port In the *Francis* of Ipswich M' JOHN CUTTING:
bound for New England the last of Aprill 1634

WILL: WESTWOOD:* { JOHN LEA ....aged 13 yeres
                 { GRACE NEWELL ...aged 13 yeres

* [The " braces " are not in the original, but have been inserted for the sake of clearness.]

Robt: Rose:	JOHN ROSE ....aged 15 [yeeres]
	ROBERT ROSE ....aged 15
	ELIZ: ROSE ....aged 13
	MARY ROSE ....aged 11
	SAMUELL ROSE ......aged 9
	SARAH ROSE............aged 7
	DANYELL ROSE ......aged 3
	DARCAS ROSE ....aged 2
WILL: FREEBOURN:...	MARY FREEBOURNE . aged 7
	SARAH FREEBOURNE aged 2
	JOHN ALDBURGH......aged 14
J^{no}: BERNARD:	FAYTH NEWELL ......aged 14
	HENRY HAWARD..... aged 7
ABRAHĀ: NEWELL...	ABRAHAM NEWELL...aged 8
	JOHN NEWELL ....aged 5
	ISAACKE NEWELL ...aged 2
EDWARD: BUGBY......	SARAH BUGBYE ......aged 4
JOHN: PEASE:	FAYTH CLEARKE......aged 15
	ROBERT PEASE........aged 3
	DARCAS GREENE......aged 15
ROWLAND: STEBING:	THOMAS STEBING ...aged 14
	SARAH STEBING ......aged 11
	ELIZ: STEBING ....aged 6
	JOHN STEBING........aged 8
	MARY WINCHE........aged 15
MARY: BLOSSE:	RICHARD BLOSSE......aged 11
THO: SHERWOOD: ...	ANNA SHERWOOD ...aged 14
	ROSE SHERWOOD......aged 11
	THOMAS SHERWOOD . aged 10
	REBECCA SHERWOOD aged 9
ROB^t: COOE:	JOHN COOE ....aged 8
	ROBERT COOE ....aged 7
	BENIAMIN COOE ......aged 5
RICH: PEPPER:.........	MARY PEPP [PEPPER] aged 3 and halfe
	STEPHEN BECKETT...aged 11

ELIZ: HAMOND: .. ... $\begin{cases} \text{ELIZ: HAMOND ....aged 15 [yeeres]} \\ \text{SARAH HAMOND ....aged 10} \\ \text{JOHN HAMOND ....aged 7} \end{cases}$

Ipswich Customehouse this xij[th] of Nouember 1634

PHIL: BROWNE   EDW: MANN Compt
  ꝑ Custr.

PSWICH   A Note of the names and ages of all the Passengers which tooke shipping In the *Francis* of Ipswich M' JOHN CUTTING bound for new England the last of Aprill 1634

	yeeres		[yeeres]
JOHN BEETES.............aged	40	ROBERT PEASE ....aged	27
WILLIAM HAULTON......aged	23	HUGH MASON .... ⎱ aged ⎱	28
NICHOLAS JENNING'S ...aged	22	HESTER his wife ...... ⎰ aged ⎰	22
WILLIAM WESTWOODE ⎱ aged ⎱	28	ROWLAND STEBING ... ⎱ aged ⎱	40
BRIDGETT his wife...... ⎰ aged ⎰	32	SARAH his wife .... ⎰ aged ⎰	43
CLEARE DRAꝑ [DRAPER] aged	30	THOMAS SHERWOOD... ⎱ aged	48
ROBERT ROSE .... ⎱ aged ⎱	40	ALICE his wife .... ⎰ aged	47
MARGERY his wife...... ⎰ aged ⎰	40	THOMAS KING ....aged	19
JOHN BERNARD......... ⎱ aged ⎱	36	JOHN MAPES ....aged	21
MARY his wife .... ⎰ aged ⎰	38	MARY BLOSSE ....aged	40
WILLIAM FREBOURNE ⎱ aged ⎱	40	ROBERT COOE .... ⎱ aged ⎱	38
MARY his wife .... ⎰ aged ⎰	33	ANNA his wife .... ⎰ aged ⎰	43
ANTHONY WHITE........aged	27	MARY ONGE ....aged	27
EDWARD BUGBYE ...... ⎱ aged ⎱	40	THOMAS BOYDEN ....aged	21
REBECCA his wife ...... ⎰ aged ⎰	32	RICHARD WATTLIN ......aged	28
ABRAHAM NEWELL ... ⎱ aged ⎱	50	JOHN LYUERMORE .....aged	28
FRANCIS his wife ...... ⎰ aged ⎰	40	RICHARD PEPꝑ [PEPPER] ⎱ aged	27
JUST HOULDING ....aged	23	MARY his wife .... ⎰ aged	30
JOHN PEASE ....aged	27	RICHARD HOULDING ...aged	25
ROBERT WINGE... ....aged	60	JUDETH GARNETT ......aged	26
JUDITH his wife...........aged	43	ELIZ: HAMOND ....aged	47
JOHN GREENE ....aged	27	THURSTON CLEARKE ...aged	44

These psons aboue named tooke the Oath of Allegeance and Supremacy at his Maties Custome house in Ips^wch before vs his Maties Officers according to the order of the Lords & others of his Maties most hono^ble Priuy Councell: This xij^th of Nouember 1634

    Ipswich Customehouse   THO CLERI scr

                 EDW: MANN Compt

        PHIL BROWNE

          p Custr.

IPSWICH   A Note of the names and ages of all the Passengers which tooke shipping In the *Elizabeth* of Ipswich M' WILLIĀ ANDREWS bound for new EngLand the last of Aprill 1634

	yeeres		[yeeres]
JOHN SHERMAN .... aged	20	JOHN BERNARD......... } aged	30
JOSEPH MOSSE .... aged	24	PHEBE his wife .... } aged	27
RICHARD WOODWARD } aged	45	THOMAS KILBORNE ... } aged	24
ROSE his wife............ } aged	50	ELIZABETH his wife ... } aged	20
EDMOND LEWIS......... } aged	33	JOHN CROSSE............ } aged	50
MARY his wife .... } aged	32	ANNE his wife .... } aged	38
JOHN SPRING............ } aged	45	ROBERT SHERIN ....aged	32
ELINOR his wife......... } aged	46	HUMPHRY BRADSTREET } aged	40
THURSTON RAYNOR... } aged	40	BRIDGETT his wife ...... } aged	30
ELIZABETH his wife ... } aged	36	HENERY GLOUER ....aged	24
THOMAS SKOTT......... } aged	40	WILLIAM BLOMFIELD . } aged	30
ELIZABETH his wife ... } aged	40	SARAH his wife .... } aged	25
HENERY KEMBALL ... } aged	44	ROBERT DAY .... } aged	30
SUSAN his wife .... } aged	35	MARY his wife .... } aged	28
RICHARD KEMBALL ... } aged	39	SARAH REYNOLD'S ......aged	20
VRSULA his wife......... } aged		ROBERT GOODALL...... } aged	30
ISAACKE MIXER ...... } aged	31	KATHERIN his wife ... } aged	28
SARAH his wife .... } aged	33	SAMUELL SMITHE...... } aged	32
MARTHA SCOTT............aged	60	ELIZABETH his wife ... } aged	32
GEORGE MUNNING'S... } aged	37	THOMAS HASTING'S ... } aged	29
ELIZABETH his wife ... } aged	41	SUSAN his wife .... } aged	34

	[yeeres]			[yeeres]
SUSAN MUNSON ....aged	25		JOHN PALMER ....aged	24
MARTIN VNDERWOOD ⎫ aged	38		DANYELL PIERCE ....aged	23
MARTHA his wife ...... ⎭ aged	31		JOHN CLEARKE...........aged	22
HENERY GOULDSON... ⎫ aged	43		JOHN FIRMIN..............aged	46
ANNE his wife ....⎭ aged	45		REBECCA ISAACKE ......aged	36
ANNE GOULDSTON ......aged	18		ANNE DORIFALL ....aged	24
WILLIAM CUTTING ......aged	26			

These psons aboue named tooke the Oath of Allegeance and Supremacy, at his Mat's Custome house in Ipswich before vs his Maties Officers according to the order of the Lords & others of his Mat's most Honoble Priuy Councell : This xijth of Nouember, 1634.

THO CLERI Scr

Ipswich Custome House

PHIL. BROWNE   EDW: MAN

ꝑ Custr   Compt

PSWICH A Note of all the names and ages of all those which did not take the oath of Allegiance or Supremacy being vnder age shipped in o' Port In the *Elizabeth* of Ipswich Mr WILLIA ANDREWES, bound for New England the last of Aprill 1634

ED: LEWIS: .... ⎰ JOHN LEWIS: aged 3 yeeres
           ⎱ THOMAS LEWIS: aged 3 quarters

RICH: WOODWARD:...... ⎰ GEORGE WOODWARD: aged 13
           ⎱ JOHN WOODWARD: aged 13

JOHN: SPRING: .... ⎧ MARY SPRING: aged 11.
           ⎪ HENRY SPRING aged 6
           ⎨ JOHN SPRING aged 4
           ⎩ WILLIAM SPRING aged 3 quarters

THURSTON: RAYNOR.... ⎧ THURSTON RAYNER aged 13
           ⎪ JOSEPH RAYNOR aged 11
           ⎪ ELIZABETH RAYNOR aged 9
           ⎨ SARAH RAYNOR aged 7
           ⎪ LIDIA RAYNOR, aged 1
           ⎪ EDWARD RAYNOR aged 10
           ⎩ ELIZABETH KEMBALL aged 13

36

THO: SCOTT: ....
{ ELIZABETH SCOTT aged 9 [yeeres]
ABIGAIL SCOTT aged 7
THOMAS SCOTT aged 6

ISAACK MIXER aged 4

HEN: KEMBALL...........
{ ELIZABETH KEMBALL aged 4
SUSAN KEMBALL aged 1 and halfe
RICHARD CUTTING aged 11

RICH: KEMBALL ....
{ HENRY KEMBALL aged 15 yeeres
RICHARD KEMBALL aged 11
MARY KEMBALL aged 9
MARTHA KEMBALL aged 5
JOHN KEMBALL aged 3
THOMAS KEMBALL aged 1

JOHN LAUERICKE aged 15

GEORGE: MUNNINGS:...
{ ELIZ: MUNNING'S aged 12
ABIGAIL MUNNING'S aged 7

JNO: BERNARD: ....
{ JOHN BERNARD aged 2
SAMUELL BERNARD aged 1
THO: KING aged 15

HUMP: BRADSTREET:...
{ ANNA BRADSTREET aged 9
JOHN BRADSTREET aged 3
MARTHA BRADSTREET aged 2
MARY BRADSTREET aged 1

WILLI: BLOMFIELD: ...
SARAH BLOMFIELD aged 1

SAM: SMITH: ....
{ SAMUELL SMITH aged 9
MARY SMITH aged 4
ELIZ: SMITH aged 7
PHILLIP SMITH aged 1

ROBᵀ: GOODALE: ....
{ MARY GOODALE aged 4
ABRAHAM GOODALE aged 2
ISAACKE GOODALE aged halfe a yeere

HEN: GOULDSON: ......
MARY GOULDSON aged 15

Ipswich Custome house this xij^th of Nouember 1634

PHIL: BROWNE.

THO CLERI scr

p Custr.

EDW: MAN

Compt

BOUND FOR NEW ENGLAND

WAYMOUTH
    ye 20th of
March 1635* }

 1 JOSEPH HALL of Somerst a Ministr aged 40 year
 2 AGNIS HALL his Wife aged .... 25 yr
 3 JOANE HALL his daughtr aged 15 Yeare
 4 JOSEPH HALL his sonne aged 13 Yeare.
 5 TRISTRAM his son aged......... 11 Yeare
 6 ELIZABETH HALL his daughtr aged 7 Yeare
 7 TEMPERANCE his daughtr aged 9 Yeare
 8 GRISSELL HALL† his daughtr aged 5 Yeare
 9 DOROTHY HALL† his daughtr aged 3 Yeare
10 JUDETH FRENCH his s'vamt aged 20 Yeare
11 JOHN WOOD his s'vaunt aged 20 yeare
12 ROBT DABYN his s'vamt aged 28 Yeare
13 MUSACHIELL BERNARD of batcombe Clothier
        in the County of Somersett 24 Yeare
14 MARY BERNARD his wife aged 28 yeare
15 JOHN BERNARD his sonne aged 3 Yeare
16 NATHANIELL his sonne aged 1 Yeare
17 RICH: PERSONS salter ℓ his s'vant: 30: yeare
18 FRANCIS BABER Chandler aged 36 yeare
19 JESOPE Joyner aged 22 Yeare
20 WALTER JESOP Weaver aged 21 Yeare
21 TIMOTHY TABOR of Som'st of Batcombe
        taylor aged 35 Yeare ———————
22 JANE TABOR his Wife aged 35 Yeare
23 JANE TABOR his daughtr aged 10 Yeare
24 ANNE TABOR his daughtr: aged 8 yeare
25 SARAH TABOR his daughtr aged 5 Yeare

* [Really 163⅚.]   † [So in the original.]

26   WiℲℲᴍ Fever his s'vaunt aged 20 Yeare

27   Jɴᵒ: Whitmarck   aged 39 yeare

28   Alce Whitmarke his Wife aged 35 yeare

29   Jᴍᵒ* Whitmarcke his sonne aged 11 yeare

Portus
Waymouth 30   Jane his daughtʳ aged   7 Yeare

31   Ouseph [*or* Onseph] Whitmarke his sonne
        aged 5 yeare

32   Ricʜ̄: Whytemark his sonne aged 2 Yeare

33   WiℲℲᴍ Read of Batcombe Taylor in

34† Som'sᵗᵗ aged 28 Yeare ————————

35   Susan Read his Wife aged 29 Yeare

36   Hanna Read his daughtʳ aged 3 yeare

37   Lusan‡ Read his daughtʳ aged 1 yeare

38   Ricʜ̄: Adams his s'vante 29 Yeare

39   Mary his Wife   aged 26 yeare

40   Mary Cheame his daughtʳ aged 1 yeare

41   Zachary Bickewell   aged 45 Yeare

42   Agnis Bickwell his Wife aged 27 yeare

43   Jɴᵒ Bickwell his sonne aged 11 Yeare

44   Jɴᵒ Kitchin his servaunt   23 yeare

46§ George Allin   aged 24 Yeare

47   Katherin Allyn his Wife aged
        30 yeare ——————

48   George Allyn his sonne aged 16 yeare

49   WiℲℲᴍ Allyn his sonne aged 8 year

50: Mathew Allyn his sonne aged 6 yeare

51   Edward Poole his s'vaunt aged 26 yeare

52   Henry Kingman   aged 40 Yeares

53   Joane his wife beinge aged 39

54   Edward Kingman his son aged 16 year

55   Joane his daughtʳ aged 11: yeeare

---

* [Sic. But doubtless intended for Joʜɴ.]

† [It will be noticed that No. 34 is placed against the name of a place instead of that of a person.]

‡ [Probably intended for Susan.]   § [There is no No. 45.]

56 ANNE his daught[r] aged ...... 9 Yeare

57 THOMAS KINGMAN his sonne aged 7 Yeare

58 JOHN KINGHMAN his sonne aged 2 yeare

59 J[n] FORD his servaunt aged 30 Yeare

60 WILLIAM KINGE   aged 40* Yeare

61 DOROTHY his Wife   aged 34 yeare

62 MARY KINGE his daught[r] aged 12 year

63 KATHERYN his daught[r] aged 10 Yeare

64 Wiłłm KINGE his sonne aged 8 year

65 HANNA KINGE his daught[r]: aged 6 year

66† Somm'. [Somerset.]

THOMAS HOLBROOKE of Broudway aged 34: yeare

67 JANE HOLBROOKE his wife aged 34 Yeare

68 JOHN HOLBROOKE his sonne aged 11 yeare

69 THOMAS HOLBROOKE his sonne aged 10 yeare

70 ANNE HOLBROOKE his daught[r] aged 5 yea[re]

71 ELIZABETH his daught[r] aged 1 yeare

72 THOMAS DIBLE husbandm̄ aged 22 yeare

73 FRANCIS DIBLE soror aged   24 Yeare

74 ROBERT LOVELL husbandman aged 40 Year

75 ELIZABETH LOVELL his Wife aged 35 year

76 ZACHEUS LOVELL his sonne 15 yeares

78‡ ANNE LOVELL his daught[r]: aged 16 yeare

79 JOHN LOVELL his sonne aged 8 yeare

ELLYN his daught[r] aged ... 1 yeare

80 JAMES his sonne aged......... 1 yeare

81 JOSEPH CHICKIN his servant 16 year

82 ALICE KINHAM aged......... 22 yeare

83 ANGELL HOLLARD aged ... 21 yeare

84 KATHERYN his Wife 22 yeare

85 GEORGE LAND his servaunt   22 yeare

86 SARAH LAND§ his kinswoman 18 yeare

---

* [*Or* 30. One figure is written over the other, and I cannot tell which is the later.]

† [Thus in the original. This number should evidently come against the next line.]

‡ [There is no No. 77 ; but it will be observed that two lines below there is a name without number.]   § [Originally written LANG.]

	87	RICHARD JOANES of Dinder.........	
	88	ROB^T MARTYN of Badcombe husbandm̄	44
	89	HUMFREY SHEPHEARD husbandm̄...	32
	90	JOHN VPHAM husbandman	35 ......
	91	JOANE MARTYN	44 ......
	92	ELIZABETH VPHAM	32 ......
	93	JOHN VPHAM Juñ........................	07 ......
	94	WILLIAM GRAUE [GRAVE]	12 ......
	95	SARAH VPHAM	26 ......
	96	NATHANIELL VPHAM	05 ......
	97	ELIZABETH VPHAM	03.
Dors^t		RICHARD WADE of Simstuly	
	98*	Cop [Cooper] aged	60 ......
	99	ELIZABETH WADE his Wife	6†......
	100:	DINAH his daugh^r......................	22 ......
	101	HENRY LUSH his s'vant aged	17 ......
	102	ANDREWE HALLETT his s'vaunt	28 ......
	103	JOHN HOBLE husbandm̄	13 ......
	104	ROB^T HUSTE husbandm̄	40 ......
	105	JOHN WOODCOOKE	2 ......
	106	RICH̄ PORTER husband	3 ......

JOHN PORTER Deputy
Cleark to EDW:
THOROUGHGOOD

---

* [This number should be in the line above.]　　　　† [Sic in orig.]

A Register of the . . . .

of such persons a . . . .

and vpwards and haue t . . . .

to passe into forraigne partes from . .

march 1637 to the 29th * day of [S]ept. .

by vertu of a commission granted to

m^r thomas mayhew gentleman.

---

* [The list does not go beyond the 19th of September 1637 ; the above date must therefore be an error.   It should be mentioned that many passages to Holland are included in the original document : these we omit, as not pertinent to our object.   The last passage for *America* is dated May 15.   The dots indicate parts of the indorsement eaten away by age.]

[A REGISTER OF PERSONS ABOUT TO PASS INTO FOREIGN PARTS.

1637.]

THESE people went to New England: with WILLIAM:*ANDREWES:
of Ipswich M^r of the: *John: and Dorethey:* of Ipswich and
With WILLIAM ANDREWES his Sone. M^r of the *Rose:* of Yarmouth.

Aprill the / 8th / 1637. The examinaction of JOHN: BAKER: borne in
Norwch in Norffolck Grocar / ageed / 39 yeres and ELIZABETH:
his Wife / ageed / 31 yeares with 3 Children ELIZABETH: JOHN:
and THOMAS—and 4 Saruants. MAREY: ALXARSON: aged / 24
yeares ANNE: ALXARSON: aged / 20 yeares / BRIDGETT
BOULLE: aged / 32 yeares / and SAMUELL: ARRES: aged 14
yeares ar all desiroues to goe for / Charles Towne in New
England ther to inhabitt and Remaine ///

Aprill. the / 8th / 1637. The examinaction of NICHO: BUSBIE: of Norwch
in Norff / Weauer / aged / 50 yeares and / BRIDGETT: his Wife
/ aged / 53 yeares with / 4 / Children. NICHO: JOHN: ABRAHAM:
and SARATH: ar desirous to goe to boston in New England to
in habitt ///

Aprill. the / 8th / 1637 The examinaction of MICHILL: METCALFE: of
Norwch Dornix Weauear / aged. 45 yeares and / SARRAH: his
Wif / aged / 39 yeares with. / 8 Children / MICHILL: THOMAS:
MAREY: SARRAH: ELIZABETH: MARTHA: JOANE: and REBECA:

---

* [We follow the very peculiar punctuation of this list throughout.]

37

and his Saruant THOMAS COMBERBACH: aged / 16 / yeares ar
desirous to passe to boston in New England to inhabitt /!/

Aprill. the / 8ᵗʰ / 1637   The examinaction of JOHN: PERS: of Noᵗwch in
Noᵗff Weauear ageed 49 yeares / and ELIZABETH: his Wife aged /
36 yeares / with 4 Children. JOHN: BARBRE: ELIZABETH: and
JUDETH and one Saruant / JOHN: GEDNEY aged / 19 yeares.
are desirous to passe to boston in New England to inhabitt /!/

Aprill. the / 8ᵗʰ / 1637. The examinaction of WILLIAM: LUDKEN: of
Noᵗwch in Noᵗff / Locksmith ther boᵗne / ageed 33 yeares /
and ELIZABETH: his Wife / ageed. / 34 yeares. With one Child
and one Saruant / THOMAS: HOMES: are desirous to goe to
Bostone in Newe England there to inhabitt / and Remaine /!/

.... *ES: of Noᵗwch in Noᵗff / Cordwynar aged /
28 yeares and. / ....
with / 4 / Children SAMUELL: JOHN: ELIZABETH: and DEBRA:
......................NS: aged / 18 years and ANNE:
WILLIAMES: aged / 15 years / ....
.... England to Inhabitt /!/

.... RANCIS: LAWES: boᵗne in Noᵗwch in Noᵗff
and their liuing Weauear / aged ....nd LIDDEA:
his Wife / ageed / 49 yeares / With one Child MAREY: and 2
saruants. SAMUELL: LINCORNE: aged 18 yeares / and ANNE:
SMITH: aged. 19 yeares ar desirous to passe foᵗ New-England
to inhabitt /!/

.........8 1637. The examinaction of WILLIAM: NICKERSON: of
Noᵗwch in Noᵗff / Weauear / ageed 33 yeares. and. ANNE: his
Wife / aged / 28 yeares with / 4 Children / NICHO: ROBARTT:
ELIZABETH: and ANNE: ar desirous to goe to Bostone in
New England ther to Inhabitt /!/

Aprill the / 8ᵗʰ / 1637. The examinaction of SAMUELL: DIX: of Noᵗwch
in Noᵗff Joynar ageed 43 yeares / and JOANE: his / Wife / aged
38 yeares with 2 Children PRESELLA: and ABEGELL: and 2
Saruantes WILLIAM: / STOREY: and DANIELL: LINSEY: the
one aged / 23 the other / 18 yeares / ar all desirous to pass
to Boston in New England there to Inhabitt /!/

* [The dots here and after indicate parts of the original MS. eaten away by age or damp.]

Aprill. the / 11th / 1637 The examinaction. of HENRY: SKERRY: of great yarmouth in the County of Norff / Cordwynar. / ageed / 31 yeares and ELIZABETH : his Wife / ageed / 25 yeares / with one Child HENRY: and / one Aprentics / EDMUND: TOWNE: aged / 18 yeares. / ar desirous to passe for New England to inhabitt ///

Aprill. the / 11th / 1637 The examinaction of JOHN: MOULTON: of Ormsby in Norff husbandman. aged. 38 yeares., and. ANNE: his Wife / ageed / 38 yeares with 5 Children. HENRY: MAREY: ANNE: JANE: and / BRIDGETT: and / 2 Saruants. ADAM: GOODDENS: aged. 20 yeares and ALLES: EDEN: aged 18 yers / ar all desirous to passe to New England there to inhabitt // and abide ///

Aprill. the / 11th / 1637 The examinaction of MAREY: MOULTON: of Ormsby in Norff / Wydow, ageed / 30 yeares and 2 / Saruants. JOHN : MASTON: aged / 20 yeares and MERREAN: MOULTON: ageed / 23 yeares / are desirous to goe to New England to inhabitt and dwell //

Aprill. the / 11th / 1637 The examinaction of RICHARD: CARUEAR: of Skratby.* in the County of Norff / husbandman / ageed / 60, yeares, and GRACE: his Wife. ageed, 40 yeares. with / 2 Children. ELIZABETH: /// ageed / 18 yeares and, SUSANNA: aged 18, yeares. being twynes. / mor 3 Saruants ISACKE: HARTT: ageed, 22 yeares and THOMAS: FLEGE: aged / 21 yeares. and one MARABLE: VNDERWOOD: a mayd. Saruant / ageed, 20 yeares. goes all for New England to Inhabitt / and Remaine ////

Aprill. the / 11th / 1637 The examinaction of RUTH: MOULTON: of Ormsby in Norff. Singlewoman. ageed / 20 yeares. is desirous to passe for New England there to Inhabitt and dwell //

Aprill. the / 11th / 1637 The examinaction of ROBERTT: PAGE: of Ormsby in Norff. husbandman, ageed 33 yeares and / LUCEA: his Wife. aged 30 yeares with / 3 Children / FRANCES: MARGRETT: and SUSANNA: // and 2 Saruants / WILLIAM: MOULTON: and ANNE: WADD: the one aged 20 yeres the other / 15 yeares. and are all desirous to passe for New England to inhabitt and Remaine. //

---

* [Perhaps Scratley, a part of Ormsby.]   37—2

Aprill. the / 11th / 1637   The examinaction of HENREY: DOWE: of Ormsby in No^{rff} husbandman, aageed, 29 yeares. / and JOANE: his Wife / aged 30 yeares with 4 Children, and one Saruant / ANNE: MANING, aaged / 17 ycares. are desirous to passe into New England to inhabitt ///

Aprill. the / 11th / 1637   The examinaction of ROBERTT:.............. Singleman. is desirous to passe ....

Aprill. the / 11th / 1637   The examinaction of ELLEN: ROBENSONE: of g............. desirous to passe into New England ther to in............

Aprill. the / 11th / 1637.   The examinaction of WILLIAM: WILLIAMES: of great yarm .... 40 yeares. and ALLES: his Wife / aged. 38 yeares with / 2 Children .... ar desirous to goe fo^r New England to inhabitt ///

Aprill. the / 11th / 1637   The examinaction of ELIZABETH: WILLIAMES: of Ya^rmouth. in No^{rff} / Singlewoman aaged 31 yeares / is desirous to passe into New England ther to inhabitt and Remaine ///

Aprill. the / 12th / 1637   The examinaction of KATHREN: RABEY: of Yarmouth / a Wattermanes. Wydow. / aged. 68 yeares. is desirous to passe into New England there to Remaine With her Sone /

Aprill. the / 12th / 1637   The examinaction of RICHARD: LEEDS: of great ya'mouth. Marrinar. aged 32 yeares. and JOANE: his Wife /aged. 23 yeares / with one Child / are desirous to passe fo^r New England and there to inhabitt / and dwell ///

Aprill. the / 12th / 1637   The examinaction of HENRY: SMITH: of New-bucknam husbandman / aaged 30 yeares. / and ELIZABETH: his Wife aged. 34 / yeares. with 2 / Children JOHN: and SITHE: ar desirous to passe into New England /// to inhabitt ///

Aprill. the / 13th / 1637   The examinaction of JOHN: ROPEAR: of New Bucknam Carpentar. / aged. 26 yeares. and ALLES: his Wife / aged, 23 yeares / with / 2 Children. ALLES: and ELIZABETH: are desirous to goe for New England there to Remaine* ///

---

* [Here come a number of entries of passages for Holland.]

.. ese people went to New England with WILLIAM: / GOOSE: m^r of the
Marey: Anne: of Yarmouth: ///

. . . . 1637   The examinaction of THOMAS: PAINE: of Wrentom
in Suffolcke / Wcaucar / ageed / 50 yeares / and ELIZABETH: his
Wife / ageed / 53 ycares with / 6 / Children / THOMAS: JOHN:
MAREY: / ELIZABETH: DORETHEY: and SARAH: are desirous
to goe for Salame in New England to inhabitt

May: the / 10th / 1637   The examinaction of MARGRETT: NEAUE: of
great yarmouth in No^rff / Wydow. / ageed / 58 ycres / and
RACHELL: DIXSON: her grand Child is desirous to passe into
New England to inhabitt /

May: the / 10th / 1637   The examinaction of BENIEMEN: COOPER: of
Bramton in Suffolck / husbandman / ageed / 50 / Yeares / and.
ELIZABETH: his Wife / ageed / 48 ycares With / 5 Children
LARWANCE: MAREY: REBECA: BENIEMEN: and FRANCIES:
FILLINGHAM: his Sone / in Lawe / ageed / 32 yeares allso his
Sister ageed / 48 yeares / and 2 Saruants / JOHN: KILIN: and
FELEAMAN: DICKERSON: ar all desirous to goe for Salam in
New England and there. to inhabitt ///

May: the / 10th / 1637.   The examinaction of ABRAHAM: TOPPAN: of
yarmouth Cooper / aged / 31 yeares and SUSANNA: his Wife /
ageed. 30 yeares With / 2 Children PETTER: and ELIZABETH:
and one Mayd / Saruant / ANNE: GOODIN: ageed / 18 ycares
are desirous to passe to New England to / inhabitt ///

May: the / 10th / 1637   The examinaction of WILLIAM: THOMAS: of
great Comberton in Wo^rstershire husbandman / Singleman /
ageed / 26 yeares. is desirous to passe to Exerden / in New
England to inhabitt

May: the / 10th / 1637   The examinaction of JOHN: THURSTON: of
Wrentom in Suff / Carpentar / ageed, 30 ycares. and MAR-
GRETT: his Wife / ageed. 32 yeares. With / 2 Children THOMAS.
and JOHN: ar / desirous to passe to New England /// to inhabitt ///

May: the / 10th / 1637   The examinaction of LUCE: POYETT: of No^rwch
Spinster / ageed. 23 yeares is desirous to pass into New
England and there to Remaine ///

May: the / 10th / 1637   The examinaction of JOHN: BOROWE of yarmouth
Cooper / aged 28 yeares. and ANNE: his / Wife / ageed / 40 /
yeares is desirous to passe to Salam in New England and ther
to inhabitt

May: the / 11th / 1637   The examinaction of WILLIAM: GAULT: of yarmouth Cordwynar / Singleman / ageed 29 / yeares is desirous to
passe to New England and there to Remaine ///

May: the / 11th / 1637   The examinaction of JOANE: AMES: of yarmouth.
Wydow / ageed / 50 yeares with / 3 Children RUTII: ageed / 18
yeares WILLIAM: and JOHN: are desirous to passe for. New
England and there to inhabitt and Remaine ///

May: the / 11th / 1637   The examinaction of AUGSTEN: CALL........
.... ALLES: his Wife / ageed / 40 / yeares...........
desirous to goe to Salam in New Eng.............

May: the / 11th / 1637   The examinaction of JOHN: DARRELL: of......
....passe into Salam in New England and there...........

May: the / 11th / 1637   The examinaction of JOHN: GEDNEY: of No^rwch
in No^rff Weauear.... to passe fo^r New England / with his Wife
SARAII: aged 25 yeares. .... LEDIA: HANAH:
and JOHN: mo^r / 2 Saruantes / WILLIAM: WALKER: ageed ....
.... BURGES : ageed / 26 yeares / ar desirous
to passe fo^r Salam ///

May: the / 11th / 1637   The examinaction of SAMUELL: AIRES: of No^rwch
an apintes / ageed / 15 yeares is desirous [to] passe into New
England to his Mr JOHN: BAKER: as he had apointed him ///

This man was
for byden pas-
sage. by. the
Commission^{rs}
and went.
not.from.
yramouth

The examinaction of JOHN: YONGES: of St Margretts: Suff /
Minister / ageed 35 yeares. and. / JOAN: his Wife / ageed / 34 /
yeares with / 6 / Children / JOHN: THO: ANNE: RACHELL:
MAREY: and / JOSUEPH: ar desirous to passe fo^r Salam: in
New England to inhabitt ///

May: the / 12 / 1637   The examinaction of SAMUELL: GRENSILD: of
No^rwch Weauear / ageed, 27 yeares, and BARBREY: his Wife /
ageed / 35 yeares. With two Children MAREY: and BARBREY:
and JOHN: TEED: his Saruant / ageed, 19 yeares ar all desirous to passe into New England to inhabitt ///

May: the / 12th / 1637 The examinaction of THOMAS: JOANES: of Elzing in No^rff, Buchar / Singleman / ageed. 25 yeres is desirous to passe into New England: and there to Remaine ///

May: the / 13th / 1637 The examinaction of THOMAS: OLLIUER: of No^rwch Calinder / ageed / 36 yeares. and MAREY: his Wife / ageed. 34 yeares, with 2 Children. THO: and JOHN: and 2 Saruants / THOMAS: DOGED: aged, 30 yeares and MAREY: SAPE: ageed / 12 yeares ar desirous to passe fo^r New England. to inhabit

May: the / 15th / 1637 The examinaction of WILLIAM: COCKRAM: of Southould in Suff / Marinrar / ageed 28 yeares. / and CHRISTEN: his Wife ageed. 26 yeares with 2 Children and / 2 Saruantes desirous to passe fo^r new england to inhabitt ///

[*Then follow more passages for Holland; and the whole is signed :*]

HENRY: HILL Deputy for m' THOMAS MAYHEW Gentleman.//

SOUTHAMPTON.

ORTUS SOUTHTON. A List of the Names of such Passengers as were shipped in the *Virgin* of Hampton of 60 tonnes JOHN WEARE M^r for the Barbathoes, & JOHN DE LA. HAY merchant who haue taken the oathes of Allegiance & Supremacy the 30th of Marche. 1639 [1640]. Viz^t.

Aged.

*57. yeares.	MICHAELL EDMOND'S of Crawley Com Southt husband.
28.	JEREMY ROBINSON of Singleton Com Suss hoopmaker.
29.	JOHN VENNELL de eod Cordwayner.
25.	W^M FRANCIS of Catterington Com Southt sergweau'. [serge-weaver]
20.	JAMES WILSON of Glascowe husbandm.
20.	W^M BARNES of Wimborne Com Southt shoemak^r
22.	NICHAS BARDIN of Southton Smith
22.	ANDREWE DRUDG of Southton p'd husbandm
27.	ABRAHAM SAD of Southton p'd sergeweau'
24.	JAMES BARREY of Dorchester husbandm
16.	JOHN STEVENS of Ringwood Com Southt husbandm
15.	GYLES WEEKEHAM of Bansteed Com Surr husbandm.
18.	PETER WOODLAND of Southton Ropemaker.
16.	RICHARD SHINGLE of Bevis hill nere Southton.
17.	JAMES HACKER of Andiver Com Southt.
15.	WIHM TUCKE of Husborne nere Andiver p'd.
30.	JOHN HUDLICE of Newport in ye Isle of wight taylo^r.
16.	JAMES BLANCHE of the Isle of Wight p'd.
31.	RICHARD TRODD of Southstoneham husbandm.

* [The first figure is almost effaced.]

Aged.
 14. Robt Clitson of Andiver p'd.
 12. Henry Harris of Southton p'd.
 12. Wiłłm Decke of Wimborne p'd.
 14. Walter Smalle of the Isle of Wight p'd.
 12. John Bassett of Christchurch.
 11. Robt Bruton of Andiver p'd.

These sixe vnder yeares, & not sworne.

HE names of such as were sworne the 8th of Aprill, & passed in the same Shipp.

Aged.
 29. yeares. Andrewe Bullaker of Southton barbo^r.
 24. Michaell Oxford of Bevis hill husbandm.
 24. Robt Maijor of Southton, Chaundler.
19. 14. Thomas Gretrick & Rich. Warren serv^{ts}
 14. Thomas Turner vnder age & not sworne.
 22. Daniell de la Hay seaman.
 45. John Newman of Brading in the Isle of wight.
 30. Thomas Holmes of Southton Currier.
 24. Wiłłm Cockerell. Com Staff Taylo^r.
 24. Henry Dainty of Bymest^r Com Dors^t shoemak^r.
 25 Henry Pressey of Hamsteed Com Berk glou' [Glover]
 26. Gerrart Sister a form' Inh'itant there.
 29. Charles Darvall. of Southton clothworker.

---

 14. Francis Desart of Southton.
 14. Wiłłm Gilbert of Southton p'd.
    eight serv^t maydes,   Not sworne.
    These & the former which passe in this
     Shipp were noe Subsidy men, but
     people & servants of meane condiçon.

PORTUS SOUTHTON ;

28. June   REGNALD ALLEN* of Kent of 30. yeares gent, GERRARD
  1639.   HAUGHTON of 30. yeares Com̄ Oxōn geñ ꝑ DAVID
           BIXE of 35. yeares Com̄ Kanc̄ geñ free planters
           of the Barbathoes.
           JOHN EVENSON of the County of Chestr ꝑ THO: EVENSON
           his brothr, ANDREW WALLER of 18. yeares Com̄
           Hertf, HUMPHRY BURGIS of 19. yeares of Cornewall,
           JOHN WETHERED of 22—yeares in the County of
           Yeorke servt's to the Planters aboue named, they
           passe in the *Boldadventure* of Hampton for the
           Isle of Guarnzey, ꝑ from thence they take shipping
           for the Barbathoes, who haue taken the oathes
           vt supᵃ [ut supra]

[*May* 1638.]

SOUTHTON   The list of the names of Passengrs Intended to shipe
        themselues, In the *Beuis* of Hampton of Cl Tonnes, ROBERT
BATTEN Mr for Newengland ; And thus by vertue of the Lord Tre-
surers Warrant of the second of May. wch was after the restrayne[t] &
they some Dayes gone to sea Before the Kings Mates.. Proclamacōn
Came vnto Southton.

Ages.
 JOHN FREY of Basing wlclwrite. [wheelwright] his wife. ⎫
05—& three Children.   ⎭

40—RICHARD AUSTIN tayler of Bishopstocke. his wife ⎱
05—& two Children.   ⎰

 ROBERT KNIGHT his seruant Carpenter. ⎱

---

* [Three entries of passengers for Jersey and Guernsey precede this in the original.]

[Ages]

37—CHRISTOPHER BATT of Sarum Tanner. }

32—ANNE his wife. }

20—DOROTHIE BATT there sister. & fiue

10 & vnder. Children vnder tenne yeares.

24.—THOMAS GOOD ....)

22.—ELIZA: BLACKSTON .... } serv^ts

18.—REBECCA POND...............)

62.—WILLIAM CARPENTER...... } of Horwell Carpent^rs

33.—WILLIAM CARPENT jun ...)

32.—ABIGAEL CARPENTER.

10 & vnder & fower Children.

14—THO: BANSHOTT Servt

38—ANNIS LITTLEFEILD & six Children

JOHN KNIGHT Carpenter... } seru^ts

HEUGH DURDAL ....)

26—HENERY BYLEY of Sarū tanner.

22—MARY BYLEY ....

THO: REEUES Serv^ts

20—JOHN BYLEY............

40 | RICHARD DUM' [DUMMER] of Newengland.

35 | ALCE DUM'

19 | THO: DUM'

19 | JOANE DUM'

10 | JANE DUM'

*09 | STEEPHEN DUM' husbandman.

06 | DORATHIE DUM'.

04 | RICHARD DUM'.

02 | THO: DUM'.

---

* [Evidently either the age or the occupation must be wrong here.]

[Ages]		
30	JOHN HUCHINSON Carpent'	
26	FRAUNCIS ALCOCKE Virg.	
19	ADAM MOTT tayler..........................	
22	Will WACKEFEILD.	
20	NATHANUEL PARKER of London Backer	
18	SAMUEL POORE	Serv^ts
14	DAVELL POORE	
20	ALCE POORE.................................	
15	RICHARD BAYLEY	
20	ANNE WACKEFEILD	

The numb' of the passeng's aboue mentioned are Sixtie & one Soules,

HEN: CHAMPANTE Cust^r   THO: WULFRIS Coll & Fa^r

        N. DINGLEY Compt^r

[THE SOMMER ISLANDS.

1673—1679.]

[THE SOMMER ISLANDS.]

August the 23d 1673

THE Names of yᵉ Govern' & Councill of yᵉ Assembly

J HEYDON: D. G. [Deputy Governor.]

HENRY TUCKER seni'.
RICHARD WOLRICH
HENRY MOORE
JOHN HUBBARD
JOHN WAINWRIGHT seni'.
THOMAS WOOD
JONATHAN TURNER senir.
THOMAS LECRAIFT
CORNELIUS WHITE secretary

CHARLES WHETENHALL Speaker
JOHN BRISTOW Juni'.
SAMUELL BRANGMAN
BOAZ SHARP
THOMAS SHAW
JAMES FARMER
JOHN WELCH
THOMAS STOW
EDWARD SHERLOCK Sen'.
ROBERT DICKONSON

Sᵗ* GEORG TUCKER
THOMAS KERSEY
EDWARD CHAPLAIN
GEORG BASCOMB
WILLIAM BASDEN
PHILLIP LEA
JOHN RAWLINS sen'.
NICHOLAS THORNTON
JOHN ARTHUR
JOHN STOW
JOHN SQIRE
JOHN HUTCHINS
RICHARD HANGER
GEORG HUBBARD
WILLIAM MILBORN
LAWRENCE DILL
JOHN COX
JOHN SOMERSALL Sen'.
RICHARD JENNINS
RICHARD PENISTON

---

* [But possibly Sₜ, *i.e.* Sir.]

SEVERN VICARS	THOMAS FORSTER
WILLIAM RIGHTON Seni'	RICHARD MATHELIN
THOMAS HALL	NATHANIELL BUTTERFIELD
GEORG BALL	HAMOND JOHNSON Clerk
JOHN MORRICE Seni'.	of ye Assembly
WiH. BURCH	

N Accompt of the Generall Lands belonging to the Somer Islands Comp^a taken out Mr RICHARD NORWOODS Survey booke by him made in the yeares 1662: 1663:

GENERALL LANDS*

N^o		acr': roo: Perch

Begining with St Georges Island

1 The Governo' holds of the Hono^ble Comp^a as belonging to his place Twelve Shares of Land at the East End of St Georges Island Containeing p Estimacon .... } 300 00 00

Namely in the Occupacon of

DAVID STOKES p Estimation ....1: share

JOSEPH GOODFAITH p Estimat...............1: sha:

JOHN MILLS p Estimat .... ½ sha:

JOHN BEDWELL p Estimat 1½

JOHN MILLS p Estimat ....1 sha:

ROBERT POWELL p Estimat ....1 sha.

CORNELIUS EVANS MATTHEW NORMAN } 1 sha
    and ROGER BROWNE p Estimat ...... }

ALEXANDER SMITH p Estimacon............1 sha:

JOHN WELSH JOHN BRISTOWE MARSHALL, ROGER BAYLEY HANNAH HOLLOWAY, EDWARD MIDDLETON, THO: SHAW JOHN HURT, these seaven hold p Estimacon 2 sha:

The residue of these twelve Shares are in the Occupacon of the Governo' himselfe.

---

* [There are two copies of this list, one going down to No. 26 only (see p. 307), the other to the end, as here. We have printed from the longer and more complete one. There are, however, no important variations in them, so far as they both extend.]

Nº		acr:	roo:	Perch
2	Gleabe in the Tenure of mᵣ: SAMᴸᴸ SMITH the psent Minister there Two shares Containeing p stimat. [estimation]	50	00	00
3	The Sheriffe Mʳ JOHN NICHOLLS as belonging to his Office Fower Shares of Land containeing p Estimat.	100	00	00
4	The Secrary Mʳ HENRY TUCKER as belonging to his Office holds of the Honoᵇˡᵉ Compᵃ 2 shares Containeing p Estimat	050	—	—
5	Mʳ JOHN VAUGHAN holdeth by Lease from mʳ CASE-WELL of the Compᵃˢ Land 1 sha: containeing p Estimat.....................	025	00	00
6	Leut: EDWARD BRACKLEY holdeth of the Honoᵇˡᵉ Compᵃ at Will 2 sha: containeing p Estimat......	050	00	00
7	Mʳ JOHN BRISTOWE Marshall holdeth of the Honoᵇˡᵉ Compᵃ as belonging to his Office 2 sha: Containeing p estimat	050	00	00
8	Mʳˢ STALVERS holdeth of the Honoᵇˡᵉ Compᵃ as belonging to the Ferry 2 sha: Containeing Estimat	50	00	00

Sume 27: shares

But the whole Island (as formerly measured) conteynes 706: acres that is 28: sha: and Six acres.

The Small Islands neare Sᵗ Georges,

9	Two Islands against the East End of Sᵗ Georges Lyeing in Comon containeing	05	00	06
10	Pagetts Fort whereof Captaine FRANCIS TUCKER is Comander wᵗʰ the Island whereon it stands sometimes called Penestons Island and a Tenemᵗ or Dwelling house there in the Occupacon of Leivt: JONATHAN STOKES as belonging to the Fort cont	31	01	18

N°	Generall	acr	roo:	perch.
11	Smiths Fort whereof Captaine GODHEARD ASER is Comander the Island Containeing	00	02	30
12	Smiths Island in the tenure of Captaine GODHEARD ASER from the Honoᵇˡᵉ Compᵃ as Comander of Smiths Fort cont	61	02	10
13	An Island Called Hen-Island neare the West End of Smiths Island Lyeing in Comon and Containeing	03	01	04
*13	A small Island Lyeing betweene Hen-Island aforesaid and Smiths Island Lyeing in Comon ℯ Containeing	00	01	20
*14	Long Bird Island in the Tenure and Occupacon of JAMES STIRRUP and RALPH WRIGHT Weavers wᶜʰ they hold of the Honoᵇˡᵉ Compᵃ containeing	46	02	06
*15	Conny Island Lyeing at Burnt Point in the Occupacon of Mᴵ HENRY STALVERS containeing	14	03	02
*16	Certaine small Islands in yᵉ towne harbor Mullett bay ℯ towards burnt point about Tenn in number cont p estim..	02 : 00 : 00

Sum of all these Islands lyeing neare S Georges ......   165 : 2 : 16

Davids Island and first the Easterne part thereof which is Called yᵉ Companyes land there

17	Capt FRANCIS TUCKER Comand' of Pagetts Fort			
18	holdeth of yᵉ honoᵇˡᵉ Compᵃ A parcell of Land neare Davids head in yᵉ occupacon of his Leivetennt JONATHAN STOKES			
	Item another pcell there in yᵉ occupacon of JOHN HURT, both pcells lyeing together ℯ cont p estim	60: 00: 00
19	MILES HIGGES holdeth of yᵉ honoᵇˡᵉ Compa 1 sha: cont p est...	25: 00: 00

---

* [This and the succeeding numbers, in the other list, read—14, 15, 16, 16.]

N°:	Landes	Acr:	roo:	per
20	HUGH HARDING holdeth of ye hono^{ble} Compa 1 Share cont p estimat..	25:	00:	00
21	WILLIAM ALLEN holds as aforesaid 1 share cont p est	25:	00:	00
22	Capt RICHARD JENNYNGS of Smiths tribe comand^r of Southampton fort holds of ye hono^{ble} Compā as belonging to ye Fort ℈ in ye occupacõn of JOHN GRAZBURY ℈ RANDALL DAVIS p estim 2 sha: of Land cont	50:	00:	00
23	Lievt THO: HILTON holds of ye hono^{ble} Compā p est 2 sh: con:	50:	00:	00
24	ROBT. BURCHER holds as afores^d p est 1 sh: cont......	25:	00:	00
25	Lievt EDWARD BRANGMAN and his sonne SAMUEL BRANGMAN holds as aforesaid p est 1 sha: cont ...	25:	00:	00
26	WILLIAM BELL holds of the Hono^{ble} Compā two pcells of Land namely one pcell on the South side cont p est 13 acres and another pcell on ye North side next ye Bay cont p est 12 acres both pcells cont p est one Share or	25:	00:	00

		acr:		
The sume of these Lands in S Davids called ye Companyes		310:	00:	00

The Lands in S Davids Island given by ye hono^{ble} Company to Harrington al̃s Hamilton tribe

		acr:	roo:	Per
27	THO: SPARKE of Davids Island holdeth freely a pcell of land wch formerly belonged to two shares in Hamilton tribe that sometimes were Capt JOHN BERNARDS and are there marked (No: 19) cont p estimat	10:	00:	00
28	THO: SPARKE afores^d holdeth of m^r JOHN MILNER as belonging to ye two shares in Hamilton tribe where he dwells and another share In ye occupacõn of M^{’s} COX widdow In all three Shares being ye Lands of Mr PERIENT TROTT ℈ numbred there: 9 ℈ 20 he holdeth I say as belonging to these 3 sh p est	15:	00:	00

	Generall	acr:	roo:	Per
29	WILLIAM ADAMS holdeth of JACOB AXTON as belonging to ye Share of Mr MATTHEW WICKS in Hamilton tribe (No there 11th) p est	05:	00:	00

29 WILLIAM ADAMS holdeth of JACOB AXTON as belonging to ye Share of Mr MATTHEW WICKS in Hamilton tribe (No there 11th) p est 05: 00: 00

30: Mrs MARY MOUNTAINE (formerly MARY STOW) holdeth a pcell of Tenn acres belonging to two Shares in Hamilton tribe now Mr SOUTHERNES (No: 21) Item another pcell of Five acres belonging to a share in Hamilton tribe in ye free tenure of JOHN PLACE (No 30: both pcells lyeing together ℓ cont p estimat 15: 00: 00

31 MARY MOUNTAINE afores^d holdeth as belonging to two shares in Hamilton tribe being the Shares of Capt GEORGE HUBBART of Devonsheire tribe (No 12) a pcell cont p est 10: 00: 00

32 Leivt JOHN FOX holdeth of Capt GODHEARD ASSER as apperteyneing to ye 3 shares in Hamilton tribe whereon he the said Capt ASSER dwells wch were Late M' DELBRIDGE A pcell cont p estimat......... 15: 00: 00

33   HENRY SHARPE holdeth freely a pcell of thirty acres
34   of wch 15 acres did formerly belong to ye three shares of Capt COVELLS in Hamilton tribe (No 27: 28) the whole lyeing together ℓ Cont p est............ 30: 00: 00

35 JOHN LYDDALE holdeth of M' SAM^{l} WHITNEY of Sandys tribe as apteyneing to ye Land formerly m' DYKES in Hamilton tribe a pcell Cont p estimacon.. 30: 00: 00

36: M' JOHN MOORE holdeth freely a pcell wch was heretofore JOHN DAY and apperteyneing to a share in Hamilton tribe now M' WEBBS (No 16) cont p estimat 05: 00: 00

37 JOHN MOORE afores^d holdeth of M' MIHIL BURROUGHES a parcell of Land apperteyneing to Two shares in Hamilton tribe in ye occupacon of ye said MIHIL BURROWES (No 22) cont p est 10: 00: 00

N°	Landes	acr:	roo:	per
38	ELIZABETH NAILER holdeth of M' WATERMAN (wch was heretofore M' RICH: CASWELLS a pcell of Land belonging to Five shares in Hamilton tribe wch are thought to be the shares in the tenure of Mr STAF-FORD M' STRINGER ℓ M' WRIGHTON cont p est (No: 13: 14: 15)	25:	00:	00
39	THO: STOW of Davids Island holdeth freely A pcell of Island belonging to a share now or Late in ye tenure of Capt CANTER (No. 29) cont p est	05:	00:	00
40	THO STOW afores^d holdeth of M' JOHN STOWE ℓ he of M' PERIENT TROTT a pcell of Land lyeing at ye Stocks pointe belonging to Five shares in Hamilton tribe whereof Fower were ye Earle of WAR-WICKS (Nom': 23 24 25 26: ℓ one y^t Lyes at ye Flatts No: 36. the whole pcell here Lyeing together ℓ Cont p estimat............................	25:	00:	00

The sume of these lands in Davids Island belonging to: 40: sh: in Hamilt tribe is p estim 200: 00: 00

Soe ye whole Islands of S Davids divided as aforesaid cont p estimat 510: acres

But as it was formerly measured it cont 527: acres

The Islands in Southampton halbo' als Castle Harbor

		acr:	roo:	per
41	Certaine small Islands to ye Nomber of Tenn lyeing in Comon neare to Davids Islands, and on the South side thereof (for the most pt) cont p estimat	08:	00:	00
42	The Island called Coopers Island in the tenure and occupacon of DAVID MING wch he holds of ye hono^{ble} Comp^a conteyneing	77:	2:	20
43	Foure small Islands lyeing in Comon betweene Davids Island ℓ Coopers Island cont p estimat	03:	2:	20
44:	Five other small Islands lyeing in Comon neare ye South end of Coopers Island cont p estimat.........	02:	2:	00

	Generall	acr:	roo:	per
45:	The Island called None-such lyeing in Comon cont	15:	2:	13
46.	Three Small Islands about Nonesuch lyeing in.Comon cont	01:	00:	00
47	South-hampton Fort vnder ye Comand of Capt RICH JENYNGS wth ye Island whereon it stands cont p estimat..	01:	2:	24
48	The Fellow of it lyeing next toward ye Northeast in Comon	00:	3:	30
49	Kings Castle vnder ye Comand of our hono^{ble} Gover-no' Capt FLORENTIO SEYMOR, wth ye Island whereon it stands cont.	03:	2:	00
50	Charles Fort now de~ayed (onely there remaine two peeces of ordinanc dismounted, ye Island cont p estimat	03:	3:	00
51	Three Islands lyeing neare Charles Fort Island cont p estimat	01:	00:	00
52	Some other Small Islands lyeing in Comon in South-ampton harbor als Castle Harbor cont p estimat ...	01:	3:	00
	Suñe of these Islands in Southampton harbor ...	120:	3:	27

		acr;	roo:	per
N^o	## The Generall Land at Tuckers Towne.			
53	Gleab Land in the tenure of m' Abo=Cromby wth the Gleabe house cont p estimat 2 sha:	50:	00:	00
54	M' Wm MOORE ꝑ M' JOSEPH MOORE his sonne holdeth of y^e hono^{ble} Compã two Tenem^{ts} ꝑ two shares of Land cont p estimat	50:	00:	00
55	SAM^{ll} ATKINSON holdeth of the Hono^{ble} Compã a Tenem^t ꝑ 1 share of Land cont p estimat	25,	00:	00
56:	DANIEL MARROW holdeth as aforesaid a Tenem^t and One share of Land cont p est	25:	00:	00
57	NATHANAEL NORTH holdeth of ye Hono^{ble} Compã a Tenem^t ꝑ one share of Land cont p estimat	25:	00:	00
58	PARNEL WILKINSON Widd holdeth of ye hono^{ble} Compã a tenem^t ꝑ one share of Land cont p estimat some thinke she hath more.	25:	00:	00

No.	Landes:	acr:	roo:	per
59	Leivetennt Wᴹ Jones, Leift at yᵉ Castle holds as belonging to his place A tenemᵗ in his owne occupacon, Item another tenemᵗ in the occupacon of James Grazebury Item another tenemᵗ in yᵉ occupacon of his Mother Mary Jones wᵗʰ two Shares of Land in yᵉ occupacon of himselfe and his said assignes cont p estimat...................................	50:	00:	00
60	Tho Clinch Wᴹ Newman John Browne each of them a Tenemᵗ ℓ some pcells of Land wᶜʰ together wᵗʰ yᵉ wast ℓ Comon Land extending from Tuckers towne bay allmost to yᵉ Castle cont p estimat	95:	00:	00
	Sume of these Generall Lands at Tuckers towne and extending thence to yᵉ point neare yᵉ Castle is	345:	00:	00

Touching some of yᵉ Lands at Tuckers towne as alsoe in Davids Island I could not bee throughly Informed though I made seu'all Journyes ℓ Inquiries, but have sett them downe according to yᵉ best Informacon I could Gather.

	acr:	roo:	per
The Island called s Georges conteyneing by estimat 27 shares but by measure	706:	2:	00
The other Lands in yᵉ towne Harbor ℓ soe to Burnt pointe cont	165:	2:	16
Davids Island cont by estimacon 510 acres but by measure	527:	3:	00
Coopers Island Nonesuch and the other small Islands there cont............................	120:	3:	27
The Generall Land at Tuckers Towne and extending to yᵉ pointe neare yᵉ Castle conteynes by estimacon 345 acr but there seemes to be neare one share more by measure namely............................	370:	00:	00

	acr:	ro	pe
Sume totall of yᵉ Generall Lands	1890:	03:	3:

Islands ~~in~~ Com̃on

No:

The Islands in yᵉ Great ſ Little Sound lyeing in
Comon to all the Tribes...................................... acr: rɔ.   per.

No: 1 The Bigger Island at yᵉ bottome of yᵉ Little Sound
against yᵉ Lands of mʳ JOHN HUBBART cont p
estimat 01: 02: 20

2 The Two Lesser conteyneing p estimat.................. 00: 00: 20

3 Another Small Island in yᵉ Little Sound neare to
Diggs his Dale in Smiths tribe Cont p estimat 00: 02: 00

4 An Island Att Bailyes Bay on yᵉ North side of
Hamilton tribe cont p estimat .... 00: 02: 30.

5 Another there more Westerly cont p estimat............ 00: 01: 00

6 The Greater of yᵉ Islands in yᵉ Little Sound called
Trunck Islands in yᵉ occupacõn of JOHN ROBERTS
cont 03: 00: 00

7 The next there to yᵉ Northwards in yᵉ occupacõn of
yᵉ said JOHN ROBERTS cont p estimat 01: 00: 10

8 Two other small Islands there conteyneing p estimat 00: 01· 26

In the Greate Sound

9 An Island in Crow Lane (lyeing against yᵉ Share of
Schoole Land given by Mʳ COPELAND) in yᵉ occupacõn of EVAN OWEN for yearely rent wᶜʰ he payes
to yᵉ Governo' or Sheriffe for public vses as doe yᵉ
rest of these Islands yᵗ are Lett out this Island cont
p estimat 03: 00: 00

10 Another Island in Crow lane over agᵗ Mʳ STOWES
house to yᵉ Southward lyeing in Comõn ſ and cont
estimat.. 03: 00: 00

11 Six small Islands at yᵉ Entring of Crow Lane lyeing
over from Mʳ STOWES pointe to Salt Kettle pointe
lyeing in Comon ſ Cont p estimation 03: 01: 00

No.	To all the Tribes:	acr	ro:	per
12	Another Island there in ye occupacon of THO: ACK-LAND wth the Tenem^t thereon cont p estimat	28:	2:	20
13	Two small Islands lyeing betweene y^t last before entred and warwicke tribe cont. p estimat	00:	3:	00
14	An Island in Bosses hole lyeing as aforesaid in Comon and Cont p estimat	00:	21:	00
15	Another Island there at ye Mill or Mouth of Mangrow bay &c cont p estimat	00:	1:	00
16	Another more Southerly Lyeing in Comon & cont p estimat..	00:	2:	30
17	Another there more Southerly lyeing &c & cont p estimat..	01:	00:	00
18	Another there more Southerly lyeing &c & cont p estimat..	00:	2:	00
19	A Long Island at ye Entrance of Daniels bay wth a smaller further into ye bay, both lyeing in Comon & Cont p estimat	01:	1:	00
20	A Bigger Island lyeing agt M' STOWES pointe shares to ye westward lyeing in Comon & Cont p estimat......	03:	01:	00
21	Foure Smaller Islands to ye Westwards lyeing &c cont	01:	01:	00
22	An Island wth a bay on ye South side of it wth another Lesser Island toward's ye Northeast both in ye oc-cupacon of LAZARUS OWEN wth the Tenem^t there Cont p estimat	28:	1:	30
23	Another Small Island next ye Two former lyeing in Comon & cont p estimat	00:	3:	10
24	Three small Islands to ye Westwards of LAZARUS OWEN lyeing in Comon & Cont p estimat	01:	2:	00
25	A Bigger Island Northwest from LAZARUS OWEN in ye occupacon of NATHANAEL VEAZEY or his assignes cont p est	13:	3:	00
26	Another Island neare adioyneing to ye West end in ye occupation of ye said NAT VEAZEY or his assignes cont p estimat..	09:	2:	00

39*

No	Islands in Comon	acr:	ro:	per
27	Elizabeth Island wth a tenem^t there in the occupacon of JOHN BURT cont p estimat	21:	00:	10
28	An Island at ye North head of Elizabeth Island lyeing in Comon ℈ cont p estimat	00:	03:	20
29	Another Island at ye Northwest end of Elizabeth Island lyeing in Comon ℈ Cont p estimat	01:	02:	00
30	The Island called pearle Island wth another small Island at Spanish pointe ℈ another neare Ireland all lyeing in Comon ℈ cont p estimat	02:	01:	00
31	An Island to ye Southwestward of ye West end of Elizabth Island lyeing in Comon ℈ Cont p estimat	01:	02:	00
32:	Another Island there more Southerly lyeing in comon cont p estimat	02:	01:	30
33	Three small Islands more Southerly comon cont p estimat	03:	00:	00
34	An Island called Roundhill Island in ye occupacon of HENRY WARD cont p estimat	16:	01:	20
35	A smaller Island to ye Southward of y^t last entred in ye occupacon of ye said HENRY WARD cont p estimat	02:	00:	00
36	An Island called Tuckers Island wth a Tenem^t there in ye occupacon of NATHANIEL CONYARD cont p estimat	21:	00:	00
37	The next on ye Northside called ye Lesser Tuckers Isťd in ye occupat of THO WARD cont p estimat	07:	03:	00
38	Two Small Islands to ye Westward of ye Two Last lyeing in Comon ℈ Cont p estimat	00:	02:	00
39	An Island betweene Tuckers Island ℈ Brother Islands sometimes called Graves Island lyeing in comon ℈ cont	06:	02:	00
40	The Westermost of ye Brother Islands lyeing next to Georges pointe wth a Tenem^t there in ye occupat of JOHN RIVERS cont p estimat	20:	01:	20
41	The eastermost of ye Brother Islands lyeing in comon ℈ Cont p estimat	13:	3:	30

No	To all the Tribes:	acr:	roo:	per
42	An Island neare ye Shore at ye Partition line betweene the Lands formerly ye Earle of Southamptons ꝑ Mr Scotts lyeing in Comon ꝑ Cont p estimat.........	02:	01:	20
43	Two small Islands neare Jews bay lyeing in Comon cont p estimat...	03:	00:	00
44	Two Islands before ye Entrance of Hearne bay one			
45	in ye occupacon of JOHN HELYN ye other in ye occupacon of his mother wth a tenem^t both Cont p estimat	17:	01:	00
46	Two other small Islands w^thin White hearne bay lyeing in Comon ꝑ Cont p estimation	01:	00:	10

The sume of these Islands lyeing in Comon to
all ye tribes is 253: acr: 2 roo: 36 per:

The totall of all ye shares of land sett apart for publique use
as p this booke are eighty six shares

vera Copia Ex ꝑ   HENRY DANDG
                                       RI: BANNER.

[Indorsed:]
  " Rec^d from Mr BANNER Secry to y^e Company 25 Sept: 1684."

[MONMOUTH'S REBELLION OF 1685.

LISTS OF THE "CONVICTED REBELS" SENT TO
THE BARBADOES AND OTHER PLANTATIONS
IN AMERICA.]

[MONMOUTH'S REBELLION OF 1685.]

RECEIPT for one hundred Prisoners to be transported from Taunton by JOHN ROSE of London Merchant.

DANIELL RUTTER	PERCIVALL NOWIS
JEREMIAH POOLE	WILLIAM SAUNDERS
JOHN BAKER	WILLIAM VEIYARD
ROBERT PEARCE	HENRY CHAMBERS
LEONARD STAPLE	THOMAS ROWSEWELL
EDWARD KENT	MATHEW COOKE
CHARLES BENNETT	JOHN CRANE
JOHN PARSONS	CHARLES BURRAGE
JOHN GIBBS	WILLIAM LEY
JOHN BRYER	JOHN ROBINS
THOMAS GOOLD	LUKE PORTER
JOHN HARTEY	THOMAS PREIST
WILLIAM PITTS	CORNELIUS RADFORD.
JAMES WEBB	PHILLIP CHEEKE
NICHOLAS COLLINS junr	ROBERT EARLE
RICHARD KING	JOHN MOGRIDGE
EMANUELL MARCHANT	HENRY RANDALL
WILLIAM MARCHANT	JAMES MAYNARD
JOHN SLADE	JOHN CULVERWELL
SAMUELL BOND	GEORGE TRUBBS
JOHN ROGERS	SYLVESTER LYDE
BERNARD LOVERIDGE	WILLIAM PHELPES

Elias Lockbeare	Robert Richards
Sylvester Poole	Christopher Row
Thomas Moore	Mathew Craft junᵣ
Lawrence Preist	Richard Peircy
William Gould	John Miller
Henry Preist	George Snow
Enock Gould	Samuell Collins
John Bennett	John Cockram
John Baker	James Cockram
Samuell Mountstephen	Christopher Hoblyn
Thomas Buglar	John Marwood
Stephen Jeffreyes	John Timothy
John Morse	Thomas Austin
William Scurrier	Moses Osborne
John England	Walter Hucker
Jacob Powell	Randall Babington
John Godsall	John Knight
John Andrewes	Job Hunt
Samuell Sweeting	William Woodcocke
George Rowsell	John Adams
Edward Bellamy	Thomas Pomfrett
William Crosse	James Patten
Jonas Browne	Thomas Bambury
John Crosse	James Clift
Christopher Knight	Thomas Chamberlyne
Thomas Meade	Humfrey Justine
John Needes	Isack Dyer
Thomas Pitts	Richard Symons

Receiued according to his Maᵗⁱᵉˢ order the warrant from the Lord Cheife Justice wᵗʰ a Sohedule therevnto annexed of one hundred persons attainted of High Treason wᶜʰ are by John Rose Merchᵗ to be transported into his Maᵗⁱᵉˢ Island of Barbadoes or other his Maᵗⁱᵉˢ plantaco͞as [plantations] in America according to a Condic͞on of a Recognizance entred into by me for that purpose In Wittnesse whereof I haue herevnto put my hand this 12th day of October in the first yeare of his Maties Raigne. Annoq̃ Dñi 1685°

JOHN ROSE

Wittnesse herevnto
ROB^T HYDE
GILES CLARKE.

MR ROSE'S LIST*

NUOICE of Sixty Eight Men Seruants Shipped on board Capⁿ CHARLES GARDNER in y^e *Jamaica Merchant* for accot of Mr JOHN ROSE & Comp^a, they being to be Sold for ten Yeares theire Names as followeth Viz:

	Age		Trades
ISAACK DYER	25 year		Comber
JAMES WEBB	18	,,	Hosbanman
WILLIAM WOODCOKE	19	,,	Comber
HUMPHRY JUSTIN	17	,,	Ditto.
RICHARD PEARCEY	20	,,	Ditto.
JAMES COCKRAM	21	,,	Ditto.
DANIEL RUTTER	20	,,	Sarge Weauer
JAMES CLIFT	20	,,	Weauer
XOPHER HOLBIN	40	,,	Ditto
THOMAS PITT	18	,,	Comber
JOHN TIMOTHY	29	,,	Riben Veauer
ENOCH GOULD	15	,,	Wauer
JERIMIAH POOLE	30	,,	Clothier
WILLIAM SCURRIER	22	,,	Weauer
EMANUEL MERCHANT	20	,,	Plowman
EDWARD BELLAMY	27	,,	Carpenter
JOHN GODSALL	27	,,	Boucher
GEORGE ROUSELL	30	,,	Woolle Comber

* [It will be noticed that so far as names are concerned, this list is in large part a repetition of that previously given.]

	Age	Trades
THOMAS GOULD	35 years	Tayler
LUKE PORTER	20 ,,	Showmaker
JOHN MAGERIDGE	23 ,,	Weauer
JOHN CROSS	18 ,,	Plowman
JOHN ROGERS	38 ,,	Clothier
ROBERT RICHARDS	28 ,,	Tayler
JAMES MAYNARD	22 ,,	Plowman
ROBERT PEARCE	25 ,,	Clothier
NICHOLAS COLLINGS	20 ,,	Weauer
JOHN GIBBS	19 ,,	Plowman
THOMAS MEADE	22 ,,	Glouer
RICHARD SIMONS	33 ,,	Weauer
JOHN COCKRAM	18 ,,	Comber
BERNARD LOUERIDGE	22 ,,	Sope boyler
ROBERT EARLE	24 ,,	Plowman
SAMUEL BOND	20 ,,	Serge Weauer
PERCIFULL NOWES	23 ,,	Hatter
WILLIAM LEE	20 ,,	Plowman
WILLIAM PHILLIP	26 ,,	Plowman
SILUESTER POOLE	24 ,,	Boucher
EDWARD KENT	19 ,,	
WILLIAM SANDERS	19 ,,	Clothier
CORNELIUS RADFORD	20 ,,	Weaer
CHARLES BURRAGE	27 ,,	Comber
JOBE HUNT	26 ,,	Carrier
LEONARD STAPLES	20 ,,	Plowman
JOHN SLADE	25 ,,	Sergeweauer
JONAS BROWNE	20 ,,	Plowman
JOHN BAKER	35 ,,	Sergeweauer
PHILLIP CHEEKE	16 ,,	Plowman
THOMAS PREIST	20 ,,	Sergeweauer
WILLIAM VERRYARD	17 ,,	Carpenter
MATHEW COOKE	21 ,,	Plowman
MATHEW CRAFT	19 ,,	Weauer
JOHN BAKER	27 ,,	Mason

	Age	Trades
JOHN CHAMBERLIN	20 years	Shoomaker
SILUESTER LYDE	27 „	Boucher
JOHN BRUER	25 „	Mason
GEORGE tRUBBS	28 „	Plowman
WILLIAM PITTS	28 „	Woollecomer
RICHARD KING	18 „	Plowman
JOHN ANDREWS	27 „	Woollecomer
JOHN MILLER	35 „	Plowman
HENRY PREIST	22 „	Ditto
GEORGE SNOW	19 „	Commer
ELIAS LOCKEBEAR	18 „	Tanner
XTOPHER ROW	34 „	Weauer
HENRY CHAMBER	25 „	Woollcomer
THOMAS AAUSTIN	27 „	Mercer

(in dorso) 9 *Dec:* 1685

The men whose names are conteined in the within written list are Shipt upon the acc^t of JOHN ROSE & company on board the *Jam^a Merch^t* to be landed & disposed of in Barbados or in Jamaica :

JOHN ROSE

RECEIPT for one hundred Prisoners on Mr NEPHO'S Acc° to be sent to Barbudos*

Prisoners in Dorchester Goale to bee Transported

JOHN MEGGERIDGE	JOHN FACY
THOMAS QUICK	W^M GREENWAY
NICHOLAS SALTER	RICHARD DANIEL
FRANCIS SMITH	PETER KENT
RICHARD GREEN	CHRISTOPHER JEWELL
W^M MATHEWES	ABRAHAM THOMAS

* [There are three copies of this list, as well as the certificate given in p. 320, each differing in some points from the other. Important variations are mentioned in the footnotes ; the differences in spelling, common at that time, I have not indicated. I have chosen as "copy" that which appears, from the signatures, to have been the original document.]

JOHN BAKER	Wm DEALE
SAMUEL PINSON	Wm HAYNES
ROBERT CLARKE	THOMAS FRANKLYN‖
GEORGE EBDON	Wm GUPPY
SAMUEL DOLEBEER	~~MALACHI MALLOCKE~~ ⎱ being
BENJAMIN WHICKER*	AZARIAS PINNEY ⎰ wittnesse¶
JOHN WHICKER	JOHN BOVETT
JOHN HITCHCOTT	ROBERT SANDY
THOMAS FORCEY	THOMAS DOLLING
Wm GYLES	EDWARD MARSH
JOSEPH GAGE	JOHN EASEMOND
ROBERT MULLENS	JOHN VINCENT
ROGER BRYANT	ALLEN ENGLAND
CHARLES BROUGHTON	ROBERT VATER
RICHARD PARKER	JOHN PREW
JOHN HAYNE	OLIVER HOBBS
JOHN CONNETT	PHILIP COX
BARNARD† LOWMAN	PETER TICKIN**
JOHN HEATHFEILD	WM CLARKE
EDWARD VENN	WALTER OSBORNE
RICHARD PINE	RICHARD HOARE
THOMAS PESTER‡ [not found there	ROBERT FOANE
and so not deliuered to me]	DANIELL PARKER
JOHN SAM	P^r†† BAGWELL
HENRY SIMES§	

   * [Thus in two lists ; WHITKER in one.]   † [BERNARD in the other two lists.]

   ‡ [In two copies of this list he is called LESTER : in *this* list it was first so written, and then altered to a P. The bracketed words are found only in *one* of the copies.

   § [In one copy clearly written SUNES.]

   ‖ FRANCLYON in one of the copies ; FRANCKLYN in the other.

   ¶ In both the copies MALACHI MALLOCKE's name is left unerased : one differs from the original only in using the word "evidences" instead of "witnesses." The other reads thus :—

        MALACHI MALLOCKE taken out of my custody for a wittnes

        AZARIAS PINNEY sent away to Bristoll.

This explains why MALLOCKE's name is erased ; for PINNEY, see the letter in note *, p. 320.]

   ** [Written thus in two lists ; TINKIN in one.]

   †† [PETER in two lists.]

Prisoners in Exeter Goale to bee transported

ABRAHAM HUNT

CHRISTOPHER COOPER

EDMUND* BOVETT

JOHN FOLLETT

PETER BIRD

JOHN KEMPLYN†

WALTER TEAPE

Prisoners att Wells to bee Transported

JOHN JOLIFFE

ROBERT PEIRCE

JOHN DODDS

HENRY PITTMAN

NATHANIEL BEATON

PETER‡ CORDYLION

WᴹBIGGS§

WᴹPUTTMAN

JOHN COOKE

JOHN HARCOMBE

JOHN COLLINS

NATHANIEL STANDERWICK‖

RICHARD DYKE

JOHN DENHAM

ABRAHAM GOODEN

JOHN MEAD

JOHN BRICE ¶

ANDREW HOLCOMBE

JOHN HOOPER**

THOMAS VENNER

LAWRENCE CASWELL

THOMAS CHYN

SAMUEL WEAVER

ROBERT BATT

JOHN HOOPER**

JOHN GOALD

JOHN COOKE

JOHN JOHNSON

JOHN WILLIS

RICHARD NASH aℓs LYLLANT

JOHN FOOT

JOHN REEVES

JOHN GILL juñ

Reĉd according to his Maᵗⁱᵉˢ direccõns yᵉ Warrᵗ from yᵉ LORD CHEIFE JUSTICE wᵗʰ a Schedule thereunto annexed of one hundred psons attainted of High Treason wᶜʰ are by JEROM NEPHO to bee transported into some of His Majesties Plantacõns in America according to a Condicõn of a Recognizance entred into by me for that purpose In witnes

---

* [Thus in two lists ; EDMOND in one.]   † [SCAMPLYN in the two other lists.]

‡ [PETARD in one list.]   § [Thus in two lists ; BRIGGS in one.]

‖ [SANDERWICK in one of the two copies ; SANDERWICKE in the other.]

¶ [Thus in two lists. PRICE in the other.]

** [Thus repeated in the original and other lists.]

whereof I have hereunto putt my hand this six ℓ Twentieth day of September In the first yeare of his now Majesties reigne Añoᵹ Dñi 1685

GEORGE PENNE

CHARLES WHITE

Witness
   ROBᵀ HYDE
   SAMᴸ GEE *

CERTIFICATE of Mʳ NEPHO's Prisoners Landed at Barbados.†

LIST of the Convicted Rebells put on Board the *Betty* of London
at the Port of Waymouth in the County of Dorsett, JAMES MAY
Comander, and is according to Bill of Ladeing by him signed bound for
the Island of Barbados, Uizᵗ·

JOHN WHICKER	PETER BAGWELL
BENJAMIN WHICKER	ABRAHAM THOMAS
ROGER BRYANT	JOHN BAKER

---

* [At the end of one of the copies the following is written :

These men are to bee transported to Barbados.
GEO: PENNE.

That same list is preceded by the following letter :

Mʳ NEPHO'S Acct of Prisoners.

Sʳ

   Where as you haue signified to me that you are ordered to giue me an exact Acctt of yᵉ hundred Rebells
which his Mates was pleased to grant you, in whome you haue transported your Right unto me to be
transported according to his Mates order to some of his Plantacions In America pursuant to yᵉ Recognizance which I have entered Into, I doe assure you that there are in Goale sixty fiue of them at Dorchester one wounded man by name EDMUND BOUETT now Remaining In Exeter Goale, and three and thirty
at Ilchester besides AZARIAS PINXEY who was sent in Custody to Bristoll to be transported who it will be
made appeare upon yᵉ Return of my Express sent for that purpose hath been shipd for some one of his
Mates Plantacions according to his Mates order, of yᵉ Rest I haue here annexed an exact List and èxpect
with in feue daies by my afore-mentioned messenger the Cirtificat there of   I am

21ˢᵗ Oct. —85. |

yʳ humble Seruant
GEORGE PENNE

The men that are to bee transported as in the list annexed, are to bee Sentt in the Ship
Rebecca, the Commander is Capt JAMES MAY: wittness my hand   GEORGE PENNE.

   It will be observed that the ship in which the men sailed is called the *Betty*, in the certificate
given above.

   † [There is another copy of this list—an "Invoyce" of the prisoners made out before they
started for the Barbadoes.   The following are all the important differences in spelling of names
&c., as given by it and in the above-printed list.   See list for the corresponding numbers.

WILLIAM BIGGS
JOHN FOOT
JOHN DODDS
RICHARD PARKER
THOMAS QUICKE
NICHOLAS SALTER
EDWARD VENN
JOSEPH GAICH
SAMUELL PINSON
PETER KENT
CHRISTOPHER JEWELL
FRANCIS SMITH
JOHN UINCENT
JOHN EASTMOND
PHILLIP COX
JOHN REEUES
ROBERT MULLENS
JOHN CONNET (1)
JOHN FACEY
JOHN HAYNE
THOMAS FRANCKLYN
DANIELL PARKER
JOHN HEATCHFEILD (2)
JOHN MOGERIDGE
ABRAHAM HUNT
WILLIAM CLARKE
JOHN SAM
ROBERT VAWTER.
WILLIAM MADDER.
JOHN FOLLETT
JOHN COLLINS
JOHN COOKE (3)

WILLIAM GREENWAY
WILLIAM GUPPY
ALLEN ENGLAND
EDWARD HOARE (4)
RICHARD DANIELL
LAWRENCE CASWELL
RICHARD PINE
SAMUELL DOLBEARE
ROBERT CLARKE
ROBERT PEARE (5)
OLIVER HOBES (6)
RICHARD GREEN
JOHN WILLIS
ROBERT SANDY
THOMAS PESTOR
THOMAS VENNER
WILLIAM HAYNE
JOHN HITCHCOCK
WILLIAM GYLES
CHARLS BRAGHTON (7)
JOHN KEMPLIN (8)
PETER BIRD
RICHARD NASH
ANDREW HAULKON (9)
THOMAS FORCY
CHRISTOPHER COOPER
JOHN HILL (10)
JOHN HARCOMB
PETER CORDELON (11)
JOHN BOVETT
HENRY SIMS
WILLIAM DALE (12)

(1) CUNNET,
(2) HEATHFEILD.
(3) COCKE.
(4) RICHARD HOARE,
(5) PEARCE.
(6) HOBBS.
(7) BROUGHTON.
(8) KAMPLINN.
(9) HAWLKOM.
(10) GILL.
(11) PETARD CORDELION,
(12) DEALE.

NATHANIELL STANDERWICK (13)
THOMAS DOLLEN
ABRAHAM GODEN
EDWARD BOVETT (14)
EDWARD MARSH
JOHN PREW

ROBERT FAWN (15)
SAMUELL WEAVER
HENRY PITMAN
WILLIAM PITMAN
and one Servant woman by name
SUSANNAH TOLEMAN (16)

The Bill of mortallity of the said Rebells that dyed Since they were reced on Board and were thrown over board out of the said Ship are these uiz. December the sixteenth THOMAS VENNER, Seaventeenth Wᴹ GUPPY, Eighteenth JOHN WILLIS, Nineteenth EDWARD VENN, the same day PHILLIP COX one and Twentieth ROBERT VAWTER, Five and Twentieth Wᴹ GREENWAY Jannuary the First PETER BIRD, Witnessed by the Comander, Marchᵗ and officers of the said Ship this Eighth day of Janu'y 1685*

JOHN MAY
JOHN PENNE
JOHN MADDISON
GABRIEL WHITHORN
MALCUM FRASER

Barbados.

By the Rᵗ Honᵇˡᵉ the Leiuᵗ Gouernor

CAPTAINE JAMES MAY Comander of the ship *Betty*, JOHN PENNE Marchᵗ Jⁿᵒ MADDISON Mate, GABRIELL WHITHORN Boatswain & MALCUM FRASER Dᶜᵒr of sᶜʰ Shipp, personally appeared before mee and made oath on the Holly Evangelists of Allmighty God, that the within servants or Convicted Rebells by the said MAY taken in at the Port of Waymouth in the County of Dorsett, are the very same Convicted Rebells that were delivered to, and by the said MAY brought in the said Ship to this Island, and that they were all of them here

---

(13) STANDERICK.   (14) EDMUND.   (15) FOWNE.   (16) SUSAN DOLEMAN.
* [1685-6.]

landed and delivered to m' CHARLS THOMAS and Company Factors to
JEROM NEPHO or his assignes Except Eight of them wch dyed on
board the said ship in the voyage, and buried in the sea, whose names
are mentioned in the within Bill of Mortallity. Giuen vnder my hand
the 8th day of Jannuary 1685*

A true Coppy attested this
    Nineth day of Janu'y 1685*   EDWYN STEDE
      JN^o WHETSTONE Dep^{ty} Secr^{ty}

Warr for Delivery of Rebells convict to Mr NEPHO.

AUG^T S^s

Whereas the severall persons whose names are conteyned in
a Schedule hereunto annexed remaine now in yo' custody being
attainted of high Treason for leavying Warr against his Sacred
Matie vnder the late Duke of Monmouth, before mee and other
his Maties Justices of Oyer and Terminer for this Westerne
Circuit ; And whereas his Matie has been pleased to signifie to
mee, his Royall pleasure of his gratious intentions to extend
his mercy to the s^d persons, and to pardon them their lives
vpon Cond_icon of Transportation into some of his Maties Plantacons beyond the Seas And for that purpose the said persons
should bee delivered to JEROME NEPHO or Order, he haveing
allready pursuant to his Maties Comands entred into a Recognizance for their safe and speedy transportacon into his s^d Maties
Plantations beyond the Seas according to his Royall directions,
and is alsoe obliedged to discharge you and all yo' Officers &
Ministers from further trouble and the Country from further
charge, relateing to the said persons within tenn dayes after the
date of these p'sents, and upon such other Conditions as his
Matie has required.

Jeffreys

These are therefore in his Maties name to will and require you forth-
wth vpon sight hereof to deliver unto the said JEROME NEPHO or his

---

Order the said severall persons in the s^d Schedule named, in order to
their Transportaçon as aforesaid, and you are hereby directed to take a
receipt from the person or persons to whome you shall deliver the said
Prisoners Pursuant to this Order of the Receipt of them, and for soe
doeing this shall bee yo' Warrant   Giuen vnder my hand and seale this
p'sent 25th day of September, in the first yeare of the Reigne of our
Soveraigne Lord King James &c   Annoq̧ Dñi 1685.

> To the High Sherriffs of the Counties of Dorsett
>   Devon and Somersett, & to his ℮ their
>   Deputies & all other Officers whome these
>   may concerne.

A true Coppy attested this
9th day of Jannuary 1685
JN° WHETSTONE Dep^ty Secr^ty

[BARBADOES.]

LIST* of Seaventy two Rebells by his Ma^tyes Mercy granted to
GEROME NEPHO to bee transported to this Island by the *Betty*
JAMES MAY Master received by CHARLS THOMAS and JOHN PENNE,
by order of GEORGE PENNE Esq' being the order of JEROM NEPHO

Masters.	Rebells
	WILLIAM BIGGS
	WILLIAM HAYNE
RICHARD WALTERS	WILLIAM DEALE
	EDMOND BOVETT
	SAMUELL WEAVER
	ROBERT MULLINS
MICHAELL CHILD....................	WILLIAM GILES
	DANIELL PARKER
	JOHN FACEY

---

* [The names of the "Rebels" in this List have been given in "*A Receipt for* 100 *Prisoners
on Mr. Nepho's Account,*" on page 317*; but it was deemed advisable to print the following
second list, made on their arrival in the Barbadoes, because of its including the names of the
Masters to whom they were sold. The variations in the orthography of names have been already
referred to.]

Masters.	Rebells
THOMAS GIBBS	JOHN EASMAN
RICHARD CHEESMAN	HENRY SIMS
Cap^tn JOHN SUTTON.	JOHN COLLINS
Cap^tn ROBERT HARISON	JOSEPH GAICH JOHN FOLLETT
WILLIAM CHESTER Esq'	THOMAS DOLLEN
Cap^tn JOHN GIBBS....................	LAWRENCE CASEWELL JOHN FOOT RICHARD PINE
NICHOLAS MAYNARD	PETER BAGWELL JOHN HEATHFEILD
JOHN SMART	JOHN HERCOMBE JOHN REEVES JOHN DODDS
JOHN CHACE	RICHARD PARKER
THOMAS BERRESFORD	EDWARD MARSH JOHN SAMS NATHANIELL STANDERICKE
THOMAS PEARCE	THOMAS FRANKLYN JOHN COOKE
PETER FLEWILLING	ROBERT CLARKE ANDREW HAUKOM JOHN PREW SAMUELL PINSON
REBECCA BEAL	JOHN GILL CHRISTOPHER JEWELL RICHARD NASH THOMAS PESTOR

41—2

Masters	Rebells
BARNABAS CHATER	BENJAMINE WHICKER
Lᵗ Colloˡˡ RICHARD VINTER	JOHN HAYNES THOMAS FAUCEY
THOMAS HOLEMAN	ROBERT PEIRCE
WILLIAM MARCHANT	SAMUELL DOLBEARE JOHN CONNETT
JOHN SHAHANY	OLIVER HOBBS
RALPH LANE...........................	ROBERT FOANE NICHOLAS SALTER ABRAHAM THOMAS THOMAS QUICKE JOHN BAKER WILLIAM CLARKE
Colloˡˡ JOHN WATERMAN............	ALLEN ENGLAND
CHRISTOPHER WILLIAMS	RICHARD GREEN
MATHEW CHAPMAN	RICHARD HOARE
THOMAS PROTHERS	PETER KENT
THOMAS AUSTIN	JOHN HITCHCOCKE
ELIZABETH FOSTER	JOHN MOGERIDGE
THOMAS LINTON	ROGER BRYANT
JOHN GOLDINGHAM	ROBERT SANDY
Capᵗⁿ JOHN KING	JOHN VINCENT
DANIELL DEUSBURY	CHARLS BRAUGHTON
Majʳ GEORGE BUSHELL	FRANCIS SMITH
EDWARD HENLEY	ABRAHAM HUNT

Masters	Rebells
RICHARD SCOTT	ABRAHAM GODDING
JOHN JACKMAN.......................	PETTARD CORDELION
CHARLS THOMAS and Company ..	JOHN WHICKER
	CHRISTOPHER COOPER
	JOHN BOVETT
	RICHARD DANIELL
ROBERT BISHOPP	HENRY PITMAN
	WILLIAM PITTMAN
HESTER FOSTER	JOHN KEMPLIN
	Wᵡ MADER dead

CERTIFICATE of the Disposall of the Rebells sent by Mʳ NEPHO.

Barbados'

By the Rᵗ Hon'ᵇˡᵉ the Leiuᵗ Gouernor.

M' CHARLS THOMAS and m' JOHN PENNY Factors for JEROME NEPHO Esqʳ to whom the within Convicted Rebells menconed in this List were consigned, personally appeared before mee and made oath on the Holy Evangelists of Almighty God, that the said Rebells were delivered them out of the ship *Betty* of London, whereof JAMES MAY is Comander, and were all of them by the said THOMAS and PENNY, Sold and disposed of here to the Seuerall persons menconed in the Said List, Except one of the said Rebells by name WILLIAM MADDER that dyed on Shoar Since the Arriveall of the said Ship Giuen vnder my hand the First day of February 1685*

EDWYN STEDE

A true Coppy attested this ⎫
Second day of February 1685* ⎭

JNᵒ WHETSTONE Depᵗʸ Seerᵗʸ

* [1685-6.]

S̲IR WILLIAM BOOTH'S Receipt for the Prisoners within men-
con'd on the Account of JAMES KENDALL Esqr to be sent to
Barbados*

Prisoners in Dorchester Gaole to bee Transported

EDWARD LUTHER(1)

JOHN DOWNE

BENJ: CROWE

THOMAS BENNETT

JOHN FISHER

JOHN MANNING

ROBERT LUMBARD(2)

WM WADFORD(3)

RICHARD KEECH(4)

GEORGE PLUMLEY

THOMAS ALLEN

JOHN REASON

JOHN SPEERING

MATHEW PORTER

ROBERT SPURWAY(5)

JOHN EDWARDS

JOHN HARDIMAN

BARNARD BRYANT

JOHN MINIFIE(6)

JOHN WHITE(7)

JAMES POMEROY(8)

ROBERT SHALE(9)

THOMAS HOARE

PETER ROW

JOHN LOVERIDGE

ELIAS STEPHENS(10)

JOHN BRIDLE

THOMAS PARSONS(11)

NICHOLAS PALMER

THOMAS WILLIAMS

MATHEW HUTCHINS(12)

NICHOLAS SMITH

EMANUELL COLLINS

ROGER HOBBS(13)

JOHN GAY(14)

JOSEPH HALLETT(15)

NATHANIEL WEBBER(16)

EDWARD MORETON(17)

JAMES SALTER

WILLIAM LOVERIDGE(18)

AMBROSE ASHFORD

ROGER FRENCH(19)

NICHOLAS WARREN(20)

WILLIAM WILLS(21)

* [There is an "attested copy" of this Receipt, in which the following (see references after
the names in list) are the more important alterations in spelling, &c. :—

(1) LUTTER.	(8) POMREY.	(15) *Left out.*
(2) LUMBERD.	(9) *Left out.*	(16) WHEELER.
(3) MADFORD.	(10) STEVENS.	(17) MORTEN.
(4) KEATCH.	(11) PASSENS.	(18) *Left out.*
(5) SPURNAY.	(12) HUGHENS.	(19) *Left out.*
(6) *Left out.*	(13) HOBES.	(20) *Left out.*
(7) WITTE.	(14) GUY.	(21) WILLIAMS.

John Pryor

W^M Tucker

W^M Browne

Samuel Lawrence

John Hutchins (22)

W^M Clarke

John Browne

Robert Burridge

Henry Tucker

Thomas Burridge

John Allambridge (23)

Thomas Cornelius

Humphry Moleton

Edward Willmott (24)

W^M Williams (25)

Thomas Marshall

Richard Paul

Joseph Paul

Hugh Willmott (26)

John Johnson

Richard Allens

John Pitts

Stephen Gammage (27)

Andrew Rapson

W^M Cozens (28)

Thomas Townesend

Jasper Dyamond (29)

Thomas Gregory

John Allen (30)

Robert Hellyer (31)

Thomas Allen (32)

Thomas Best

Thomas Hellyer (31)

John Long

W^M Bennett (32)

John Markes (32)

John Mitchell

John Madders

Thomas Hallett

John Alston

George Macy

John Pinney (33)

Charles Strong

W^M Foode (34)

W^M Saunders

James Spence (35)

John Wilson

Edward Adams

John Adams

Arthur Lush (36)

John Hutchins (37)

Thomas Bovett

John Truren (38)

James Fowler

John White (39)

Francis Langbridge

---

(22) Hugens.

(23) Alimbridge.

(24) Willmatt.

(25) Wills.

(26) Willmatt.

(27) Gamidge.

(28) Coussens.

(29) Dimand.

(30) Allens.

(31) Hillier, and Thomas's name is twice given

(32) *Left out.*

(33) Penny.

(34) *Left out.*

(35) John Spence.

(36) Luch.

(37) Hugens.

(38) *Left out.*

(39) Wittes.]

Recd according to his Majesties direccons the Warr[t] from the LORD CHEIFE JUSTICE wth a Schedule thereunto annexed of One hundred persons attainted of High Treason w[ch] are by JAMES KENDALL Esq[r] to bee transported into his Majesties Island of Barbadoes or other his Majesties Plantacons in America according to a Condicon of a Recognizance entred into by me for that purpose In witnes whereof I have hereunto putt my hand this Five and twentieth day of September In the first yeare of his now Majesties reigne Ano q̄ Dñi 1685

WILL: BOOTH

Wittness herevnto
        SAM: GEE
        ROBT: HYDE*

CERTIFICAT of the Disposall of CAPTAIN KENDALLS Rebells.

BARBADOS. A List of Ninety Rebells by the *Happy Returne* of Pool Cap[tn] ROGER WADHAM Comander, with the Names of their Masters to whom they were disposed to, by the Hon'[ble] Collo[ll] JOHN HALLETT and Company for acco[t] of S[r] WILLIAM BOOTH and Cap[tn] JAMES KENDALL, December 1685†

Servants Names	Masters Names
BENJAMIN CROW	
JOHN GUY	
JOHN ALSTONE	Collo[ll] JOHN HALLETT
WILLIAM BROWN:	
EDWARD WILLMOTT	PETER FLEWELLIN
RICHARD ALLEN	WILLIAM LEWGAR Esq[r].
JOHN BROWN	BENJAMIN BIRD

* [The attested copy (dated Jan. 9, 1685 [1685-6]) states that the prisoners were put on board the *Happy Returne*, at Weymouth, in Portland Road, ROGER WADHAM Commander, &c. They were delivered to Mr. JOHN BROWNE and Company, Factors for Sir WILLIAM BOOTH, Knt., at the Barbadoes.]

† [It will be noticed that the same names are in some cases very differently spelt in this and the preceding list.]

Servants Names	Masters Names
ELIAS STEVENS........................	Cap^{tn} JOHN STEWART
WILLIAM CLARKE	
WILLIAM WILLS	
JAMES POMREY	Cap^{tn} W^M MARSHALL
EDWARD MORTON	
JAMES SALTER	AGNIS FENTON
JOHN EDWARDS	Cap_jⁿ MATHEW HAVILAND
JAMES FOWLER	
THOMAS CORNELIUS	Collo^{ll} JOHN FARMER
ROBERT SPURWEY	
THOMAS TOUNSEND.................	
JOHN HUGENS	Cap^{tn} TOBIAS FRERE
NATHANIELL WEBBER..............	
JOHN LOVERIDGE....................	WILLIAM WEAVER
JOHN SPEERING	Maj^r GEORGE LILLINGTON
THOMAS HALLETT	Collo^{ll} SAM^{LL} TITCOMB
JASPER DIAMOND	RICHARD HARWOOD Esqr.
WILLIAM WILLIAMS.................	
ROBERT BURRIDGE	Maj^r JOHN JOHNSON
PETER ROW	
FRANCIS LAUGHBRIDGE	HESTER FOSTER
JOHN WILSON	STEPHEN GIBBS
NICHOLAS SMITH	HUGH WILLIAMS
W^M COSSENS	RALPH FRETWELL
JOHN ADAMS.........................	
EDWARD ADAMS	JAMES THORPE
THOMAS BOVETT	PHILLIP FOUSHER
THOMAS ALLEN	
ROBERT HELLIER....................	
SAMUELL LAWRENCE	
JOHN PITTS	
THOMAS HELLIER	
JOHN FISHER	Collo^{ll} RICHARD WILLIAMS
JOHN ALAMBRIDGE	

Servants Names	Masters Names
THOMAS HOAR	
ARTHUR LUSH	
JOHN PRIOR	
JOHN LONG	
WILLIAM MADFORD	
THOMAS ALLEN	
RICHARD KEATCH	
W'LLIAM TUCKER	RICHARD LINTOTT
STEPHEN GAMADGE	
JOHN WHITE	
JOHN MADDERS.......................	
EMANUELL COLLINS	
MATHER PORTER	
GEORGE PLUMLEY	NICHOLAS PRIDEAUX
THOMAS WILLIAMS	
JOHN MANNING	
JOHN JOHNSON	
ANDREW RAPSON.....................	
THOMAS BURRIDGE	JOHN HETHERSELL Esq'
THOMAS BENNETT	
HENRY TUCKER	
BARNARD BRYANT*	
THOMAS BEST	
THOMAS MARSHALL..................	JOHN BURSTON
HUGH WILLMATT......................	
JOHN BRIDLE	
JOHN HARDEMAN.....................	JOHN HOW
NICHOLAS PALMER	Cap^{tn} GEO: TERWIGHT
JOHN PENNY	
CHARLS STRONG	
EDWARD LUTHER....................	Collo^{ll} J^{no}: SAMPSON.
WILLIAM SANDERS	
THOMAS REASON	

* [The "brace" against this and the four following names is not in the original.]

Servants Names	Masters
JOHN MITTCHELL......................	
THOMAS PARSONS....................	
JAMES SPENCE	
JOHN ALLIN	Cap.^{tn} J.^{no} PARNELL
JOSEPH PAUL.........................	
THOMAS GREGORY	
RICHARD PAUL	
JOHN HUTCHINS	JOHN HAYWOOD
MATHEW HUTCHINS	THOMAS HAYSE
HUMPHRY MOULTON	
AMBROSE ASHFORD	Cap.^{tn} WALTER SCOT
GEORGE MASEY......................	
ROGER HOBES	Cap.^{tn} ROBERT HARRISSON
JOHN DOWNE	STEPHEN DEVORAX
JOHN WITTE	
ROBERT LAMBERT	RICHARD ADAMSON

Barbados,

By the R.^t Hon'^{ble} the Lt Gouernor.

Mr JOHN BROWNE one of the Factors for s.^r Wm BOOTH K.^t to whom the aboue and within Convicted Rebells menconed in this List were consigned personaly appeared before mee and made oath on the Holy Evangelists of Allmighty God that they were delivered him and Company, out of the ship *Happy Returne* of Pool, ROGER WADHAM Comander, and were all of them by him and Company sold and disposed of here to the severall persons menconed in the said List, Giuen vnder my hand the 8th day of Janu'y 1685*

EDWYN STEDE

A true Coppy Attested this
Nineth day of Janu'y. 1685.*
J.^{No}: WHETSTONE Dep.^{ty} Secr.^{ty}

---

* [1685-6.]

R WILL: BOOTH'S LIST of Prisoners sent to Barbados.*

Summersett. Shire.

Will: DREW of Bridgwater
JOHN SEAMER of Chilton
WILLIAM SMITH of Road
WILLIAM HALL of Cheard
JUSTINEAN GUPPY of Tanton (1)
GEORGE CARROW of Bridgwater
THOMAS DENNIS of Bridgwater
AMBROSS WINTER of West Buckland
THOMAS GALHAMTON(2) of West Zoyland
WILLIAM DAW of Tanton
HENRY GIBBONS of Tanton
ROB: EASTON of Tanton
GEORGE MICELL of Bridgwater
DANIEL PUMREY(3) of Tanton.
EDWARD COUNSELL of Allerton
JOHN. WALL of Bridgwater
JOHN LEAKER(4) of Hunspill [Huntspill]
EDWARD VILDY of Tanton
ROBERT TEAPE of Bridgwater
JOSEPH WICKHAM of Burnam
JEREMIAH ATKINS of Tanton
SAMUEL BOONE of Tanton
JOHN BUSTON of Milverton
JOHN WALTERS of Tanton
ROB: SEASE of Tanton (5)
GEORGE MULLINS of Tanton
THOMAS BROCKE of Tanton

* [In an "attested copy" the under-named differences of spelling of names occur (see the reference numbers) :—

(1) JUZTIPHER GUPPY.   (3) JUMREY.   (5) SEARS.
(2) GILHAMTON.   (4) LEAKE.

ROB: SEAMAN of Tanton
LAURANCE HUSSEY of Wellington
Will. TIVERTON of Bridgwater
GEORGE WARREN of Milverton
ROB: COWARD of Road
JOHN CHAPPELL of Petherton
WILL: BURROW'S of Corfe (6)
Will: HAYNES of Beckington
GEORGE KEELE of Chilton (6)
STEPHEN RODEWAY (7) of Frome
HENRY QUANT of Tanton
WILL: MEAD of Bridgwater
THOMAS GAMAGE of Tanton
JAMES BAKER of Milverton
HUMPHERY POPE of Tanton
JOHN WARRIN of Milverton
JOSEPH VINICOTT(8) of Bridg Water
HENRY MIRE of Bridgwater
JOHN HARRIS of Hunspill
FRANCIS CAME of Hunspill
RICHARD STEPHENS(9) of North Carre
GEORGE NOWELL of Tanton
MORRIS FUSSE of Milverton
JAMES HILLMAN of Milverton
JOHN STOODLY of Trent
Will: BARNARD of Hust
BARTHOLOMEW RANDALL (10) of West Coter
JOHN RODGERS (11) of Mackington
ROB: MITCHELL of Illton
JONAS CROSSE of Cullington
RICHARD ALLIN of Creech
THOMAS MIDLETON of Tanton

---

(6) *Left out.*   (9) STEVENS.
(7) RODWAY.   (10) RENDELL.
(8) VINCOTT.   (11) ROGERS.

RICHARD BICKHAM (12) of Dosin
JOHN BUDGE of Cheard
ROBART PAUL of Illton
OSMOND READ (13) of Tanton
JOHN BURGES of Tanton
WILLIAM PARKER of Tanton
JOHN FARMER of Tanton
ABRAHAM POLLARD of Cheard

Devon—Shire

TIMOTHY HAWKER of Thorn Combe
JOHN MITCHILL of Thorn Come
JOHN BAGG of Thorncome
WILLIAM SMITH jun: of Vpportre [Uppottery]
MICELL POWELL of Neath Glomorging
WILLIAM WALTER'S of Membery
HUMPHERY TRUMP of West Sanford
JOHN BARTLETT of Pitmisser
JOHN CHILCOT (14) of Tiverton.
WILLIAM HARVEY of Memrc
WILLIAM HUTCHINGS (15) of Vpportre
JOHN SMITH of Hunington
JOHN CLODE of Vppertre
JOHN CANTLEBURY of Sanford Pefrin
RICHARD WADHAM of Froome
WILLIAM WOOLRIDGE of Tiverton
SIMON POOLE of Bemister
WILLIAM COMBE of Broad Winser
RICHARD EDGAR of Mosterton.
Will: PHIPPIN (16) of High Church
JOHN GALE (17) of Coscam

(12) BRICKHAM.
(13) SYMOND REID.
(14) CHILLICOTT.
(15) HUTCHINS.
(16) SHIPPIN.
(17) JOSEPH GALL.

Thomas Matthews of Chiddicke
John Keele of Chilton

Put on board the *John frigget* cap Will: Stokes comand^r ninty Prisonners consined for the burbadous dated at Dorchester oc^{br} the 24 1685

WILL: BOOTH

    Shipt at Bristoll

Barbados *

By the Right Honble the Leiv^t Governo':

John Rogers Cheife Mate, and William Alexander Second Mate of the Ship *John Friggott* of Bristoll, whereof William Stoakes deceased was lately Master, personally appeared before mee, and made Oath on the holy Evangelist of Almighty God, that the above convicted Rebells by the s^d Stoakes taken in att the Port of Bristoll, are the very same Rebells, that were delivered to, and by the said Stoakes brought in the said Shipp to this Island, and that they were all of them here landed, and delivered to M' John Browne and Company Factors for S' William Booth Kn^t except Joseph Wickham who dyed on board the said Shipp in Kingroad, and was from thence carryed on Shoare in the Port of Bristoll and there buryed, as alsoe twelve more of them which dyed on board the said Shipp on the voyage and were buryed in the Sea, whose names are as followeth vizt Justipher Guppy, Thomas Gilhampton, George Micell, Edward Councell, George Keale, William Smith jun'. William Hutchins, Symon Poole, Wm Mead Francis Came Jonas Cross and Robert Paul Given under my hand this 28th day of January 1685.†

EDWYN STEDE

A true Coppy Attested this }
  First day of February 1685† }
    J^{No} WHETSTONE Dep^{ty} Secr^{ty}

---

* [This certificate, as will be seen from its ending, is taken from the attested copy.
† [1685-6.]

list of seaventy seaven Convicted Rebells by the *John Friggat* of
Bristoll Cap^tn Wm STOAKS Comander Imported this Island arc
all the very same Rebells that was taken on board the said ship at the
Port of Bristoll, Except thirteen of them that dyed before the Arriveall,
and one since the arriveall of the said ship to this Island:

Masters	Rebells
Cap^tn WALTER SCOTT	JOHN LEAKE EDWARD VILDY ROBERT EASTON JOHN STOODLY RICHARD BICKHAM THOMAS DENNIS GEORGE CARROW WILLIAM SMITH jun' JOHN BARTLETT ROBERT MITCHELL MICHAELL POWELL HENRY QUANT JOHN FARMER RICHARD ALLEN
J^no & Wm HOLDER	JOHN WALL AMBROSE WINTER JOHN CANTLEBURY RICHARD EDGAR RICHARD STEVENS Wm TIVERTON.
	THOMAS GAMADGE ROBERT COWARD GEORGE WARREN

Masters	Rebells
Ann Gallop.........................	John Walters
	Stephen Rodway
	George Nowell
	John Warrin
	John Burgis
	William Parker
	John Chilcott
	George Seaman
Colloll John Farmer	John Seamar
Henry Quintyne Esqr	William Haynes
	Robert Sease
	John Bagg
Samuell Smart	William Phiffin
John Buston	William Burrowes
	William Drew
	Humphry Pope
	John Clood
	John Gale
	Osman Read
	William Coomb
	John Budge
Colloll John Hallett..............	Humphry Trumpe
	Thomas Brocke
Wm Hectrop........	George Mullins
Richard Harwood Esqr	Thomas Middleton
	James Hilman
	John Smith

43

Masters	Rebells
Collo^{ll} JOHN SAMPSON	TIMOTHY HAWKER JOHN MITCHELL RICHARD WADHAM W^M BARNARD
Cap^{tn} STOAKS	JAMES BAKER BARTHOLOMEW RANDALL
D͞cor BATTYN	HENRY MYRE MORRIS FUSS
D͞cor JOHN SPRINGHAM	HENRY GIBBONS
JOHN ALCHORNE	THOMAS MATHEWS
OTHNIELL HAGGAT..................	JOHN BUSTON
JOHN SUMERS	JOSEPH VINICOTT
SILUS MARCHANT	WILLIAM HALL
Major JOHNSON	JOHN RODGERS
JOHN HETHERSELL Esqr...........	JOHN HARRIS
HUGH WILLIAMS	ROBERT TEAP
WILLIAM ALLAMBY	JOHN CHAPPELL
JOHN DENNER	DANIELL POMRE
THOMAS BURKE	WILLIAM HARVEY
WILLIAM SLOGRAVE	LAWRENCE HUSSE
SAMUELL WARNER	WILLIAM WALTERS
ANTHONY PALMER	WILLIAM DAW
WILLIAM MARCH^T	ABRAHAM POLLARD

Masters	Rebells
	JEREMIA ATKINS
JOHN BROWNE	SAMUELL BOON
	WILLIAM WOOLRIDGE

JOHN KEAL Dead

Barbados

By the R^t Honble the Leiu^t Gowernor.

Mr JOHN BROWNE one of the Factors for Sr WILLIAM BOOTH K^t to whom the within convicted Rebells menconed in this List were consigned; and m' DANIELL RICHARDSON personally appeared before mee and made oath on the Holy Evangelists of Allmighty God, that the said Rebells were delivered him the said JOHN BROWNE and Company out of the ship *John Friggat* of Bristoll, whereof WILLIAM STOAKS deceased was lately Master, and were all of them by him the said BROWNE and Company sold and disposed of here to the seuerall persons menconed in the said List, Except one of the said Rebells by name JOHN KEALE that dyed on shoar Since the arriveall of the said Ship Giuen vnder my hand the 29th Jann'y: 1685

EDWYN STEDE

A true Coppy Attested this }
First day of February 1685 }

J^{no} WHETSTONE Dep^{ly} Secr^{ty}

S^R WILLIAM BOOTH'S Receipt for the Prisóners within men- con'd

Att the Bridewell at Taunton

RICHARD STEVENS	CHARLES LUCAS
*RICHARD EDGAR	GEORGE GRAY

* [The names marked with an asterisk are mentioned in previous Lists.]

John Bartlett
*John Stoodley
*Robt Paul
*Robt Mitchell
*John Gale
*Bartho: Randall
*John Rogers
*Wᵐ Haynes
*Wiłłm Barnard
*Thomas Mathewes
*Henry Meyer
John Bressett
*Richard Allen
John Poole
*John Burges
*John Farmer
*Richard Bickham
*Henry Gibbons
John Bason
*George Nowell
*Morris Furse aƚs Voss
*Humphrey Trump
*John Warren
*George Warren
*Humphrey Pope
*Osmond Read
*Henry Quant
*Wiłłm Burroughs
*Wᵐ Daw
*Wᵐ Parker
*Robt Sease
*Thomas Midleton
*James Hillman
John Bray
*Ambrose Winter

*Laurence Hussey
*Robt Seaman
Edward Lyde
*John Chappell
*Robt Easton
*John Walter
*Thomas Brocke
George Mollins
*Daniell Pumroy
*Jeremy Atkins
*Samˡˡ Boone
John Edwards

Out of Bridgwater Prison's that came from Taunton

*George Michill
*Wᵐ Drew
*Thomas Dennis
John Avoake
*Wᵐ Tiverton
*Joseph Vinicott
John Seymer
*John Leaker
*Symon Poole
*John Wale
*Richard Wadham
*Stephen Rodway
*Francis Came
*Michell Powell
*John Kerle
*Thomas Galhampton
*George Carrow
*Abraham Pollard
*John Budge

*W^M HARVEY
*W^M HALL
*W^M PHIPPEN
*JOHN CHILCOTT
*ROBT COWARD
*JOHN CANTLEBURY
*W^M WOOLRIDGE
*W^M SMYTH
JOHN SMYTH
*W^M MEAD
*GEORGE KEEL
*EDWARD COUNCELL
*JOSEPH WICKHAM
JOHN HARRIS

Out of the Prison's that came from
Exeter to Taunton.

*ROBT TEAP
*TYMOTHY HAWKER
*W^M SMYTH
JOSEPH NEWBERRY
*JOHN SMYTH
JOHN CLODE
*JONAS CROSS
*JOHN BRAGG
*WIllM HUTCHINS
*JOHN MITCHELL
*EDWARD VILDY
*JUSTINIAN GUPPY
W^M COMBE
*JAMES BAKER
*THOMAS GAMAGE
*W^M WALTER

Received According to his Maties direccons the Warr^t from the Ld CHEIF JUSTICE wth a Schedule therevnto annexed of One hundred persons attainted of high Treason wch are by me to be transported in to his Maties Island of Barbadoes according to a Condicon of a Recognizance entred into by me for that purpose in Wittness whereof I have herevnto put my hand this present 25th of September in the 1st year of his now Maties reigne Annoq, Dom 1685.

WILL: BOOTH

Witness
ROB^T: HYDE
SAM^L GEE

(in-dorso)   Prison's 100

Bridwell at Taunton .. 56
Bridgewater Prison's at Taunton 33
Exeter Prison's att Taunton 11
———
100

HE sale of Sixty Seaven Rebells delivered by Cap^{tn} CHARLS GARDNER Comander of the *Jamaica Marchant* to CHARLS THOMAS and THOMAS SADLER for acco^t of Messrs JOHN PALMER JOHN RICHARDSON SAMUELL YOUNG and WILLIAM ROSE the 12th day March 1685. Viz^t

Masters	Rebells
WILLIAM CHESTER Esqr	THOMAS PITT
FRANCIS BOND esq^r	JOHN BRUER
	WILLIAM CROSS
	ROBERT RICHARDS
	JOHN MILLER
	JOHN CROSS
BENJAMIN MIDDLETON	LUKE PORTER
EDWARD JOURDEN	JOHN SLATE
	DANIELL RUTTER
DANIELL PARSONS	ISACK DOYER
	SAMUELL BOND
MATHEW GRAY	JOHN MAGRIDGE
NICHOLAS GIBBS	JAMES COCKRAM
THOMAS ESTWICKE	WILLIAM SANDERS
RICHARD FORSTALL..................	JOHN ADAMS
JOHN GRAY	CHRISTOPHER HOLBIN
Maj^r RICHARD SALTER	HENRY CHAMBERS
FRANCIS YOUNG	SILVESTER LOYD
JOSEPH JONES	PERCYFULL NOWIS
WILLIAM BARON	JOHN CHAMBERLIN
ARCHIBALD JOHNSON	GEORGE RUSSELL
	HUMPHRY JUSTIN
	LEONARD STAPLE
	THOMAS GOOLD
	GEORGE SCRUBS
	WILLIAM VARIER
	ROBERT PEARCE

Masters	Rebells
Maj^r ABELL ALLEN	RICHARD SIMMONS
	ENOCK GOOLD
	JEREMIAH POOL
	JAMES CLIFT
	EMANUELL MARCH^T
GEORGE HANNAY esq^r	GEORG SNOW
	WILLIAM CURRIER
	JOHN COCKRAM
JOHN BAWDEN Esqr	JAMES WEBB
	RICHARD KING
JOHN HETHERSALL Esqr...	RICHARD PEARCE
	EDWARD BELLEMIE
GEORGE HARPER	CORNELIUS RADFORD
	JOB HUNT
Maj^r GEORGE BUSHELL	JOHN BAKER
Collo^{ll} THOMAS COLLETON	THOMAS BUGLER
	NICHOLAS COLLINS
	MATHEW COOKE
	CHRISTOPHER ROE
	THOMAS MEADE
	JOHN BAKER
	THOMAS PREIST
NICHOLAS PRIDEAUX	WILLIAM PHILLIPS
	JAMES MAYNARD
ROBERT KELLY.......................	HENRY PREIST
WILLIAM ALEMBY	EDWARD KENT
MICHAELL CHILD....................	JOHN GIBBS
Cap^{tn} JOHN SUTTON................	ROBERT EARLE
	WILLIAM PITTS
MUSE WALFORD	JOHN GODSAL
Maj^r GEORGE LILLINGTON	SILVESTER POOL
	JONAS BROWNE
JOHN SUMMERS......................	JOHN ROGGERS
ANN WALTERS	JOHN TIMOTHY

Masters	Rebells
Cap^{tn} THOMAS MORRIS	MATHEW CRAFTS
	BARNARD LOVERIDGE
CHARLS THOMAS & THOMAS SAD- ⎫ LER ....⎬	WILLIAM WOODCOCKE
	THOMAS AUSTIN
EDWARD HURLSTONE	PHILLIP CHEEK
	CHARLS BURRAGE

WILLIAM LEE dead before the ship arrived in Barbados

Barbados

By the R Hon'^{ble} the Lt Gouernor.

Mr THOMAS SADLER one of the Factors to whom the within convicted Rebells menconed in this List were consigned to, personally appeared before mee and made oath on the Holy Evangelists of Allmighty God that they are the very same Rebells that were delivered him and m' CHARLS THOMAS the other Factor for Messrs JOHN PALMER, JOHN RICHARDSON SAMUELL YOUNG & Wm ROSE out of the Ship *Jamaica March^t*, whereof CHARLS GARDNER is Comand^r and where all of them by the said SADLER disposed of there to the Severall persons menconed in the said List, Except one of the said Rebells that dyed at Sea by name WILLIAM LEE, and was thrown over board, as appeared by the oaths of the Said Comander, and JOHN LLOYD Mate of the Said Shipp, Giuen vnder my hand this 24th day of March (1685)

EDWYN STEDE

A true Coppy attested this ⎫
　25th day of March 1686 　⎬

J^{no} WHETSTONE Dep^{ty} Secr^{ty}*

---

* [There is "An Account of one Hundred and three Convict Rebells taken on board the *Jamaica March^t* CHARLS GARDNER Comander, at the Port of Waymouth in old England, vizt. thirty ffive p bill of loading, for acco^t of s^r CHRISTOPHER MUSGRAVE, and to bee delivered to Cap^{tn} SYMON MUSGRAVE in Jamaica, and sixty Eight for acco^t of Messrs JOHN PALMER, JOHN RICHARDSON, SAMUELL YOUNG and Wm ROSE, delivered on the Island of Barbados to m' CHARLS THOMAS and THOMAS SADLER, the 12th March 1685." But all the names contained in this account have been mentioned in other Lists printed in this book.]

[TICKETS GRANTED

TO EMIGRANTS FROM BARBADOES, TO NEW ENGLAND, CAROLINA, VIRGINIA, NEW YORK, ANTIGUA, JAMAICA, NEWFOUNDLAND, AND OTHER PLACES.

1678—1679.]

[BARBADOS.—TICKETS.]

LIST of what TICQ̄ᵀᵀˢ· have been granted out of the Secrᵗʸˢ Office of the Island aforesaid for the departure off this Island of the several psones hereafter menconed begining in January 1678 ꝑ ending in December following. (Vizᵗ.)—

February yᵉ 26ᵗʰ 1678:

ALBERCHT HENNIGO in the Ship *Judith*, for London ROBERT KINGS-LAND Commandʳ·   time out

March yᵉ 11ᵗʰ 1678

ARMITAGE HENRY in the ship *Society*, for Boston, WILLIAM GUARD Comander.   Security

March yᵉ 20ᵗʰ 1678:

ARIS JOHN in the ship *Indeavour* for London, JAMES GILBERT Comander   time out

Aprill the 26ᵗʰ: 1679

ADAMSON GEORGE in the Ketch *Vnity* for Virginia JAMES RAINY, Comander   time out

Aprill yᵉ 26ᵗʰ 1679:

ADAMS THOMAS in the Ship *Defeyance* for London Wˣ CREED Comander.   time out

44—2

Aprill the 28th 1679.

ALBERT ANN in the ship *Mary* for Carolina NICH⁰ LOCKWOOD
Comander   time out

Aprill y[e] 28th 1679

ANDERSON MARGRET in the Ketch *Unity* for Virginia JAMES RAINY
Comander.   time out

Aprill y[e] 29th 1679

ARMSTRONG ANN in the Ship *Francis* for Antegoa PETER JEFFERYS
Comander.   time out

May the first 1679

ABRAHAM AGNUS in the Ketch *Francis & Susan* for Boston PHILLIP
KNELL Comand[r].   time out

May 2[d] 1679

ARTHUR KATHERINE in the Ketch *Prosperous* for Virginia DAVID
FOGG Comander   time out

May the 2[d] 1679

ADAMS GEORGE in the Ship *Adventure* for Lond⁰ W[M] JOHNSON
Comand[r].   security

May y[e] 22 1679

AUST HENRY in the Ship *Industry* for Bristoll JAMES PORTER Comand[r]
                                                 time out

May the 27th 1679

ALLIN ELIAZER in the ship *Prudence and Ma:y* for Boston JACOB
GREEN Comand[r]   time out

June the 14th 1679

ALLISON THOMAS in the ship *Johns Adventure* for Jamaica EDWARD
WINSLOW Comand[r]   time out

July the 8ᵗʰ 1679

ALDERSON THOMAS in the ship *Friendship* for London JOHN WILLIAMS
  Comander   time out

August the 18ᵗʰ 1679

AVERY MARY in the Ship *Golden Fleece* for London HENRY PASCALL
  Comandʳ   time out

October the 4 1679

ATHERTON Wᴹ in the Ship *Nathaniell* for Boston Wᴹ CLARKE Comandʳ
         time out

November the 25ᵗʰ: 1679

ABUDIENT ABRAHAM in the Ketch *Phœnix* for Antegoa ROBERT
  FLEXNY, Comand   security

November the 25. 1679

ARE SARAH in the Sloop *Katherine* for Antegoa ANDREW GALL,
  Comandʳ   security

Novembʳ 27ᵗʰ 1679

ALSOP KATHERINE in the Sloop *Katherine* for Antegoa ANDREW
  GALL Comandʳ   security

Februray 13 1678*

BOWDLER ANDREW in the ship *James* for New Yorke WILLIAM
  SWEETLAND Comander   time out

February the 17ᵗʰ 1678

BROWN RACHAELL, in the Barq, *Adventure* for Antegoa CHRISTOPHER
  BERROW Comander   security

February 18ᵗʰ 1678

BLAKE JOHN in the sloop *Resolution* for Montseratt JOHN INGLEBY
  Comander   time outᵗ

* [1678-9.]

March first 1678

BARWELL JOHN in the *Constant Warwick* friggott for Lond⁰ Capᵗ RALPH
  DELAVALL Comandʳ   time out

March the 5ᵗʰ 1678

BILFORD JAMES in the Pink *Seaventure* for Antegoa GEORGE BAT-
  TERSBY Comandʳ   time out

March the 12ᵗʰ 1678

BARTON JAMES in the Ketch *Wᵐ and Susan* for New England RALPH
  PARKER Comandʳ   time out

March the 22 1678

BANCKS JOSEPH in the Ketch *Wᵐ & Susan* for New England RALPH
  PARKER Comander   time out

March the 27ᵗʰ 1679

BARNARD HUMPHRY Senior and Junʳ in the Ketch *Mary and Sarah* for
  Carolina GEO: CONWAY Comandʳ   time out

Aprill the first 1679

BATES RICHARD in the ship *Expedition* for London JOHN HARDING
  Comander   time out

Aprill the third 1679

BROWNING ANN in the Ship *Martin* for Newfoundland CHRISTOPHER
  MARTIN Comander.   time out

Aprill 4ᵗʰ 1679

BAGNALL JOHN in the Sloop *Rutter* for Jamaica EDWARD DUFFEILD
  Comander   time out

Aprill the 7ᵗʰ 1679

BICKLE THOMAS in the Sloop *May Flower*, for Bermudes EDWARD
  HUBBERT Comandʳ   security

Aprill the 11ᵗʰ 1679

BURGOSS ABRAHAM in the Ketch *Wᵐ & John* for New England JOHN SANDERS Comander   time out

Aprill the 15ᵗʰ 1679

BRETT JOHN in the Ship *Honor* for London THOMAS WARREN Comander   time out

Aprill the 17ʰ 1679

BARNES NICHOLAS in the Barq, *Blessing* for Prouidence FRANCIS WAT-LINGTON Comandʳ.   time out

Aprill the 17ᵗʰ 1679

BUSHELL Wᴹ in the Ship *Pearle* for Antegoa, RICHᴰ WILLIAMS Comandʳ   time out

Aprill the 19ᵗʰ 1679

BALL JAMES in the ship *Pelican*, for London JOHN COCKE, Comander   security

Aprill the 22ᵈ 1679

BALRICK THOMAS in the Ship *Hope* for London JOSEPH BALL Co-mander.   security

Aprill yᵉ 29ᵗʰ 1679

BAGWELL FRANCIS in the Keatch *Calieta* for Topsham SAMUELL PAUL Comandʳ   time out

May yᵉ 5ᵗʰ 1679

BINCKS CHARLES Esqʳ in the Ship *Experimᵗ* for London ALLAN COCK Comandʳ   time out

May the 5ᵗʰ 1679

BREARLY MARTIN in the Ship *White Fox* London JOHN LEE Comandʳ   time out

May the Sixth 1679

Box Ann in the Ketch *Prosperous* for Virginia Dauid Fogg, Comander   time out

May the 6ᵗʰ 1679

Burne Dennis A servant belonging to Mʳ· Henry Aplewhite in
the Ketch *Prosperous* for Virginia David Fogg Comander

May the 7ᵗʰ 1679

Brown Wᴹ in the Ship *Merchants Adventure* for Leverpool John
Greigs Comandʳ   time out

May yᵉ 8ᵗʰ 1679

Blackleech John Senior and Junʳ for Boston in yᵉ Ketch *May Flower*
Robert Kitchin Comandʳ   time out

May the 10ᵗʰ 1679

Bishop Robert in the ship *experiment* for London Allan Cock
Comandʳ·   security

May the 16ᵗʰ 1679.

Brome John in the Ketch *Prouidence* for Boston Marke Hunking
Comandʳ   time out

May the 17ᵗʰ 1679.

Bolton Ambross in the ship *New Concord,* for Londo James Strutt
Comandʳ   time out

May yᵉ 29ᵗʰ 1679

Bond Thomas in the Ketch *Elizᵃ·* for Boston John Fletcher
Comander   time out

May the 21ˢᵗ 1679

Berrow Christopher in the ship *Society,* of Bristoll Edmond Ditty
Comandʳ   time out

June the 2ᵈ 1679

BOWHANE TEAG in the ship *Society,* for Bristoll EDMOND DITTY Comandʳ·   time out

June yᵉ 22ᵈ 1679

BREAD THOMAS, in the Ship *Prouidence* for Boston TIMOTHY PROUT Comandʳ   time out

July the first 1679

BIRD HENRY in the Ship *Amity* for London BENJᴬ GROVE Comandʳ   time out

July the 2ᵈ 1679

BRADLEY MICHAELL in the ship *Amity* for London BENJᴬ GROVE Comandʳ   time out

July yᵉ 4ᵗʰ 1679

BUTLER JOHN in the Ketch *New London* for ditto ADAM PICKETT Comander   time out

July the 7ᵗʰ 1679

BOLTON SAMUELL in the Ship *Bare* for London Wᴹ DICKINS Comandʳ   security

July yᵉ 12ᵗʰ 1679

BROWNE HUGH in the ship *Bachelor* for London Wᴹ KNOTT Comandʳ   time out

July the 21 1679

BROGRAVE HENRY in the Ship *Malligoe Merchᵗᵗ* for London ROGER HOMER Comandʳ   time out

August the first 1679

BODKIN MARTIN in the ship *Young Wᵐ* for Virginia THO. CORNISH Comander   time out

August the third 1679
BODKIN NICH⁰ in the ship *Young William* for Virginia THO CORNISH
Comander   time out

August the 9ᵗʰ 1679
BARKER JOHN Laborer in the ship *friendship* for London JOHN Wᴹˢ
Comander   time out

August the 11ᵗʰ 1679
BEVENISTER ELIAM* in the Ship *friendship* for London JOHN WIL-
LIAMS Comander   time out

August. yᵉ 12ᵗʰ 1679
BEARD JOHN in the ship *friendship* for Lond⁰ JOHN WILLIAMS
Comandʳ   time out

August the 15ᵗʰ 1679
BODINGHAM JOHN in the Ship *friendship* for New Engtᵈ Wᴹ MURPHY
Comander   security

August yᵉ 19ᵗʰ 1679
BUTLER ELINOR A Seruᵗ belonging to Mʳ Wᴹ BULKLEY in the Ketch
Neptune for Virginia JO: KNOTT Comand

September yᵉ 16: 1679
BROWNE FRANCIS in the Barq, *blessing* for Burmudos FRANCIS WAT-
LINGTON Comander   time out

September the 30ᵗʰ 1679
BRANDBY ELIZᴬ a Servant belonging to DAVID WATKINS in the sloop
Rutter for Jamaica ED: DUFFEILD, Comd

---

* [There is a doubt as to this name; it has been written over another which is only par-
tially erased.]

October y^r 2^d 1679

BLUNT GEORGE in the Ship *Lixboa Merch^u* for New Yorke ROGER
WHITFEILD Comander   time out

October the third 1679

BARTON CHRISTOPHER in the Ship *Barbados Merchant* for Virginia
JAMES COCK Comand^r security

October the 4th 1679

BELFOUR JAMES in the Sloop *true friendship* for Antegua CHARLES
KALLAHANE Comand^r·   time out

October ye 4th 1679

BISHOP THOMAS in the Ship *Virgin* for Leward Islands THOMAS
ALUMBY Comander   security

October ye 4th 1679

BANISTER RICH^D in the sloop *true Freindship* for Antegoa CHARLES
KALLAHANE Comander   time out

October ye 6th 1679

BUTCHER JOHN in the Sloop *true friendship* for Antegua CHARLES
KALLAHANE Comand^r security

October ye 9th 1679

BENSON MARY in the Sloop *Endeavor* for Carolina THOMAS SHAW
Comand^r security

October ye 13th 1679

BATTISON JULIAN in the Barq, *Endeavor* for Carolina THOMAS SHAW
Comand^r time out

October the 20th 1679

BUTTLER WALTER in the Keatch *John & Sarah* for New Yorke JAMES
SHOARE Comander   security

45—2

November y^c 7th 1679

BABBINGTON THOMAS a Servant belonging to THO: GLADDIN in the
Barq, *Adventure* for Jamaica EDWARD DUFFEILD Comand^r

November y^c 20th 1679

BENTLY MARTIN in the Ketch *Mary & Sarah* for providence GEORGE
CONWAY Comander   security

November 25th 1679

BREAD THOMAS in the Ketch *Phœnix* for Leward Islands ROBERT
FLEXNY Comander   security

November y^c 25 1679

BREAD ARTHUR in the Ketch *Phœnix* for the Lew^d. Islands ROBERT
FLEXNY Comander   security

December the 18th 1679

BARROW, REBECCA in the ship *Ann and Jane* for London RICH^D RAD-
FORD Comander   time out

December the 24th 1679

BROOK THOMAS in the ship *Recouery* for Jamaica JAMES BROWN
Comander   time out

December 24th 1679

BULKLY W^M in the ship *Ann & Jane* for London RICHARD RATFORD
Comander   security

December the 29th 1679

BARNEWELL ROBERT in the Ship *Recouery* for Jamaica JAMES BROWN
Comander   time out

December the 30th 1679

BURKE JEOFFERY in the Sloop *true friendship* for Antegoa CHARLES
KALLAHANE Comand^r   time out

January the 4ᵗʰ 1678*

CRILLICK JANE a Servant belonging to JOHN FOLLITT in the ship *Old head* of Kingsale ROBERT BARKER Comandʳ for Lewᵈ.

January the 7ᵗʰ 1678

CARTER ELINOR in the ship *Joseph and Ann* for Carolina SAMUELL EVANS Comander   security

January the 15ᵗʰ 1678

CHAPLIN JEREMIAH in the Ship *Joseph ℓ Ann* for Carolina SAMUELL EVANS, Comandʳ   security

January the 31ˢᵗ 1678

CRAGG JOHN in the Ketch *Freindship* for New England JOSEPH HARDY Comandʳ   time out

February yᵉ 22ᵈ 1678

CLAYPOOLE NORTON in the Ship *Bachelors Delight* for NYorke ROBERT GREENWAY Comander   time out

March the first 1678

CLARKE ANN in the ship *Samuell* for London JOHN CLARKE Comander   time out

March the 5ᵗʰ 1678

CLAYPOOL JOHN in the Ship *Patience* for Londᵒ THOMAS HUDSON, Comander   time out

March the 6ᵗʰ 1678

COOPER THOMAS in the Pinke *Blessing* for New Yorke JOHN THWING Comandʳ   time out

March the 10ᵗʰ 1678

CARY RICHARD in the Pink *Seaventure* for Antegua GEORGE BATTERSBY Comander   security

March the 10*th* 1678

CANTING DENNIS in the Ship *Mary* for Carolina NICHᵒ LOCKWOOD,
Comandʳ   time out

March the 11*th* 1678

COLLYER AMBROSS in the Ship *Society* for Boston Wᴹ GUARD Comander
time out

March the 21 1678

COLWELL SAMUELL in the Ketch *Wᵐ ℓ Susan* for New England
RALPH PARKER Comandʳ   time out

March the 21*st* 1678

CORNELIUS FRANCIS in the Barq͜ *Joseph* for Saltertudos STEPHEN
CLAY Comander   time out

March yᵉ 24*th* 1678

CLARKE PORCAS in the ship *Supply* for London JOSEPH FREEMAN
Comandʳ   time out

Aprill the first 1679

CHAMBERLAINE MARMADUKE in the Ship *Endeavor* for London JAMES
GILBERT Comander   time out

Aprill the first 1679

CAMPANELL MORDICAY in the Ketch *Swallow* for Newengland JOSEPH
HARDY Comandʳ   time out

Aprill the first 1679

CROSSING Wᴹ in the Ship *Blessing* for Boston SAMᴸᴸ RICKARD Comandʳ
security

Aprill the third 1679

COOPER MARY in the Ship *Mary* for Carolina NICHOLAS LOCKWOOD
Comandʳ the said COOPER a seruᵗᵗ of ROBᵀ DANIELL.

Aprill the 22^d 1679

CAREW THOMAS in the Ship *Benj^a* of Topsham ROBERT LYDE
Comander time out

April ye 25th 1679

COLTHROUGH PETER in the Ship *Samuell and Eliz^a* for London
THOMAS ORCHARD Comander time out

May the 3^d 1679

CURSTIS JOHN in the Ship *Concord* for London JAMES STRUTT, Comander time out

---

May the 10th 1679

CLARKE MARY in the Ship *Experiment* for Londo ALLAN COCK
Comander security

May the 22: 1679

COULBURNE JOHN in the Ship *Conclusion* for London W^M BEEDING
Comand^r

May the 28th 1679

CORNISH EDWARD A Serv^{tt} belonging to JOHN HARRIS in the ship
W^m & John for Boston, SAM^{LL} LEGG Comand^r

May the 31st 1679

CLOVAN THO.* in the Sloop *true friendship* for Neuis CHARLES KALLA-
HANE Comand^r security

July the first 1679

COLE THOMAS Junr in the Ship *Prevention* for Surranam BARNARD
BOOGHERT Comander time out

---

* [See the entry of Oct. 2nd, where this man is re-entered as for Antegua.]

July the 2^d 1679

COLLINS JOHN in the Ketch *Neptune* for Carolina JOSEPH KNOTT
    Comander   time out

July the 28th 1679

CAWFEILD RICH^D in the Ship *Young William* for Virginia THOMAS
    CORNISH Comand^r   security

August the 2^d 1679

COTTINGHAM KATHERINE in the Ship *Eliz^{a.}* for Jamaica SILVANUS
    PAINE Comander   time out

August the 9th 1679

COLLINS JOHN in the Barq_h *Platacon* for Carolina ASER SHARPE
    Comander

August the thirteenth 1679

CALLAY THOMAS in the Keatch *Neptune* for Virginia JOSEPH KNOTT
    Comander   time out

August y^e 25th 1679

COX FRANCIS in the ship *John and James* for New England GILES
    HAMLIN Comand^r   time out

September 2^d 1679

COLE JAMES in the Sloop *John and Francis* for Antequa JOHN HOW-
    ARD Comander   security

September the 18th 1679

COLLIS ALEXANDER in the Ship *Hope* for New England JOHN PRICE
    Comander   time out

September ye 20th 1679

CHESTER SAMPSON in the Ship *Malligo Merchant* ROGER HOMER
    Comander for Lond^o   time out

September 22^d 1679

CHAPLIN THOMAS in the Ship *Malligo Merch^{tt}* for London ROGER HOMER Comander   time out

October the 2^d 1679

CLOVAN* THOMAS in the Sloop *true friendship* for Antegua CHARLES KALLAHANE Comander   time out

October the 6th 1679

CHARLES EUAN in the Sloop *true friendship* for Antegua CHARLES KALLAHANE Comander   time out

November the 3^d 1679

COTINHO MOSES HENRIQUES in the Barq, *Adventure* for Jamaica EDWARD DUFFEILD Comander   time out

November ye 6th 1679

COURTNEY W^m in the Sloop *Hopewell* for Antegua Wm MURPHY Comander   time out

November the: 27th 1679

CORBETT WILLIAM in the Sloop *Katherine* for Antegua ANDREW GALL Comander   time out

December the 15th 1679

CRISP ROGER in the Ship *Ann and Jane* for Lond^o RICH^D RADFORD, Comand^r   time out

February 14th 1678

DANG MARGARETT in the Sloop *Resolution* for Nevis JOHN INGLEBY Comander   time out

* [In the entry of May 31st he is bound for Nevis.]

February 21st 1678

DENTON JOHN in the Ship *Endeavour* for Virginia ABRAHAM NEWMAN
Comander   time out

March the first 1678

DOLDRON GRACE in the Ship *Samuell* for London JOHN CLARKE
Comander   time out

March the 10th 1678

DOLEBERRY ANDREW in the Ship *Society* for Boston W^M GUARD
Comander   time out

March the 20th 1678

DEVENISH JOHN in the Ship *Endeavor* for London JAMES GILBERT
Comander   time out

Aprill the first 1679

DICKINSON FRANCIS in the ship *Blessing* for Boston SAMUELL RICK-
ARD Comander   security

Aprill the fourth 1679

DANIELL ROBERT in the Ship *Mary* for Carolina NICHOLAS LOCK-
WOOD Comander   time out

Aprill the 7th 1679

DUKES W^M in the Barq$_b$ *Adventure* for Carolina DANIELL RIDLEY
Comand^r time out

April the 9th 1679

DANIELL JOHN in the Barq$_b$ *Johns Adventure* for Antegua JOHN WELCH
Comand^r time out

April 22: 1679

DAVIES ELIZ^A A serv^{tt} belonging to HILLIARD HOLDIP in the ship
Lond^o Merch^{tt} for Lond^o EDW: DESWORTH, Comd

A brill the 22ᵈ 1679

DRAX HENRY Esqʳ in the Ship *Honor* for Londᵒ THOMAS WARREN
Comander   time out

Aprill the 22 1679

DENSY JANE in the Ship *Hope* for London JOSEPH BALL Comander
                                          security

Aprill the 25ᵗʰ 1679

DRAYTON THOMAS junʳ in the ship *Mary* for Carolina NICHOLAS
LOCKWOOD Comandʳ   time out

Aprill the 28ᵗʰ 1679

DAVIES JANE A Servant to RICHᴰ TOWNSEND in yᵉ Ship *Nathaniell*
for Boston Wᴹ CLARKE Comandʳ

May the 2ᵈ 1679

DAVIES SAMUELL in the Ketch *Prosperous* for Virginia DAVID FOGG
Comander   time out

May the 13: 1679

DAVIES JOHN junʳ in the Ship *Roe Buck* for London Wᴹ SHAFTO
Comandʳ   security

May 13ᵗʰ 1679

DOWELL DENNIS in the Ship *Industry* for Bristoll JAMES PORTER
Comander   time out

May the 14ᵗʰ 1679

DANGERFEILD WALCUP in the ship *Bachelor* for Bristoll ROGER BAGG
Comander   time out

May the 23ᵈ 1679

DUNNOHOE TEAG in the ship *Margaret* for Bew Morris* ALEXANDER
WOOD Comandʳ   time out

---

* [*i.e.*, Beaumaris.]

May the 24 1679

DUBOYES JOHN in the Ship *Supply* for Boston JOHN MELLOWES
Comander   time out

June the 11th 1679

DUNNOHOE CORNELIUS and JEFFORY in the ship *Margrett* for Bew
Morris ALEXANDER WOOD Comand[r]   time out

June the 11th 1679

DAVIES, JOHN in the ship *Coast Friggott* for Lond[o.] PHILLIP VARLOE
Comander   time out

June the 11th 1679

DAVIES JOHN of Christ Church in the Ketch *Joseph* for New Yorke
ABRAHAM KNOTT Comander   security

July the 21 1679

DAVIES PETER in the Pinke *Neptune* for Carolina JOSEPH KNOTT
Comander   time out

July the 29th 1679

DRAN MAREN A servant belonging to JACOB LEROUX in the Ketch
Dove for Antegoa JOHN GRAFTON Comand[r]

August the first 1679

DUNDAS W[M] in the ship *Young William* for Virginia THO: CORNISH
Comander   time out

August the 2[d] 1679

DAWSON TREMMIT in the ship *Eliz[a]* for Jamaica SILVANUS PAYNE
Comander   time out

August the 2[d] 1679

DAVIES KATHERINE a servant belonging to JOHN AUSTIN in the ship
Young William for Virginia THOMAS CORNISH

Septemb' the 27th 1679

DANIELL WILBERT in the Ship *Supply* for Virginia JOHN ADY Comander   time out

---

November ye 15th 1679

DEWER STEPHEN in the Barq. *Resolution* for Antegoa THO GILBERT Comander   time out

---

Decemb^r the 15th 1679

DEXTER W^M in the Ship *Ann and Jane* for Lond^o RICHARD RATFORD Comander   time out

---

December the 22^d 1679

DOUSE BRIDGETT in the Ship *Ann & Jane* for Lond^o RICHARD RATT-FORD Comander   time out

---

December the 22: 1679

DOWNING JOHN in the Ship *Lawrell* for Nevis ROBERT OX Comander   time out

---

December the 24th 1679

DAVY ROBERT in the Ship *Ann and Jane* for London RICH^D RATFORD Comander   time out

---

December y^e 24th 1679

DE WEVER LEWIN in the ship *Blossom* for Surranam RICH^D MARTIN Comander   security

===

March the 13th 1678

ENDERBEE OLIUER in the Ship *Ann and Mary* for Antegua JOHN JOHNSON Comander   security

---

March the 20th 1678

ELSON W^M in the Ketch *Begining* for New Yorke W^M PLAY Comander   time out

Aprill the 25 1679

EVANS LEWIS in the Ketch *Unity* for Virginia JAMES RAINY Comander

time out

Aprill the 26th 1679

EARLE JOHN in the ship *Defyance* for Londo. W[M] CREED Comand[r]

security

Aprill the 26th 1679

ELLISTON GEORGE in the ship *Nathaniell* for Boston W[M] CLARKE Comander

time out

Aprill the 28th 1679

EDWARDS JOHN in the ship *Society* for Bristoll EDMOND DITTY Comander

time out

May the 24 1679

ELLICOTT VINES in the ship *Supply* for Boston JOHN MELLOWES Comander

security

June the 20th 1679

EUANS W[M] in the ship *W[m] and Robert* for London GILES BOND Comander

time out

July y[e] 21: 1679

EVANS EDWARD in the Pink *Neptune* for Carolina JOSEPH KNOTT Comander

time out

July the 26th 1679

EASTCHURCH WILLIAM in the Ship *Joseph* for Lond.

July the 31 1679

EMERY JOHN a Servant belonging to Liev[t.] Coll[o.] HALLETT in the Ship *Young William* for Virginia THO CORNISH Comand[r]

September the 12*th* 1679

ELLINSWORTH W^M in the Pink *Portsmouth* for Road Island JOSEPH
BRIAR Comand^r   time out

October the 2*d* 1679

ELLIOTT HENRY in the Sloop *true friendship* for Antegoa CHARLES
CALLAHANE Comand^r   time out

Feb^{ry} the 6*th* 1678

FANNING ANDREW a servant belonging to DANIELL STANTON in the
Ship *Diligence* for New England JER: JACKSON

February the 13*th* 1678

FORBUSH JAMES in the Ship *two Brothers* for Jamaica RICE JEFFERYES
Comander   time out

March the 4*th* 1678

FITZRANDOLPH PHILLIP in the ship *Vnity* for Saltertudos ABRAHAM
WISE Comand^r   security

March the 19*th* 1678

FYERS JONE in the ship *Katherine* for Bristoll ROBERT DAPWELL
Comander   time out

March the 24*th* 1678

FITZ JAMES EDWARD in the Ship *Merch^{tt} Bonadventure* for London
W^M BULKLEY Comander   time out

March the 26*th* 1679

FRANKLIN THOMAS in the Ship *Supply* for Lond^o JOSEPH FREEMAN
Comander   time out

March the 29th 1679

FOX STEPHEN in the ship *Mary* for Carolina NICH^o LOCKWOOD Comander   time out

March the 29th 1679

FOX PHILLIS in the ship *Mary* for Carolina NICH^o LOCKWOOD Comander   time out

March the 31: 1679

FRANSUM JOSEPH in the Barq, *Blessing* for Prouidence FRANCIS WAT-LINGTON Comander   time out

April the 29th 1679

FITZ NICHOLS MARY a Serv^{tt.} belonging to RICH^D MICHELL sen^r in the ship *Nathaniell* for Boston W^M CLARKE Comander

May the Sixth 1679

FEAGHERY THOMAS in the Ship *John & Tho:* for Prouidence THO. JENOUR Comander   time out

May the 8th 1679

FINN TEAGE in the Ship *Industry* for Bristoll JAMES PORTER Comander   time out

May the 14th 1679

FOSTER HESTER in the ship *Ann and Eliz^a.* for Leverpoole HUGH REYNOLDS Comander   time out

May the 21 1679

FITZ JARRELL JOHN in the ship *Swallow* for Leverpoole THO WITH-INGTON Comander   time out

May the 23 1679

FONTLEROY JAMES in the ship *Prudence and Mary* for Boston JACOB GREEN Comander   time out

---

May the 26th 1679

FARRER JAMES in the ship *Conclusion* for Lond^{o.} W^M BEEDING Comander   time out

---

May the 28th 1679

FRENCH SAMUELL in the Ketch *Joseph and Mary* for New Yorke ABRAHAM KNOTT Comand^r   time out

---

May the thirtieth 1679.

FOWLER JOSHUA in the ship *John and Mary* for London JOHN UREE Comand^r·   security

---

June the fourth 1679

FLEMG [? FLEMING] EDMOND in the ship *Society* for Bristoll EDMOND DITTY Comand^r   time out

---

June the 11th 1679

FELL LIDIA in the Ketch *John and Sarah* for New Yorke PETER CAROW Comander   time out

---

July the 21: 1679

FRITH SAMUELL in the Pinke *Rebecca* for Virginia THOMAS WILLIAMS Comander   time out

---

July the 26th 1679

FORD FRANCIS in the ship *Mallego Merch^{tt.}* for London ROGER HOMER Comand^r   time out

October the first 1679

FEAR FRANCIS in the ship *Barbados Merchant* for Virginia JAMES COCK
    Comander   time out

October y⁶ 29ᵗʰ 1679

FARRELL HUGH in the Barq; *Dove* for Nevis ANTHONY JENOUR
    Comander   time out

November the 26ᵗʰ 1679

FARRELL ROGER in the Sloop *Katherine* for Antegua ANDREW GALL
    Comander   security

December the 22 1679

FAVELL CHRISTOPHER in the ship *Ann and Jane* for London RICHᴰ
    RATTFORD Comandʳ   time out

December 24ᵗʰ 1679

FARROR EDMOND in the ship *Ann & Jane* for London RICHᴰ RATT-
    FORD Comandʳ   time out

===

March the 10ᵗʰ 1678

GRIGG ROBERT & ALCE GRIGG in the ship *Mary* for Carolin[a] NICHO-
    LAS LOCKWOOD Comander   time out

March the 11ᵗʰ 1678

GARDNER GEORGE in the Ship *Samaritan* for Leverpo[ol] VALENTINE
    TRIM Comandʳ   time out

March the 18ᵗʰ 1678

GRESTNINII JACOBUS in the Pink *Desire* for Pool THO WADHAM
    Comander   security

March the 20th 1678

GOLDING PERSIVALL in the ship *White Fox* for London JOHN LEE
Comander   time out

March the 22^d 1678

GERISH BENJAMIN in the Ketch *Mary* for Boston JOHN GARDNER
Comander   time out

Aprill the 7th 1679

GODFRY MARY in the Ship *Mary* for Carolina NICH^o LOCKWOOD
Comand^r   time out

Aprill the 12th 1679

GOODING JOSEPH in the Barq_h *Boneta* RICH^D RIPLY Comand^r for
Jamaica   time out

Aprill the 25th 1679

GITTES HENRY in the Ship *Mary* for Carolina NICHOLAS LOCKWOOD
Comander   time out

May the 6th 1679

GOLDING PERCIVALL in the Ship *Concord* for London JAMES STRUTT
Comand^r

May the 6th 1679

GIBBS RICH^D in the ship *Bachelor* for Bristoll ROGER BAGG Comand^r
                                                                            time out

---

May the 14th 1679

GIBBS EDWARD in the ship *Roe Buck* for Lond^o W^M SHAFTO Comander
                                                                            time out

May the 23 1679

GOGIN WILLIAM in the ship *Bachelor* for Bristoll ROGER BAGG Comander   time out

---

July the 22^d 1679

GRAY ROBERT in the Keatch *Endeavor* for New England LAWRENCE CUTT Comander   time out

---

August the 9th 1679

GORDEN GEORGE in the ship *Plantacon* for Carolina ASER SHARPE Comander   time out

---

August the 16th 1679

GORTON JOHN A servant belonging to JOHN BROWNE in the Ketch *Neptune* for Virginia JOSEPH KNOTT Comand^r

---

August the 19th 1679

GODFFREE GILBERT a seru^{tt} belonging to Mr W^M BULKLY in the Ketch *Neptune* for Virginia JOSEPH KNOTT Comand

---

September ye 2^d 1679

GRIFFIN DENNIS in the sloop *John and Francis* for Antegua JOHN HOWARD Comand^r

---

October the first 1679

GOTHER HENRY in the Sloop *Rutter* for Jamaica EDWARD DUFFEILD Comander   time out

---

October the 2^d 1679

GORTON RICH^D in the Sloop *Rutter* for Jamaica EDWARD DUFFEILD Comander   time out

October the 7th 1679

GREENSLATT THOMAS in the Sloop *true friendship* for Antegua
CHARLES KALLAHANE Comandr   security

Novembr the 25th 1679

GIDION ROWLAND in the Ketch *Phænix* for Antegua ROBERT
FLEXNY Comandr   security

February 11th 1678

HAYEM ABRAHAM in the ship *James* for New Yorke Wᴹ SWEETLAND
Comander   time out

March the 3d 1678

HATTON ROBERT in the Sloop *Hunter* for Surranam WALTE[R] ASSU-
EROS Comander   time out

March the 3d 1678

HOLLARD THOMAS in the *Constant Warwick* Frigott for London Capt
RALPH DELAVALL Comandr   security

March the 11th 1678

HOLLOWAY RICHᴰ in the ship *Samaritan* for Leverpool VALENTINE
TRIM Comander   time out

March the 12th 1678

HERRICK ISAAC in the Ketch *Wᵐ & Susan,* for New Engla[nd]
RALPH PARKER Comander   time out

March the 20th 1678

HARVEY, GRIFFITH, in the ship *Merchtt Bonadventure,* fo[r] London
Wᴹ BULKLY Comander   time out

March the 21 1678

HAMILTON ADAM in the Ketch *W^m ℓ Susan* for New England RALPH
PARKER Comand^r   time out

March the 24th 1678

HEYWOOD JOHN in the Pinke *Submission* for London CHRISTOPHER
NEWHAM Comander   time out

March the 24th 1678

HIGLEY JOHN in the Ketch *Mary* for Boston JOHN GARDNER Comander   time out

---

March the 28th 1678 [? *should be* 1679].

HASELL WILLIAM in the Ship *Oliue Tree* for Bristoll THOMAS SHEL-
LAM Comander   time out

Aprill the first 1679

HAWTON GERARD in the ship *Expedition* for London JOHN HARDING
Comander   time out

Aprill the first 1679

HAVILAND MILES in the Ketch *Swallow* for Rhoad Island JOSEPH
HARDY Comander   time out

April the 2^d 1679

HENDLY DANIELL and ELIZ^A in the ship *Olive Tree* for Bristoll THOMAS
SHELLAM Comand^r   time out

Aprill the 9th 1679

HETHERINGTON KATHERINE in the Pink *Greyhound* for London
JOSEPH WASEY Comander   time out

Aprill the 10th 1679

HOWELL SARAH in the Barq, *Prouidence* for Burmudos FRANCIS WAT-
LINGTON Comander   time out

Aprill the 10th 1679

HURLES, ELIZ^A in the ship *Martin* for Newfoundland CHRISTOPHER
MARTIN Comand^r   time out

Aprill the 19th 1679

HIGGISON HENRY in the ship *freinds Adventure* for Lond^o JOHN
BLADES Comander   time out

Aprill the 19th 1679

HOLLIDAY MARY in the ship *Recouery* for New Yorke THOMAS CHIN-
NERY Comander   time out

Aprill the 22^d 1679

HOLDIP HILLIARD in the Ship *Lond^o Merch^{tt}* for London EDWARD
DESWORTH Comander   security

Aprill the 22 1679

HOLT ROWLAND in the Ship *Honor* for London THOMAS WARREN
Comander   time out

Aprill the 30th 1679

HACKER FERDINANDO in the ship *Faireffax* for London NICH^o FAIRE-
FAX Comander   time out

May the 2^d 1679

HEALY W^M in the ship *Society* for Bristoll EDM^D DITTY Comander
                                                                 time out

May the third 1679

HURST W^M in the Ship *Adventure* for Lond^o W^M JOHNSON Comand^r
time out

May the third 1679

HOLSEY RICHARD in the Sloop *Batchelor* for Leward PETER SWAINE
Comand^r   time out

May the 23th 1679

HACKETT ROBERT in the ship *Society* for Bristoll EDMOND DITTY
Comand^r   time out

May the 23^d 1679

HALEY DENNIS in the ship *Society* for Bristoll EDMOND DITTY
Comander   time out

May the 31 1679

HELMES JOHN in the Ketch *Nich^o ę Rebecca* for New Yorke NICHOLAS
BLAKE Comand^r   time out

June the 2^d 1679

HOOK W^M in the Barq, *Hopewell* for Boston NICHOLAS MORRELL
Comander   security

June the 13 1679

HUNT DENNIS in the ship *Coast Friggott* for London PHILLIP VAR-
LOE Comander   time out

June the 14 1679

HOW ELIZ^A in the Ship *Johns Adventure* for Jamaica EDWARD WIN-
SLOW Comander   time out

June the 17*th* 1679

HOOPER DANIELL in the Ketch *Joseph* for New Yorke ABRAHAM
KNOTT, Comand[r]   time out

June the 21 1679

HARRIS EDWARD in the Ship *Experiment* for Lond°, HENRY SUTTON
Comand[r]   time out

June the 21 1679

HILL JOHN in the ship *Charles* for Lond° THOMAS NASH Comander
                                                                                                  security

---

June the 21 1679

HOUGH W[m] in the Ship *W[m] ℓ Robert* for London GILES BOND
Comander   time out

June the 28 1679

HUNT JOHN in the ship *Prouidence* for Boston TIMOTHY PROUT
Comander   time out

July the third 1679

HORNE GUSTAVUS ADOLPHUS in the ship *W[m] ℓ Ann* for London
PHILLIP HANGER Comander   time out

July the 10*th* 1679

HUGHS ANDREW in the ship *Amity* for Lond° BENJ[A] GROVE
Comand[r]   time out

July the 31 1679

HALL GILES ju[r] in the Ketch *John ℓ Mary* for Boston JOHN PARRECK
Comand[r]   security

August the 14 1679

HERBERT HENRY in the Ship *John & Henry* for Bristo[l] THOMAS
CADES Comander   time out

August the 20th 1679

HOBBS ELIZ[A] in the ship *Robert* for Lond[o] RICHARD COCK Comander
                                                                 time out

---

September the 17th 1679

HARKER JOHN in the ship *Hope* for New Engl[d] JOHN PRICE Comander
                                                                 time out

---

September the 18th 1679

HOLDSWORTH ARTHER in the Ship *Thomas & Sarah* for Lon[don]
JAMES DAY Comander   time out

October the 7th 1679

HOTEN MARGERY in the Sloop *Affrica* for Leward Islands ANTHONY
BURGESS Comander   security

October the 7th 1679

HILK JOHN in the Sloop *true friendship* for Antegua CHARLES KAL-
LAHANE Comander   security

October the 7th 1679

HANCOCK ALEXANDER in the Sloop *true freindship* for Antequa
CHARLES KALLAHANE Comander   security

October the 20th 1679

HASELL PETER in the Ship *Happy returne* for London ISAAC RAGG
Comand[r]   time out

October the 29*th* 1679

HALE BARNABIE and THO HOW Seru*tts* belonging tu Coll⁰ CHRISTO-
PHER CODRINGTON in the Barq, *Doue* for Nevis ANTHONY JENOUX
Comander

October the 29*th* 1679

HOLT JOSEPH in the Sloop *Hopewell* for Antegoa JOHN AYRES
Comand*r*   time out

November y*e* 6*th* 1679

HUNT LUKE in the Barq, *Adventure* for Jamaica EDWARD DUFFEILD
Comander   time out

November the 27*th* 1679

HANNAH, ANDREW a Serv*tt* belonging to W*M* STICKLAND in the Sloop
Katherine for Antegua ANDREW GALL Comander

December the 24*th* 1679

HOLEMAN ROGER in the Sloop *true freindship* for Antegua CHARLES
KALLAHANE Comand*r*   time out

March the 11*th* 1678

JARMIN SYMON in the Ship *Society* for Boston W*M* GUARD Comander
                                                                  time out

---

March the 14*th* 1678

JACCSON W*M* in the ship *Ann and Mary* for Antegoa JOHN JOHNSON
Comander   time out

March the 20*th* 1678

JACCSON GEORGE in the Ship *Merch*tt *Bonadventure* for London W*M*
BULKLEY Comand*r*   time out

48—2

March the 29th 1679

JIPSON SARAH in the ship *Mary* for Carolina NICH[o] LOCKWOOD
Comand[r] time out

Aprill the 9th 1679

JACOB JOHN in the Ketch *Providence* for New England MARKE HUNK-
ING Comander time out

Aprill the 19th 1679

JOHNSON NATHANIELL in the *friends Adventure* for Antegua, JOHN
LONG Comander time out

May the 9th [? 19] 1679

JONES JOHN jun[r] in the ship *Ann and Eliz[a]* for Leverpool HUGH REY-
NOLDS Comander time out

May the 20th 1679

JONES ROBERT in the Ship *Rose and Crown* for London THOMAS
CROFTS Comander security

May the 22[d] 1679

JORDAN W[m], in the Ship *Prudence and Mary* for Boston JACOB GREEN
Comander

May the 22[d] 1679

JOHNSON JOHN in the Ketch *Joseph* for New Yorke ABRAHAM KNOTT
Comander time out

May the 22[d] 1679

JONES RICH[d] in the Ship *Battchelor* for Bristoll ROGER BAGG Comander
time out

May the 23ᵈ 1679

JAMES WILLIAM in the Ship *Society* for Bristoll EDMOND DITTY
Comander   time out

June the 11ᵗʰ 1679

JELSON JOELL in the Ship *Bachelor* for Bristoll ROGER BAGG Comander
time out

June the 11ᵗʰ 1679

IRISH GEORGE in the ship *Bachelor* for Bristoll ROGER BAGG Comander
time out

June the 17ᵗʰ 1679

JENKINS OWEN in the Ketch *Johns Adventure* for Jamaica EDWARD
WINSLOE Comandʳ   time out

June the 18ᵗʰ 1679

JONES SAMUELL in the Ketch *Johns Adventure* for Jamaica EDWARD
WINSLOE Comandʳ   security

June the 27ᵗʰ 1679

INGLEBY NICHOLAS in the ship *Prouidence* for Boston TIMOTHY PROUT
Comandʳ   security

August the 13ᵗʰ 1679

JACCSON JAMES in the Barqₕ *Hopewell* for Virginia THO CURLE
Comander   time out

August the 14ᵗʰ 1679

JONES ELIZᴬ· in the Barqₕ *Plantacon* for Carolina ASER SHARPE
Comander   security

September the fourth 1679

JAMES RICH^D A serv^{tt} belonging to Coll^o SAM^{LL} NEWTON in the ship *Joseph* for New Yorke STEPHEN CLAY Comand^r

---

September the 13th 1679

JOHNSON NATHANIELL in the Sloop *true freindship* for Antegua CHARLES KALLAHANE Comander　　　　　　　　time out

---

September the 13 1679

JORDAN JAMES in the ship *Mallego Merch^{tt}* for London ROGER HOMER Comander　　　　　　　　time out

---

September the 19th 1679

JENKINS JANE in the Ship *Lixboa Merch^{tt}* for New Yor[k] ROGER WHITFEILD Comander　　　　　　　　security

---

September the 26th 1679

JENNINGS MICHAELL in the Sloop *Rutter* for Jamaica EDWARD DUF-FEILD Comand^r　　　　　　　　time out

---

October the 7th 1679

JENNINGS WILLIAM, in the Sloop *True friendship* for Antegu[a] CHARLES KALLAHANE Comand^r　　　　　　　　security

---

October the 29th 1679

JOHN MORGAN in the Barq_b *Dove* for Neuis ANTHONY JENNOR, Comander.　　　　　　　　time out.

Nouember the 7 1679

JONES WILLIAM in the Sloop *Hopewell* for Antegua W^M MURPHY Comand^r　　　　　　　　time out

Nouember the 7th 1679

JONES HECTOR in the Sloop *Hopewell* for Antegua W^M MURPHY
Comander   time out

Aprill the 24th 1679

KING WILLIAM in the ship *friends Adventure* for Lond^o EDWARD
BLADES Comander   security

May the 2^d 1679

KENNEDY JOHN and ELLINOR his wife in the Ship *Society* for Bristoll
EDMOND DITTY Comander   time out

May the 28th 1679

KYTE JOHN in the Ship *Prudence and Mary* for Boston JACOB GREEN
Comand^r   time out

August the 2^d 1679

KEITH HENRY in the Ship *Young William* for Virginia THO: CORNISH
Comand^r   time out

November the 29th 1679

KEW NICHOLAS in the Barq_h *Resolution* for Antegua THO GILBERT
Comander   security

Feb^{ry} 17th 1678

LYNCH NICHOLAS and ALICE his Wife in the Barq_h *Adventure* for
Antegua CHRISTOPHER BERROW Comand^r   time out

March the 18th 1679 [167⅞]

LOCK ANN in the Ketch, *W^m ℮ Susan* for New England RALPH
PARKER Comand^r   time out

March the 20th 1679 [167⅞]

LYTTCOT LEONARD in the Ship *Supply* for Lond⁰ JOSEPH FREEMAN
Comander   security

Aprill the first 1679

LEE HENRY in the Ketch *Unity* for Virginia JAMES RAINY Comander
time out

Aprill the third 1679

LEE HENRY in the Ship *Martin* for Newfoundland CHRISTOPHER
MARTIN Comand^r   time out

Aprill the 16th 1679

LANGLEY W^M in the Ship *Brothers Adventure* for New Yorke JOHN
SELLOCK Comand^r   time out

Aprill the 21st 1679

LOPES ABRAHAM in the ship *Hope* for Lond⁰ JOSEPH BALL Comand^r
time out

Aprill the 22^d 1679

LOWTHER CHRISTOPHER a servant belonging to Coll⁰ HENRY DRAX
in the Ship *Honor* for Lond⁰ THO WARREN Comand^r

May the 12th 1679

LANGTON THOMAS in the Ketch *Prosperous* for Virginia DAUID FOGG
Comand^r   time out

May the 28th 1679

LYDIATT TIMOTHY in the Ship *W^m ℓ John* for Boston SAMUELL LEGG
Comander   time out

June the 17*th* 1679

LONGSON WILLIAM in the Ketch *John's Adventure* for Jamaica EDWARD
   WINSLOW Comand[r]   security

July the 17*th* 1679

LEE RICH[D] in the Pinke *Rebecca* for Virginia THOMAS W[ms] Comander   time out

---

July the 29*th* 1679

LEROUX JACOB in the Ketch *Dove* for Antegua JOHN GRAFTON
   Comand[r]   security

August the 8*th* 1679

LEWGAR JOHN in the ship *freindship* for London JOHN WILLIAMS
   Comand[r]   time out

August the 13*th* 1679

LADSON JOHN in the Barq[,] *Plantacon* for Carolina ASER SHARPE
   Comander   time out

August the 28*th* 1679

LLOYD JOHN in the ship *Barbados Merch[tt]* for Leward Islands
                                                                      time out

---

September the 2*d* 1679

LANGFORD HARRY in the Ship *Joseph* for New Yorke STEPHEN CLAY
   Comander   time out

September the 15*th* 1679

LYNN ROBERT in the Ship *Mallego Merch[tt]* for Lond[o] ROGER HOMER
   Comand[r]   time out

49

September the 16th 1679

LYNCH RICHARD in the Sloop *true friendship* for Nevis CHARLES KALLAHANE Comand^r   time out

---

October the 25th 1679

LEE HENRY in the Ship *Happy returne* for Lond^o ISAAC RAND Comand^r   security

---

Nouember the 24th 1679

LILBURNE RICH^D in the Ketch *Mary & Sarah* for Prouidence GEORGE CONOWAY Comand^r   security

---

November the 29th 1679

LYNCH MORGAN in the Barq resolution for Antegua THOMAS GIL-BERT Comand^r the said LYNCH being a Seru^{tt} belonging to JOHN CODRINGTON Esqr.

December the 22: 1679

LYNE CHRISTOPHER Esqr in the Ship *Recouery* for Jamaica JAMES BROWNE Comand^r

---

December the 31. 1679

LOPEZ TELLES ABRAHAM in the ship *Recouery* for Jamaica JAMES BROWN Comand^r   time out

---

January the 4th 1678

MAYNARD JAMES A Seru^{tt} belonging to MATHEW W^{ms.} in the ship *Old head* of Kingsale for Lew^d ROBERT BARKER Comand

---

January the 28th 1678

MARSHALL JARVIS in the Ship *James* for New Yorke JAMES SWEET-LAND Comander   time out

Feby 11^*th*^ 1678

MASTUS JOSEPH and MARTHA MASTUS in the Ship *Patience* for
London THOMAS HUDSON Comand^r^   time out

March the 10^*th*^ 1679 [1678]

MORRIS W^M^ in the Ship *Society* for Boston W^M^ GUARD Comand^r^
    time out

March the 14^*th*^ 1678

MELONY TIMOTHY in the Ship *Ann and Mary* for Antegua JOHN
JOHNSON Comand^r^   security

March the 18^*th*^ 1678

MORRIS ISAAC in the Ketch *Begining* for New Yorke W^M^ PLAY
Comand^r^   time out

March the 19^*th*^ 1678

MADDOX JONE in the Ketch *Begining* for New Yorke W^M^ PLAY
Comand^r^   time out

Aprill the 7^*th*^ 1679

MATTSON BENJ^A^ in the Ship *John and Mary* for Lond^o^ EDWARD
CALCOTT Comand^r^   time out

Aprill the 8^*th*^ 1679

MANNEN ANDREW in the Ship *Mary* for Carolina NICHOLAS LOCK-
WOOD Comand^r^   time out

Aprill the 10^*th*^ 1679

MAUL THOMAS in the Ketch *W^m^ & John* for New England JOHN
SAUNDERS Comand^r^   time out

Aprill the 17th 1679

MAJOR W^{M} in the Barq$_{t}$ *Blessing* for Prouidence FRANCIS WATLINGTON
Comander   time out

Aprill the 28th 1679

MAHONY DANIELL in the ship *freinds Adventure* for Antegua JOHN
LONG Comand^{r} time out

Aprill the 25th 1679

MICHELL RICH^{D} in the Ship *Nathan^{ll}* for Boston W^{M} CLARKE
Comander   security

Aprill the 25 1679

MICHELL JOHN in the Ship *Nathan^{ll}* for Boston W^{M} CLARKE
Comander   time out

May the 8th 1679

MORGAN JOHN in the Ship *Society* for Bristoll EDMOND DITTY Comander   time out

---

May the 8th 1679

MACCMASH CHARLES in the Ship *Roe Buck* for Londo W^{M} SHAFTO
Comander   security

May the 13th 1679

MURPHY DANIELL in the Ship *Industry* for Bristoll JAMES PORTER
Comander   time out

May the 14th 1679

MORGAN THOMAS in the Ship *Bachelor* for Bristoll ROGER BAGG
Comand^{r} time out

May the 14th 1679

MAGWAINE OWEN in the ship *Industry* for Bristoll JAMES PORTER
Comand^r time out

May the 17th 1679

MATHER GEORGE in the Ship *Hannah and Eliz^a* for Lond^o RICH^D PIX
Comand^r security

May the 19th 1679

MASON SYLAM in the Ship *W^m & John* for Boston SAMUELL LEGG
Comander   time out

May the 23^{d} 1679

MARROW CORNELIUS & KATHERINE in the Ship *Society* for Bristoll
EDMOND DITTY Comander   time out

May the 24th 1679

MOSELY RICHARD in the Ship *W^m & John* for Boston SAMUELL
LEGG Comander   time out

May the 24th 1679

MORGAN EDWARD in the Ship *Society* for Bristoll EDMOND DITTY
Comander   time out

May the 24th 1679

MAHANE JOHN in the ship *Industry* for Bristoll JAMES PORTER
Comand^r time out

May the 28th 1679

MORRELL NICHOLAS in the Ship *Prudence and Mary* for Boston JACOB
GREEN Comander   time out

May the 30th 1679

MACCLAHEN OWEN in the Ship *Society* for Bristoll EDMOND DITTY Comander   time out

June the 18th 1679

MATTSON MATHEW in the Ship *Concord* for Lond^o Wm FOSTER Comander   time out

June the 14th 1679

MAROH THOMAS, MARY ᵱ SARAH in the Ship *Society* for Bristoll EDMOND DITTY Comand^r   time out

July the 7th 1679

MACCENREE JOHN in the Pink *Revecca* for Virginia THOMAS W^{ms} Comand^r   time out

July the 16th 1679

MATTHEWS GEORGE in the Pink *Eliz^a* for Boston JOHN BONNER Comander   time out

July the 21st 1679

MANSELL ROBERT in the Ship *Rich^d and Mary* for New England SAMUELL FITCH Comand^r   security

August the 12th 1679

MAHONE JAMES A Seruant belonging to HENRY QUINTYNE Esqr in the Barq_h *Plantacon* for Carolina ASER SHARPE Comand^r

August the 13th 1679

MACCDANIELL PATRICK in the Ketch *Neptune* for Virginia JOSEPH KNOTT Comand^r   time out

August the 14th 1679.

MIDLETON ARTHUR in the Barq, *Plantacon* for Carolina ASER
SHARPE Comand^r time out

September the 16th 1679

MOUNTACK ANDREW in the Ship *Eliz^a* for Holland ALLEXANDER
MATTISON Comand^r security

October the first 1679

MADEN PATRICK in the Sloop *true friendship* for Antegua CHARLES
KALLAHANE Comand^r time out

October the 2^d 1679

MUSKETT W^M in the Sloop *Rutter* for Jamaica EDWARD DUFFEILD
Comander   time out

October the fourth 1679

MELLOLY JAMES in the Ship *Virgin* for Virginia THO : ALLUMBY
Comander   security

October the 7th 1679

MOUNTAINE JOHN in the Sloop *true freindship* for Antegua CHARLES
KALLAHANE Comand^r security

October the 25th 1679

MORECOCK THOMAS in the Ship *Happy returne* for London ISAAC
RAND Comand^r security

November the 21 1679

MANERICK NATHANIELL in the Ketch *Phœnix* for Antegua ROBERT
FLEXNY Comander   security

December the 23ᵈ 1679
MARRIOTT ROBERT in the Ship *Recouery* for Jamaica JAMES BROWNE .Comandʳ   time out

March the 7ᵗʰ 1678
NEUILL JOHN in the ship *Society* for Boston Wᴹ GUARD Comander
                                                                                     time out

July the 15ᵗʰ 1679
NEWTON ABIGALL in the Ship *Elizᵃ* for Boston JOHN BONNER Co-
mandʳ   time out

July the 22ᵈ 1679
NEEDLER JOHN in the Pink *Rebecca* for Virginia THOMAS WILLIAMS
Comandʳ   time out

August the 4ᵗʰ 1679
NEAGLE MARTIN in the Ship *Young William* for Virginia THOMAS
CORNISH Comandʳ   time out

September the 4ᵗʰ 1679
NEUILL JOHN in the Ship *Pearle* for Leward Islands EDWARD PEIR-
SON Comander   security

September yᵉ 18ᵗʰ 1679
NASY DANIELL in the ship *Hope* for New England JOHN PRICE
Comander   time out

October the 14ᵗʰ 1679
NUTTALL THOMAS in the ship *Happy returne* for Londᵒ ISAAC RAND
Comandʳ   time out

October y[e] *2*[d] *1679*

ONEAL ANN in the Sloop *Rutter* for Jamaica EDWARD DUFFEILD
Comand[r]   time out

Nouemb[r] *the* 10th *1679*

OLDRIDGE ABELL in the Sloop *Hopewell* for Antegua W[M] MURPHY
Comand[r]   time out

Nouember y[e] *20*[th] *1679*

OGLE JOHN in the Ketch *Mary and Sarah* for Prouiden [Providence]
GEORGE CONOWAY Comand[r]   security

Nouember y[e] *24*[th] *1679*

OSBURNE ROBERT a Seru[tt] belonging to RICH[D] LILBURNE in y[e] Ketch
Mary and Sarah for Prouidence GEORGE CONWAY Comand[r]

January the 13th *1678*

PATY ELIZ[A] in the Ship *Joseph and Ann* for Carolina SAMUELL EVANS
Comand[r]   time out

February the 21: *1678*

PEIRCE JOHN in the Ship *Judith* for Lond[o] ROBERT KINGSLAND
Comander   time out

February 28th *1678*

PEARSON JOHN in the Ship *Samuell* for London JOHN CLARKE
Comander

March the third 1678

PIPER W[M] in the Ship *begining* for Virginia THO: BOSSINGER
Comand[r]   time out

March the third 1678

PERRIN MARGARETT in the ship *Arthur* for Londo HENRY COSKER
Comand^r   security

March the fifth 1678

PERWIDGE JOB in the ship *Expedition* for Virginia JOHN HARDING
Comander   time out

March the 13 1678

PILE W^m in the Barq Susanna for Carolina HUGH BABELL Comander
                                                           time out

March the 21 1678

PARRIS OWEN in the Barq *Joseph* for Saltertudos STEPHEN CLAY
Comand^r   security

March the 28th 1679

PERWIDG JOB in the Ship *Endeauor* for London JAMES GILBERT
Comander   renewed

Aprill the first 1679

PEAD THOMAS in the Keatch *Swallow* for Road Island JOSEPH HARDY
Comand^r   time out

Aprill the fifth 1679

PLUMER JOHN in the Barq *May ffower* for Prouidence EDWARD
HUBBERT Comander   time out

Aprill the 5th 1679

PENISTON SAMUELL in the Barq *May ffower* for Providence EDWARD
HUBBART Comand^r   time out

Aprill the 16th 1679

PRIMATT HUMPHRY in the *Honor* for London THO: WARREN
Comand[r]   security

Aprill the 16th 1679

POLEGREEN JOHN in the Ship *Honor* for London THOMAS WARREN
Comander   security

Aprill the 22[d] 1679

POPE CHARLES in the Ship *Honor* for Lond[o] THOMAS WARREN
Comander   time out

Aprill the 22[d] 1679

PENNIMAN JANE in the Ship *Honnor* for London THOMAS WARREN
Comand[r]   time out

Aprill the 25th 1679

PIDDOCK W[M] in the Ship *Freinds Adventure* for London EDW[D] BLADES
Comand[r]   time out

Aprill the 28th 1679

POSLETT RICH[D] in the Ship *Conclusion* for Lond[o] W[M] BEEDING Comander   time out

---

May the 2[d] 1679

PINKE JOHN in the Ketch *Prosperous* for Virginia DAVID FOGG
Comander   time out

May the 8th 1679

PARSONES FRANCIS in the Ship *Concord* for Lond[o] JAMES STRUTT
Comand[r]   time out

May the 13th 1679

POTTLE CHRISTOPHER in the Pink *Dymond* for Topsham EZEKIAH
VASS Comander   time out

May the 14th 1679

PRICE JOHN in the Ship *Bachelor* for Bristoll ROGER BAGG Comandr   time out

May the 19th 1679

PRICE JOHN in the Ship *Bachelor* for Bristoll ROGER BAGG Comandr   time out

May the 19th 1679

PEMMELL THOMAS in the Ship *Rose and Crown* for Londo THOMAS
CROFTS Comandr   time out

*June the 16th 1679

PLATT JOHN in the Ketch *Joseph* for New Yorke ABRAHAM KNOTT
Comandr   time out

June the 17th 1679

PECHEY LAMBERT in the ship *Ruth* for Londo Wm TAYLOR Comandr   time out

June the 28th 1679

PHILLIPS ELIAZER in the Ship *Providence* for Boston TIMOTHY PROUT
Comandr   time out

†July the 22d 1679

PEARSHOUSE CHESTER in the Pink *Rebecca* for Virginia THO Wms
Comandr   time out

* [In the original the name of RICORD precedes this; but in order to keep to the alphabetical arrangement I have transposed it among the R's, and to its proper date (see p. 400).]

† [A similar remark applies to the name RICHARD, which stands here in the original (see p. 401).]

July the 29th 1679

POOR MILES in the KETCH *Doue* for Antegua JOHN GRAFTON Comand^r
time out

August the 9th 1679

POWELL ARTHUR in the Ship *Friendship* for Lond^o JOHN WILLIAMS
Comand^r

August the 18th 1679

POOR MARY A seru^{tt} belonging to Mr Wm BULKLEY in the Ketch *Neptune* for Virginia JOSEPH KNOTT Comander

---

August the 19th 1679

PICKFORD ROBERT in the Ketch *Neptune* for Virginia JOSEPH KNOTT
Comand^r
time out

September the 1st 1679

POLLARD JOSEPH in the Pinke *Trent* for Boston GEORGE MUNJOY
Comand^r
time out

September the 4th 1679

PICKFORD ROBERT in the Ship *Pearle* EDW^D PEIRSON Comand^r for
Lew^d Islands
renewed

September the 8th 1679

PENDLETON MARY in the Ship *Trent* for Boston GEORGE MUNJOY
Comand^r
time out

September the 15th 1679

PILSON EDWARD in the Ship *Hope* for New England JOHN PRICE
Comander
time out

October the 11ᵗʰ 1679

PORTMAN CHRISTOPHER in the Sloop *Endeavor* for Carolina THOMAS
SHAW Comandʳ   time out

October the 11ᵗʰ 1679

POPPLE MAGNUS in the Sloop *Endeauor* for Carolina THOMAS SHAW
Comandʳ   time out

October the 29ᵗʰ 1679

PARKER JOHN a Seruant belonging to Collᵒ CHRISTOPHER CODRING-
TON in the Barq̄ *Doue* for Neuis ANTHONY JENNOR Comandʳ

October the 29 1679

PAGE JOHN a Seruant belonging to Collᵒ CHR: CODRINGTON in the
Barq̄ *Doue* for Neuis ANTHONY JENOUR Comand

Nouember the 27ᵗʰ 1679

PARRIS OWEN in the Barq̄ *Resolution* for Antegua THOMAS GILBERT
Comandʳ   time out

December the 23ᵈ 1679

PERSIVALL ANDREW in the Ship *Ann & Jane* for Londᵒ RICHᴰ RATT-
FORD Comandʳ   security

March the 13ᵗʰ 1678

QUERK JOHN a Servant belonging to THOMAS ALLEN in the Ketch
Wᵐ & Susan for New England RALPH PARKER Comandʳ

August the 12ᵗʰ 1679

QUINTYNE RICHᴰ in the Barq̄ *Plantacōn* for Carolina ASER SHARPE
Comandʳ   time out

February the 25*th* 1678

ROSE CHRISTOPHER in the Ship *Patience* for Lond⁰ THOMAS HUDSON
Comand^r   security

February the 27*th* 1679 [1678]

ROYDON W^m in the *Constant Warwick* Friggott for London Capt RALPH
DELAUALL Comand^r   time out

March the 3*d* 1678

RYDER SYMON A seruant belonging to GEORGE MOOR in the Ship
Vineyard for Virginia HENRY PERRIN Comand^r

March the third 1678

ROANE BANCKS in the Sloop *Hunter* for Surranam WALTER ASSUEROS
Comand^r   time out

March the 12*th* 1678

ROBINSON ALLEXANDER in the Ship *Ann & Mary* for Antegua JOHN
JOHNSON Comand^r   security

March the 21 1678

ROSS WILLIAM in the Ketch *W^m & Susan* for New England RALPH
PARKER Comand^r   time out

March the 26: 1679

ROBERTS W^m in the Pinke *Endeauor* for Lond⁰ JAMES GILBERTS
Comand^r   time out

Aprill the 2*d* 1679

RIDLEY GEORGE in the Sloop *Rutter* for Jamaica EDW^D DUFFEILD
Comand^r   time out

Aprill the 12ᵗʰ 1679

ROW LAWRENCE in the ship *Robert* for Boston NATHAN HAYMAN
Comander   time out

Aprill the 19ᵗʰ 1679

ROTH RICHᴼ in the Ship *Recovery* for New Yorke THOMAS CHINERY
Comander   time out

Aprill the 30ᵗʰ 1679

REMNANT JAMES and JONE his Wife in the Ship *Industry* for Bristoll
JAMES PORTER Comandʳ   time out

May the 6ᵗʰ 1679

RAINY LUKE A servant belonging to Mʳ HENRY APLEWHITE in the
Ketch *Prosperous* for Virginia DAUID FOGG Comandʳ

May the 13ᵗʰ 1679

RICHBELL RICHARD in the Ship *Experimᵗᵗ* for London ALLEN COCK
Comander   security

May the 19ᵗʰ 1679

RAVENSCROFT BENJᴬ in the Ship *Rose and Crowne* for Londᵒ THOMAS
CROFTS Comandʳ   time out

May the 20ᵗʰ 1679

REMNANT JAMES ℓ JONE in the Ship *New Concord* for Londᵒ JAMES
STRUTT Comandʳ   renewed

[May the 24ᵗʰ 1679

RICORD CHARLES in the Ship *Society* for Bristoll EDMOND DITTY
Comander   time out]

* [This name is entered among the P's in the original, as is the case with RICHARD, JAMES,
at bottom of next page.]

May the 28th 1679

RAINSFORD EDWARD in the Ship *W[m] & John* for Boston SAMUELL
LEGG Comand[r] time out

May the 28th 1679

RUSSELL EDWARD in the Ship *W[m] & John* for Boston SAMUELL
LEGG Comand[r] time out

May the 28th 1679

RICHBELL ROBERT in the Ship *W[m] & John* for Boston SAMUELL LEGG
Comander time out

June the 28th 1679

RICH ROBERT Senior in the Ship *Amity* for London BENJ[A] GROVES
Comander time out

July the first 1679

RICHBELL JOHN in the ship *Prouidence* for Boston TIMOTHY PROUT
Comander security

July the 10th 1679

RULE THOMAS in the Pinke *Rebecca* for Virginia THO: WILLIAMS
Comander time out

July the 17th 1679

RUDGE THOMAS in the Briganteen *Brother's Aduenture* for New Yorke
ROBERT DARKIN Comand[r] security

[*July the* 21 1679

RICHARD JAMES in the Pinke *Rebecca* for Virginia THOMAS WILLIAMS
Comand[r] time out]

51

August the third 1679

RICE JAMES and JOHN in the Ship *Young W^m* for Virginia THOMAS
CORNISH Comand^r time out

August ye 15th 1679

RICH ROBERT in the ship *Postilion* for New England JOHN PRAUL
Comand^r security

August ye 15th 1679

RUDLE ROBERT in the Ship *John and Henry* for Bristoll THOMAS
CADES Comander time out

September the 4th 1679

ROBOTHAM WILLIAM in the Ship *Joseph* for New Yorke STEPHEN
CLAY Comand^r a serv^tt belonging to Coll^o SAM^{LL} NEWTON

Nouember the third 1679

REDDIN KATHERINE a Serv^tt belonging to MARTIN HAYES for
Jamaica in the Barq, *Aduenture* EDW^D DUFFEILD Comander

January the fourteenth 1678

SLAUGHTER WILLIAM a Serv^tt belonging to JOHN JENNINGS in the
ship *Joseph & Ann* for Carolina SAM^{LL} EUANS Comand^r

January the 14th 168 [1678]

SERJEANT RICH^D in the Ship *Joseph and Ann* for Carolina SAMUELL
EVANS Comander security

January the 28th 1678

SMITH PHILLIP in the Ship *James* for New Yorke W^M SWEETLAND
Comand^r time out

February the 11th 1678

SYMONS SAMUELL in the Ship *James* for New Yorke W^M SWEETLAND
Comand^r   time out

February the 13: 1678

STOCKLEY JOHN and MARY in the ship *two Brothers* for Jamaica
RICE JEFFERYS Comander   time out

February the 13th 1678

SHERWOOD SAMUELL in the ship *Two Brothers* for Jamaica RICE
JEFFERYS Comand^r   time out

February the 17th 1678

STEEL MARY in the ship *Merch^{tt} Bonaduenture* for London W^M BUCK-
LEY Comand^r   time out

February the 25th 1678

SMITH HESTER in the Barq̣ *Plantacon* for Carolina ASER SHARPE
Comand^r   time out

March the 8th 1678

STOAKES MICHAELL in the Ship *Society* for Boston WILLIAM GUARD
Comander   time out

March the 11th 1678

STACY W in the Ship *Society* for Boston W^M GUARD Comand^r
                                                                                          time out

March the 12th 1678

SMITH EDWARD in the Barq̣ *Susannah* for Carolina HUGH BABELL
Comander   security

51—2

March the 18th 1678

SANDERS BENJ^A in the Ketch *begining* for New Yorke W^M PLAY
    Comand^r   time out

March the 26th 1679

STEEL MARY* in the Ship *Supply* for London JOSEPH FREEMAN
    Comand^r   renewed

March the 29th 1679

SAILES RICH^D in the Ketch *Swallow* for New England JOSEPH
    HARDY Comander   time out

March the 31st 1679

SEWER JOHN in the ship *John and Thomas* for Prouidence THOMAS
    JENOUR Comander   time out

March the 31st 1679

SCOTT BENJ^A in the Ship *Expedition* for Lond^o JOHN HARDING
    Comand^r   time out

Aprill the first 1679

SMITH W^M in the Ketch *Unity* for Virginia JAMES RAINY Comand^r
                                                                time out

---

Aprill the 3^d 1679

SALT SAMUELL in the Ship *Change* for London W^M KING Comander
                                                                time out

---

Aprill the 12th 1679

SANDIFORD HENRY in the ship *Robert* for Boston NATHAN HAYMAN
    Comander   time out

---

* [See under date Feb. 17, in previous page.]

Aprill the 15th 1679

SFRANE ALMONS in the Ship *Eliz^a* for Neuis PETER MAJOR Comand^r   time out

---

Aprill the 19th 1679

STEPHENS NATHANIELL in the Ship *Recouery* for New Yorke THOMAS CHINERY Comander   time out

---

Aprill the 19th 1679

SEDGWICK RALPH in the Ketch *Unity* for Virginia JAMES RAINY Comander   time out

---

Aprill the 22^d 1679

SPICER SAMUELL in the Ship *Hope* for London JOSEPH BALL Comander   tim e out

---

Aprill the 26th 1679

SMITH MARGERETT a Seru^{tt} belonging to THOMAS DOXEY in the Ship *Brother's Aduenture* for New Yorke J^{no} SELLECK Com^r

---

Aprill the 28th 1679

SNACKNELL RICH^D in the Ship *Nathan^{ll}* for Boston W^M CLARKE Comand^r   time out

---

May the 2^d 1679

SOUTHWORTH FRANCIS in the Ketch *Prosperous* for Virginia DAUID FOGG Comander   time out

---

May the fifth 1679

STAPLETON WALTER in the Ship *Society* for Bristoll EDMOND DITTY Comander   time out

May the 10th 1679

STANTON PEARCE in the Barq, *Resolution* for Antegua JOHN INGLE-
BEE Comand^r   time out

May the 12th 1679

SHORT WALTER in the Ship *Bachelor* for Bristoll ROGER BAGG
Comand^r   time out

May the 14th 1679

SKAHANE TEIGE in the Ship *Industry* for Bristoll JAMES PORTER
Comand^r   time out

May the 14th 1679

SMITH ISAAC in the Ship *Supply* for Boston JOHN MELLOWES
Comand^r   time out

May the 19th 1679

SANDOME RICH^D in the Ship *Swallow* for Leuerpoole THO WITH-
INGTUN Comander   time out

May the 20th 1679

SMITH WILLIAM in the Ship *New Concord* for Lond^o JAMES STRUTT
Comand^r   time out

May the 20th 1679

STEPHENS SYLVESTER in the Ketch *Nich^o & Rebecca* for New Yorke
NICHOLAS BLAKE Comand^r   time out

May the 22^d 1679

SHERLAND JOHN jun^r in the Ship *Prudence and Mary* for Boston
JACOB GREEN Comand^r   time out

May the 28ᵗʰ 1679

SERFATTY JOSHUA in the Ship *Morneing Starr* for Surranam JOHN
UANDERSPIKE Comandʳ   security

May the 29ᵗʰ 1679

SPARKES SAMUELL in the Ship *Wᵐ & John* for Boston SAMˡˡ LEGG
Comandʳ   time out

May the 29ᵗʰ 1679

SALTER RICH in the Ketch *Wᵐ & John* for Boston SAMˡˡ LEGG
Comander   time out

June the 25ᵗʰ 1679

SUTTON JOHN in the ship *Prosperous* for Londo THOMAS WOOD-
COCK Comandʳ   time out

July the 9ᵗʰ 1679

SMITH THOMAS in the Ship *Bachelor* for London Wᴺ KNOTT Comander   time out

---

July the 15ᵗʰ 1679

SCOTT THOMAS in the Pink *Rebecca* for Virginia THOMAS WILLIAMS
Comander   time out

July the 22ᵈ 1679

STANNADGE THOMAS in the Pinke *Rebecca* for Virginia THOMAS
WILLIAMS Comandʳ   time out

July the 22ᵈ 1679

STRAUSE ELIAS in the Ship *Experimᵗᵗ* for London THOMAS AUBONY
Comandʳ   time out

August the 2ᵈ 1679

STONE JOHN in the ship *Bachelors Delight* for Londᵒ ROBERT
GREENWAY Comander   time out

August the 16ᵗʰ 1679

SEALY HENRY in the Ketch *Neptune* for Virginia JOSEPH KNOTT
Comandʳ   time out

August the 16ᵗʰ 1679

SMITH THURLO a Servᵗᵗ belonging to HENRY SEALY in the Keatch
Neptune for Virginia JOSEPH KNOTT Comandʳ

September the 16ᵗʰ 1679

SONE GEORGE in the Barqₕ *Blessing* for Burmudos FRANCIS WATLING-
TON Comander   security

September the 20ᵗʰ 1679

STANLEY ROBERT in the Ship *Malligo Merchᵗᵗ* for London ROGER
HOMER Comander   time out

September the 22ᵈ 1679

SEAMAN THOMAS in the Ship *Thomas & Sarah* for London JAMES
DAY Comander   time out

October the first 1679

SHORT MARTHA in the Ship *Barbados Merchᵗᵗ* for Virginia JAMES
COCK Comand.   time out

October the first 1679

SANDFORD JOHN in the Ship *Barbados Merchᵗᵗ* for Virginia JAMES
COCK Comandʳ   time out

October the 2ᵈ 1679

SEARLE RICHᴰ A Servᵗᵗ belonging to JAMES COATES in the Sloop *Rutter* for Jamaica EDWᴰ DUFFEILD Comandʳ

October the 7ᵗʰ 1679

SWINNY THOMAS in the Sloop *true friendship* for Antego CHARLES KALLAHANE Comander   security

October the 29ᵗʰ 1679

SENIOR JACOB in the Barq, *Doue* for Neuis ANTHONY JENOUR Comandʳ   security

October the 29ᵗʰ 1679

SMITH JOHN a Servᵗᵗ belonging to Colloᵒ CHRISTOPHER CODRINGTON in the Barq, *Doue* for Nevis ANTHᵒ JENOR

Nouember the 3ᵈ 1679

SWEETING RICHᴰ in the Barq, *Aduenture* for Jamaica EDWARD DUFFEILD Comander   time out

Nouember the 6ᵗʰ 1679

SIDDY HENRY in the Barq, *Aduenture* for Jamaica EDWARD DUFFEILD Comandʳ   security

Nouember the 7ᵗʰ 1679

SALTER GEORGE in the Sloop *Hopewell* for Antegua Wᴹ MURPHY Comandʳ   time out

Nouember the 29ᵗʰ 1679

SPITTLE ROBERT in the Sloop *Katherine* for Antegua ANDREW GALL Comandʳ   time out

December the 15ᵗʰ 1679

SIDNEY JOHN in the Ship *Lawrell* for Lewᵈ ROBERT OXE Comandʳ
security

December the 22ᵈ 1679

SMITH JOHN in the Ship *Ann and Jane* for Londᵒ RICHᴰ RATT-
FORD Comander
time out

December the 24ᵗʰ 1679

SMART JOHN in the ship *Ann & Jane* for Londᵒ RICHᴰ RATT-
FORD Comander
security

December 24ᵗʰ 1679

SHERWIN JOHN in the Ship *Ann & Jane* for Londᵒ RICHᴰ RATT-
FORD Comander
security

December the 24ᵗʰ 1679

SINDRY JOHN in the ship *Recouery* for Jamaica JAMES BROWNE
Comander
time out

December the 30ᵗʰ 1679

SWANLEY ROBERT in the Ship *Ann and Jane* for London RICHᴰ
RATTFORD Comander
time out

December the 31ˢᵗ 1679

SHARPE MARY in the Ship *Recouery* for Jamaica JAMES BROWNE
Comandʳ
time out

February the 21ˢᵗ 1678

TRAVIS RICHARD in the Ship *Fellowship* for Antegua THOMAS PIM
Comandʳ
time out

March the first 1678:

TIPPIN JOHN in the *Constant Warwick* Friggott for London Capt
RALPH DELAVALL Comander   time out

Aprill the 11th 1679

TINICO JACOB in the Ketch *W^m and John* for New England JOHN
SANDERS Comander   time out

Aprill the 19th 1679

TOOLES MORGAN in the Ship *Freinds Aduenture* for London EDWARD
BLADES Comander   time out

Aprill the 25th 1679

THORNTON W^M in the ship *Freinds Adventure* for Lond^o EDWARD
BLADES Comander   time out

Aprill the 28th 1679

TOWNSEND RICHARD in the Ship *Nathan^{ll}* for Boston W^M CLARKE
Comander   time out

Aprill the 29: 1679

TURNER JOHN in the ship *Nathaniell* for Boston W^M CLARKE
Comander   time out

May the 10th 1679

TERRY CHRISTOPHER jun^r in the Ship *Experiment* for London
ALLAN COCK Comander   time out

May the 24th 1679

THOMAS GEORGE in the Ship *Prudence and Mary* for Boston JACOB
GREEN Comander   time out

June the 26 : 1679

TEAGE JOHN in the ship *Freindship* for London JOHN WILLIAMS
Comander   time out

July the 12th 1679

TOLLO DEMEUEREZ LEWIS in the ship *Bachelor* for Londo WM KNOTT
Comander   time out

July the 17th 1679

THAYER NATHANIELL in the ship *Society* for Boston WM GUARD
Comander   time out

August the 16th 1679

TURDALL JOHN in the Ketch *Neptune* for Virginia JOSEPH KNOTT
Comandr a Servtt belonging to HENRY SEALY

September ye 18th 1679

TAPPER THOMAS in the ship *Malligo Merchtt* ROGER HOMER Comander for London   time out

---

Nouember the 7th 1679

TREMILLS WM in the Sloop *Hopewell* for Antegua WM MURPHY
Comander   time out

December the 11th 1679

THORPE JOHN in the ship *Ann and Jane* for London RICHD RATT-
FORD Comander   time out

March the 10th 1678

VINER ANTHONY in the Ship *James* for Antegua PAUL CREAN
Comander   time out

May the 2^d 1679

VAUX JOHN in the Ship *Roe Buck* for London W^M SHAFTO Comander   time out

---

July the 16th 1679

VERIN NATHANIELL in the Pink *Rebecca* for Virginia THOMAS
WILLIAMS Comander   time out

Nouember ye 8th 1679

URQUHART ALLEXANDER in the Sloop *Hopewell* for Antegua W^M
MURPHY Comander   time out

December ye 24^t 1679

VERNON PETER in the ship *Ann and Jane* for Lond^o RICH^D RATT-
FORD Comander   security

January the 4th 1678

WILLIAMS MATTHEW in the Ship *Old head* of Kingsale for Leward
ROBERT BARKER Comander   time out

February 11th 1678

WILLIS HENRY in the Ship *Dilligence* for Boston JEREMIAH JACSON
Comander   time out

February the 17th 1678

WILLS JOHN in the ship *Endeauour* for Virginia ABRAHAM NEWMAN
Comand^r time out

March the 10th 1678

WELTDEN ANTHONY in the Ship *Society* for Boston W^M GUARD
Comander   security

March the 12th 1678

WHITELIFF GEORGE in the Ship *Samaritan* for Leverpool VALENTINE
TRIm [? TRIMMER] Comand[r]   security

March the 19th 1678

WHITTEE MARY in the Ketch *begining* for New Yorke W[M] PLAY
Comand[r]   time out

March the 19th 1679 [1678]

WRIGHT ROBERT and MARY in the Ketch *begining* for New Yorke
W[M] PLAY Comand[r]   time out

March the 21st 1678

WILKS NATHANIELL in the ship Merch[tt] *Bonadventure* for London
W[M] BUCKLEY Comander   security

March the 27th 1679

WRIGHT RICH[D] in the Ketch *Mary and Sarah* for Carolina GEORGE
CONOWAY Comand[r]   time out

March the 31st 1679

WHITEFOOT AMOS in the ship *Robert* for Boston NATHAN HAYMAN
Comand[r]   time out

Aprill the 10th 1679

WILKINSON DANIELL in the Barq[b] *Resolution* for Prouidence DANIELL
ACKLIN Comand[r] y[e] said WILKINSON a Seru[tt] belonging to
ROBERT HALL

Aprill the 15th 1679

WEBSTER HENRY in the ship *Robert* for Boston NATHAN HAYMAN
Comand[r]   time out

Aprill the 19*th* 1679

WILSE FRANCIS in the ship *Hope* for Lond° JOSEPH BALL Comand[r]   time out

---

Aprill the 26*th* 1679

WEBSTER EDWARD in the Ship *Nathan[u]* for Boston W[M] CLARKE
Comand[r]   time out

Aprill the 26*th* 1679

WILKINS JOHN in the ship *Nathan[u]* for Boston W[M] CLARKE
Comander   time out

Aprill the 26*th* 1679

WILLIAMS SYMON in the ship *Francis* for Leward PETER JEFFERYS
Comander   security

May the 2*d* 1679

WHITFEILD MATHEW in the Ketch *Presperous* for Virginia DAVID
FOGG Comand[r]   time out

May the 5*th* 1679

WHEELER W[M] in the Sloop *Bachelor* for Leward PETER SWAINE
Comander   time out

May the 8*th* 1679

WINGATT JOHN in the Ketch *Prosperous* for Virginia DAVID FOGG
Comand[r]   time out

May the 20*th* 1679

WICKHAM BENJ[A] in the Barq, *Resolution* for Antegoa JOHN INGLEBE
Comand[r]   security

May the 26th 1679

WHITEING W^M in the ship *Francis and Susan* for Boston PHILLIP KNELL Comander   time out

---

May the 26th 1679

WATTKINS PHILLIP in the ship *Prudence and Mary* for Boston JACOB GREEN Comander   time out

---

June the 18th 1679

WOLFE EMANUELL in the Ship *Thomas and Susan* for Boston DAVID EDWARDS Comand^r   security

---

June the 18th 1679

WOOD JAMES in the ship *Thomas and Susan* for Boston DAUID EDW^DS Comand^r   time out

---

July the 15th 1679

WILLSON W^M in the Barq_b *Rebecca* for Virginia THO WILLIAMS Comand^r   time out

---

July the 18th 1679

WELCH EDMOND a Seru^tt belonging to JOHN HOPCROFT in the Pink *Rebecca* for Virginia THO: W^MS Comander

---

August the first 1679

WHEELER JOHN jun^r in the Ship *Returne* for New Engl^d THOMAS HARVEY Comand^r   security

---

August the 19th 1679

WOLFINDEN JEREMIAH in the Sloop *true freindship* for Nevis CHARLES KALLAHANE Comand^r   time out

August ye 28th 1679

WHELER CHRISTOPHER in the Ship *Robert* for London RICH^D COCK
Comander   security

September the first 1679

WICKHAM ELIZ^A in the Sloop *John & Francis* for Antegua JOHN
HOWARD Comander   time out

September the first 1679

WESTBURY THOMAS in the Ship *Barbados Merch^{tt}* for Lew^d Islands
EDWARD GRIFFIN Comand^r   time out

September the 3^d 1679

WATLINGTON MARY in the Sloop *John & Frances* for Antegua
JOHN HOWARD Comand^r   time out

September the 16th 1679

WEAVER THOMAS in the Ship *Mallego Merch^{tt}* for London ROGER
HOMER Comander   time out

September ye 22 1679

WOODCOCK THO: in the ship *Thomas & Sarah* for Lond^o JAMES
DAY Comand^r   time out

October the 6th 1679

WICKHAM THOMAS in the Sloop *True freindship* for Antegoa
CHARLES KALLAHANE Comand^r   security

October ye 7th 1679

WALL SAMUELL in the Sloop *true freindship* for Antegua CHARLES
KALLAHANE Comand^r   security

October ye 8th 1679

WILLOUGHBY OLIVER in the Sloop *Affrica* for Antegoa ANTHONY
BURGESS Comand^r   security

53

October y^e *17*th *1679*

WILDE W^M in the Ship *Happy Returne* for Lond° ISAAC RAND
    Comand^r time out

October y^e *24*th *1679*

WAINWRIGHT JAMES in the ship *Happy Returne* for London ISAAC
    RAND Comand^r time out

Nouember y^e *first 1679*

WHITEHEAD JOSEPH in the Ship *Three Brothers* for New Yorke PETER
    BOSS Comand^r security

Nouemb^r *y*^{e} *7*th *1679*

WILLIAMS ARTHUR in the Sloop *Hopewell* for Antegua W^M MURPHY
    Comand^r time out

Decemb^r *y*^{e} *6*th *1679*

WARNER NATHANIELL in the Sloop *Unity* for Jamaica LAWRENCE
    SLUCE Comander   time out

May the 2^d *1679*

YATES THOMAS A Seru^{tt} belonging to FRAN: SOUTHWORTH in the
    Keatch *Prosperous* for Virginia DAUID FOGG Comd.

July y^e *18*th *1679*

YOUNG MATHEW in the Pink *Rebecca* for Virginia THOMAS WIL-
    LIAMS Comand^r time out

Nouemb^r *y*^{e} *4*th *1679*

YARWOOD THOMAS in the Barq$_b$ *Endeavor* for Carolina THOMAS SHAW
    Comand^r time out

Total of Men   523
Total of Women 60

In all 583

BARBADOES.

PARISH REGISTERS :— BIRTHS AND DEATHS, LISTS OF INHABITANTS, LANDED PROPRIETORS, SERVANTS, &c.

1678—1679.]

[PARISH REGISTERS.]

BARBADOS — *The Parish of St Michaels.*

BAPTISMS.

1678

March 31. JOICE ye daughter of CHARLS & MARGARET YATES.
THOMAS ye Son of HENRY & ANNE SMITH.
April. 2. ESTHER ye daughter of FRANCIS & ELISABETH HALL.
16. MARY ye daughter of CALEB & ELISABETH POWEL.
25. MARY ye daughter of JANE SCOT.
LOVEL ye Son of JOHN & ELINOR HOBCRAFT.
JANE ye daughter of JONE DAVIS.
May. 5. MARY ye daughter of WILLIAM & MARY STANDON.
7. SUSANNA ye daughter of JOHN & ANNE HALL.
15. WILLIAM ye Son of STEVEN & MARGARET LANSDALE.
19. MARY ye daughter of FRANCIS & KATHARINE HARDING
DAVID ye Son of JOHN & ELISABETH MURRAL.
19. JOHN ye Son of RICHARD & ELISABETH PERKIN.
EDWARD ye Son of THOMAS & KATHARINE PROUT.
20. EDWARD ye Son of EDWARD & HANNAH MATTHEWS.
28. RICHARD ye Son of Majr THOMAS JELLY & MARY his Wife.
June. 3. MARGARET ye daughter of Mr JOHN CRISP & SARAH his wife.

1678.

June. 9. WILLIAM yᶜ Son of WILLIAM & MARGARET STICKLAND.
ELISABETH yᵉ daughter of JOHN & ELISABETH GOSNEL.
KATHARIN yᵉ daughter of SIMON & ANN WILLIAMS, Christian Negroes.

16. ELISABETH yᵉ daughter of URSULA PEASE.
MARY yᵉ daughter of JOHN & JUDITH SMITH.

20. ANDREW yᵉ Son of ANDREW & SARAH GODFREY.

24. ARTHUR yᵉ Son of RICHARD & SARAH MENDAM.

25. PETRONILIA yᵉ daughter of GEORG & ELISABETH PARR.

28. ANN yᵉ daughter of THOMAS & ELISABETH CLARK.

July. 25. HANNAH yᵉ daughter of Dʳ JOHN SPRINGHAM, & SARAH his wife.

26. JANE yᵉ daughter of Mʳ SAMUEL SHENTON & GRACE his wife.

August. 9. WILLIAM yᵉ Son of STEPHEN & MARGARET LANDSDALE.

19. MARY yᵉ daughter of NICHOLAS & ELISABETH MAYNARD.
LAKE yᵉ Son of Capt WILL. MARSHAL.

21. CLEMENT yᵉ Son of ROBERT & REBECCA LANIERE.

25. ELISABETH yᵉ daughter of JOHN & SUSANNA NEWPORT.

September. 7. FRANCES yᵉ daughter of Mʳ ROBERT CODRINGTON & ELISABETH his Wife.

8. WILLIAM yᵉ Son of ROBERT & MARY ELLIS.

22. HANNAH yᵉ daughter of JOHN & MARY LISWEL.

26. THOMAS yᵉ Son of RICHARD & ELEN WHITE.

28. DAVID yᵉ Son of HUGH & JANE DAVIS.

October. 7. CHRISTOPHER yᵉ Son of Major JOHN HALLET & MARY his Wife.

13. JOHN yᵉ Son of JOHN & MARGARET AWMAN.
EDWARD yᵉ Son of BRASIL & REBECCAH BENFIELD.

14. ELISABETH yᵉ daughter of Mʳ THOMAS PIERCE & ELISABETH his Wife.

20. MARY yᵉ daughter of Mʳ JOHN SMITH & PHILIPPA his Wife.
SARAH yᵉ daughter of SAMUEL & SARAH h̶i̶s̶ ̶W̶i̶f̶e̶ *PERROT.

November. 3. MARY yᵉ daughter of THOMAS & ANN KANNIDAY.

---

* [Thus crossed through in the original.]

1678.

November. 10. PETER, alias THOMAS ye Son of ROBERT & JANE PORTER.

 11. JONATHAN ye Son of JONATHAN & SARAH PEACH.

 14. EDWARD ye Son of Mr NATHANIEL BRANCKER & MARY his Wife.

 17 ELISABETH ye daughter of JACOB & PRISCILLA ALLEN.

December. 8. RICHARD ye Son of JOHN & MARY BUTCHER.

 12. FRANCIS ye Son of Mr FRANCIS BOND & ELISABETH his Wife.

 13. WILLIAM ye Son of WILLIAM & ANN PARIS.

 15. THOMAS ye Son of DANIEL & ELISABETH FRISEL.

 17. ELISABETH ye daughter of Mr WILLIAM BARNS & SARAH his Wife.

 22. ANN ye daughter of NICHOLAS & DORCAS WILLOUGHBY.

 27. JOHN ye Son of STEPHEN & ELISABETH CORNISH.

 ANN ye daughter of JOHN & MARY HARWOOD.

January. 1. WILLIAM ye Son of WILLIAM & MARGARET ROPER,

 JOHN ye Son of LAWRENCE & MARY ENGLAND.

 8. THOMAS ye Son of Mr THOMAS FERGUSSON & ELISABETH his Wife.

 9. THOMAS ye Son of JOHN & ELISABETH WILLIS.

 12. KATHARIN ye daughter of Mr JOHN SUTTON & MARY his Wife.

 14. CHARLS ye Son of CHARLS CAVENAUGH.

 20. NICHOLAS ye Son of ARCHIBALD & FRANCES MACQUIN.

 22. JOHN ye Son of HILLIARD HOLDIP & FRANCES his Wife.

February. 6. DOROTHY & THOMASIN ye daughters of Capt. THOMAS MORRIS & SARAH his Wife.

 ROGER ye Son of Mr ROGERS & MARY his Wife.

 9. ELISABETH ye daughter of Mr GEORG CHENEY & MARY his Wife.

 23. SAMUEL ye Son of FRANCIS & MARY THATCHER.

 27. ELISABETH ye daughter of ROGER COWLEY Esqr, & SUSANNA his Wife.

March. 6. FRANCIS ye Son of Capt. FRANCIS BURTON & JUDITH his Wife.

1678.

March. 13. SARAH yͤ daughter of CHARLS & MARTHA LEIGH.

19. REBECCA yͤ daughter of NICHOLAS PRIDEAUX & REBECCA his Wife.

22. FRANCES yͤ daughter of Mʳ JOHN OGILBY & ELISABETH his Wife.

—— 23. ANN yͤ daughter of DANIEL & BARBARA LAWRENCE.

1679 30. JAMES yͤ Son of JOHN & ELENOR FITZGERARD.

JOHN yͤ Son of JOHN & SUSANNA CRAG.

April. 13. CORNELIUS yͤ Son of JOHN & SUSANNA MACKENNY.

14. ABRAHAM yͤ Son of THOMAS & MARY HAWKINS.

19. ALICE yͤ daughter of THOMAS & BRIDGET JOHNSON.

25. JOSEPH yͤ Son of GEORG & HANNAH OATS.

May. 13. GILES yͤ Son of GILES & MARY ELDRIDG.

June. 3. JOHN yͤ Son of Mʳ JOHN STEWARD & MARGARET his Wife.

4. THOMAS yͤ Son of MARY KING.

8. JOHN yͤ Son of ANTHONY & ELISABETH SUILLIVANT.

16. MATTHEW yͤ Son of FRANCIS & THOMASIN CHRISTIAN.

22. THOMAS yͤ Son of JOHN & JANE JANES.

JOHN yͤ Son of THOMAS & JANE WEST.

July. 15. WILLIAM yͤ Son of WILLIAM & ELISABETH HERBERT.

24. ELISABETH ERPEY.

25. THOMAS yͤ Son of DANIEL & SARAH GUN.

MARY yͤ daughter of MARTHA TURNER.

27. EDWARD yͤ Son of JEFFRY & PRISCILLA BATLEY.

29. HENRY yͤ Son of ANN SMITH, Wid.

August. 5. ELISABETH yͤ daughter of Mʳ RICHARD BUNNY and HANNAH his Wife.

10. TIMOTHY yͤ Son of TIMOTHY & MARGARET ENNYS

NICHOLAS yͤ Son of NICHOLAS & MARGARET MORREL.

DARBY yͤ Son of LANTHIL & MARY HALLOWAY.

17. SUSANNA yͤ daughter of ROBERT & ELISABETH PAIN.

ELISABETH yͤ daughter of JOHN & MARGARET TINE.

22. EDWYN yͤ Son of EDWYN STEED Esqʳ & CALIA his Wife.

26. MUNDUSIA yͤ daughter of JOHN & ELISABETH SMITH.

28. ELISABETH yͤ daughter of Mʳ ROBERT & SUSANNA BECKLES.

1679.

September. 2. MARY ye daughter of ANDREW & MARY MAIN.

      5. WILLIAM ye Son of LEONARD & ANN ROBINSON.

      10. ESTHER ye daughter of EDMUND & ELISABETH MORGAN.

      12. GEORG ye Son of Capt. FRANCIS BURTON & JUDITH his Wife.

      21. ELISABETH & MARGARET ye daughters of Mr BENJAMIN & MARGARET MATSON.

      25. MARGARET ye daughter of Mr THOMAS & MARGARET DOD·

107.

BARBADOS

The Parish of
St Michaels.

BURIALS.

1678

March 26th JOHN SWAN Master of y^e *Hope* of Amsterdam.

      28. Mr WILLIAM FLETCHER.

      30. FRANCIS BOYS'S child.

      31. FRANCIS VARNAM.

April. 1. WILLIAM FELLOW.

      2. VRSULA GREY.
         ROSE FORD.

      3. ALICE ye daughter of HENRY & MARY LELAM.
         ROGER JONES from ye Almshous.

      4. MARTHA CLAY.

      8. EDWARD ROBERTS.
         Mr ROBERT RAMSEY.

      14. JOHN HUGHS.

      15. JONE ALLEN a Widdow.

      16. WILLIAM TRUSDAL.
         HENRY JENNISON.

      17. Mr THOMAS PARIS, Merch^t
         WILLIAM MILLER.

1678.

April. 18. MARY yͤ daughter of CALEB & ELISABETH POWEL.

19. AGNES yͤ daughter of Mʳ THOMAS FORRESTER & JANE his Wife.

MARGARET yͤ daughter of· RICHARD & ELISABETH RICHARDSON.

22. ELISABETH yͤ daughter of JOHN & JANE CARN.*

HANNAH yͤ wife of JOHN WADE.

MARGARET, a distracted Woman.

24. RALPH WARNER.

WILLIAM FERRIMAN.

27. KATHARINE MILLER.

Mʳ HECTOR STEVENS.

28. PATRIC KILHAMMY.

29. SUSANNA WITHERS.

May. 4. EDMUND JOY.

5. Mʳ JOHN JONES chief Mate of yͤ *Arany Marchant,* Mʳ JOHN HALL, Mʳ

SUSANNA STEDMAN.

THOMAS yͤ Son of HENRY & ANN SMITH.

6. SUSANNA ROSE.

7. GEORG HILL.

9. THOMAS STEVENS Gunner of yͤ *Thomas & Susan* of London, GEORG PYE Commander.

11. JANE yͤ Wife of Capt. HENRY HAWLEY.

13. THOMAS WALKER.

15. JOHN ROBINSON.

16. HUMILITY HOBS, from yͤ Almshous.

18. JONE WILEY.

20. ANDREW WOOD.

JOHN WASHBURN.

DANIEL SUILLIVANT.

THOMAS ENGLISH, from yͤ Almshous.

21. SARAH BUNTING.

EDWARD RUSSEL, from yͤ Almshous.

---

* [Seems to have been originally written CORN, and then altered to CARN.]

1678.

May. 22. EDWARD MATTHEWS.

27. THOMAS JAMES.

28. JOHN HOLLIN.

29. JOHN WILLIAMS, from yᵉ prison.

31. KATHARINE yᵉ daughter of DENIS & ALICE DAYLEY.

June. 4. WILLIAM RAYNER.

5. MARY COPELAND.

15. HUMPHREY ROSSER.

17. ELISABETH yᵉ daughter of URSULA PEASE.

19. THOMAS BAL.

20. ROBERT HORTON Mate to WILLIAM SHACKERLY.
HENRY GRIFFIN.

21. JOHN yᵉ Son of Mʳ THOMAS WARNER & ANN his Wife.
THOMAS   * a Servᵗ to L.Col. JOHN CODRINGTON.
MARY yᵉ daughter of JOHN & JUDITH SMITH.

23. MARY JACKSON.

25. ARTHUR yᵉ Son of RICHARD & SARAH MENDAM.

28. JOHN yᵉ Son of ANN AUSTIN, Widdow.

29. ANN yᵉ daughter of THOMAS & ELISABETH CLARK.
PHILLIP LE VOH.
ROGER yᵉ Son of THOMAS & LÆTITIA CLARK.
GEORG yᵉ Son of GEORG & ELISABETH DODSON.

July 3. JOHN FILKS, a Servᵗ to RICHARD WHITING.
KATHARIN MORRIS.

5. NOAH FLETCHER.

7. JOHN WILSON.

8. JAMES REYNOLDS.
SAMUEL PEACOCK, mate of yᵉ *Africa* C JOHN HURLOCK
Comᵈᵉʳ.

9. DAVID ROGERS.

10. JOHN DAN.

12. FRANCES yᵉ daughter of Mʳ JOHN OGILSBY & ELISABETH
his Wife.

* [Blank in original.]

1678.

July 13. Two daughters of JOHN PEARSON, infants.
   15. GUALTER GRIFFIN.
   15. MARGARET SUILLIVANT.
   16. ALICE y daughter of Mr ROBERT CODRINGTON.
         KATHARIN HOSKINS.
   17. MARGARET ADAUDLY.
         HENRY OVERBURY.
   20. RICHARD HUGHS.
         BENJAMIN MIDDLETON, an Infant.
   21. ISABELLA LEVANT.
   22. ANN SMAL.
         EDMUND SHIP.
   24. An Irishwoman.
   27. ELISABETH FEE.
   28. Mr WILLIAM DAVIS Citisen & Merchant of London.
   29. RICHARD HOWES.
   30. WILLIAM ASTIN.
August. 1. Capt. THOMAS BROWN, from ye Almshous.
         ANTHONY HALL.
    2. DANIEL NEAL, from ye Almshous.
    3. MARTHA NEAL.
         RICHARD MENDAM, a child.
    5. MARGARET BLAND.
         WILLIAM BUNNEL.
    7. MARY CONNET.
         Ms SARAH FRITH.
    9. JOHN TAYLOR.
   12. ELISABETH GUY.
   14. Mr THOMAS LARKHAM.
   16. MARY HORN, Widdow.
         ANDREW, from ye Almshous.
         ALICE TOWNSEND.
   17. MARY WHITE.
         WILLIAM LEIGH ye Son of CHARLS & MARTHA LEIGH.
   19. JOHN RADFORD.

1678.

August. 19. SARAH COOK.

        EDWARD CHAMBERLAIN.

    20. Mr RICHARD DUTTON.

        BARTHOLOMEW JONES.

    22. ALEXANDER HILGROVE.

    26. THOMAS WILLIAMS.

        MARY HACKWOOD.

    28. LAKE ye Son of Capt. WILLIAM MARSHAL.

    30. ELISABETH ye daughter of JOHN & SUSANNA NEWPORT.

    31. RALPH HENLY.

September. 1. HENRY BANKS.

        MARY SMITH.

    4. KATHARIN CRADDOCK.

    5. LAWRENCE PETERSON.

    7. SUSANNA MOYSE.

    8. SAMUEL JONES.

        A Child of DANIEL & MARGARET SUILLIVANT.

        FRANCES ye daughter of ROBERT & ELISABETH CODRINGTON.

    10. ANN MARSHAL.

    12. JANE y Wife of ROBERT HOLMAN.

    15. ELISABETH ye Wife of JOHN PEERS, Esqr

    19. NICHOLAS BREWER.

    21. THOMAS HOG.

    22. HAGAR a Christian Negro.

        ELISABETH PIERCE.

    25. HANNAH ye daughter of Mr BERNARD SCKENKEN.

        RALPH ye Son of CHRISTOPHER & JANE SMITH.

    26. ROBERT ALDRIDG.

    28. Mr EDWARD BUSHEL Merch^t

        HUGH DAVIS.

    29. NICHOLAS CONEY.

    30. M^s PICKERING.

        JONE PERRY.

October. 1. JONE ye wife of CHRISTOPHER HODGES.

        ELISABETH ye daughter of ROBERT & ELISABETH WEBSTER.

1678.

October. 2. Mr THOMAS ORESBY.

    3. Mr HUGH STONE.
ROBERT READING.
ELISABETH WEBSTER.

    9. ROGER ye Son of ROGER COWLEY Esq^s & SUSANNA his Wife.
ANN ye Wife of THOMAS HATTON.

  10. MARY ye Wife of PATRIC GOLANE.

  13. ANN ye daughter of JOHN SMITH.
MARGARET ye Wife of ROBERT CHANDLER.

  14. JOHN HART.

  15. DEARMAN SUILLIVANT, out of prison.

  16. CHRISTOPHER ye Son of Major JOHN HALLET & MARY his wife.

  17. JOHN LOCKTON.
JANE ELLIOT.

  19. SAMUEL OKELLY.

  21. MARY ye daughter of WILLIAM RICHARDSON.

  23. JAMES BAYNS.
JOHN KELLEY from ye Almshous.

  24. ELISABETH BLANCHFLOWER.
THOMAS MARSHAL.

  31. Mr JOSEPH RUMSEY from ye prison.
WILLIAM SHIRLEY.

November. 1. SARAH BLACKMAN.
JOHN ye Son of WILLIAM & DORCAS MORRIS.

  3. SUSANNA ye daughter of HENRY & ANN BUNTING.

  4. JOHN ye Son of JOHN & ELISABETH MURRIL.

  5. ELISABETH HUNT.

  6. GEORG ELLIOT.

  7. ZECHARIAH DUNSTHORP.

  15. KATHARIN ye Wife of DANIEL ONEAL.

  16. MARY ye Wife of ABEL DEAN.

  18. JOHN ye Son of JOHN BAILY & JANE CONNER.

  19. MARY ye Wife of Mr RICHARD TUDOR.

1678.

November. 23. MARY yᵉ Wife of JOHN BRUSH.

    24. Mʳ THOMAS BONNET.

    26. THOMAS GRANT.

        ANNA HENRY yᵉ daughter of ANTHONY HENRY.

    27. WILLIAM yᵉ Son of JOHN & ANN SHREWSBURY.

    30. JAMES JONAS.

December. 2. ELISABETH SMITH.

        ROBERT CLARK.

     3. GEORG POET.

     5. FRANCIS PETERSON.

     6. Mʳ JOSEPH HUSSEY.

    11. HANNAH HARRIS.

        WILLIAM BROUGHTON.

    12. ELISABETH yᵉ daughter of MARY TANNER.

    15. JANE DAVIS.

    16. JOHN WALKER.

    17. MARY yᵉ daughter of WILLIAM BLACKMAN.

        A poor woman from Dʳ DE VILLERMARSK.

    19. PHOEBE yᵉ Wife of Mʳ WILLIAM CAPS.

    24. THOMAS yᵉ Son of THOMAS & JANE PARIS.

    25. ANN yᵉ Wife of Mʳ JOSEPH WARREN.

    26. ABIGAIL yᵉ Wife, and ELISABETH yᵉ daughter of THOMAS
        COOPER.

    29. NATHANIEL LANE.

        ELISABETH MACKARTEE.

    30. BENJAMIN GODBEHERE.

January. 4. WILLIAM PARSONS.

     7. HENRY FERN.

     8. ROBERT GILBERT.

    10. BENJAMIN yᵉ Son of BENJAMIN & AMEY JONES.

    11. EDWARD MACKLOGHLIN.

        ELISABETH yᵉ Wife of JOHN ADAMS, alias ADAMSON.

    12. ELISABETH yᵉ Wife of CHRISTOPHER BANCROFT.

        JOHN HORTON.

        ELISABETH RUMLEY.

1678.

January. 14. M<sup>s</sup> BARNET y<sup>e</sup> Wife of M<sup>r</sup> WILLIAM BARNET.

    15. M<sup>r</sup> EDWARD CRISP, Merch<sup>t</sup>
        CHARLS y<sup>e</sup> Son of CHARLS CAVENAUGH.

    17. DAVID MAYO.

    30. SAMUEL COLLINS.

    31. CORNELIUS SUILLIVANT.

February. 4. DAVID MILLER.

    6. JOHN y<sup>e</sup> Son of M<sup>r</sup> JOHN HAM & SUSANNA his Wife.
        BERNARD CORNELIUS, a Norman belonging to y<sup>e</sup> *Endeavor*
           of N. England, SAM. SMITH, Com<sup>r</sup>

    9. EDWARD BERRIDG.

    10. ELISABETH y<sup>e</sup> daughter of EDWARD & JONE GISLINGHAM.

    12. MARGARET y<sup>e</sup> Wife of PETER BEAL.

    13. REBECCA y<sup>e</sup> daughter of ROBERT & GRACE GRIFFITH.

    14. ANN PATRIC Serv<sup>t</sup> to SUSAN HALL.
        BARBARA y<sup>e</sup> daughter of MARY TAILOR.

    15. EDWARD FARTHING belonging to y<sup>e</sup> *Endeavor* of London,
        JAMES GILBERT Com<sup>r</sup>

    20. MARY y<sup>e</sup> daughter of M<sup>r</sup> JOHN SMITH & PHILIPPA his Wife.
        JAMES y<sup>e</sup> Son of ROGER & SARAH DYER.

    21. MICHAEL ROGERS, belonging to his M<sup>ties</sup> Frigat, y<sup>e</sup> *Europa*,
        Capt. WILL. LONG Com<sup>r</sup>

    26. JOHN BUCKLY Serv<sup>t</sup> to M<sup>r</sup> BROOKS.

    27. JONATHAN y<sup>e</sup> Son of THOMAS & SARAH ELLARCE.*

    28. JOHN RICHARDSON.

March 3. GEORG ADSON.

    6. HENRY SMITH.

    9. JONATHAN y<sup>e</sup> Son of ROBERT & ELISABETH PAIN.

    10. WILLIAM ROSE.
        ELISABETH BROWN.
        ELISABETH TESTER.

    12. GEORG BRADLEY.

    13. ELISABETH y<sup>e</sup> daughter of MUES WALFORD.

    21. MARY LETHERLAND.

* [This name *may* be read ELLAREE.]

1679.

March. 26. WALTER BUSH.

28. Capt. ANDREW RICHES Com^r of y^e *White Fox* of London, & his Son SAMUEL RICHES, who were both killd by ye bursting of a gun.

31. JACOB BASTIONS, Servt to Mr LATIMER RICHARDS of St Georges.

April. 1. JAMES FOWLER.
GRISSEL ALLEN.

2. ELISABETH WILSON, from ye almshous.
SARAH ye daughter of CHARLS & MARTHA LEIGH.

5. RICHARD THOROGOOD.

12. JOHN SUTTON.

14. ZEBULON ye Son of Mr JOHN CUNNINGHAM & ANN his Wife.
ELISABETH ELLIOT, Widdow.

15. THOMAS ye Son of DANIEL & ELISABETH FRISSEL.

17. THOMAS STRANFELLOW.
ELISABETH WILLIAMS.

18. ELISABETH ye daughter of STEPHEN & MARY WILSON.

20. MARY ye Wife of Mr JOSEPH SMITH, Merch^t
CORNELIUS MACKELLY.

21. ELISABETH DICK.
STEPHEN ye Son of JOHN LIZARD.

22. ELISABETH BEACHAM.
WILLIAM AVERY.

24. HENRY GITLY.

26. MARY UNDERWOOD.

27. THOMAS FERRIMAN.

May. 1. JOSEPH ye Son of GEORG & HANNAH OATS.

2. EDWARD LEEK.
GEORG SPAR.

3. JOHN BRUNCOCK.

4. ELIAS BLACKWELLER.

6. ANN TROWSDALE.
THOMAS BOON.

1679.

May.	7.	Mr ROBERT BLAKE.

May. 7. Mr ROBERT BLAKE.

    9. MARY ye Wife of DENIS COCKLIN.

    .,. HUMPHREY KELLEY.

       JANE ATKINS.

       Mr GREGORY HALLET.

    23. ANN RAYMENT.

    24. TEAG MULLINS.

       ROBERT DANES.

    25. PHILLIS ye Wife of JOHN KINGSTON.

    29. JOHN JONES

    30. JAMES ye Son of Mr WILLIAM BOWEN.

    31. Mr JOHN GILLIARD of y^e *Guianabo* of London, SAM. JONES Com^r

June. 1. SAGE ye Wife of JAMES ANDREWS.

       ELISABETH ye Wife of THOMAS LAMBERT.

       RICHARD HENDY of y^e *Coast Frigat*, Capt. VARLOW, Com^{r.}

    2. SUSAN ye wife of EDWARD WALKER.

       ISAAC HOGDON.

       GEORG POTTER.

    3. PRUDENCE ye wife of Mr GEORG PEARSON.

    4. EDWARD REEVS.

       Mr WILLIAM BRAG.

    5. ARTHUR Servt to JOHN RICHARDSON.

    7. JOYCE ye daughter of EDENDEN.

    8. Capt. HENRY HAWLEY.

    9. ANN ye Wife of HENRY BRADLEY.

    11. HENRY KIRBY, a Seaman.

       WILLIAM WATSON of y^e *Ruth*, THEOPHILUS POMEROY, Com^r

       ISAAC COLE belonging to a Guiney-ship, JEHU HAL Com^{r.}

    12. JOHN ye Son of ANTHONY & ELISABETH SUILLIVANT.

       ANN ye Wife of THOMAS HENWOOD.

    13. ELISABETH ye Wife of Mr EDWARD PARIS.

    16. JOHN BROWN of y^e *Friendship*, JOHN WILLIAMS Com^{r.}

    17. THOMAS ATKINS.

    18. ELISABETH TAGGARD.

1679.

June. 19. RICHARD MAY.

20. NICHOLAS FRANCKLIN.

21. SARAH ye daughter of Mr GABRIEL MORGAN & MARY his Wife.

23. WILLIAM MANSFIELD.

24. Mr RICHARD PIERCE.

KATHARIN CARVIS.

EDWARD ye Son of EDWARD WALKER.

27. ROBERT LANE, from ye almshous.

28. BARNS PASTOR.

MATTHEW BENTHAM, Servt to L.Col. CODRINGTON.

29. SARAH BLACKWELLER.

30. ANTHONY HAYLEY.

July. 2. ELISABETH ye daughter of GABRIEL & MARY MORGAN.

3. Capt. EVAN MORGAN.

4. Capt. WILLIAM LONG Com^r of his M^{ties} Ship y^e *Europa,* buried in ye Sea.

6. GRACE HARVEY, Widdow.

7. MARY ye Wife of THOMAS STRATTON.

8. JOHN DICK.

JOHN BUCKLY, from ye almshous.

9. GABRIEL MORGAN.

DAVID FOGO, from ye almshous.

Mr THOMAS BALDWIN.

11. JANE ye Wife of HENRY KARVIS.

Mr JOHN CUNNINGHAM.

12. Mr EDMUND DAWSON.

13. TIMOTHY GARMAN.

14. CASSANDRA ye wife of EDWARD WILLIAMS.

Mr JOHN COTTON.

15. JANE BAGGET.

ROBERT ye Son of JANE DEMPSTER, Widd.

17. JANE WARD.

18. JOHN ROBERTS, from ye prison.

1679.

July 18. PETER GASCOIGN.

     19. MARY BUCKLY.

          MARTIN STITH.

          PHILLIP BRIAN.

     21. RICHARD VANLANG.

          SARAH ABBEY.

          WILLIAM BUNNEY, from yᵉ almshous.

          ELENOR daughter of MARY BRIAN, Widd.

     22. MARY MORRIS a Christian Negro.

          PHILIPPA yᵉ Wife of Mʳ JOHN SMITH, Mercht.

     23. Sʳ THOMAS WARNER, Kᵗ

     24. GEORG SMITH, a Trumpetter to C. ROBINSON.

     25. MARY yᵉ daughter of JOHN WOODLAND.

          Mʳ JOHN RICHARDSON.

     26. WILLIAM ABRAHAM.

          JOHN yᵉ Son of MARY WOODYARD.

     27. NATHANIEL THOMAS.

August.4. WILLIAM ANDERSON.

          ANN yᵉ wife of PATRIC CAMPEL.

          SARAH yᵉ daughter of C. JOHN JOHNSON & SARAH his Wife.

      5. EDWARD PARSONS.

      6. FRANCIS yᵉ son of C. FRANCIS BURTON & JUDITH his Wife.

      7. JOHN VINCENT.

      8. ELISABETH yᵉ daughter of Mʳ RICHARD & HANNAH
              BUNNY.

          Col. GEORG THORNBURGH.

      9. RALPH MONTREVERS.

          JAMES DODSWORTH.

          JOHN WILLIAMSON.

     15. MARY yᵉ Wife of Mʳ JOHN COCK.

          THOMAS BANKS.

     17. ELISABETH FREEMAN.

          Mʳ GULLIVER.

     18. ISAAC yᵉ Son of ANTHONY SANDS.

          DANIEL LAWRENCE.

1679.

August. 18. JANE, from ye almshous.

    JAMES, ditto.

  19. ELISABETH DICK.

  20. TEAG CONNER.

  21. ELISABETH JEFFRYS.

    MANUS CALLEN.

  23. MARY ye Wife of JOHN WORSAM, Esqr

  26. JOHN BAL.

  27. ELISABETH ye daughter of Mr WILLIAM BARNS & SARAH his Wife.

  28. THOMAS STRAFFORD.

    CHARLS HARRISON.

    MUNDUSIA ye daughter of JOHN & ELISABETH SMITH.

September. 2. CICILY ye Wife of JOHN MILES.

  4. ESTHER ye daughter of FRANCIS & ELISABETH HAL.

  5. M^s JULIAN NELSON Widd. aged 92 years.

  6. Mr ROBERT PALMER aged 95 years.

  7. JOHN GREENWOOD.

    JANE DEMPSTER.

    Capt. THOMAS CRUTCHFIELD Com^{r.} of y^e *Lisbon Merch^t* of London.

  11. EDWARD HARDING aged 70 & odd years.

    DOROTHY SUTTON.

  12. JOSEPH ye Son of JOSEPH & MARGARET SALMON.

  14. NICHOLAS BARNWEL from Mr REYNOLDS'S.

  16. DANIEL OREE, from ye almshous.

    ESTHER MORGAN.

    ELISABETH ERPEY.

    MARTIN SWAIN.

  17. THOMAS SMITH.

  18. MARY ye Wife of JOHN HARE.

  19. ALICE ye Wife of THOMAS FOLINSBY.

  20. Mr HENRY TURPIN aged 87 years.

  23. KATHARIN CARYL.

1679.

September. 24. Mr EDWARD PRESTON.

        GEORG ye Son of Capt. FRANCIS BURTON & JUDITH his Wife.

     25. ALEXANDER MACKRERY from L.Col. JELLY'S.

        ELISABETH RUL.

        RICHARD ye Son of RICHARD & JONE ELLIOT.

     26. SUSANNA ye daughter of Mr THOMAS & SUSANNA REYNOLDS.

        WILLIAM LAWLESS, out of prison.

     27. JOHN COOPER.

     29. JOHN ye Son of Mr THOMAS & JANE FORRESTER.

421.

Año: 1680

BARBADOS

LIST of the Inhabitants in and about the Towne of St Michaells wth their children hired Seruants, Prentices, bought Seruants and Negroes.

	childrn	hired Seru^{ts} & Preñt	bought Seru^{ts}	Neg^{rs}
ALLAN LYDE & wife............	3	..	..	6
HENRY MOSELY & wife	..	..	..	6
WIll^m BISHOP & wife......... ...	5	..	..	5
EDWARD DUFFEILD & wife......	I	..	..	2
BENJ^a GRACE jun^r & wife........	2	..	..	2
ANTHONY MICHELL & wife......	5	..	..	2
THOMAS GARROTT & wife	2	..	..	2
SARAH WAKER	..	..	O	2
ABRAHAM LANGFORD	..	..	..	I
GEORGE PEARCE & wife	..	I	O	2

	children	hired Seru.ts & Preñt	bought Seru.ts	Neg.rs
JOHN BARKER	..	I	O	I
JOHN BORROWS................	..	2	..	I
GEORGE TUTHILL..............	..	..	..	3
OLLIUER HUTTON & wife	I	..	..	4
SAMUELL BRUNTTS & Comp.a ...	..	..	..	4
DANIELL CLANEY & wife	I	..	..	2
REBECCAH JONES	..	..	..	3
JOHN ORPEN & wife...........	..	3	2	5
JOSEPH SMITH	..	..	..	4
W.M BULKLY	..	I	..	I
ALLEXANDER HARBIN & wife ..	..	..	..	I
W.M HARDING & wife	I	I	..	6
WALTER BENTHALL & wife	..	..	..	6
SAMUELL CARPENDER	..	..	..	4
JOHN COSTEEN & wife.........	..	3	..	8
JOSEPH HARBIN & wife	3	I	..	8
W.M STICKLAND & wife.........	I	..	..	3
THOMAS EMPEROR & wife	2	..	I	10
RICHARD WILLIAMS & wife	3	..	2	3
STEPHEN LANGTON & wife......	..	..	I	4
HENRY DEUILLERMAS & wife ..	2	I	I	2
JAMES SICKLEMORE	..	..	..	2
JOHN BUSSHELL Senior & wife ..	2	..	..	7
THOMAS DOXY & wife	I	I	..	3
JOHN HUTTON & wife	5	..	..	..
THOMAS WATTSON & wife	I	2	2	8
LUCY BUTTLER................	..	I	..	3
JOHN WHETTSTON & wife	2	..	..	5
HENRY CROFTS & wife	2	..	..	5
CHRISTOPHER FOWLER	..	I	..	5
RICH.D DEARSLEY & wife	..	..	..	2
THOMAS SMITH & wife	I	5	..	3
PETER BAKER & wife	..	..	..	2

	children	hired Serᵗᵗˢ & Preñttˢ	bought Seruᵗᵗˢ	Slaues
THOMAS CLARKE & wife	1	..	2	1
Jnᵒ OGLESBY & wife	4	3	1	6
LETTECIA BATE	..	1	..	4
Robᵗᵗ DRAPER	..	2	..	5
Jnᵒ SMITH	2	3	1	12
Jnᵒ HARUEY	1	..	..	3
Richᴰ FORSTALL	..	..	2	..
JOSEPH GROUE	..	1	..	4
Jnᵒ MERCER	..	..	..	1
THOMAS PERCE & wife	2	4	5	8
Richᴰ LENNON & wife	..	..	..	4
Jnᵒ FELTON & wife	1	3	5	16
JAMES POKE & wife	6	2	1	4
FRANCIS CRISTIAN & wife	7	3	2	3
MUSE WALFORD & wife	4	..	1	1
ANNE OWEN	..	..	2	6
CHARLES COLLINS & wife	2	1	..	8
Richᴰ SHETMAN & wife	..	..	..	3
Wᴹ CRITCHLOW & wife	2	1	2	7
GEORGE HARPER & wife	..	2	..	..
Collᵒ BATTE	..	1	..	1
Capᵗᵗ Jnᵒ JOHNSON & wife	4	4	3	20
OLLIUER SMITTH	..	4	..	..
Jnᵒ SMARTT	..	1	..	2
THOMAS BREARLY & wife	..	1	1	6
JEREMIAH COOKE & Compᵃ	..	6	..	5
ELIZABETH BANCKS	2	..	..	4
Wᴹ SMITH & wife	..	..	..	1
Jnᵒ PITT	..	..	..	3
OWEN DAUIS	..	..	..	1
Widᵈᵒ CRISP	1	..	..	4
PAUL GWYNE & wife	1	..	..	6
Wᴹ GOLD & wife	..	..	..	5

	children	hired scrut^ts & Prett^s	bought seru^tts	Slaues
HUMRY BROWNE & wife	..	..	..	3
J^no COSSENS	..	..	..	1
GEORGE FLETTCHER & wife	..	4	2	12
Capt THOMAS MORRIS & wife....	3	3	..	11
J^no RAYMON	..	1	..	
THOMAS MOUNTAINE & wife	..	..	..	1
JAMES SHARPE & wife	2	..	..	3
THOMAS HOLLARD & wife	3	2	11	18
J^no HIGGINBOTHAM & wife	..	..	2	3
J^no NEWBOTT & wife	..	7	..	1
J^no COCK	..	..	..	1
Widd^o THORNBRUGH	3	..	1	8
THOMAS SEARLE & wife	1	..	..	6
THO: BLAKE & wife	..	..	..	2
THO: ASHENDINE...............	..	..	..	2
GEORGE MASON	..	..	..	1
M^rs: MAGETTESS	..	..	..	4
KATH: TOYER	..	..	..	1
THOMAS LAMBORNE & wife	..	..	..	2
RICH^D BRISTOW & wife	..	2	..	
Wm HOLLYDAY & wife	4	..	1	
Wm BROOKE & wife	3	..	..	5
J^no HALLETT Esqr & wife	5	3	2	14
ROGER CORBITT & wife	..	..	..	9
ANTH^o PRINCE & wife	..	1	..	5
Wm BICKNALL	..	0	1	2
MARTIN CREAMER	..	..	..	2
J^no CHOLEMLEY	..	..	..	2
Wm EMBEREE.................	..	..	2	2
J^no CRISP jun^r & wife	..	..	..	2
RICH^D PARKER & wife	1	1	..	4
J^no STUARD & wife	..	1	..	8
RICH^D TRANTT	..	..	1	4

56

	children	hired scru^{tts} & Pren^{tts}	boug^t scru^{tts}	Slaus
HUGH ARCHER & wife..........	..	3	..	6
GEORGE SNOUKS	..	1	..	
GEORGE NEDHAM & wife	2	1	..	6
W^M SANDERS	..	1	..	1
Widd^o TURPIN	..	0	..	..
ROB^{TT} TATT'S..................	..	02	..	..
W^M PRICE	..	..		
W^M BAYNES & wife	..	0	0	0
JAMES VICKARS & wife..........	..	2	2	1
THOMAS BISHOP & wife	..	..	..	2
ROGER DYER & wife	..	0	..	1
RICH^D BUNNEY & wife	1	1	..	3
CHARLES JUES [?IVES] & wife....	1	1	..	2
J^{No} HANCOCK & wife	..	1	..	
RICH^D NUSOM & wife	1	..	1	4
MARY DOUE	..	..	..	1
RICH^D ATTWOOD & wife	..	2	..	5
Mrs DAUIS	..	..	..	1
SAMUELL MEAD & wife	3	..	..	9
Widd^o LAROCH	..	..	..	2
W^M CAPPS	..	..	1	3
J^{No} PUDDIFORD & wife..........	..	1	..	3
DANIELL BREWER	..	1	..	1
GAMALIELL ELLIS	..	..	..	2
Widd^o BUSH	..	1	..	..
STEPHEN SCAR & wife	..	1	..	3
NATHANIELL ELDRED & wife....	..	1	..	2
J^{No} JOHNSON & wife	..	..	..	1
RICH^D POORE & wife............	..	1	..	1
ROGER ANDERSON & wife	1	..	..	3
J^{No} BOLES	..	..	..	2
NICHOLAS MOLDER & wife	..	..	..	4
J^{No} HUDSON & wife............	..	2	..	2

	children	hired scrutts & Prentts	bought scruts	Slaues
J^{no} PRINCE & wife	..	..	..	I
J^{no} HOPCROFTT & wife	..	O	I	2
ROB^{TT} LANDALL & wife	..	..	5	..
ROB^{TT} GRAY & wife	..	3	..	4
Widd^o SMITH	..	..	..	I
ABELL DEANE	..	I	..	I
THOMAS FORRESTOR & wife	..	I	I	5
XTOPHER AKERS & wife........	..	3	..	..
J^{no} CRESWELL & wife	..	..	..	2
ANDREW HAWKINS & wife......	..	..	I	I
HESTER LANE	..	..	..	I
HENRY JACOBS & wife..........	..	..	I	5
THOMAS WRIGHTT & wife	..	..	..	3
J^{no} COOCKE & wife	..	..	..	4
THO: READ & wife	..	..	..	I
J^{no} COPPIN sen^r & wife	..	..	..	5
THOMAS SIMSON & wife	..	..	..	I
FRANCIS BESTT & wife..........	..	..	..	2
AMBROSS ADDAMS	..	..	..	I
W^M CRAGG...................	..	..	..	I
W^M PARRIS....................	..	..	..	2
ROB^{TT} LANIER & wife	..	3	..	..
XTOPHER FRANKLING & wife ..	..	..	..	2
ABRAHAM FIFEILD & wife	I	..	..	I
JOHN OLLIUER & wife..........	..	I	..	I
Widd^o BAINES	4	..	..	4
BENIAMIN RAWLINGS & wife	..	..	..	2
J^{no} PEIRCESON	..	..	..	3
SAMUELL SOURTON	..	4	..	I
RICH^D HALLETT	..	I	..	4
BENJ^A MATTSON & wife	2	..	..	2
EDWARD STURDIUANTT	..	..	..	I
HUGH HALL & wife...........	2	..	..	8

	child[r]	hired seruan[tts] & Prett[s]	bought seru[tts]	Slaues
J[no] BARNES	..	..	I	2
J[no] DEUENISH & wife	2	..	..	4
J[no] FIREBRASS & wife	..	..	I	
ROB[tt] HUSSEY & wife	2	..	..	6
MATHEW HAUILAND	..	2	..	I
JACOB LEGAY	..	I	I	3
J[no] MAN & wife	5	..	..	6
ROB[tt] BECKLES & wife	3	..	I	4
JUDITH SPARROW	I	..	..	11
HENRY FISSHER & wife	3	..	..	11
ROB[tt] RICH jun[r] & wife	I	..	..	13
Widd[o] BRAGG	3	..	..	2
SAMUELL GIFFORD & wife	2	..	I	5
MARTIN HAYES & wife	I	..	I	
SAMUELL STOKER & wife	2	..	..	4
THOMAS WARNER & wife	3	..	I	7
W[m] CANNINGS & wife	2	..	..	8
BRIDGETT COLLETT	2	I	..	4
THOMAS LOWE & wife	..	I	..	2
SAMUELL BALLARD & wife	I	I	..	I
THOMAS FERCHARSON & wife	5	2	..	17
PHILLIP TRAUERS	..	..	I	10
GEORGE NEWTON	..	..	I	I
J[no] BAYLEY & wife	2	I	..	5
EDWARD PARSONS & wife	2	2	..	12
Widd[o] BARROWMAN	..	..	..	2
GABRIELL NEWMAN & wife	3	..	..	4
MARY CHAPMAN	I	..	..	5
RICH[D] ADDAMSON & wife	4	I	..	9
BENJ[A] HASSELL	..	..	I	2
ROB[tt] STONE & wife	I	..	..	I
THOMAS DOD & wife	5	I	..	2
W[m] WILSON & wife	2	3	..	11

	children	hired seruantˢ & Prenttˢ	bougtt seruttˢ	Slaues
JOSEPH BORDEN & wife	2	I	..	14
SAMUELL PARRIS	..	I	..	I
RICHᴰ TUDAR & wife	2	..	3	16
MATHEW DEANE & wife	2	2	O	2
JNᵒ HASELL & wife	3	2	..	20
SAMUELL SHENTON & wife......	..	2	..	3
GUY & wife	..	I	..	..
Wᴹ LITTON & wife	5	I	..	I
HENRY LELLAND & wife........	3	..	..	3
JNᵒ LEGAY	2	I	..	II
THOMAS HESLERTON & wife	I	..	..	3
EDMOND JEFFERRES & wife	..	..	..	6
Widdᵒ SEAY	2	..	..	6
THOMAS PILGRIM & wife........	..	2	..	..
GEORGE BREAD & wife	..	..	..	3
Wᴹ JORDAN & wife	I	I	I	5
Wᴹ COPE & wife	5	..	..	6
THOMAS ELES & wife	I	4	..	4
THOMAS HORNER & wife	2	..	..	3
Wᴹ PRESWELL	..	2	..	..
THEOPHILUS BARRODALL	3	..	..	2
DOWNES DANIELL	..	..	..	2
JAMES TAGGARTT & wife........	..	..	..	4
NATHANIELL CLAIRE & wife	..	3	I	10
JNᵒ HUDSON & wife	2	I	2	3
OLLIUER GILHAMPTON & wife ..	3	..	I	3
THOMAS CLOUAN & wife........	2	..	..	I
NICHOLAS MAYNARD & wife	5	..	..	2
GEORGE OATES & wife.........	..	I	..	2
BARNARD MAN & wife	..	I	..	2
JNᵒ DAUIS & wife	..	..	..	2
JNᵒ MURRELL & wife	2	..	..	2
Widdᵒ BOUEY	..	..	I	..

	children	hired seruant & Prentt[s]	bougtt serutt.	Slaues
W[M] HARDING Vintner & wife	..	1	1	1
THOMAS TICKNER & wife	..	..	2	3
VALLENTINE COPMAN & wife....	1	..	..	4
W[M] SHIPTON & wife	1	2	..	5
GEORGE CHEYNEY & wife	1	1	..	2
J[NO] BRADHAM	..	1	..	..
OWEN DAYLEY & wife..........	1	1	1	1
FRANCIS WOOD & wife	1	..	..	4
HENRY BYRCH & wife	1	1	..	6
ROB[TT] HOLE & wife	1	..	1	8
MATHEW WILLOX & wife	1	..	1	3
J[NO] HEATON	..	..	1	1
RICH[D] WILSON & wife	2	1	..	4
W[M] BIDDLE & wife	2	1	..	3
M[RS] HOSKINS	2	..	1	0
BENJ[A] ELLY & wife	1	..	1	
GEORGE HANNAH & wife	2	4	2	10
J[NO] HUNTER & wife...........	..	..	1	4
RICH[D] ALFORD & wife	2	3	3	5
THOMAS WHITEING & wife.....	1	8	3	14
THOMAS BRINGHURST & wife....	..	5	2	5
J[NO] HAYWOOD & wife	1	..	..	3
HENRY FREMAN & wife	2	5	1	3
J[NO] PLUMLY p EL: BROWNE ...	..	..	..	9
EDWARD TOWNE & wife	..	..	..	3
LAUGHLINE BAYNE & wife	..	1	..	0
THOMAS WALDEN & wife	1	..	..	2
BENJ[A] JONES & wife	..	..	..	1
W[M] CLIGGATT & wife	1	3	1	
LAWRANCE REED & wife.......	..	..	..	1
ROB[TT] HEWITT & wife..........	1	3	..	13
EDWARD HUNTT & wife	3	..	..	5
NATHANIELL BRANKER & wife ..	1	..	..	5

	children	hired seru^{tts} & Pren^{tts}	bough^t seru^{tts}	Slaues
NATHANIELL SMITH & wife	2	..	..	1
STEPHEN GASCOYNE Esqr & wife .	..	7	1	0
EDWINE STEED Esqr & wife	2	1	..	7
BENJ^A DWEIGHTT & wife ,.......	3	..	..	12
THOMAS REYNOLDSON & wife ..	..	..	3	3
HENRY STEBING	..	3	..	1
RICH^D FORD & wife	1	..	..	2
HENRY HARUEY & wife	..	1	..	3
J^{NO} FREDERICK & wife..........	..	6	..	
THOMAS PARKER	..	1	3	1
JAMES ELY & wife	3	1	1	13
JONATHAN HUTCHINSON........	..	..	..	5
URSELAH PEA	..	..	..	4
RICH^{D:} HALL & wife	3	..	..	7
W^M WELDING	1	..	..	3
THEOPHILUS BOWDEN	..	..	..	1
J^{NO} LEGARD	..	..	..	2
J^{NO} SANDERS & wife...........	2	..	..	1
STEPHEN CLAY & wife..........	1	..	..	2
JACOB: MACKERNESS & wife	..	2	..	4
W^M SIDNEY & wife	5	3	..	7
THOMAS BIFFIN & wife	2	..	..	2
RICH^D BARRETT	..	..	..	7
THOMAS ROWSE & wife	..	7	..	3
Mrs TOTHILL	1	..	..	1
SAMUELL SMARTT & wife	1	2	..	13
SUSANAH BEEKE	..	..	..	5
W^M MICHLEBORNE & wife	..	1	..	2
J^{NO} FISHER	..	..	..	1
JACOB: LEGAY sen^r	2	1	..	3
CHRISTOPHER JACSON & wife....	1	1	..	5
W^M MACKERNESS	1	3	..	2
Widd^o HAYWOOD	..	..	..	2

	children	hired serutts & Prentts	bought serutts	Slaues
EDWARD PRESTTON	..	..	..	I
Widdᵒ BALDWINE	..	I	..	7
Jᴺᵒ TOWNSEND & wife	2	..	..	4
Jᴺᵒ MUNROW & wife	..	..	..	I
Jᴺᵒ SHROESBERRY & wife	I	..	..	I
Jᴺᵒ MILLS & wife	..	..	..	7
ISAAC ROETT..................	..	I	I	5
CHARLES LEE & wife	..	..	..	I
BENJᴬ BIRD & wife	2	I	..	I
BASELL DUNKLY & wife	..	I	..	
MARTIN DALLISON & wife	..	2	..	6
MARY LISTER	..	..	..	I
ANNE KEW	..	..	..	I
KATHRINE WHITEING..........	..	..	..	2
Jᴺᵒ HUNTER	2	..	..	I
Jᴺᵒ SPENCER & wife...........	2	3	..	3
Wᴹ MAXWELL & wife	I	..	..	I
Doctor RICHARD LAWFORD	..	..	..	I
THOMAS PARRIS & wife	2	..	..	I
EDWARD RAINSFORD	..	2	..	4
SAMUELL DYER	..	I	..	2
EDWARD PEIRESON & wife	I	..	..	I
MARKE NOBLE & wife	I	I	..	4
FRANCIS LOUELL..............	..	I	..	9
JOHN CHASON & wife	2	I	..	..
Wᴹ BEALE	..	..	..	2
DANIELL JONES	..	I	..	5
PETER SWAINE & wife.........	3	..	I	4
Jᴺᵒ LADSTON & wife	..	..	..	3
ELLINOR WALTER	2	..	..	2
Jᴺᵒ WILLIAMS & wife	4	..	..	2
Jᴺᵒ LAMPLY & wife	I	..	..	I
MARY BUSHER	..	..	..	3

	children	hired seruen^{ts} & Pren^{ts}	bought scru^{tt}	Slaues
MARY WILSON	..	..	..	I
J^{NO} RAWLINGS & wife	..	..	2	I
JAMES MILLER & wife	..	I	..	I
EDWARD FENNELL & wife	I	..	..	4
JONATHAN TAYLOR & wife	..	..	..	3
W^M SIMMES & wife	I	..	..	8
ROB^{TT} WEBSTER & wife	..	..	I	..
ROB^{TT} PAINE & wife	6	I	I	2
J^{NO} PAINE & wife	..	..	..	I
J^{NO} STEDHAM	..	..	..	2
MADAM FITS JAMES............	..	..	..	2
THE JEWES	Jewes			
JACOB FRANCO NUNES..........	4	..	..	I
ARON NAUARO	7	..	..	I I
ARON BARRUCH	5	..	..	5
PAUL DEUREDE.................	2	..	..	3
ISAAC PERERA	2	..	..	4
DAUID RALPH DEMEREADO	3	..	..	I I
LEWIS DIAS	6	..	..	8
ABRAHAM QAY	2	..	..	2
ABRAHAM BARRUCH	3	..	..	3
DAUID ISRAELL................	5	..	..	3
ANTHONY RODRIGUS	3	..	..	10
ABRAHAM SOUSA	2	..	..	2
LEAH MEDINAH	7			
ISACK ABOF	2	..	..	I
ABRAHAM BURGES ARON	2	..	..	2
MOSES HAMIAS	2	..	..	I
M^{RS} LEAH DECOMPAS	3	..	..	I
HESTER BAR SIMON............	5	..	..	I
DANIELL BOYNA	3	..	..	I I
ABRAHAM LOPES	2	..	..	I
ABR: VALUERDE	2	..	..	4

	Psons	slaues		Psons	slaues
JUDIEAH TOREZ	2	2	SAMUELL NAUARRO....	4	I
MOSES MERCADO	5	2	RACHELL BURGES	6	2
JAELL SERANO	I	5	MORDECAH PALACHE ..	I	
ELIAH LOPEZ.........	5	2	REBECAH PACHECO	2	4
ISAAC GOMEZ	3	2	REBECAH BARRUCH	I	I
JOSEPH SENIOR	3	4	JACOB PACHECO........	5	4
ISAAC PERERA	6	3	RACHELL LOPEZ	4	I
ISACK MEZA	3	4	JACOB FONCECO VALE..	5	4
SOLOMAN CORDOZA	3	2	MORDECAH SARAH	4	I
ABRAHAM OBEDIENTE..	2	2	SAMUELL DECHAUIS ..	2	4
JUDITH RISSON	4	2	DAUID SWARIS	5	2
DAUID NAMIAS	9	5	JUDITH NAUARO	2	I
MOSES ARROBAS	4	2	HESTER NOY..........	2	
GABRIELL ANTUNES ..	2	4	JUDIH ISRAELL	2	
JACOB PREETT	I	I	MOSES DESAUIDO	5	3
SARAH ATKINS........	I	..	ISACC NOY	6	2
ABRAHAM COSTANIO ..	2	6			

Total of Inhabit.......... 404.

Mem^d that y^e Town of St Michael
only has returnd an Acco^t. of
Children

Total of Inhabitants .. $\left\{ \begin{array}{l} \text{Men......404} \\ \text{Children ..402} \end{array} \right\}$ 806.

Total of White servants 412

Total of Negroes .... 1325.

[BARBADOES.]

LIST of Owners and possessors of land Hired Seruants & Apprentices, Bought Seruants & Negroes in ye Parish of St. Michaells.*

A	acres land	hired Seru^ts	bought Seru^ts	Neg^rs
THOMAS ASHENDINE	5	..	..	3
BARTHO ALDSWORTH	46	..	..	16
ANTHONY ANTHONY	1ç	1	..	15
CORNELIOUS AUSTRIAN	6	..	..	6
ALLIN THOMAS................	7	3	..	10
ALEXANDER ANTOR	7	..	..	2
JACOB. ALLEN	..	1	..	3
B	Ac'			
THEO: BARRADALL	4	..	..	1
BORDEN JOSEPH	9	..	..	..
BONETT EDW^D PLANT^A	88	2	1	94
FRANCIS BOND Esqr...........	160	3	5	93
Coll^o Wm BATE	125	1	1	60
FRANCIS BURTON	130	—	—	60
THOMAS BATSON	35	2	3	20
J^no BATTYNE jun^r	32	1	..	21
J^no BOUCHER	3	2	..	1
GEORGE BIRKEHEAD	8	1	..	10
HUGH BRANDON	25	1	—	6
J^no BIRD	6	..	..	2
J^no BARRON	14	..	..	6
HUMPHRY BROGDON	10	..	..	14
ALLICE BAINES	30	1	2	16
J^no BARNES	15	1	3	11

* [Totals are given in the original at the end of every page of MS., but are not carried forward ; as it is impossible to keep page for page with the MS., we have omitted them altogether, with the exception of the sum totals at end.]

	acres land	hired serutts	bougt Serlll	Negrs
Wᴹ Barron	19	I	..	15
Wᴹ Barnett..................	15	..	I	11
Jɴᵒ Brett	4	..	..	5
Joseph Beedle..............	8	..	3	4
Wᴹ Busshey	10	I	..	14
Jɴᵒ Bignall senʳ	7	...	4	11
Jɴᵒ Bignall junʳ	10	I	2	14
Mʳˢ Burnell..................	6	..	..	2
Wᴹ Bragg	10	..	..	2
Allexander Barraman	4	..	..	8
Jerreard Boucher	..	..	..	3
Phillip Brewster	5	..	..	3
Cornelious Bryan...........	14	I	I	9
Daniell Boyna	10	I	..	14

C	ac'	hired serutts	bougtt Sertts	Slau.
Capps. William	12	I	..	5
Jɴᵒ Crisp senʳ	56	I	2	7
Roger Cowley Esqʳ	88	I	3	40
Wᴹ Cannings	7	..	..	5
Mʳˢ Coather	15	I	..	8
Tho: Carnock Powis*	8	I	..	2
Jɴᵒ Chace..................	60	I	2	24
Patick Carney	5	..	..	I
Kathrin Cleaner †	20	I	..	4
Wᴹ Cliggatt	13	I	I	6
Chrictopher Coalē	5	..	..	I
James Cissell	22	I	..	16
Jɴᵒ Cleaner†	10	..	..	—
Tho: Clark dead*	20	..	..	—
Nicho. Chandler	5	..	..	—
Henry Cleauer	20	I	..	3

* [Thus erased in the original.]

† [So in the original : but see Cleauer [Cleaver] at the bottom of the page.]

	ac'	hired seru^tts	boug^tt Ser^tts	Slau^e
THO: COALE	39	..	..	4
J^no CODDRINGTON Esqr	300	I	5	137
THO. CHILD	7	I	..	13
BENJ^A CAIME	13	2	..	8
W^M COCKMAN	14	3	—	11
GEORGE CLARKE	20	..	..	6
SYMON COOPER	80	3	2	26
ALLEX: COACHMAN his Estate ..	8	..	..	..
HENRY CLARK	8	..	..	..
CORDIU PAULUS	..	..	..	7
J^no CATTLIN	5	..	..	..
BOHAM CARTER	5	..	..	..

D.	land	hired Seru^tts	bog^tt Ser^tts	Slaues
BENJ^A DWIGHT	25	I	..	13
DAUIS W^M	101	2	..	35
DUNIDGE W^M	15	I	..	4
THOMAS DRAYTON	12	I	I	7
JAMES DANEFF	5	..	..	4
J^no DICK	5	..	..	2
GILES DEBOYCE	16	I	2	7
DENNIS DOWELL	5	..	..	..
ROGER DUNN	7	..	..	2

E	acres land	boug^tt serutt^e	hired seru^tts	Negros
W^M EMBREE	10	..	..	I
J^no ELLIOTT	35	I	..	6
JAMES ARD	7	..	I	I
Mrs ELLACOTT	27	I	2	6
LAWRANCE ENGLAND ju^r	10	..	..	3
SEABORNE EGGINTON	2	..	..	I

	acres land	hired seru[tts]	bough[t] seru[tts]	Negroes
F.				
RICH[D] FORSTALL	294	4	6	129
GEORGE FLETCHER	10	..	..	..
J[NO] FARMER	179	3	5	93
HENRY FEAKE	8	1	..	3
RICH[D] FIFEILD	12	..	1	8
J[NO] FOWLER	8	1	..	1
PHILIP FONSEIRE	25	1	3	19
ROGER FAUELL...............				
ROB[TT] FEAUER	10	..	..	3
JOANE FULLER	30	1	1	16
FRANCIS FROSTT	..	..	..	7
G.				
BENJAMIN GRACE	10	1	2	10
RICH[D] GAYTON	26	1	1	26
ELLIZAB: GRITTON	50	1	2	26
ELLZ: GOODMAN	10	1	..	8
J[NO] GRIGGORY	204	1	4	85
PETER GODING	7	..	..	4

	land Ac'.	hired seru[tts]	boug[tt] Seru[tts]	Neg[rs]
H.				
HARRIS J[NO]	20	1	..	6
HALLETT J[NO] Esq[r]	220	4	5	84
HUTCHINSON J[NO].............	5	..	..	5
HAWKSWORTH J[NO]	63	1	..	18
SAMIELL HANSON	101	..	..	..
RALPH HASSELL	10	1	..	10
RICH[D] HOWELL & GUY Esq[rs]	605	5	20	405
SYMON HUNTT dead	40	1	..	24
FRANCIS HARDING	10	..	..	..

	land Ac'.	hired serv^{tts}	boug^{tt} Seru^{ts}	Neg^{rs}:
DANIELL HURLOW	17	1	1	5
CHRISTOPHER HOOPER	25	1	..	10
FRANCIS HALL	26	1	..	30
EDWARD HUNTT	5	..	..	..
J^{no} HAWKSWORTH*...........	63	1	1	20
DANIELL HARWOOD...........	10	..	..	2
J^{no} HANDY	56	1	2	49
EDWARD HARDING	3	..	..	3
SAMUELL HYATT	30	..	..	7
FRANCIS HARDWICK	10	..	..	..
J^{no} HAM.....................	20	..	..	..
Widd^{o} HAMBLIN	4	..	..	1
GEORG HARPER	20	1	..	10
Wm HECTHROP	14	..	..	12
Wm HEARST	10	..	..	9
J^{no} HILL	10	..	1	5
J^{no} HARE	..	..	..	3
J^{no} HIGGINBOTHAM	5	..	..	..
RALPH HOLLINSWORTH	10	..	..	5
SAMUELL HATHWAY	10	..	..	5

I	ac'	hired seru^{ts}	boug^{t} Seru^{ts}	Negroes
JACSON XTOPH:...............	11	1	2	28
THOMAS JELLY	200	3	10	70
J^{no} JEFFERRES	5	2	—	4
ALLEX JENNISON	3	..	..	..
J^{no} JOHNSON................	6	..	..	..
Wm JACOBS	..	..	..	3

K.

| HUMRY KENTT............... | 52 | 1 | 1 | 17 |

* [This name will also be found six lines from the bottom in p. 454; the number of servants, however, is different.]

	ac'	hired seru[tts]	boug[t] Seru[tts]	Negroes
L				
LEER THOMAS	234	2	18	160
ROGER LOUELL.................	13	..	..	5
XTOPHER LYNE	53	..	..	..
PHILLIP LANCASTER	50	1	2	25
J[no] LEDRA....................	27	..	..	7
W[m] LITTON	4	..	..	3
RICH[d] LAYTON	50	1	2	27
M[rs] LUCOMB	9	..	..	6
NICHOLAS LANGWORTHY	12	..	..	11
GEORGER LILLINGTON	32	..	..	..
M[rs] LOUELL	7	1	..	27
THOMAS LINKS................	6	..	..	12
THOMAS LUCOMB	9	..	..	5
M				
MORRIS THOMAS	144	3	..	100
EUAN MORGAN	140	2	3	72
GABRIELL MARTIN	10	..	..	5
W[m.]MARCHALL	180	1	2	52
RICH[d] MORRIS	35	1	1	12
J[no] MACKLAIRE	6	..	..	6
W[m] MURRELL	11	..	..	8
M[rs] MULLINAX	7	..	..	3
RICH[d] MULLINAX	9	..	..	5
ANTHONY MICHELL............	5	1	..	4
BRYAN MURPHE	9	3	..	14
J[no] MURROW.................	3	..	..	3
J[no] MURRELL	..	..	..	2
N.				
NEALE THO:	50	2	1	16

	ac'			
O				
SAMELL OSBORNE	40	0	1	33
THOMAS ODIARNE	101	1	..	17
FRANCIS OAKLEY	6	..	..	..
Jnᵒ ODELL	5	..	..	2
P				
NICHOLAS PRIDEAUX	230	2	6	76
RICHᴰ PEARCE	15	..	..	80
THOMAS PILGRIM	20	1	..	34
EDWARD PARRIS	35	1	..	12
Jnᵒ PIGGOTT	5	..	..	1
Mʳˢ PANTON	3	..	..	3
GEORGE PARRIS	32	1	..	23
ADRIAN PAILY	5	..	..	1
Widdᵒ PIRKINS	16	..	..	6
Jnᵒ PERRIMAN	7	..	..	..
JOB PERRIDGE	7	..	..	4
SAMUELL PERRY	4	..	..	7
HENRY PRICE	5	..	..	..
Jnᵒ PLUMLEY	15	1	..	6
Jnᵒ POLLARD	5	..	..	..
RICHᴰ POLLARD	3	..	..	..
R				
EDWARD RUNDALL	11	1	..	16
ANNE ROWE	22	..	..	3
RICHᴰ ROBINSON	12	0	..	3
Wᴹ ROBINSON	186	2	3	76
THOMAS REYNOLDS	28	..	..	12
ISACC ROETT	5	..	..	..

	land ac'	hired Scru^tts	bougt Seru^tts	Negroes
S				
BARNARD SHENKINGH	10	..	..	..
Jⁿᵒ STRODE	50	1	2	40
Mʳˢ STANLY	10	..	..	4
BENJᴬ SCOTT	10	..	..	..
SIMMONS PHILL.	39	..	..	18
Mʳˢ SPENSWICK	30	1	..	22
SIMMONS PHILLIP*	39	..	..	18
STEEDE EDWYNE Esqʳ	12	2	..	30
Capt Jⁿᵒ SUTTON	129	1	3	105
ALICE SMITH	12	..	..	6
Jⁿᵒ SPRINGHAM	22	1	..	28
JOSEPH SALMON	10	1	..	12
ALLEX: SINKLAIRE	10	1	..	7
RICHᴰ SWEETING	19	1	..	8
T				
TURPIN HENRY Senʳ	10	..	..	3
TUDAR RICHARD	8	..	..	..
ALLEX TAGGARTT	4	..	..	2
FRANCIS TURTON.............	25	..	..	3
XTOPHER TERRY	12	..	..	3
Widdo TWINE	10	..	..	6
GEORGE TYRWHITT	49	1	2	33
ROGER THOMAS	5	3	..	4
HERCULOUS TYRWILL	5	..	..	4
HENRY TURPIN junʳ	7	..	..	5
DAUID THOMAS	4	..	..	4
PHILL. TROWELL	9	..	..	..

W	ac'			
WILLIS JNᵒ	5	1	..	5
WARREN JOSEPH	6	1	..	14
FRANCIS WOOD	10	..	..	10
Wᴹ WELDING	10	..	..	..
Wᴹ WITHINGTON	20	..	..	9
MARY WATERS	15	1	..	9
JNᵒ WILLOUGHBY	5	..	..	..
GEORGE WALTON	30	..	..	6
GEORGE WILLOUGHBY	26	..	1	8
SAMUELL WARNER	10	..	..	8
JNᵒ WILLIAMS	..	..	..	2
DAUID WELCH	5	..	..	..
NATH: WHITE	13	1	..	13
BRIDGET FERRELL (*sic*)	5	..	..	..
Y				
JOHN YOUNG	40	1	..	13
	*			

Tot. of Inhabitants.............. 225.
Total of Acres.................. 7063.
Total of Servᵗˢ.................. 303.
Total of Negro's .... 3746.

* [There are 227 names entered, but 2 have been entered twice, viz. HAWKSWORTH and SIMMONS.]

[BARBADOES.]

Masters & mistreses names y' are Owners of Land in the Parish of St Georges in ye Island of Barbados taken by the command of his Excellency Sr Jonathan Atkins Kt ye 23th Day of December: 1679	Number of Acres	Number of White Seruants	Number of Negroes
ROBERT DAUERS Esqr	305	8	200
Mr ROBERT DAUERS Junior........	47	..	..
Mr JAMES ROBINSON	6	2	1
Mr JOHN ROBINSON	12	..	4
Mr WILLIAM DAUIS	10	1	10
Mr JOHN KOKER	..	..	5
Mr THOMAS BROWNE	..	..	3
Mrs SARAH HORSWOOD	..	..	4
Mrs MARGARET ROE.............	40	..	6
M's ELLINOR BOWDLER	..	..	2
Mr JOB: LULLMAN	6	..	2
EDWARD PYE Esqr	400	..	190
Mr THOMAS PROTHERS	55	..	15
Mr WILLIAM CATLINE...........	..	..	5
Mr HENRY EUANS	106	..	42
Mrs FRANCIS HOLDIP	19	..	9
Mr JOHN HOLDIP	..	..	7
Mr BRIAN BLACKMAN	10	1	10
Mr FRAN: SMITH Jujo'..........	6	..	18
Mr MILES TOPPIN...............	30	..	38
Mr HENRY BURRELL	15	..	3
Mr MICHAELL WEYLY	10	..	10
Mr FRAN: BELL.................	12	..	8
Mr JOHN JEMOT	8	..	5
Mr HENRY EASTWICK	50	1	37
Mr JOHN GOLDINGHAM	118	..	76
Mr RICHARD EASTWICK	40	..	20

Masters & mistreses names y, are owners of Land in the Parish of St Georges in ye Island of Barbados taken by the command of his Ex- cellency S, Jonathan Atkins K, y, 23th Day of December: 1679	Number of Acres	Number of White Seruants	Number of Negroes
Mr MARMADUKE NICHOLES	30	..	13
Mr FRAN: BOND	105	1	60
Mr JOHN GIBBONS	7	..	3
Mr EDWARD CLEYPOLE	325	12	86
Mr RICHARD SUTTON	106	5	60
Mr GEORGE BRIGGS	140	1	64
Mr JOHN BATTINE Senjo^r	172	1	81
Mr SAMUELL WEBB	..	..	1
Mr THOMAS BLACKMAN	..	1	1
The Lady ANN WILLOUGHBY	317	..	160
Mr SAMUELL COWARD...........	20	..	4
Mrs GRACE SILUESTER	515	10	220
M^r THO: WILBRAHAM	20	..	6
Mr HENRY HARDING	95	..	54
Coll^o XTOPHER LINE & Sonn......	272	..	..
Mr WALTER CHAMELL	33	..	27
Mrs MARTHA ALT................	36	1	22
Mr JOHN WILKINS	40	..	8
Mr JOSEPH MILES	..	2	6
Mr JOSEPH ROBINSON	5	1	3
Majo^r PAULE LYTE	235	8	120
capt JOHN COUSSINS.............	70	1	50
Mr JOHN COUSSINS Senjo^r	60	..	50
Mr WILLIAM SNIPE	..	..	4
Mr LATYMORE RICHARDS	12	..	8
Mr SAMUELL SEDGWICK	12	..	5
Mr JOHN SEDGWICK.............	10	..	5
Mr JOHN LAHANE...............	10	..	4
Mr PHILLIP FUSHEIR	7	..	3
Mr WILLIAM WEAUER	100	..	30
Mrs MARY RIDGWAY.............	39	..	5

Masters & M^{rs}: names that are owners of Land in ye Parish of S^tGeorges in The Island of Barbados Taken by the Command of His Excellency Sr Jonathan Atkins K^t ye 23th December —1679—	Number of Acres	Number: of White Seru^{ts}	Number of Negroes
Mrs Elizabeth Barnes	57	..	40
Mrs Elizabeth Woluerstone	20	..	6
Mr John Price	10	..	1
Mr Joseph Ridgway	40	..	6
Mr Edward Robert's............	10	..	7
Mr William Bradshaw..........	10	..	8
Mr Robert Custis	10	..	7
Mr Richard Lintott............	144	2	60
Mr William Sapster	46	..	14
Mr John Marshall	..	..	2
Mr Henry Gorges	125	..	58
Mr Benja Middleton	379	..	130
Mr John Wiltsheir	140	..	43
Mr Basill Dixwell	37	..	19
Mr William Greene	100	..	42
Mr Robert Hooper	219	2	117
Mr Richard Salter	217	4	120
Mr Samuell Hanson............	57	6	105
Mr William Harmer............	32	1	12
Mr Samuell Warner	4	..	16
Mr John Battine Jujo^r	190	5	80
Mr John Tull	10	..	8
Mr Dauid Morgan	20	..	19
Mr Thomas Gunstone	165	1	42
Mr John Renney	15	..	8
Mr William Harris	29	..	2
Mr Gabrill Deane.............	22		14
Mr George Keyser.............	104	1	42
Mr John Morecott	55	..	27
Mr Barnes Widdoe	15	..	13
Mr Richard Britland	25	..	19

Masters & mistreses Names yᵗ are owners of Land in yᵉ Parish of Sᵗ Georges in yᵉ Island of Barbados taken by the command of his Excellency Sᵣ Jonathan Atkins Kᵗ yᵉ 23ᵗʰ December —1679—	Number of Acres	Number of White Seruᵗˢ	Number of Negroes
Mʳ GEORGE WILLSON	16	2	7
Mʳ JAMES BUTLER	..	1	3
Mʳ THOMAS LEARE	127	1	75
Sʳ PETER LEARE	336	8	123
Mʳ THOMAS BATTSON	110	4	75
Mʳ SAMUELL PALMER	70	..	35
Mʳ CHARLES BUTTALL	48	1	44
Mʳ GEORGE GREENE his Plantā	258	..	52
Collonell HEN: DRAX	705	7	327
WILLIAM BULKELY Esqʳ ʃ his sonn	380	2	174
SAMUELL HUSBANTS Esqʳ	420	3	220
Mʳ THO: WILTSHEIR Deceased	·180	3	93
Mʳ JAMES BUTT & MARY MIDDLETON	42	..	2
Mʳ SAM: SMITH	26	..	6
Mʳ JOHN WHEELER	20	..	..
Mʳ ROBERT RICH	40	..	..
Mʳ JONATHAN ANDREWES	37	..	..
Mʳ PEIRSE POOR	9	..	..
Mʳˢ. APPLEWHITE Widdoe	169	..	..
Mʳˢ BOOTH Widdoe	10	..	..
Mʳ JOHN RENNEY Jujoʳ	7	..	..
Mʳ JOHN ROBINS	7	..	..
Mʳ JOHN ELLIOTT	10	..	..
Sʳ THOMAS BENDISH	72	..	..
Mʳ JOHN EVANS	10	..	..
Mʳ DARBY MACKONE	7	..	..
Mʳ WILLIAM CLARKE	6	..	..
Mʳ MICHAELL POORE	6	..	..
Mʳ ANTHO: LORD	6	..	..

Master & mistreses Names y[t] are owners of Land in y[e] Parish of S[t] Georges in y[e] Island of Barbados taken by the command of his Excellency S[r] Jonathan Atkins K[t] y[e] 23th December —1679—	Number of Acres	Number of White Seru[ts]	Number of Negroes
M[r] ROBERT DAWSON	15	..	..
M[r] BITLER & COLETON ....,......	15	..	..
Sume Totall	9569	111	4316

Baptized in The aboue S[d] pish p the Register Booke from y[e] 25 march 78: to y[e] 29: 7[ber] 1679 .... } 36

Buried in S[d] Parish in y[t] time.................... 66

p J[No] COUSSINS & PAULE LYTE, Church Wardens

(In-dorso

Acco[t] of Inhabitants   122
Land &c in the parish
of S[t] George.

Rec[d] 3[d] June 1680.

BARBADOS.   BAPTISMES:

CHILDREN BAPTIZED in the parish of St Georges from march the 25th. 1678. till September ye 29th 1679

                                                                                          d

MILES ye Sonne of MILES TUPPIN: ....baptized......Aprill—01—78

JOHN ye Sonne of JOHN PITTS ....baptized......Aprill—04—·

JOHN ye Sonne of LAWLAND CLAREE ..baptized......Aprill—12—

JDETH ye daughter of JOHN ROBBISON..baptized ......May—30—

ANNE ye Daughter of MICHAEL PORE;..baptiz'd .....July—06—

MARY, & ELIZABETH ye daughters of THOMAS WHITE ..July—18—

SAMUEL, ye Sonnne [*sic*] of JAMES DOWNING.. baptiz'd ..July—21—

SARAH ye daughter of MARMADUKE NICOLLS.. baptiz'd ..July—26—

GEORGE ye Sonne of JOHN SEDGEWICKE ....baptized ..July—30—

ELIZABETH ye daughter of WILLIAM GREENE, baptized August—07—

ANNE ye daughter of MATTHEW JENNINS ....baptized august—25—

PAUL ye Sonne of PAUL LYTE ....baptized august—31—

HENRY ye Sonne of DANIEL GUNNE ....baptized ..7ber.—14—

JOHN ye Sonne of EDWARD MORGAN ....baptized...7ber.—22—

MARGARET ye daughter of GEORGE KEYZAR............8ber—03—

SAMUEL ye Son of BONAVENTURE JELLFES baptized....8ber—13—

JOHN ye Sonne of JOHN WHITING baptized ....8ber—25—

THOMAS ye Sonne of JOHN DOLLSTAN baptized........8ber—31—

HESTER ye daughter of ALEXANDER CROOKSHANK ....9ber—03—

JOHN y^e Sonne of WILLIAM ALLEN baptized ....9ber—24—

HENRY y^e Sonne of JOHN GOULDINGHAM .... xber—04—

ELIZABETH y^e Daughter of ANNE REES widdow ......xber—06—

JOHN y^e Sonne of ROBERT PART baptized ....xber—09—

JOHN y^e Sonne. of JOHN BRADFORD baptized........January—26—$\frac{78}{9}$

JOHN y^e Sonne of JOHN JEMMOT baptized ....february—19—

ELIZABETH y^e daughter of CHARLES SAWYERS ....march—06

SARAH yᵉ daughter of EDWARD GIBBS baptized ....march—21—
GEORGE yᵉ Sonne of JOHN PITTS baptized ....Aprill. 23–1679
BENJAMIN yᵉ Sonne of Widdow WILTSHEIR ....Aprill—25—
NATHANAEL yᵉ Sonne of HENRY HARDING baptiz'd......June—10—
WILLIAM yᵉ Sonne of JONATHAN ANDREWES baptiz'd ...June—15—
ELIZABETH the daughter of JOHN HANDY baptized.........July—20—
MARMADUKE yᵉ Sonne of MARMADUKE NICOLLS............July—22—
RICHARD yᵉ Sonne of JOHN TULLS baptized ....7ber—04—
JOHN yᵉ Sonne of JOHN IPSLEY baptized ....7ber.—07—
WILLIAM yᵉ Sonne of MILES TAPPIN; baptiz'd ....7ber—15—

Coppied out of yᵉ register-   p. me. DANIEL DYKE Cleric̄
    booke for yᵉ parish of Sᵗ Georges—
  in yᵉ Island of Barbados. December yᵉ 8ᵗʰ 1679.

BARBADOS.

BURIALLS in yᵉ parish of Sᵗ Georges from yᵉ 25ᵗʰ of March: 1678. untill yᵉ 29ᵗʰ September. 1679.

BURIALLS

JOHN yᵉ Sonne of LAWLAND CLARKE ....buried   Aprill–14–1678
WILLIAM PLOWMAN ....buried ......May—12—
THOMAS, yᵉ Sonne of BARBARY STEELE ......buried ......May—31—
SARAH yᵉ Wife of WILLIAM DAVIS ....buried ......June—13—
JOHN BOOTH ....buried ......June—14—
JOHN yᵉ Sonne of THOMAS NEALE..............buried ......July—07—
ANNE yᵉ daughter of MICHAEL PORE .... buried ......July—07—
SARAH yᵉ daughter of MARMADUKE NICOLLS ....august—01—
RICHARD LACON's daughter ....buried ...august—05—
NICHOLAS WILLSON ....buried ...august—26—

Burialls

WILLIAM yᵉ Sonne of JOHN PALMER ....buried......7ber—07—

THOMAS WILTSHEIR Junioʳ ....buried......7ber—19—

JOYCE WILLIAMS...buried......7ber—20—

AMY yᵉ Wife of WILLIAM BRETTLAND ....buried......7ber—28—

AMY yᵉ Wife of THOMAS BROOKMAN ....buried......8ber—07—

ELIZABETH yᵉ daughter of WILLIAM GREENE buried.. ...8ber—09—

ROBERT QUARREE* ....buried......8ber—14—

RICHARD HARRIS ....buried......8ber—25—

JOHN WHITING ....buried......8ber—28—

JAMES yᵉ Sonne of JOHN HOLMAN ....buried......8ber—29—

WILLIAM yᵉ Sonne of WILLIAM MATTHEWES, buried......8ber—30—

ELIZABETH JONES ....9ber—02—

NATHAN MORRIS ....9ber—11—

ROBERT HOSKINS ....buried......9ber—20—

CHARLES yᵉ Sonne of CHARLES CHEYNY ......buried......xber—17—

ANNE yᵉ Wife of JAMES GAD ....buried......xber—28—

THOMAS WILTSHEIR Senioʳ ....buried......xber—31—

BRIDGET yᵉ daughter of EDWARD MORRIS ...buried...January—04-$\frac{1678}{9}$

PETER LITTLEWOOD..............................buried...January—30—

RICHARD POSSLET .. ..buried...January—30—

BRIDGET yᵉ wife of WILLIAM SAPSTER.........buried February—01—

ROSE yᵉ daughter of ROBERT GRAVES ....buried......Febʳ—02—

MATTHEW MACKLOND ....buried......Febʳ—09—

JOHN CRAGE ....buried......Febʳ—12—

DANIEL MORTON ....buried.....Febʳ—28—

SARAH yᵉ wife of JOHN WEAVER ....buried... march—02—

RICHARD FOOT ....buried... march—19—

MOSES NASEBY ....buried...March—27-1679

SAMUELL BROOKES ....buried...Aprill—03-1679

JOHN TEENE ....buried...Aprill—04—

MARY GRAVES ....buried...Aprill – 16—

PEIRCE PORE ....buried...Aprill—17—

GEORGE NICE ....buried......May—02—

* [The first letter in the MS. is blotted, but I do not think there can be much doubt as to the name.]

59—2

Burialls

PETER MORE ....buried......May-04-1679

THOMAS COLTON......................................buried......May—05—

MARY yͤ Daughter of SAMUEL BOYS..........................May—06—

ALEXANDER BUCKLE..................................buried......May—07—

CHARLES ANDREWES................................buried......May—22—

JOHN HOLLOWELL....................................buried......June—05—

BENJAMIN WOLVERSTON ....buried......June—11—

TEAGE ONAN ....buried........June—14—

·HENRY JONES...buried......June—24—

FRANCES yͤ Wife of OLIVER COTTOM ....buried......July—01—

ABIGAIL yͤ daughter of EDWARD CLAYPOLE.................July—16—

JANE yͤ daughter of WILLIAM AVERY ....July—25—

MARGARET yͤ Wife of JOHN PRICE ....July—28—

GEORGE yͤ Sonne of BARBARY STEELE ....buried......July—31—

JOHN yͤ Sonne of RICHARD HARLOW............buried...august—10—

MARY yͤ daughter of THOMAS READ ....buried...august—11—

MARTHA yͤ wife of ANGUIS BANES ....buried...august—12—

WILLIAM DAVIS ....buried...august—25—

LAWRENCE yͤ Sonne of THOMAS WILTSHEIR

       Junior, deceasd ....buried......7ber. 03—

BENJAMIN yͤ Sonne of THOMAS WILTSHEIR

       junioʳ deceasd ....buried......7ber—06—

WILLIAM CRAFTS ....buried......7ber—07.—

SAMUEL yͤ Sonne of BONAVENTURE JELLFES buried......7ber—23—

MARY yͤ Daughter of ROBERT PART ....buried......7ber—23—

(66)

Coppied out of yͤ register-   December yͤ 8th
booke for yͨ parish of Sͭ Georges.   1679.
in yͤ Island of Barbados.   pʳ. me DANIEL DYKE Cleric.

[endorsed]   BARBADOS

                Accoͭ of Christnings. 36.

                Burials........... 66.

                in the Parish of
                St. George.

                    Recᵈ 3ᵈ June. 1680.

List of the Masters & Mistresses names wth what Lands & Seruants & negrees they haue, & Asoe what Christenings & Burialls hath been in the Parish of St. Andrews,

Masters & Mistris names	Acres of Land	Seruants:	Negroes:	Christnings	Burialls:
Leut BASSILL GIBBES	130	2: men	045	one MARY	1: man
JOHN FOORD Esqr:	280	4: men	120	one ELIZa: BURGES	4: men
Captn JOHN GIBBES	200	1: man	093	....	2: Children
THOMAS LEAKE Esqr	150	......	060		
Mr RICHARD EDWARDS	30	......	031	one SARAH	1: SARAH
Captn ABBLL* ALLEYNE	316	1: man	115	....	1: man
Captn SAMUELL WOODWORD ..	120	......	046		
Mr JOHN HOULDER	57	......	041	....	3: men
The Widdow HUTCHINS......	10	......	003		
Mr JOHN SWANN	42	......	014		
Mr SAMUELL AUSTEN	6	......	002		
JOHN BODEN Esqr	250	12:men	143	....	1: man
Mr RICHARD MORRIS	115	1:man	035		
Mr EDWARD JORDAN	28	......	010	....	2:
THOMAS RICHARDS	12	......	008	....	1:
Doctor EDWARD LAMMY......	14	......	005		
Mrs MARTHA HAMERLY	86	......	019	....	2:
Mr GEORGE HURST	110	1: man	040		
JOHN SAVERY	53				
Mr WILLIAM HAWKSWORTH ..	18	......	006		
Captn TYMOTHY THORNHILL ..	170	1: man	150	....	3: men
Mrs ANNE JOHNSTON	105	......	041	....	3: men
Lt CHARLES SANDIFORD......	15	......	004	one RICHARD	
Lt WILLIAM HALL	40	......	009	one ANNE	
Captn ARCHIBALD JOHNSTON..	60	3: men	036	two Sonns	1: boy
Mr WM DOTTEN	109	3: men	60		

* [? ABELL,]

Masters & mistris names	Acres of Land	Seruants:	Negroes:	Christnings	Burialls:
Lᵗ JOHN SANDIFORD	75	1: man	033		
Doctoʳ JOHN HAYWARD	30	......	006	....	1: Boy
JOHN SOMERHAIES Esqʳ	140	2: men	051	one ANNE	1: Girle
JOHN MERRICK Esqʳ	266	6: men	167		
Mʳ ALEXANDER BARTLETT ..	12	......	006		
Mʳ JOHN JEPHSON	10	......	003		
WILLIAM ROACH	4	......	001	....	1: Boy
Mʳ JOHN BURGES	40	......	016		
Mʳ DAVID SMITH	6	......			
Mʳ STEPHEN SMITH..........	50	......	008		
Mʳˢ MARY COBHAM	87	2:	26	....	2:
Mʳ ROBERT HAYTE	18	......	005		
Doctor STEPHEN GIBBES......	28	......	014		
Mʳ HUGH WILLIAMS	10	......	005		
Mʳ THOMAS BROOKES	12	......	021		
Mʳ Wᵐ RAWLINGS............	9	......	004		
The Widdow ELLICOTT	86	......	010		
Mʳ JOHN TAYTE	16	......	005		
Mʳ HUGH DUNN	10				
Mʳ JOHN BELFORD	8	......	002	....	1:
DENNIS MURFEY	14	......	..	1	
Mʳ THOMAS CADLE	9	......	..	1:	1:
JOHN BOOTHMAN	5	......	001		
DANIELL DONAVAN..........	4	......	000	....	1:
CALEB ROUSE*			003		
Mʳ JOHN SWAN..............			14		
Mʳ HENRY COLLETT			·02		
JOHN THOMAS			003		
ANDREW FALLIN			001		
DANIELL SHANIS			001		
JAMES STOLLARD			001		
WILLIAM ROCH*			001		

* [A pen has been drawn through these names in the Orig. MS.]

Masters & mistris names	Acres of Land	Seruants:	Negroes:	Christnings	Burialls:
GEORGE DENT			006		
JAMES WEBB			001		
Mr ROBERT ENGLISH			004		
PHILIP CHARLES			001		
JOHN SMITH			002		
TEAGUE Boy			001		
Mr JOHN SLYE	26	......	005		
Mr THOMAS COPPIN..........	12	......	009		
Capt ABELL GAY	100	......	028		
The Widdow GAY...........	100	......	019		
Lt JOHN MILLS..............	260	......	90	....	3:
Mr HENRY JEENES	68	......	12	....	2:
Mr ANDREW FOLLYN	26	......	01	one ANDREW	1:
Mr DANIELL SHAHANISSE	10	......		....	2:
Mr GEORGE BUSTIAN	10	......	001		
Mr JOHN WELCH	19	......	001		
Mr ROBERT HIUE...........	10	......		two Sonns	
Mr ROBERT HEWITT	10	......	005	two Sonns	
Mr HENRY KELSOLL	105	......	030	one Daughter	1:
Mrs HELLEN CANTEY	20	......	007		
Mr BARTHOLOMEW REESE	152	......	051	....	1:
Mr THOMAS BERESFORD	180	2	028	1:	
Lt BENNETT REESE..........	60	......	006		
Mr NATHANIELL SNOW	180	......	048		
Mr CALEB ROUSE............	76	......	003		
Mr EDWARD PAINE	5	......		1:	
Lt HUMPHERY WATERMAN ..	186	......	092		
Mr ROBERT RICHARDS	60	3:	25		
Mr WILLIAM DAVIES	82	1:	22		
Mr JOHN WAYTE	93	......	050		
Mr PHILLIP ROSSE	12	......	004	....	1:
Mr RICHARD WILLIS	5	......	001		
DANILL DYNEGELL	5	......			

masters & mistris names	Acres of Land	Seruants	Negroes	Christnings	Burialls
RALPH FRETTWELL Esqr		1:			
Mr JOHN LOCKE		......	006		
Mr THOMAS RUSSELL	25	......	005		
Mr ANDREW BLACK	20	......	014		
Mr DAVID MICHELL	10				
JOHN NOBB			003		
W^M CAMPION..................			005		
JAMES BINNEY			003		
W^M HENDERSON			001		
W^M PURSS			002		
THOMAS JOHNSTON			008		
SYMON RUD			001		
RICHARD WILLIS			001		
DANIELL DOUGLE			001		
DERMOTT MAHONT			002		
DENNIS MACKHALA			002		
JOHN DANIELL...............			003		
THOMAS LAYTON			003		
HENRY LAYTON & JANE WEBB......			005		
Total............. 109	5597	47	2248	18	44

Lands in dispute between the Lady YEAMANS Madam FARMER Madam SPARKS Amo^{ts} } 719

MATTHEW GREY Minister
JOHN FOORD
BASILL GIBBES.. Churchward

Lands in this parish & the owners lives in other parishes Amounts to .... } 1260

Totall 7576

(endorsed) BARBADOS.
Acc^t of Inhabitants .. 109.
Christnings .... 18.
Burials .... 44·
Land &c in St Andrew's parish.
Rec^d 3^d June. 1680.

Año: 1680 (?)

A True and Perfect List of all yᵉ Names of yᵉ Inhabitants in yᵉ Parrish of Christ Church. with an Exact accompt of all yᵉ Land, white Seruants; and Neg's within yᵉ Said parrish Taken This 22ᵗʰ Decemb' 1679

A	acres Land	wᵗᵗ Seruants	Negʳˢ
ADAM ......JOHN	.. 192	 3	64
ARNETT ....DAUID	.. 50	 1	20
ANDREWS ..ROGER	.. 10	......	18
ADAMS......CONRADT	.. 10	......	21
ALCORN ....JOHN	5	 2	 5
ANDERSON ..ADAM............	5	......	......
ASHBURNER .WILLIAM	.. 13	......	 6
AUSTINE....THOMAS	5	......	......
ALSOPP ....RICHARD	5	......	 1
ADDICE ....EDWARD...........	.. 20	......	11
ADDIS JOHN ORPHANT	3	......	......
ANDERSON ..WILLIAM	2	......	......
AUSTINE ....JOHN	.. 30	......	16
ALSOPP ....EDWARD	.. 10	......	 2
ASHURST....JOHN	.. 33	......	11
ASHURST....BENIAMIN	......	......	 7
ANDREWS ..THOMAS	5	......	......
ARTHUR ....MICHAELL	......	 3	......
ARNETT ....PATRICK	3	 1	 3
ARCH ......JOHN	....7½	......	......
ANDERSON ..THOMAS	....2½	......	......
	411	10	.. 185

B.	acres Land	w^{tt} Seruants	Neg's
BISHOPP ......JOAN	..202	 2	65
BUCKWORTH ..RICHARD	..188	 5	65
BONNETT ....THOMAS dečd....	..138	......	......
BOND ....FRANCIS	.. 60	......	......
BROWNE......STEPHEN	.. 85	 I	16
BARRY........JOHN	.. 14	......	12
BLANCHARD ..WILLIAM	.. 15	......	 4
BULL ....CHRISTOPH^{R}	.. 18	......	 3
BOXFIELD ....THOMAS	5	......	......
BAKER........ESIAS	5	......	 I
BRIGSTOCK....RICHARD	....7½	......	......
BARNES ......OLLIVER........	 I	......	......
BURTON ......AGNES Widdow..	.. 55	......	17
BURBON ......JOHN and Compl^{t}.	....8½	......	 2
BOURNE ......JOHN	.. 12	......	 I
BOURN........JOHN Junio'	7	 I	11
BENTLY ......MARTYN Esqu'..	..245	 5	.. 154
BROOKS ......JOHN	.. 30	......	 8
BLAKE ....NICHOLAS	9	......	 7
BAYLY ....ROBERT	7	......	 2
BOURNE ......SAMUELL	5	......	 2
BUENNO ......BENIAMIN	......	......	 I
BOULINE (?) ..HENRY	4	 I	......
BRIGGS ......WILLIAM	.. 12½	......	 7
BURK ....TOBIAS	4	......	 2
BARRY........ALCE	.. 10	......	 4
BATEMAN ....JOHN	7	......	......
BAYLY........CHARLES	.. 32	......	 3
BRADLY ......RALPH	5	......	......
BRADLY ......ROBERT	2	......	 I
BANBRIGG ....ROBERT	.. 33½	......	 9
BUTTLER ....WILLIAM	.. 10	......	 I
BOYNER ......JOHN	....3¾	......	......

	acres Land	w^{tt} Seruants	Neg's
BURK ....JAMES	....8½	......	......
BUDDING ....RICHARD........	...10	......	 8
BAYLY.......RICHARD	5	......	 6
BAXTER ......EDWARD........	8	......	......
BEARD........RICH^D dec̄d	4	......	......
	1256¼	.. 14	412

C	acres Land	w^{tt} Seruants	Neg's
CLARK ......MARGARETT	.. 167	 5	78
COOPER ......THOMAS	.. 21	......	17
CLEMENT ....WILLIAM........	.. 14	 3	 7
CLARK ......FRANCIS	.. 12	......	 6
CONOWAY ....CORNELIUS......	3	......	 1
COUGHLAN....TEAGUE	7	......	 4
CHAFFIN......DANIELL	......	 1	 2
CONNER ......BRYEN	6	......	......
COCKTON ....DANIELL........	7	......	 2
CLARK ......EDWARD	1	......	......
COPPINGER....JOHN	8	......	......
CARNER [?CARVER] MICHAELL ..	6	......	 1
CRICHLOW ....ELIZABETH......	......	......	 5
CHRICHLOW ..JAMES	9	......	 6
CLARK ......ROGER..........	.. 20	......	11
CLARK ......CHRISTOPH'	.. 60	......	31
CASON ......THOMAS	8	......	 5
CRICHLOW ....HENRY	.. 15	......	 4
CLANCEY ....CORNELIUS......	.. 10	......	 3
CUDDEN ......JOHN	8	......	 3
COLLYER ....TOBIAS	......	......	 2
COMELL ......DUGWELL	.. 10	......	 3
CLARK ....WILLIAM and Compl^t	7	......	......
CONNEY ......EDMOND........	....1½	......	......

	acres Land	w^{tt} Seruants	Neg'ᵉ
CLOUGHAN....ELIZABETH......	2	......	......
CREEDE ......JOHN	.. 26	......	 2
COLLEY ......THOMAS	.. 10	......	 4
CORTEENE ...ELLINOR........	6	......	......
CHIZELL......DANIELL........	....2½	......	......
CAUAN ......JOHN	2	......	 I
CHAPPELL ....JONAH Decd	....2½	......	 I
COOKE......MARGRETT Widdow	5	......	 3
CHASE........STEPHEN	9	......	 6
CONNEYLAND . PATT: and Compᴸᵗ	.. 12½	......	 2
COPPINE ......JOHN	5	......	......
CAREW ......RICHARD	.. 38	......	 6
CHURCHER ....THOMAS........	5	......	......
CLARK........THOMAS	.. 15	......	......
CODD ....JAMES..........	.. 13	......	......
CAMMELL ....GILBERT........	4	......	......
	558	.. 9	216

	acres Land	w^{tt} Seruants	Neg'ᵉ
D			
DORN ....JOHN	.. 56	 2	31
DORN ....FRANCIS	.. 37	......	......
DOWELL......RICHARD	3	......	 I
DAWSON......MILLES	5	......	 I
DAUIS........EDWARD	I	......	......
DANIELL ....NICHOLAS	.. 10	......	 8
DRURY ......RICHARD	.. 61	......	25
DENNIS ......JOHN	....2½	......	......
DOLLAR ......JOHN	......	......	 2
DUKE ....HENRY	.. 23	......	 4
DUMESNILL .. CAREW..........	.. 70	......	37
DAUIS........MARGARETT	.. 10	......	 2

	acres Land	w^{tt} Seruants	Neg's
DENHAM......JOHN	......	......	 1
DEMSTER ....JOHN	 6	......	......
DILLON ......GARRETT	20	......	 9
DURANT......NATTHAN	 8	......	 9
DENNIS ......JOHN	 5	......	......
DOWLING ....WILLIAM........	 3	......	......
DANIEL ......JOHN	 5	......	......
DANBY ......JOHN	 2	......	......
DURANT......THOMAS	 6	......	 4
	333	 2	134

E	acres Land	w^{tt} Seruants	Neg'
EYTON ......WILLIAM........	...98	 3	70
EDNEY ......PETER	...52	......	......
ELLIOTT......JOAN	10	......	 2
EUANS ......JOHN	 3	 2	 4
ENES ....PHILLIPP	 4	......	 3
EARL ....THOMAS	12	......	......
ELLIOTT......RICHARD........	......	 1	20
	179	 6	.. 99

F	Acres Land	w^{tt} Seruants	Neg's
FRERE........TOBIAS Esqu'....	395	 5	.. 150
FRERE........JOHN Esqu'	180	......	.. 80
FRERE........WILLIAM	120	......	.. 40
FITZGERALD ..MORRIS	.. 15	......	 9
FA'WELL [*i.e.* FAREWELL]..JAMES	.. 18	......	 2
FORESTALL....RICHARD	.. 10	......	......
FAWNE ......JOHN	5	......	......
FRERE........WILLIAM	1	......	....
FARROW ......ROBERT	1	......	......

	acres Land	w^{tt} Seruants	Neg's
FOY..........HUGH...........	3	......	......
FRAME ......WILLIAM........	.. 10	......	......
FORD ....THOMAS	.. 15	......	 9
FOSTER ......JOHN	.. 25	......	10
FIELD........ANTHONY	.. 11	......	 5
FEYFIELD ....RICHARD........	.. 23	......	......
FELL ....THOMAS	5	......	......
	842	 5	305

G.	acres Land	w^{tt} Seruants	Neg's
GUNNING ....JOHN	..267	......	...47
GRAY ....RICHARD decd ..	..150	 5	...55
GREENIDGE ..RICHARD........	.. 40	......	 9
GRAY ....ROBERT	.. 18	......	 4
GREENIDGE ..JEAN	9	......	 4
GASLEE ......JOHN	.. 20	......	16
GORMAN ......MATTHEW	.. 10	......	 1
GILHAM ......JOHN	4	......	......
GARUEY ......JAMES	5	......	 3
GOODMAN ....RICHARD	8	......	 9
GRIGGS........JOHN	.. 10	......	......
GILBERT ......NATTHAN^{ll}	5	......	 2
GARY ....EDWARD	8	......	 1
GREGORY......ORMOND	5	......	 4
GRIFFIN ......EDWARD	.. 30	......	 3
GILLES ......EDWARD........	.. 10	......	 6
GORDEN ......PETER..........	8	......	......
GILLES........EDWARD Junio'..	5	......	 1
GRIGSON ......ROBERT	.. 10	......	......
GEORGE ......THOMAS.........	......	......	 7
GIBBS ....JOHN	......	......	10
	622	 5	182

H	acres Land.	w^t Seruants	Neg's
HARDING ....HENRY Decd	220	 1	90
HARGRAUES ..ALLIS	126	 1	56
HASELWOOD ..THOMAS	170	 2	78
HOOPER ......JONATHAN	.. 50	......	17
HAWEN [or HAUSEN] SAMUELL..	.. 50	......	......
HOOPER ......CRISPINE	..100	......	......
HARLSTONE ..EDWARD	.. 30	 1	11
HORNIOLD ....WILLIAM	.. 12	......	 3
HAGTHORP....WILLIAM	9	......	......
HYDE ....HENRY	5	......	 3
HANMERRY ..NICHOLAS	6	......	......
HUTTON......OLLIUER........	.. 36	......	......
HARRIS ......ZACHARIAH	......	......	 1
HOLMES......JOHN deēd	.. 15	......	 8
HUMPHRYES ..EDWARD	.. 25	......	14
HUMPHRYES ..EDWARD	2	......	......
HOLMES......JAMES	9	......	 3
HOLDER......NICHOLAS	.. 33	......	18
HERRINGMAN WILLIAM	.. 14	......	 4
HART........EDWARD	.. 32	......	......
HALLAM ....W^M Decd........	.. 20	......	10
HALEY ......THOMAS	.. 12	......	......
HARRIS ......ANTHONY	.. 10	......	 6
HARMAN ....WILLIAM........	.. 10	......	 2
HENDERSON ..FRANCIS	5	......	......
HUGHINIS ....PATTRICK	9	......	 7
HOGMAN ....ELIZABETH......	.. 10	......	......
HATTON......CHARLES	.. 28½	......	15
HAYWOOD ....JOHN	.. 15	......	 6
HOLMES ......HENRY	.. 12	......	 4
HACKETT ....WILLIAM	7	......	......
HART ....WALTER	.. 80	......	28
HAYES........THOMAS	.. 37	......	16

	acres Land	wᵗᵗ Seruants	Negˡˢ
HARBERT ....EDWARD	.. 13	......	 6
HACKETT ....ANN & Compˡᵗ ..	.. 21	......	......
HAUGHTAINE . RICHARD........	.. 30	......	......
HANBURY ....NICHOLAS	 5	......	......
HOOPER......DANIELL	......	......	 9
HOUGH ......WILLIAM	......	......	 4
	1268	.. 10	419

I	acres Land	wᵗᵗ Seruants	Negˡˢ
IRELAND......THOMAS	.. 18	......	 6
ILAM ....RICHARD	.. 10	......	......
JONES ....ANTHONY	 3	 1	 2
JELPH'S ......JOHN	 5	......	......
JEAMES ......MARGARETT	.. 10	......	 2
JONES ....ROBERT	......	......	 1
JEAMES ......MARGARETT	......	......	 5
	.. 46	.. 1	.. 16

K.	acres Land	wᵗᵗ Seruants	Negˡˢ
KINSLAND ..NATTHANᴸᴸ Esqu'..	340	 5	170
KIRTON.. .....PHILLIPP deͨd....	360	 9	130
KIPPS........JEAN............	.. 10	......	 3
KELLY ......DAUID	.. 13	......	 3
KEZAR ......TEAGUE	 3	......	......
KEY ....WILLIAM........	.. 16	......	 1
KNIGHTS ....JOHN	.. 20	......	 6
KNOWLES ....ANDREW........	 1	......	......
KENDALL ....WILLIAM decd ..	 5	......	......
KING ....RICHARD........	.. 12	......	 2
	779	.. 14	315

L	acres Land	w᷃ᵗ Seruants	Neg'ᵴ
LEWIS .... EDMOND........	214	 8	72
LEIGH .... SARAH	172	......	52
LEWIS .... DAUID..........	 10	......	 1
LUCAS .... RICHARD	 15	 1	10
LAMBERT...... ARTHUR	 4	......	 2
LINCK .... THOMAS	 9	......	......
LEWIS .... JOHN	 15	......	 6
LEE .... JAMES..........	19	......	 4
LETTIS........ THOMAS........	42	......	24
LACON .... THOMAS........	 9	......	 1
LELAND ...... CHRISTOPH'	30	......	 9
LOCKSMITH.... THOMAS........	....3½	......	......
LOWRE .... JOHN	 7	......	 6
LOUELL........ CONSTANCE....	.. 17½	......	 6
LONGSTAFF .... ELIZABETH	 9	......	......
	576	 9	193

M	acres Land	w᷃ₜₜ Seruants	Neg's.
MAXWELL ..... THOMAS	24	 2	30
MATTSON ..... MATTHIAS	11	 2	12
MOORE .... ROBERT	 5	......	 2
MURFORD .... RICHARD	12	......	 3
MERRICKS .... JOHN decd	 5	......	......
MASON........ THOMAS........	 7	......	 3
MOORE........ ALCE	 2	......	......
MITCHELL .... THOMAS........	 1	......	......
MACC GRAUGH.. DANIELL	 2	......	 2
MOODY........ DAUID	13	......	 2
MORRIS........ WILLIAM	15	......	 2
MATTSON...... SMITHELL	20	......	 3
MACC DANIELL.. ALLEXAND'	13	......	 1
MUNROW ...... ANDREW	 5	......	 3
MORRIS .... HUGH..........	 5	......	 1

61

	acres Land	wᵗᵗ Seruants	Neg'ˢ
MARSAN ......EDWARD	10	......	 6
MARKLAND....HENRY	44	......	20
MACC GRAUGH..JOHN	 5	......	 2
MORRIS ......EDMOND........	10	......	......
MACC BREECLY BRYEN	19	......	 8
MONK ....HENRY	 2	......	 2
MOHOLLAND ..JAMES..........	10	......	 2
MAY..........JOHN	....4½	......	......
MUNROW......ALLEXAND'......	13	......	......
MILLINGTON ..JOHN	......	......	 2
	257½	.. 4	106

N	acres Land	wᵗᵗ Seruants	Neg'ˢ
NEWTON......SAMUELL Esqu'..	.. 581	15	.. 260
NEMIAS ......DAUID a Jew	20	......	12
NOBLE........MARK	 5	......	......
NORRON......KATHERINE	10	......	 7
NUSUM ......ARTHUR	48	......	 7
NUSUM ......ARTHUR Junio' ..	13	 1	12
NEWMAN......MARGARETT	28	......	 9
NIXON........MARY	 5	......	......
NURSE........ROBERT	 5	......	 2
	715	16	.. 309

O	acres Land	wᵗᵗ Seruants	Neg'ˢ
OKER ....GEORGE	69	......	22
OWTRAM.....DOROTHY	.. 116	......	28
OISTINE ......JAMES	67	 1	17
OUERTON ....ROBERT	 5	......	......
OISTINE...... NICHOLAS	 4	......	 1

	acres Land	wᵗᵗ Seruants	Neg's
OLLIUER......MARGARETT	 4	......	......
OUTRAM.....ROBERT	10	......	......
	275	 1	68

P.	Acres Land	wᵗᵗ Seruants	Neg's
PEARS ....JOHN Esqu'......	910	 8	.. 180
PERRIMAN ....RICHARD	37	 1	20
PINCHBACK ....THOMAS........	38	......	11
PILE..........THEOPHILUS	45	 1	12
PILE..........SARAH	20	......	 3
PERRY ....JOHN	15	......	......
PEAD ....JOHN	....4½	......	 7
POCKETT......WILLIAM	 3	......	......
PAYNE........ELIZABETH......	 4	......	......
PERROTT......RALPH	70	......	15
PECOCK ......ROBERT	 7	 2	 7
POYER........THOMAS	13	......	 3
PARSONS......WILLIAM deēd ..	 4	......	......
PITTMAN .....ARTHUR	15	......	 5
PITTS ....HUGH	 8	......	 2
PEAK ....CHRISTOPH'	 4	......	 2
PRICE ....MATTHEW	 5	......	 2
PRICE ....HENRY	35	......	15
PRICE ....WILLIAM	 1	......	......
PERRY........EDWARD........	 5	......	......
POTTER ......ROBERT	 4	......	......
PORTER .....ROBERT	 5	......	 7
PIKE ....OLLIú deēd......	....2½	......	......
POORE........PETER	 3	......	......
PUMFRETT ...ANN............	 5	......	......
PHELOMY ....JOHN	10	......	......
PHILLIPPS WILLIAM 5 acrs 2 Neg's			
	1273	.. 12	291

Q	acres Land	w^{tt} Seruants	Neg'$_s$
QUIGGEN......JOHN	.. 12	......	6

R	acres Land	w^{tt} Seruants	Neg'$_s$
RICHBELL ....ROBERT	..315	 8	140
RISLEY........CRESSENT	..148	 I	84
RUSHBROOK ..HENRY	.. 50	 I	13
RODMAN......SARAH..........	.. 75	......	 2
RODMAN ......JOHN	7	......	 3
RODMAN......JOHN Junio'	.. 47	......	13
RICHARDS ....JOHN	.. IO	......	 7
RICHARDSON ..MARY	.. 33	......	.... IO
RYCRAFT......SARAH	.. 45	......	12
RICHARDSON .. DAUID..........	....4½	......	 2
REYNOLD ....JEAN Widdow ..	......	......	 8
ROBINSON ....THOMAS	.. IO	......	 8
ROBINSON ....ROBERT	.. 12½	......	 6
ROGERS ......JOHN	.. 12½	......	 3
RAWLINES ....JOHN	.. 15	......	8
ROSE ....ELIZABETH......	8	......	 3
RICHARDSON ..GEORGE	.. IO	......	 7
ROBINSON ....MANUSS (?)......	.. I7	......	 6
ROSSE ....JOHN	I	......	......
ROBINSON ....WILLIAM........	......	......	 3
RAINSFORD ...JOHN	3	......	 I
RENNY ......TEAGUE	5	......	......
RENNY ....TEAGUE Jun'....	.. IO	......	 I
RYCORD ......SAMUELL	2	......	 I
RUCK ....JOHN	.. 44	......	16
REDMAN......RICHARD	.. IO	......	......
ROBINSON ....EDWARD........	7	......	......
RENTFREE ....ROBERT	.. IO	......	......
RYMORE ......ALLEXAND'	I	......	......

S	acres Land	w^{tt} Seruants	Neg's
SCAWELL .. } RICH^D Esqu' .... [*or* SEAWELL] }	550	 8	.. 206
SEARL ....JOHN Esqu'	365	11	.. 184
SILUESTER ....Madam	180	 1	40
SCOTT ....BENIAMIN	..108	 2	41
SHURLAND ....JOHN	.. 30	00	12
STANFORD ....ROBERT	.. 27	......	 9
SMITH........ELIZABETH......	5	......	 6
STEPHENS ....JOHN	5	......	......
SHELTON .....SAMUELL	....1½	 2	 3
STRODE ......HENRY	.. 30	......	32
STRAWNE .....HENRY	5	......	 2
SHERON ......GEORGE	.. 10	......	 6
SIMPSON ......JAMES	....1½	......	 1
SPEGHT ......WILLIAM	.. 22	......	21
SISTERS ......ELIZABETH......	.. 36	......	19
SNERLING ....ROBERT	......	......	 1
SADLER ......THOMAS	.. 21	......	......
SLANY ......ANTHONY	......	......	 2
STONE........JOHN	.. 20	......	 1
SKAROS ......GEORGE	5	......	 i
SPAROWHAWK ..JAMES	5	......	... 4
STRODE ......MARGRETT......	......	 1	 4
SPENCER......JOHN	.. 23	......	 7
SAUNDERSON..JOHN	4	.... .	 1
SLAUGHTER ..THOMAS	3	......	 2
STUDDY ......THOMAS	8	......	 3
SHORTE ......OWEN	6	......	......
SCRUTTON [*or* STRUTTON].. JOHN	5	......	 1
SAWYER ......MARGARETT	.. 10	......	 4
SNIPE ....JOHN	......	......	 2
SHORE........RICHARD	.. 10	......	......

	acres Land.	w^{tt} Seruants	Neg'^s
SAUNDERSON .. ROBERT	.. 10	......	......
SUTTON ...... HENRY	 5	......	......
	1511	25	615

T	acres Land.	w^{tt} Seruants.	Neg'^{s.}
THORNBURGH ... GEORGE	.. 40	....	10
TROWELL .... PHILLIPP	.. 34	......	21
TYLER .... ROBERT	.. 21	......	 4
TAYLOR ...... JOHN	.. 12	......	 6
THOMPSON .... JOHN	8	......	 4
THOROWGOOD .. THOMAS	 1	 1	 1
TERRILL ...... SAMUELL	....3¾	......	ι .. 2
TUBBS .... EDWARD	....7½	......	......
TILNEY ...... THOMAS	.. 10	......	 1
THOMAS ...... THOMPSON	8	......	 1
THISTLETHWAITE .. PETER	8	......	 1
TICHBOURN .... WINNEFRED	.. 17	......	 6
TYSOE .... WILLIAM	1	......	 1
	171¼	 1	.. 58

V	acres Land	w^{tt} Seruants	Neg's
VINTON [*or* VNITON] .. THOMAS ..	.. 17	......	 9
VFFORD .... JOHN	5	......	......
	.. 22	......	 9

W	acres Land	w^{tt} Seruants	Neg'^s
WATTKINES .. DAUID	.. 20	......	 6
WYNN .... RICHARD	.. 60	......	 8
WALTERS .... CHRISTOPH'	.. 112	......	28
WATTKINES .. ROBERT	5	......	......

	acres Land	w^{tt} Seruants	Neg's
WRIGHT ......WILLIAM	2	......	 3
WALROND ....THOMAS	..340	18	.. 170
WASLEY ......JOHN	1	......	......
WATTKINES ..THOMAS	.. 10	......	 5
WEBSTER ....JOHN	5	......	 1
WISE ....CHRISTOPH'	.. 19	......	 7
WILLIAMS ....RICHARD	..406	 2	.. 200
WRIGHT ......JOHN	.. 40	 4	 7
WARNER......STEPHEN	.. 18	......	11
WATT ....DAUID..........	.. 10	......	10
WILSON ......ANTHONY	6	......	......
WHITE........PATRICK	.. 13	......	 6
WILSON ......EDWARD........	6	......	 4
WILSON ......CHARLES	.. 20	......	 6
WILSON ......CHARLES Junio'..	5	......	 4
WALTER ......RICHARD	....$2\frac{1}{2}$	......	......
WHITE........MILICENT	....$2\frac{1}{2}$	......	......
WARD ....WILLIAM	.. 14	......	 3
WILSON ......WILLIAM	9	......	 2
WELLS........JOHN	5	......	......
WILSON ......MARGARETT	5	......	......
WARD ....RICHARD	2	......	......
WADDINE ....THOMAS	2	......	......
WYATT ......CHRISTOPH'	.. 10	......	 3
WHITEHEAD ..THO: decd	.. 25	......	 6
WALTON ......RICHARD	.. 11	......	 2
	1112	.. 24	492

Total of
Inhabitants } 410

The Sum Totall of Euery Lott Conteined in ye w^{thin}
List Alphabettically Drawne and Cast upp att ye Foote

acres Land	w^{tt} Seru^{tts}	Negros
12978¾	.. 178	4723

JN° KENNEY
RICH ELLIOTT } Church Wardens
JN° ADAMS

BARBADOS

AN Extract from ye Register of Christ Church of ye Christnings
within ye Said Parish from March ye 25: 78. to ye 29th: of 7b^r: 79

Anno Dom. 1678
Aprill.

JANE ye Daughter of THOMAS and JANE WITHERING was bap^t y^e: 2^d
GRISSEL ye Daughter of TIMOTHY and MARY HUDLEY was bap^t y^e: 26th

June
MARGRET ye Daughter of WILLIAM and MARY WALTON was bap^t y^e: 27th

July
THOMAS ye Sonn of CORNELIUS and MARGRET STAPONS bap^t y^e: 2^d
THOMAS ye Sonn of NICOLAS and MARIE CLARE............ bap^t y^e: 3^d

August
MARY ye Daughter of HUMPHREY and ELIZABETH BALL bap^t y^e: 1st
MARY ye Daughter of WILLIAM and MABELL HOWARD bap^t y^e: 18th
JOAN ye Daughter of BENJ^A and KATHERINE FINCH bap^t y^e: 25th
RICHARD ye Sonn of THOMAS and ELIZABETH HASELWOOD bap^t y^e: 26th

1678

JOHN yᵉ Sonn of THOMAS and ELIZABETH SERLE .... bapᵗ yᵉ: 30ᵗʰ
MARY yᵉ [*sic*] of JOHN and MABELL GITTINGS of yᵉ Age of
   Eighteen years and Seaven moneths was bapᵗ in yᵉ P'sence ⎫ yᵉ: 31ᵗʰ
   of EDWARD WASSON and ANNE PACKSON Wittnesses ...... ⎭

September

NICOLAS yᵉ Sonn of HUGH and MARY MORRICE ~ was bapᵗ yᵉ: 8ᵗʰ
MARY yᵉ Daughter of DOWGALL and MARY CAMPBELL   bapᵗ yᵉ: 8ᵗʰ
FRANCIS yᵉ Sonn of JOHN and ANN HANSON   was bapᵗ yᵉ: 19ᵗʰ
ROBERT yᵉ Sonn of ROBERT and MARY STANFORD   was bapᵗ yᵉ: 24ᵗʰ
JOHN yᵉ Sonn of JOHN and ABIGAILL COLLINS   was bapᵗ yᵉ: 29ᵗʰ

October

CHRISTOPHER yᵉ Son of JOHN and ANNE SNIPE   was bapᵗ yᵉ 13ᵗʰ
WILLIAM yᵉ Son of JOHN and MARGERY HINCH   was bapᵗ yᵉ: 20ᵗʰ
LANCELOTT yᵉ Son of LANCELOT and MARY THOMPSON bapᵗ yᵉ 20ᵗʰ
JANE yᵉ Daughter of Wⁿ and ELIANOR DAVIES   was bapᵗ yᵉ 24ᵗʰ
MACHELL yᵉ Daughter of EDWARD and MACHELL ALSOPE bapᵗ yᵉ 31ᵗʰ

November

RICHARD ye Sonn of RICHARD and MARY BRIDGESTOCK bapᵗ yᵉ 10ᵗʰ
ISABELL yᵉ Daughter of ROBERT and KATHERINE CHURCH bapᵗ yᵉ 17ᵗʰ
MARTHA yᵉ Daughter of JAMES and HANNA ANDERSON   bapᵗ yᵉ 24ᵗʰ
Wᴹ yᵉ Son of OBAH a Christian Negroe Woman   was bapᵗ yᵉ 24ᵗʰ
SUSANNA a Negroe Woman of JOHN OSBOURN'S   was bapᵗ yᵉ 24ᵗʰ
  whose vndertakers were HERBERT GRIFFITH, ANN KELLY, and
  ELIZ: WATKINS
Wᴹ yᵉ Son of yᵉ Said SUSANNA, whose vndertakers were RALPH
BRETTON, and EDWARD PRICE, and MARY SMITH was baptized yᵉ 24ᵗʰ
MARTHA a Moletto Daughter of yᵉ sᵈ JOⁿ OSBURN and SUSANNA
      bapᵗ yᵉ 24ᵗʰ
THEOPHILUS yᵉ Son of RICHARD and ELIZABETH LUCAS was
      baptized yᵉ 26th
ALEXANDER yᵉ Sonn of THOMAS and ANN IRELAND was bapᵗ yᵉ 28ᵗʰ

1678

MARGRET yᵉ Daughter of ROBERT and ELIZABETH BRADLY

was bapᵗ yᵉ: 28ᵗʰ

MARY yᵉ Daughter of ROBERT and ELIZABETH JONES was bapᵗ yᵉ 28ᵗʰ

December

SARAH yᵉ Daughter of GEORGE and ELVY HARE was...... bapᵗ yᵉ 1ˢᵗ

GRACE yᵉ Daughter of OLIVER and GRACE PIKE was ...... bapᵗ yᵉ: 10ᵗʰ

ANNE yᵉ Daughter of JOHN and SUSANNA WEBSTER was bapᵗ yᵉ 17ᵗʰ

RICHARD yᵉ Sonn of ZACHARIE and ELIZABETH HARRIS was

bapᵗ yᵉ 26ᵗʰ

MARY yᵉ Daughter of Wᴹ and MARY PHILLIPS   was bapᵗ yᵉ 30ᵗʰ

January 167⅞

JOB yᵉ Son of WALTER and DOROTHY HART of about.
22. years of Age his Chosen wittnesses WALTER HART } bapᵗ yᵉ 2ᵈ
and THOMAS HAYES ....

CHARITY yᵉ Daughter of WALTER and DOROTHY HART
of about 19 years of Age whose Wittnesses were
WALTER HART THOMAS HAYES and ELIZABETH } bapᵗ yᵉ 2ᵈ
JEWSON and JANE HAYES.............................

ELIZABETH of yᵉ age of 8 years, and KATHERINE of yᵉ
Age of Seaven years and AMARINZIA of yᵉ Age of 5
years, and BENJᴬ of yᵉ Age of 7 monethes, all children } bapᵗ: yᵉ 3ᵈ
of BERNARD and ELIZABETH SCHENCKINGH were bapᵗ

ELIZABETH yᵉ Daughter of NATHANIEL and ANN
RIDGEWAY of yᵉ Age: 11: years .... was bapᵗ yᵉ 4ᵗʰ

JOHN yᵉ Sonn of ROBERT and ANNE SNELLIN ...... was bapᵗ yᵉ 7ᵗʰ

ELIZABETH yᵉ Daughter of WILLIAM and ANNE MERCER

was bapᵗ yᵉ 19ᵗʰ

PHILOCLEON yᵉ Daughter of RICHARD and JANE GREENIDGE

was bapᵗ yᵉ 21ᵗʰ

CHRISTOPHER yᵉ Sonn [of] CHRISTOPHER and ANN BULL was bapᵗ yᵉ 22ᵗʰ

ARTHUR yᵉ Son of ARTHUR and SUSANNA NUSUM   was bapᵗ yᵉ 22ᵗʰ

February.

167⅘

MARY of yᵉ Age of 5 years and 6 moneths, and HENRY ⎞
  the Age of 4 months, Daughter and Son of JAMES and ⎬ bapᵗ yᵉ 13ᵗʰ
MARY SIMSON ....were ⎠

JOHN yᵉ Son of DANIELL and MIRIAM MAGRAUHAN was bapᵗ yᵉ 18ᵗʰ

KATHERINE ye Daughter of RICHARD and ELIZABETH
                                     CAREW was bapᵗ yᵉ 28ᵗʰ

ANTHONY yᵉ Sonn of GEORGE and MARY RICHARDSON was bapᵗ yᵉ 28ᵗʰ

March

ANNA yᵉ Daughter of PETER and MARY JARRET   was bapᵗ yᵉ   7ᵗʰ

ANNE yᵉ Daughter of RICHARD and ANNE PERRYMAN   bapᵗ yᵉ 11ᵗʰ

SAMUELL yᵉ Sonn of JAMES and ELIZABETH MADDER was bapᵗ yᵉ 12ᵗʰ

JNᵒ the Sonn of JOHN and MARY BYNO ....was bapᵗ yᵉ 13ᵗʰ

LUCY of yᵉ Age of 2 years and Six moneths, and ANTHONY ⎞
  ten dayes old, Daughter and Son of ANTHONY and MABELL ⎬ yᵉ 13ᵗʰ
HARRIS ....were bapᵗ ⎠

CONRAD yᵉ Son of CONRAD and ELIZABETH ADAMS...was bapᵗ yᵉ 23ᵗʰ

ROBERT yᵉ Son of ROBERT and REBECCA HANSON ...was bapᵗ yᵉ 23ᵗʰ

ELIZABETH yᵉ Daughter of Wᴹ and MARIE SPEIGHTS was bapᵗ yᵉ 23ᵗʰ

Aprill

JAMES yᵉ Son of HENRY and SUSANNA CHRUCTHLOE was bapᵗ yᵉ   4ᵗʰ

ELIZABETH yᵉ Daughter of PEREGRINE and ISABELL GUARD
                                     was bapᵗ yᵉ   6ᵗʰ

ELENOR yᵉ Daughter of ALEXANDER and ELENOR OSBOURN
                                     was bapᵗ yᵉ 19ᵗʰ

JNᵒ yᵉ Sonn of JOHN and LOWRIE SPENLOVE...........was bapᵗ yᵉ 26ᵗʰ

JAMES yᵉ Sonn of PATRICK and JANE OHAIN (or OHANI) was bapᵗ yᵉ 26ᵗʰ

KATHERINE yᵉ Daughter of ISAAC and SUSANNA RAGG was bapᵗ yᵉ 26ᵗʰ

May

MARY yᵉ Daughter of JNᵒ and HESTER ADAMS ...... was bap yᵉ   3ᵈ

1679

WILLIAM ye Son of WILLIAM and ANN BRIDGESTOCK was bap^t ye 11th
JOHN the Son of JAMES and MARY HOLMES............ was bap^t ye 15th
WILLIAM ye Son of MARGARET COOK Widdow........ was bap^t ye 14th

June

ELIZABETH ye Daughter of SMITHY and MARTHA MATSON
was bap^t ye 14th
JAMES the Sonn of JOHN and MARY JELPII .... was bap^t ye 29th

July

JAMES ye Son of JAMES and ANGELETTA OISTINS ... was bap^t ye 2^d
SUSANNA ye Daughter of JOHN and ELIZABETH GASELEE was bap^t ye 3^d
EDWARD ye Son of STEPHEN and MARGRET CHASE was bap^t ye 8th
GEORGE ye Son of GEORGE and ANN GILES was bap^t .... ye 8th
NICOLAS ye Son of NICOLAS BIDLECOMB by a Negroe Woman
was bap^t ye 9th
ANNE ye Daughter of J^{No} and ANNE CREED .... was bap^t ye 13th

August

JOHN ye Son of JOHN and ANNE DANIELL .... was bap^t ye 7th
MARY ye Daughter of ROGER and MARY CLARKE ... was bap^t ye 7th
JOHN ye Son of JOHN and ELIZABETH SMITH was .... bap^t ye 28th
DANIELL ye Son of DARBY and ELIZABETH MALLONEE was bap^t ye 17th
THOMAS ye Son of OWEN and JOAN MALLONEE ...... was bap^t ye 31th

September

WILLIAM of ye Age of ten moneths Son of WILLIAM and FRANCES
SMITH bap^t ye 3^d
WILLIAM ye Son of W^M and ELIZABETH WOODFINE was bap^t ye 7th
SAMUEL of ye Age of 7 months Son of DAVID and JANE ARNET.
was bap^t ye 9th
KATHERINE ye Daughter of TEAGE and KATHERINE KEYZAR
was bap^t ye 9th

1679

ANNE yᵉ Daughter of JOHN and KATHARINE ROGERS was bapᵗ yᵉ 15ᵗʰ

Wᴹ yᵉ Son of WILLIAM and JOAN COLE .... was bapᵗ yᵉ *ᵗʰ

WALTER yᵉ Son of RICHARD and CHARITY HICKMAN was bapᵗ yᵉ 25ᵗʰ

DAVERS yᵉ Son of RICHARD and ELIZABETH SEAWELL was bapᵗ yᵉ 26ᵗʰ

October

THOMAS yᵉ Son of THOMAS and ELIZABETH HUGHS . was bapᵗ yᵉ 13ᵗʰ

JOHN yᵉ son of JOHN and SUSANNA MERICK .... was bapᵗ yᵉ 16ᵗʰ

JOHN yᵉ Sonn of JOHN and MARY BUNNYON .... was bapᵗ yᵉ 16ᵗʰ

ELIZABETH yᵉ Daughter of JAMES and REBECCA CRUTCHLOE

was bapᵗ yᵉ 17

Total 93†

JNᵒ KENNEY
RICH: ELLIOTT } Church Wardens
JNᵒ: ADAMS

BARBADOS

AN Extract from yᵉ Register of Christ Church of yᵉ Burialls wᵗʰⁱⁿ yᵉ Said Parish from March yᵉ 25ᵗʰ 1678. to September yᵉ 29ᵗʰ 1679

Anno Dom 1678

May

JOHN yᵉ Son of JOHN MARKLAND .... buried yᵉ 31ᵗʰ

June

ANNANIAS MAN Senioʼ .... buried yᵉ 4ᵗʰ

MARY yᵉ Wife of Wᴹ HALLUM .... buried yᵉ 17ᵗʰ

JANE BRYAN.. buried yᵉ 20ᵗʰ

WILLIAM HARGROVE .... buried

---

* Date doubtful, owing to the orig. MS. being split.

† [It should be 98.]

July

1678

FRANCIS yᵉ Wife of JOHN STONE............................. buried yᵉ 12ᵗʰ

WILLIAM LEIGH .... buried yᵉ 19ᵗʰ

JANE yᵉ Wife of JOHN COPPIN .... buried yᵉ 29ᵗʰ

August

· JOHN ARCH .... buried yᵉ 5ᵗʰ

JANE the Daughter of THOMAS and ELIZABETH HASELWOOD būr yᵉ 26ᵗʰ

CHARLES the Son of THOMAS and ANNE IRELAND ...... buried yᵉ 30ᵗʰ

Septemb'

MAJ' RICHARD GRAY .... buried yᵉ 10ᵗʰ

HESTER the Wife of Jᴺᵒ PEERSE Esq' .... buried yᵉ 15ᵗʰ

October

JOSHUAH CHAPPELL .... buried yᵉ 5ᵗʰ

THOMAS CRAWFORD .... buried yᵉ 21ᵗʰ

KATHERINE the Wife of Wᴹ HORNIOLDE .... buried yᵉ 28ᵗʰ

November

SIMON REYNOLDS .... buried yᵉ 2ᵈ

CHARLES yᵉ Son of JOHN and ELIZABETH BURTON ...... buried yᵉ 28ᵗʰ

GEORGE STRODE was buried .... yᵉ 29ᵗʰ

Decemb'

ARTHUR yᵉ Son of ARTHUR and SUSANNA NUSUM ...... buried yᵉ 28ᵗʰ

January 167⅞

MARGARET OLIVER.. buried yᵉ 29ᵗʰ

JANE yᵉ Wife of Jᴺᵒ THOMPSON .... buried yᵉ 31ᵗʰ

MABEEL the Wife of ZACHARIAH HARRIS .... buried yᵉ 31ᵗʰ

167⅜

February

STEPHEN SMITH	buried yᵉ 8th
JOHN BUSSIE	buried yᵉ 9th
JOHN BURTON Junio'	buried yᵉ 10th
EDWARD ADDISON Junio'	buried yᵉ 10th
Jᴺᵒ BURTON Senio'	buried yᵉ 13th
JOHN and his Wife JANE LITTLE	buried yᵉ 13th
CHRISTIAN a Negroe Servant of MAJ' KINGSLANDS	buried yᵉ 13th
JOHN HOLMES	buried yᵉ 15th
WILLIAM KENDALL	buried yᵉ 18th
DELIVERANCE ADDISON	buried yᵉ 18th
CHRISTOPHER CLANCY	buried yᵉ 18th
JANE the Wife of EDWARD MARSON	buried yᵉ 26th

March

Wᴹ COOK	buried yᵉ 2d
S' ROBERT HACKET	buried yᵉ 3d

Aprill

HENRY HARDING	buried yᵉ 21th
OLIVER PIKE	buried yᵉ 22th
REBECCA POTTER	buried yᵉ 23th
SARAH yᵉ Daughter of ALEXANDER and MARY BLOWDEN	buried yᵉ 26th

May

SUSANNA yᵉ Wife of HENRY HOLMES	buried yᵉ 17th

June

DAVID ROBINSON	buried yᵉ 10th
MATHEW GORMON	buried yᵉ 23th
JAMES yᵉ Son of JOHN JELPH	buried yᵉ 24th
THOMAS CHESTER	buried yᵉ 30th

1679

July

PETER ALSOPE	buried ye 1st
JOHN BASHFORD	buried ye 3d
WILLIAM SILCOMB	buried ye 5th
EDWARD the Sonn of STEPHEN and MARGRET CHASE	buried ye 9th
ANTHONY RICHARDSON	buried ye 13th
HENRY HOLMES	buried ye 22th
RICHARD BEDFORD	buried ye 23th
MARTHA CAULDWALL	buried ye 28th

August

MICHAELL CLARK	buried ye 5th
DOROTHY CALLAHAN	buried ye 10th
MACHELL ye Daughter of EDWARD ALSOPE	buried ye 19th

September

SAMUELL ye Son of Capt DAVID, and JANE ARNET ...... buried ye 13th

JNo KENNEY
RICH: ELLIOTT } Church Wardens.
JNo: ADAMS

BARBADOS

AN account of all the Persons who have been baptized within the Parish of St James since the 25th of March 1678 to the 29th of September 1679

1678 May— 23—ELIZABETH ye Daughter of THOMAS SERTAIN
August 11—ELIZABETH ye Daughter of DAVID POOR
Aug— 17—MARY ye Daughter of FRANCIS WALTHO
Aug— 25—ANNE ye Daughter of JAMES WALWYN Esq'

Septemb 1—JOAN ye Daughter of WILLIAM HABBERD

1678 Sept— 5—ELIZABETH yͤ Daughter of WILLIAM THOMAS
  Sept— 8 ELIZABETH yͤ Daughter of ALEXANDER CUTHBERT
    —MARY the Daughter of RICHARD MIDDLETON
  October—10—JOHN the Son of JOHN HILL
  Octob—15—WILLIAM yͤ Son of JOHN LEECH
  Oct— 15—GEORGE yͤ Son of JOHN LEECH
  Oct— 15—SUSANNA yͤ Daughter of JOHN LEECH
  Oct— 15—WILLIAM yͤ Son of WILLIAM FOSTER
  Oct— 20—JOHN yͤ Son of JOHN MIRCH

  November—17—RALPH yͤ Son of THOMAS KEMP
  Nov—17—MARY yͤ Daughter of THOMAS KEMP
  Nov—24—ANNE yͤ Daughter of RICHARD CHOM

  December 8 HENRY yͤ Son of Mʳ WILLIAM CHESTER
  February 23 DORCAS yͤ Daughter of HENRY WRIGHT

1679 August 24 PIERCE yͤ Son of HENRY WATTY
  Aug— 27 ANDREW yͤ Son of Lᵗ Coᵗᵗ ANDREW AFFLECK
  September 5 JOHN the Son of Mʳ JOHN HOOKER
  Sept— 25 THOMAS yͤ Son of JOHN DANIEL Esq'.

      Concordat cū Registro
      C. LEGARD
       vicarius ibid

Baptized in the Parish
 of Sᵗ James since yͤ
 25ᵗʰ of march 1678 } 23
to yͤ 29 of Septemb 1679

BARBADOS

AN acctᵗ of all the Persons that have been buried within the Parish of Sᵗ James since the 25 of March 1678 to the 29 of September 1679

1678 March 28—MATTHEW yͤ son of MATTHEW PEDDER

Burialls

1678 Aprill— 8—RALPH yᵉ son of Mʳ JOHN HOOKER
      Apr — 13—HENRY YATES
      April— 29—JOHN HUDSON—who was casually drownd

      May — 6—ELEANOR PAYN
      May —· 7—ELIAS WILLIAMS
      May — 8—MARY yᵉ Daughter of JOHN SLAUGHTER
      May — 23—ROBERT BELL
      May — 31—JOHN THOMAS

      June — 1—NICOLAS LAWRENCE of Sₜ Thomas's Parish
      June — 27—MARY SLATE,—Servᵗ to Capᵗ JOSIAS COX

      July — 1—MATTHEW WHETTY
      July — 3—MARY DRISKELL
      July — 10—JOHN OSDELL

      September—4—DAVID CALLAHONE
      Sept   16—JOHN SPARKE Esq'
      Sept — 18—JOAN yᵉ Wife of RALPH CARR

      October—9—MARY yᵉ Daughter of RICHARD MIDDLETON
      Octob —14—Capₜ ROBERT ARUNDELL
      Octob —16—WILLIAM LINCKLATE,   servᵗ to Judge REID
      Octob 30—JOHN DOWNS

      Novemb 1—ALEXANDER ROBINSON
      Novem— 4·—JOHN NICOLLS
      Nov— 14—ELIZABETH COOK.

      December 1—MICHAEL yᵉ Son of JAMES GOFFE
      Decemb 22—JOHN SEATON
      February 12—WILLIAM JONES

Burialls.

1679 May— 8—FRANCES yᵉ Wife of JOHN GOEING
June— 7—MARY yᵉ Wife of MORGAN MURPHY
June— 13—EDWARD WEBB.
June— 29—JOHN DUDLEY
July— 4 ALICE yᵉ Wife of THOMAS WALTER
July 14—JAMES INNIS
July— 22—TOBIAS PAYNE
July 27—JOHN yᵉ son of Mʳ JOHN BATT
July 29—OWEN COLLOHONE

August 6 ANTHONY STEERMAN
Agu—— 7 JOHN ARMITAGE of the Parish of Sᵗ Peters who was casually drowned
August—19 FRANCIS BEARNE
Sept 6 JOHN yᵉ Son of Mʳ JOHN HOOKER
Sept 7 JAMES yᵉ Son of ALEXANDER MURREY
Sept 8—CORNELIUS yᵉ Son of DEARMAN DRISKELL
Sept 11 JAMES PURSLEY
Sept 22 ELIZABETH yᵉ Wife of WILLIAM SPENCE

Buried in yᵉ Parish of Sᵗ
James from yᵉ 25 of March 1678 } 44
to yᵉ 29 of September 1679

Concordat cū Registro

C LEGARD vicarius
ibid

[indorsed] BARBADOS

Accoᵗ of Christnings 23.
Burials . . . . 44.
in Sᵗ James Parish.
Recᵈ 3ᵈ June 1680.

ANN: Acco^t: of the: land As Itt: Stondeth: In ye church Books: With the Number of Servants And Negros With the Names: of the Owners thereof In the psh: of St James: As: Was taken by the Church Wardens of the Said Parrish the 20^d December 1679

A	Seru^ts„	land„	Neg'„
AFLICK: ANDREW; Leu^t Coll^o	 2	96	70
ANDREWS: EUEN	......	20	 7
ANDREWS: W^M	 2	......	 2
ALLING JACOB Very pore...........	......	 4	......
B.			
BAYLYE: RICHARD: Coll^o	......	.. 228	......
BOND: FRANCIS: Esqr	 2	.. 120	67
BURHALL: GEORGE	......	10	11
BANBRIG: ROBERT: Docto'	......	......	 4
BURROWES JOHN	......	10	 2
BATT: JOHN Senj'	 1	40	17
BALAM: CHARLES Capt............	......	78	22
BURGIS THOMAZING m's	......	20	 7
BURTON FRANCIS: Capt	......	...15	......
BISSEX WILLIAM m'	 1	 9	 4
BYRNE: DINNIS	 1	...10	11
BLAKE: JOHN	......	24	......
BELCHEM: JOHN Very pore.........	......	 3	......
BIGGNELL W^M Very pore..........	......	 3	......
BALL: JOHN—Dec^d his Widdow is pore	......	 3	 1
C			
CHESTER WILLIAM: m^r	 1	120	45
COX: JOSIAS: Capt................	 9	247	122

	Seru^{ts}„	land„	Neg's„
CHAMBERLAINE: FRANCIS: Capt	......	20	16
COLLINGS: JAMES	 2	121	 10
CHACE JOHN	......	27	 8
CHRISTOPHER WILLIAM	......	16	 8
COURTYERE GEORGE	......	23	 8
CAMERRAME JOHN	......	45	......
CHAPEMAN RICHARD	 I	......	 5
CHALLENER ROB^T	......	 2	 I
CRESSWELL JOHN	......	 9	......
CUTA MATHEW: DAY: THOMAS:			
MILLER: J^{No}: pore...............	......	 6	......
CLEMENTS ROBERT pore	......	 5	......

D.

DANIELL JOHN: Esq'	......	.. 160	55
DYMOCKE: WILLIAM: Capt	 3	57	60
DYER: WILLIAM Dec^d his Estates	 6	.. 317	.. 120
DOLLATHY: ELIZABETH	......	40	16
DALBEY: JOANE	 I	 8	 6
DOWNES HENRY	......	18	 3
DUCE: GYLES	......	10	 7
DAMERALL THOMAS pore	......	 3	 I
DUNEING HENRY pore	......	 4	......

E

EUENS: RICHARD Esqr	 7	171	78
ELDING: EDWARD: Capt	 3	176	70
ELMES: JOHN:....................	......	 5	 3

F.

FEAKE: HENRY	 8	.. 245	.. 120
FITTE: ROBERT:	......	30	14

	Seru^{ts}„	Land„	Negrs
FOSTER: ROBERT: Docto'	......	 7	 5
FLINT: GEORGE	......	10	 1
FUTER THOMAS.....................	......	32	......
FEAK RICHARD for: NATH^{ll}: WILLIAM-			
SON	......	 7	......
FUREY CHARLES pore	......	 4	......
FREEMAN WILLIAM pore	......	 3	......
G			
GIBBES: PHILLIP.....................	 7	.. 174	69
GIBBES: JOSEPH:...................	......	25	......
GIBBSON JOHN	......	 7	......
GIBBSON: MATHEW	......	10	......
GRAYE: WILLIAM	......	 6	 2
GILLHAM EMANUELL	......	 4	......
GARRET: EMOND	......	 4	 2
GRONEARE JOHN pore	......	 5	......
GARNER: MARY pore...............	......	 5	......
GARNER: MILLER & Comp^a pore	......	 4	......
H			
HELMES THOMAS Maj'.............	 4	.. 134	52
HELMES: THOMAS: Capt	 3	60	50
HOOKER JOHN	......	......	 7
HABING THOMAS	......	 6	 7
HIGGINSON MARG^t	......	10	 4
HALL: JOHN	......	14	 1
HEWES JOHN	......	 6	 4
HOLDER: MELITIAH	 3	100	32
HOLDER: JOHN: Jun'...............	......	98	......
HOPEKINGS SAMUELL	......	 4	 3
HILL JOHN.......................	......	......	 2

	Serv^{ts}	Land	Negros
HOUSFEILD JOHN pore	......	 5	......
HARRISON: ABRAHAM	......	 4	......

: I :

| JEFFORDS: ELIZ^A .... | ...... | ....20 | .... 6 |
| JOHN JOHNSON .... | ...... | ....13 | .... 1 |

K

KNIGHTS BENJ^A: Esqr	 3	.. 300	.. 150
KELLEY: ROB^T:	 3	62	37
KING ROB^T	......	 5	 3
KNATCHBULL JOHN	......	 4	 3
KENN MATHEW Docto'	 2	15	 9
KELLEY JOHN			
KNIGHTINGALL NATHANIELL pore ...	—— 0	 4	......
KANTY: DARBY pore................	......	 3	......

L.

LITTLETON: EDWARD: Esqr	 3	.. 205	.. 120
LANE ANTHONY Capt	......	20	 4
LOWTHER: LUKE	......	12	 6
LEACH: JOHN	......	16	 5
LOUE MARY	......	......	 3
LAWRANCE HENRY	......	10	 6
LEWIS: HUGH: Capt	......	40	15
LEGAYE JACOB Senj'	......	21	......
LUKE: ELIAS:	......	20	 3
LANGHAM THOMAS	......	 5	. ....
LEAGER: Widdow pore............	......	 7	......

M

| MELLOWS: ELISHA: Capt .... | .... 1 | ....47 | ....24 |

	Seruants"	Land"	Negros"
MUNDY: ELIZ^	 2	75	35
MULLENEX WILLIAM	....	...17	10
MERRELL THOMAS: Capt	....	35	19
MELL: WILLIAM	....	20	......
MARTING: JOHN	....	10	 1
MADDOX THOMAS pore	....	 5	...c..
MIDDLETON: RICHARD	....	....	 4
MACCONY DINNIS	....	 3	......
MASSLING WILLIAM	....	 8	 3
MUNNS: THOMAS: Ensigne	....	 2	 2
MORRAINE JOHN	....	 5	....
MORGAINE ROB^T: pore	....	 5	......
MACCONY: DINNIS pore	....	 2	......
MACKGERRY WILLIAM pore	....	 1	......
MACKWARD: FELLEN pore	....	 2	......

N.

NELSON THOMAS	....	 4	 1
NORRIS SAMUELL Capt	....	....	 3

O

ODAM WILLIAM	....	 7	 1
ODGNE: EDMOND	....	15	 6

P

PAIGE SARAH	....	30	 2
PARKER RICHARD	....	 7	......
PEREING SABASTING	....	24	13
PARE EDWARD	 1	....	 3
PEARCE: BENONY			
PAINE TOBIAS	....	26	 3
PETTER SAMUELL	....	14	 8

	Seruants	Land	Negros
Q			
QUALE HUGH............................	......	 5	......
QUERKE RICHARD...................			

: R :			
REID JOHN Esqr	 2	.. 198	85
RICHARDS THOMAS	 2	20	10
RAMSEY ROAS m's	 1	30	29
RUSSELL PHILLIP	... 2	13	 5
RIUERS WILLIAM	......'	......	 1
ROASS THOMAS: Docto'.............	......	20	 9
REID: ADAME pore	......	 6	......
RAUEN: XTOPHER pore.............	......	 5	......
RICHARDSON: NICHOLAS pore	......	 5	......
REEUES THOMAS pore	...,...	 4	...•...
ROBINSON: JOHN pore	......	......	 1

S			
STANFAST JOHN: Coᵗᵗᵒ.............	.10	0351	.. 238
SPARKS: JOYE: Madam	12	.. 133	.. 150
SCOTT: WALTER: Capt	 2	.. 107	52
STEWARD: AMEY	......	10	 1
SMITHWICKE Wᴹ	......	 10	 1
STURMAN MARY	 1	20	 7
STOUT JOHN Leu^t	......	10	 5
SMITH MARG^r	......	12	......
SUMERS THOMAS .,...............	......	 7	 2
SAMPSON JOHN: Capt	......	25	......
STROUDE JOHN m's	......	 5	......
SCOTT: JOHN	......	10	 1
STRETCH: JOHN	......	......	 1
STAYSMORE FRANCIS	......	......	 1

	Seruants,,	Land,,	Negros,,
SAGE RICHARD Liueing On: Coʰᵗᵒ BAYLYS land	......	......	 3
SPENCER: MARGᵀ Very pore	......	 6	 2
SHEPEHERD JOHN pore............	......	 5	......
SHAWE DANIELL pore:	......	 6	......
SHOUELL ELIAS pore:	......	 5	......
STEEUENS JOHN pore	......	 3	......
T			
THORNEHILL TIMOTHY: Coʰᵗᵒ........	 7	.. 268	.. 150
THORPE JAMES Capᵗ	......	96	27
TEMPROE JOHN	......	12	 2
TAYLOR WALTOR	......	13	10
THOMPSON: XTOPHER Docto'	......	 9	 3
TOUEY RICHARD	......	15	 7
THORNEHILL TIMOTHY Capᵗ	......	10	......
TUCKER ANN pore	......	 2	......
THOMAS: JOHN pore	......	 4	......
TINDALL RICHARD pore	......	 3	......
V.			
VEREING ALCE:................	......	25	11
VEREING JOSHUA	......	10	11
W			
WALWYNE JAMES: Esqʳ	 7	.. 305	.. 160
WALTORS RICHARD	 3	.. 206	.. 140
WARDLE: CHRISTOPHER	......	15	 4
WALE JOHN	......	.. 159	80
WILLIAMS THOMAS	......	 7	15
WILLIAMS WILLIAM	......	 5	 2
WHATSON RICHARD pore........	......	 5	......

	Seruants	Land	Negros
WALLEY HENRY pore	......	 2	......
WRIGHT HENRY pore	......	 2	......
WILLEY: RAWLEY pore	......	 3	......
YEAMONS ELIZᴬ	 2	50	18
Tot. of Inhabitants is 183	.. 113	6742	2895

JOH:N: STANFAST - ⎫
JAS. WALUYN   - ⎬ Church Wardens
                ⎭

CHILDREN Baptized in yᵉ: Parrish of Sᵗ Johns from yᵉ 25ᵗʰ day of March 1678 to the 29ᵗʰ day of Sepᵗ: 1679 Accordinge to the parrish Register

1678

March	31	JOHN, Sonne of JOHN JONES
May—	12	ELIZABETH, Daughter of THOMAS POOLER
	26	RICHARD, Sonne of RICHARD POOLER
June—	20	ANN Daughter of JOHN SUMMERS
	21	ELIZABETH Daughter of ROCKINGHAM BASON
	25	SAMUELL, Sonne of JEFFERY BATTALA
October—	3	JOHN, Sonne of Capᵗ: JOHN LESLIE
	20	JOANE, Daughter of HUGH HALL
November—	3	WILLIAM, Sonne of JOHN MILLWARD
	„ „	THEADOCIA, Daughter of LAWRANCE REESE
	„ „	DOROTHY, Daughter of RICHARD MOORE
	24	WILLIAM, Sonne of THOMAS GARDNER
	„ „	JOHN, Sonne of ARON JACOBSONE
	26	SARAH, Daughter of Mʳ JOHN VAUGHAN
	„ „	KATHARINE, Daughter of JOHN PEIRCE
	„ „	THOMAS, Sonne of THOMAS ROOME

1678	December	9	ELIZABETH, Daughter of Docter JAMES KEITH
		27	ANTHONY, Sonne of WILLIAM SHOREY
1679			

Aprell—	13	THOMAS & ELIZᴬ: } Sonne & Daughter of JOHN DENT
	„ „	SARAH, Daughter of HENRY POLLARD
	„ „	HENRY, Sonne of THOMAS QUINTYNE
August—	9	JOHN, Sonne of JAMES PEMBERTON
	24	MARY, Daughter of BENJAMEN CORBETT
	„ „	MARY, Daughter of Capt: THO: BALDWYN
	28	WILLIAM & CHARLES— } Sonns of Mr JAMES PEMBERTON
September—4		LEOLIN, Sonn of LEOLIN LLOYD

28: persons Baptized

BEN: CRYER: Clerk.

INDEX.

Jope, Wm., 118
Jordan, Edward, 469; *see* Jourden
——, James, 382
——, Margery, 171
——, Margrett, 210
——, Mary, 171, 210
——, Samuell, 269
——, Sisley, 171, 209
——, Thomas, 177
——, Wm., 380, 445
Jorden, Joane, 91
——, Peter, 169, 201
——, Thomas, 219
Jornall, John, 185, 246
Jostlin, Dorothy, 55
——, Eliza, 55
——, Mary, 55
——, Nathaniell, 55
——, Rebecca, 55
——, Tho., 55
Jourden, Edward, 342, *see* Jordan
Joy, Edmund, 426
——, William, 182
Joyce, Henery, 145
——, William, 261
Joyner, Jo., 52
——, Tho., 132
Judd, Harbert, 103
Jues (or Ives), Charles, 442
Juiman, John, 187
Julian, Robert, 227
——, Sara, 185, 247
——, William, 185, 247, 273
Jumrey, *see* Pomre, &c.
Justin (or Justine) Humphry, (&c.) 316*, 317, 342

KALLAHANE, Charles, 355, 356, 359, 361, 373, 378, 379, 382, 386, 391, 409, 416, 417
Kamplinn, *see* Kemplin
Kanniday, Ann, 422
——, Mary, 422
——, Thomas, 422
Kanty, Darby, 503
Karsewell, William, 123
Karvis, Jane, 435
——, Henry, 435
Kay, *see* Mac Kay
Keal, Keale, Keel, Keele, Kerle
——, George, 333, 335, 341
——, John, 335, 339, 340
Kean, Alice, 178, 228
Keatch (or Keech), Richard, 326, 330
Kedby, Tho., 138

Keech, *see* Keatch
Keel, *see* Keal
Keele, Edward, 46, *see* Keal
Keie, Sarah, 214
——, Thomas, 214
——, *see* Key
Keith, Elizabeth, 508
——, Henry, 383
——, James, 508
——, *see* Keth
Kelly, Ann, 489
——, Brian, 122
——, David, 480
——, Robert, 343, 503
Kelley, Humphrey, 434
——, John, 430, 503
Kellum, Richard, 115
Kelsoll, Henry, 471
Kelum, Robert, 117
Kemball, Elizabeth, 281, 282
——, Henery, 280, 282
——, John, 282
——, Martha, 282
——, Mary, 282
——, Richard, 280, 282
——, Susan, 280, 282
——, Thomas, 282
——, Ursula, 280
Kember, Robert, 240
Kemp, Anthony, 218
——, Edward, 73
——, Humfrey, 133
——, Isack, 112
——, Margrett, 218
——, Mary, 497
——, Ralph, 497
——, Thomas, 497
——, William, 177, 185, 218, 247
Kemplin (Kemplyn, Kamplinn, or Scamplyn), John, 319, 319*, 325
Kendall, Henry, 129
——, James, 165, 166, 326, 328
——, William, 480, 495
Kendridd, William, 109
Keninston, Thomas, 195
Keniston, Allen, 218
—— (or Kniston), Thomas, 221
Kenn, Mathew, 503
Kenneday, Jo., 117
——, Symon, 36
Kennedy, Ellinor, 383
——, John, 383
Kennell, Samuell, 183, 258
Kenney, John, 488, 493, 496
Kennyon, Geo., 85
——, Jo., 85

Kent, Edward, 316, 318, 343
——, Humfry (&c.), 215, 268
——, Joane, 215
——, Jo., 129
——, Nico., 79
——, Peter, 317*, 319*, 324
Kentt, Humry, 455
Kerbie, Jo., 130 } *see* Kirbie,
Kerby, Humfrey, 75 } Kirby
Kerfitt, Thomas, 227
Kerill, John, 193
Kerle, *see* Keal
Kersey, Thomas, 303
Kersley, Henry, 184
——, Robert, 36
Kerton, William, 191
Keth, George, 248
——, John, 248
—— (or Keyth), Mr., 188, 229, 273
——, Susan, 229
——, *see* Keith
Kett, Robert, 38
Kettell, Peter, 73
Kevynn, Robert, 101
Kew, Anne, 448
——, Nicholas, 383
Key, John, 41, 141
——, William, 480
Keyne, Ann, 107
——, Ben., 107
——, Robert, 107
Keyser, *see* Keyzar
Keysie, Lawrence, 143
Keyth, *see* Keith, Keth
Keyzar, Kezar, Keyser
——, George, 462, 465
——, Katherine, 492
——, Margaret, 465
——, Teague, 480, 492
Kibe, Jo., 81
Kid (or Kidd), Roger, 176, 221
Kiddall, Sara, 177
Kidson, Marmaduke, 101
Kiffin, David, 122
Kilborne, Dunston, 40
——, Elizabeth, 280
——, Francis [Frances], 66
——, Jo., 66
——, Lyddia, 66
——, Margaret, 66
——, Marie, 66
——, Thomas, 66, 280
Kilby, Henry, 125
Kildale, Edward, 219
Kildridge, William, 186
Kilhammy, Patric, 426
Kilin, John, 293
Killinghall, Margaret, 132

THE END.

BILLING, PRINTER, GUILDFORD, SURREY.

www.ingramcontent.com/pod-product-compliance
Lightning Source LLC
Chambersburg PA
CBHW021840020426
42334CB00013B/138